DEC 1 5 2004

IS THERE A SINGLE RIGHT INTERPRETATION?

Studies of the Greater Philadelphia Philosophy Consortium
Michael Krausz, editor

Already published:

Joseph Margolis, Michael Krausz, and Richard Burian, eds.,
Rationality, Relativism and the Human Sciences
(Martinus Nijhoff Publishers, 1986)

John Caputo and Mark Yount, eds.,
Foucault and the Critique of Institutions
(Penn State Press, 1993)

Joseph Margolis and Jacques Catudal, eds.,
*The Quarrel Between Invariance and Flux:
A Guide for Philosophers and Other Players*
(Penn State Press, 2001)

Edited, with an introduction, by Michael Krausz

IS THERE A SINGLE
RIGHT INTERPRETATION?

The Pennsylvania State University Press
University Park, Pennsylvania

Library of Congress Cataloging-in-Publication Data

Is there a single right interpretation? / edited by Michael Krausz.
   p.   cm.
   Includes index.
   ISBN 0-271-02175-6 (cloth : alk. paper)
   ISBN 0-271-02183-7 (pbk. : alk. paper)
   1. Hermeneutics. 2. Criticism.

   BD241 .I68 2002
   121'.68—dc21   2001036763

It is the policy of The Pennsylvania State University Press to use acid-free paper for the
first printing of all clothbound books. Publications on uncoated stock satisfy the
minimum requirements of American National Standard for Information
Sciences—Permanence of Paper for Printed Library Materials, ANSI Z39.48–1992.

Contents

Introduction   1
    Michael Krausz

PART I

1   *The Sun Also Rises:* Incompatible Interpretations   9
    Alan Goldman
2   "One and Only One Correct Interpretation"   26
    Joseph Margolis
3   Rightness and Success in Interpretation   45
    Paul Thom
4   Intentionality, Meaning, and Open-Endedness of Interpretation   63
    Jitendranath Mohanty
5   Are There Definitive Interpretations?   76
    Laurent Stern

PART II

6   Against Critical Pluralism   101
    David Novitz
7   Interpretation and Its Objects   122
    Michael Krausz
8   Constructive Realism and the Question of Imputation   145
    Chhanda Gupta
9   Interpretation and the Ontology of Art   159
    Robert Stecker
10   Can Novel Critical Interpretations Create Art Objects Distinct from Themselves?   181
    Philip Percival

PART III

11 The Literary Work as a Pliable Entity: Combining Realism and
    Pluralism   211
    Torsten Pettersson
12 The Multiple Interpretability of Musical Works   231
    Stephen Davies
13 Right Answers: Dworkin's Jurisprudence   251
    Rex Martin
14 Truth in Interpretation: A Hermeneutic Approach   264
    Charles Guignon
15 Appreciation and Literary Interpretation   285
    Peter Lamarque

PART IV

16 Hypothetical Intentionalism: Statement, Objections, and Replies   309
    Jerrold Levinson
17 Andy Kaufman and the Philosophy of Interpretation   319
    Noël Carroll
18 Whose Play Is It? Does It Matter?   345
    Annette Barnes
19 Tossed Salad: Ontology and Identity   360
    Susan L. Feagin
20 Wittgenstein and the Question of True Self-Interpretation   381
    Garry L. Hagberg

Contributors   407
Index   411

Introduction

Michael Krausz

Is there a single right interpretation of such representative entities as works of literature, visual artworks, works of music, legal and sacred texts, the self, and other cultural phenomena? Is there a single right performance of a play or a work of music? And if not, why not? Contributors to this volume take up a series of engrossing issues that bear on the ideals and the nature of interpretation and its objects. These issues reverberate in all domains of interpretive activity.

Numerous important philosophical strategies hang on whether one should always embrace the ideal of a single admissible interpretation or should sometimes embrace the ideal of a multiplicity of admissible interpretations. The first ideal is singularism. The second is multiplism.[1]

Singularists characteristically hold that full understanding is to be found in a singularist condition where there is a one-one relation between an interpretation and its object of interpretation. And admissible interpretations should be conjoinable into a comprehensive interpretation. According to the

---

1. Sometimes singularism is called critical monism, and sometimes multiplism is called critical pluralism. Yet, while critical pluralism holds that admissible interpretations are equally preferable, multiplism allows that admissible interpretations may be unequally preferable. The asymmetry between multiplism and critical pluralism allows for fruitful lines of inquiry that recommend the singularist/multiplist nomenclature.

singularist, no incompatible interpretations can be jointly defended. Even if one could not choose between competing interpretations on account of incomplete knowledge, that should not keep one from embracing singularism as an ideal. The singularist embraces the view that incompatible interpretations should be understood in bivalent terms and that no contradictions should be embraced as jointly defensible. Singularists such as David Novitz take objects of interpretation to exhibit a "singularity" constraint, namely, that such objects have only one set of noncontradictory properties.

In contrast, the multiplist questions whether admissibility needs to be understood in bivalent terms. Multiplists (such as Joseph Margolis, Torsten Pettersson, Jitendranath Mohanty, and others) hold that sometimes the very notion of competition between contending interpretations would be better understood in terms of opposition without bivalent exclusivity or contradiction. The multiplist affirms that admissibility may be understood in such multivalent terms as reasonableness, appropriateness, aptness, or the like. And quite apart from multiplist strategies, Annette Barnes and Paul Thom introduce still other sorts of values in the evaluation of contending interpretations, such as faithfulness or genuineness or successfulness or rightness.

One way to avoid incompatibility between opposing interpretations is to determine that what each interpretation takes as its object is not one and the same thing. If otherwise opposing interpretations address different things, then incompatibility or opposition is dissipated. Alan Goldman, for example, distinguishes between texts and the fictional worlds that texts may project. He suggests that what appear to be opposing interpretations may really address these in turn. The narrower world of the text differs from the broader world of works. In a similar vein, Peter Lamarque distinguishes between utterance meaning and complete works. If would-be incompatible interpretations really address different things (as Goldman, Lamarque, and Philip Percival suggest), then multiplism would yield to a benign "pluralism"; that is, different interpretations would address different objects of interpretation.

Yet a multiplist may counter that a cultural entity, for example, need not exhibit only one set of nonopposing properties. Further, a multiplist may urge the "imputationist" view that the identity conditions of an object of interpretation are themselves affected by interpretive practices. Margolis and Mohanty, for example, hold that cultural objects are intentional and that their identities are relative to their historical situatedness, or to their historicized "horizons" of understanding. Yet through their incarnations pertinent objects of interpretation remain sufficiently self-identical. Consequently, according to Heidegger and Gadamer, as Charles Guignon discusses, there can be a number of equally correct interpretations of the same object. Such a claim of sameness requires a distinctive treatment of identity that is typically resisted by singularists.

Hermeneutic philosophers suggest that an intentional object of interpretation is "determinable," that it can be made more determinate by imputation. But Novitz, Robert Stecker, and other realists resist this suggestion by holding that, however one might think of an object of interpretation, its properties cannot be altered in this way.

Rather than focus on interpretations as such, Mohanty focuses on interpretive acts. On his view an interpretive act would present an object as having the meaning it does from a certain perspective. Consequently the interpretive act would yield an intentional object that in turn would answer to an interpretation. Clearly, the sense in which artworks, for example, are created by artists and/or critics depends upon one's "metaphysics of existence," and that, as Percival points out, is philosophically contentious.

In response to the singularity constraint, Susan Feagin counters that the identity of a cultural entity is parasitic on a creator's conception of his or her own creative life and that the conception of such a life may undergo change. Further, the activity of self-interpretation does not require that mental events be determinate and fixed. Garry Hagberg affirms that the activity of self-interpretation does not require a single correct answer to questions concerning the meaning of a given utterance or action.

The debate between singularism and multiplism arises in other normative contexts as well. Mohanty pursues the matter when considering sacred Indian texts. And Rex Martin pursues it when considering legal texts, in his discussion and rejection of the "canonical reading" of Ronald Dworkin's "right-answer" thesis.

Margolis, Mohanty, Pettersson, Davies, and Hagberg all resist the singularity constraint by affirming that cultural objects are respectively indeterminate, plastic, pliable, indefinite, ambivalent, or ambiguous. Accordingly, they take such objects as answering to more than one admissible interpretation. But it remains an open question whether, despite relative indeterminacies and the like, pertinent objects could still answer to one and only one admissible interpretation.

Certain thinkers associate realism with singularism, and constructivism with multiplism. But these are not necessary associations. Pettersson, for example, attempts to reconcile realism with multiplism (or, as he calls it, "pluralism"). And I contend that none of the ontologies in an expanded tally—one that includes realism, constructivism, and constructive realism—entails either singularism or multiplism. In defending Hilary Putnam's internal realism—a view that one might or might not count as a version of "external" constructive realism—Chhanda Gupta affirms relational, rather than imputational, strategies. In turn, Thom and Mohanty express reservations about the need to link a theory of interpretation to any particular ontology.

Some singularists seek to fix the single admissible interpretation by locating the actual intentions of the historical creator. Yet even if one had access to such intentions, they might be equivocal. In contrast, Jerrold Levinson proposes a hypothetical intentionalism that involves projectable hypotheses about authorial intentions rather than actual intentions. In turn, Noël Carroll offers a "modest actual intentionalism." He seeks to refute the hypothetical intentionalist's claim that there is a rule against consulting authorial avowals of intention. Still, even if such consultation may be had, it remains open whether singularism or multiplism would obtain on that account. And within a phenomenological idiom, Mohanty goes further in resisting appeals to authorial intentions altogether.

Singularists typically advance their ideal on the assumption that interpretive activity seeks true interpretations. Stecker and Lamarque point out, however, that not all interpretive activity seeks truth as an aim. If one interprets artworks in pursuit of appreciation, for example, there may be a plurality of admissible interpretations. Accordingly, Stecker relativizes his singularist ideal to the aim of truth seeking.

The multiple-aims suggestion bears on the multifarious nature and application of interpretation itself. Lamarque observes that in certain domains the concept of interpretation is essentially contested. In opposition to the idea of a definitive interpretation, Laurent Stern holds that it would be self-defeating to argue for this idea directly. For if the idea of a definitive interpretation were to amount to an interpretive claim, then it would exemplify a single right interpretation to show that there is no such interpretation. And if it were a factual claim, it would be unclear how one could derive such a factual claim from an interpretive claim. And Stephen Davies catalogues five points at which interpretation enters into the performance and appreciation of musical works, for example.

The articles discuss a variety of types of objects of interpretation, including utterances, sentences, texts, scripts, whole works and worlds of literature; musical scores and performances; works of visual art; the self; and so on. Of course, not all conclusions about interpretive ideals in one practice are transferable to others. The symmetries and the asymmetries are revealing. And some practices—such as psychoanalysis—are not discussed at all. That is a matter of practicality and not of principle.

While, for the sake of convenience, the twenty essays are grouped into four parts, there is a good deal of thematic overlap between them. Part I offers revealing examples of apparently incompatible interpretations and, in the spirit of multiplism, offers several strategies for rendering them admissible. As well, it addresses the openness of interpretation and indicates puzzles in the very idea of a definitive interpretation. Part II counters with an affirmation of singularism and a critique of some of the strategies mentioned in Part I, in the context of a realist understanding of objects of interpretation. The linkage between ideals of interpretation and various ontologies of interpretanda is also analyzed. Part III explicates and criticizes imputationism and indicates alternative strategies, including those that bear on the aims of interpretation. It discusses interpretation in music and the law. And in its explication of intentionality and hermeneutics, it continues the discussion of imputation. Resisting the thought that a creator's individual intentions deserve conclusive weight in the assignment of admissibility, Part IV addresses constraints on any account of a creator's individual intentions, and it opposes hypothetical intentionalism with actual intentionalism. It probes the nature of the creator in relation to his or her product. In so doing it delves into notions of authorial identity and the self as they bear on the range of ideally admissible interpretations. Again, the concerns of these parts are overlapping, and the reader should take the grouping primarily as a device of convenience.

Grateful thanks are due to many people: mostly to the authors for their contributions; to anonymous readers who provided helpful suggestions and encouraged direct engagement between the articles; to Lorraine Kischner for her continued valued assistance; and to Sanford Thatcher, director of Penn State Press, for his steady and expert guidance.

 **PART I**

The Sun Also Rises:
Incompatible Interpretations

Alan Goldman

Philosophical claims about the nature of interpretation are best made by
reference to real examples. The examples of James's *Turn of the Screw* and
Blake's poems having grown somewhat stale, I begin with a different one,
much debated by literary critics[1] but absent from the philosophical literature.

I

Interpretation 1. In Hemingway's *Sun Also Rises,* the lead characters morally develop over the course of the novel. At the beginning, the narrator and
lead male character, Jake, has not come to grips with the person that his
war wound has left him. Despite his impotence, he harbors illusions of a

---

1. For a sampling of critical articles on this novel, see James Nagel, ed., *Critical Essays on
Ernest Hemingway's "The Sun Also Rises"* (New York: G. K. Hall, 1995); Harold Bloom, ed.,
Brett Ashley (New York: Chelsea House, 1991); Linda Wagner-Martin, ed., *New Essays on
"The Sun Also Rises"* (Cambridge: Cambridge University Press, 1987); A. Robert Lee, ed.,
Ernest Hemingway: New Critical Essays (Totowa, N.J.: Vision and Barnes & Noble, 1983). I
have drawn freely from many of these essays and others in what follows. The illustrative
interpretations are not novel, although I have combined claims from different sources.

long-term romantic relation with Brett, the lead female character. Near the beginning of the story, his picking up the prostitute Georgette and his attitude toward the homosexuals who accompany Brett in her first entrance underscore his ambivalent sexual identity, a theme involving several of the characters in that early scene. Throughout most of the story he is reluctantly at Brett's beck and call, finding relief only in the male bonding of the fishing trip he takes to Burguete. The low point of his life as a human punching bag comes in Pamplona after his pimping for Brett with the bullfighter Romero, when, like Romero, he is beaten up and knocked unconscious by Robert Cohen.

He is awakened by a carafe of water poured on him. Nature symbolism abounds in this book, and water is the motif for Jake's rebirth and development toward self-realization. After his awakening, everything looks new to him, and he begins to awaken from the unreal dream of Brett. But the process will be slow. He wants a bath, but the water will not run. His full awakening awaits his solitary trip to San Sebastian, the return to nature and his long swim there. Unable to swim in the open sea, he nevertheless dives deep, plumbing the depths of his psyche as well as the lake. He is now cleansed of his former illusions, and when he swims to the shore, he sees more clearly.

When summoned by Brett, he is willing to return to Spain despite the challenge. He does respond to her by returning, but their relation in Spain has changed. Formerly under her control, he now becomes the controlling figure. He chooses their restaurant; he keeps drinking, without becoming drunk, despite her protest; and he finishes his dinner (their former relationship?), though she wants to leave. He decides on a cab ride, tells the cab where to go in order to show her the city, and in the famous last line corrects her seeming illusion, refusing to blame their failed relation on his sexual incapacitation. He is now controlling the course of his life, as the policeman, his alter ego in that very last scene, controls the movement of the cab. He can now stoically accept his situation and become master of his life in the difficult times he continues to face.

Brett has also developed. Drunk, broke, and promiscuous, wavering between traditional and liberated new female roles throughout much of the novel, she too is changed at its end. Always a willing drinking partner before, at her last meeting with Jake she no longer drinks and urges him not to. She breaks with Romero, both for his own good and because he wants to conform her to his confining image, wants her to grow her hair long and become the traditional wife and woman from which she has struggled to liberate herself. Romero is her counterpart in the novel, as is evident from the descriptions of his good looks, his isolation even in crowds, his tight clothes, and the way he wears his hat, all reminiscent of Brett, and the way that others dance around him in the bull ring, as they dance around Brett earlier at the festival. As her lover and a real man, he helps her to shed her facades and become a real modern woman, despite trying to keep her in the more traditional role.

Her final statement to Jake is not an expression of continuing illusion but a recognition of time wasted with so many other men and a recognition that they could have had a better relationship. Water and vision, or sight, are the central symbols for Brett's states of mind, as they are for Jake's. Throughout most of the story she is always wanting to take baths, to cleanse herself of actions she probably regrets without admitting so. She is often described as squinting her eyes, blocking clear vision of the world around her. At the end of the novel, however, she wants to see Madrid, to see the world around her clearly, with eyes wide open. Like Jake, she is finally able to see the world and her role within it as they are, to accept the difficult times, the loss of innocence and psychological wounds of the war, and to make the best of her role as new woman.

Interpretation II. The lead characters do not develop. The structure of this novel is cyclical, emphasizing the tragic and monotonous repetition in the characters' irreparably damaged lives. The only villain in this novel is the war, the only hero the world that continues on despite it (as Hemingway wrote). But the characters one and all are the victims of the war, and their wounds, physical and psychological, will not heal.

Jake ends where he begins. At the end of the story, after his brief respite in San Sebastian, reminiscent of his earlier fishing trip in Burguete, he returns to Brett and to drinking. The taxi ride at the end also recalls the taxi ride at the beginning. Once more Brett presses close to him, the substitute for the sexual fulfillment they cannot have. His last line recognizes the hopelessness of their relation, but arguably he has recognized it all along. This is why he arranges affairs with other men for her despite later hating himself for doing so. At the end of the story, Jake faces the prospect of more drinking and fishing, as Brett faces more meaningless relationships.

Brett plans to return to Mike, and one cannot picture their relationship being any different from what it was before. She does not predict any change, saying they will continue to "look after each other," and undoubtedly they will continue to do so badly. She has dismissed Romero just as she has dismissed all her other lovers, backing out when the relation threatened to become long-term, and clinging to the illusion of meaning and self-sacrifice. She remains incapable of lasting relationships, except the mutually destructive one with Jake, whom she summons as usual to rescue her from the latest fiasco. Her words to Jake in Madrid recall her words when they first reunite in the book, complaining about how miserable she is and how she can't help doing whatever she does. She stays there at the Hotel Montana, recalling the Hotel Montoya in Pamplona.

The one character in the book who personifies notions of development over time, commitment, obligations, and responsibility for lasting consequences of his actions is Robert Cohen. Probably, in Hemingway's anti-Semitic caricature, these concepts are linked to that of Jewish guilt. In any case, Cohen is mercilessly ridiculed for clinging to these romantic trappings by the other characters in the book, Hemingway's postwar sophisticates. Brett in particular cannot stand Cohen's assumption that their affair could have lasting consequences, while the other characters find it alternately amusing and annoying.

Finally, an analysis of style supports the claim of cyclical, nondeveloping repetition. Critics have noted two dominant styles in this book: One is very simple and repetitive, with short sentences and repeating words, what one critic calls a "staccato" style.[2] Thematically, this style is associated with and suggestive of boredom, monotony, and the lack of purpose in the lives of the characters. The second style is flowing, rhythmical, with long sentences, suggesting freedom, movement, and, most of all, the beauty of nature. Significantly, the book ends as it begins, in the former style. The tone, when not describing nature or bullfighting, is relentlessly cynical, certainly not optimistic. In all their travels, these characters are going nowhere.

II

The two interpretations just offered have roughly equal textual support. Several of the events and locales in this novel are repeated with slight variations. The first of these interpretations emphasizes the variations, such as Jake's telling the second cab driver where to go. The second interpretation emphasizes the repetitions, which in any case could not be identical. Some critics have taken the view that one of these characters, the real hero of the

2. Harold Mosher Jr., "The Two Styles of Hemingway's *The Sun Also Rises*," *Fitzgerald/Hemingway Annual* (1971): 262–73.

novel, develops, while the other does not, and the possible permutations of the above, together with their supporting evidence, are easy to work out. I prefer the second of the above interpretations, not because I believe the text better supports it, but because I think it better fits the overall hard-nosed, cynical atmosphere of the novel, despite its interludes of lyrical descriptions of landscapes. It underlines the theme of moral malaise in the postwar generation that one can feel in Hemingway's prose. But others might prefer the more optimistic theme of coming to terms with hard times, and the psychological complexity that that theme implies. Not only are the characters more complex on this reading, but the events in the plot take on more significance as contributing to and mirroring their development, perhaps adding formal structure to the novel as well.

Thus one interpretation enhances one set of literary values, and the other, a different set. This, together with equal textual support, makes them equally acceptable. Instead of continuing to debate the merits of these opposed interpretations, I want to raise philosophical questions about interpretation that appeal to this example will help to answer. First, are these interpretations really incompatible or contradictory? Second, must we rest content with the answer to this first question? And third, can any interpretation be true? Addressing the first question, the clear answer is yes. Characters in the world of *The Sun Also Rises* either have the property of morally developing or they do not; they cannot both develop and not develop. In fact, interpretations can be incompatible in assigning properties that cannot be simultaneously possessed even if these readings do not maintain explicit contradictions. If, for example, one interpretation claims that Jake morally develops and another claims that he reacts in the same ways and maintains the same relationships throughout, these would be incompatible in virtue of having contradictory implications.

Addressing the second and third questions, that these interpretations are contradictory does not imply that they cannot be equally acceptable, although it does imply that they cannot both be true. But don't we need the notion of truth for interpretational assertions, so that we can, for example, derive implications from them and use them in arguments? Philosophers who answer this last question affirmatively might seek to avoid or resolve the contradictions. They might, for example, claim that the interpretations assert only that the book can be read in one way or the other: we can see Jake as developing, and we can see him as not developing. The latter two assertions are not contradictory. But to make this move is to confuse statements about interpretations (that one or another is possible) for interpretations themselves. The first interpretation, for example, does not say, "You (the reader) can interpret Jake Barnes as morally developing"; it says that he does develop, and supports this assertion with textual evidence. We *can* interpret Jake as developing, but actually to do so is to read his actions as having a certain significance, a significance that directs our readings of other episodes and descriptions and constrains other interpretations. Interpretations guide us toward the appreciation of certain aspects of the world of a work—for example, the psychological complexity of its characters or its consistently cynical atmosphere—and perhaps exclude the appreciation of certain other possible aspects. Potential interpretations, the ways we *can* read works so as to bring these worlds to life, remain inert until actually adopted.

A second and more interesting way to avoid the contradictions is to say that *The Sun Also Rises* is simply ambiguous or indeterminate on the question whether the characters develop. More broadly, it might be claimed that equal textual support for each of two opposing interpretations shows not that they are both acceptable but that a third interpretation of the work as ambiguous or indeterminate on the matter in question is always preferable. Indeed, isn't it simply implied by equal textual support that the work must be indeterminate in this respect? Isn't that interpretation then mandated?

If interpretation aimed simply at true description of a work, then this implication would hold. But the paradigm of a correct or good interpretation would then consist in an explication of the meanings of the words of a text in their textual context. This is not typically an interpretation at all, although many philosophers seem to have been confused on this matter. The two partial interpretations of *The Sun Also Rises* offered above are not concerned at all with the meanings of Hemingway's words, all of which are perfectly clear to any competent speaker of English. They are concerned to go beyond what the text literally asserts, to fill out the world of the work so as to make determinate answers to questions the text may raise without answering in any obvious or explicit way. They are, as indicated, to guide the reader to a rewarding experience or reading of the work, one that enhances some of the literary values it might afford.

Here it can be argued that a reading of the novel as ambiguous on the point in question is not as rewarding an experience as the other two readings. The world of the novel loses some of its impact, the feeling of the plight of characters caught in meaningless endless repetition or overcoming a hostile world in their own ways. To read the novel as ambiguous between these two is to call attention to the novel as novel at the expense of its projected world, accessible through interpretation, in which the characters either do or do not develop. (There is no world, it can be claimed, in which they do neither.) Such self-referential reading hinders the reader from getting caught up in the story, from projecting him- or herself into its fictional world. It sacrifices the feeling of subdued but determined optimism or that of consistent hard-nosed cynicism or nihilism.

On the other side, it might be argued for this one novel that an interpretation of it as ambiguous is acceptable, as supported, for example, by the ambiguity of its concluding line, which might express both Jake's recognition of his limitations and his continuing desire to dwell on illusions. Here the actions of the characters themselves within their world, including even the seemingly heroic Romero, are seen to be morally ambiguous. He, after all, has a kind of girlish beauty, is, like Jake, beaten up by Cohen, runs off with Brett in apparent violation of his own code, and cannot keep her. Even the best candidate for moral hero in this novel is therefore far less than that. But whether or not this interpretation flies, the point remains that it is not mandated by the textual support for the other two. It requires independent, indeed opposed, textual evidence, and it must apply, like the other two, to the world of the novel and not simply to its literal text.

Thus, we are left with equally acceptable but incompatible interpretations. We cannot therefore speak in this case of the interpretations as a whole being true. We can, however, continue to speak of the individual statements that combine to make them up being fictionally true in the particular worlds projected by the interpretations. This is fictional truth, what we are to imagine as true, and it is truth relative to an interpretive scheme. What is fictionally true under one interpretation may not be under another. But such truth suffices for the purposes of inference and argument for which the notion of interpretive truth is needed. If we imagine some statements to be true, we are committed to the fictional truth of others, and on this basis many interpretive arguments can proceed.

III

Other philosophical questions immediately arise, however, once we grant that the incompatibility of equally acceptable interpretations cannot be eliminated. Do such cases require more than one work; do interpretations then create (separate) works? Do such cases imply that there can be no single overriding criterion of acceptability for interpretations? Do they show that the only constraint on acceptable interpretations is the practice of the critical community? All these questions have been answered affirmatively by recent theorists of literature. But we should not jump to such radical conclusions too quickly.

In regard to the first two questions here, we should certainly say intuitively that Hemingway wrote *The Sun Also Rises,* not his critics or interpreters. Furthermore, we would certainly say that he wrote at least and at most one novel with that title. If one could create that novel by simply interpreting it, it would be far easier to be a great author than it is. But the book is there to be read; it does not await anyone's reading of it. Interpretation aims to enhance appreciation of the work in question, not to create a better one, a far more difficult task. Less intuitively but still eminently plausible: if interpretation is a kind of explanation,[3] if it must explain the characters and episodes as written, then it requires an independent explanandum existing prior to the explanations offered. If these incompatible explanations are to compete, then they must be explanations of the same object or work, a work that endures from earlier interpretations to later ones.[4] An object can endure while changing, but this requires a continuity in properties that different interpretations themselves may not possess. It is also implausible to think that one could change Hemingway's novel every few seconds by successively thinking that Jake does and does not develop. Thus, it certainly seems initially that we should answer these first two questions negatively: competing explanations explain the same work differently; they do not create new and separate works.

There are nevertheless other considerations that motivate the opposing counterintuitive intuitions (oxymoron intended). Competing interpretations appear to attribute properties, indeed incompatible properties, to the work itself. One claims that Jake develops in *The Sun Also Rises.* The other claims that he does not. I argued above that this does not mandate our interpreting Jake as neither developing nor not developing. But it seems that he cannot do both in the same story, and these interpretations are equally acceptable. Doesn't all this require two stories, one in which he develops and one in which he does not? And if the permutations between him and Brett are

3. For a full defense of this claim, see my *Aesthetic Value* (Boulder, Colo.: Westview, 1995), chap. 4.

4. Compare David Novitz, *Knowledge, Fiction, and Imagination* (Philadelphia: Temple University Press, 1987), 105.

again equally acceptable, then we seem to require four different stories just on this score. More generally, if acceptable interpretations impute properties to characters or episodes in a work, and if it is then fictionally true in the work that they have these properties, then incompatible, equally acceptable interpretations would require separate works, as many works as there are such interpretations. And if this is so, then there seems to be a clear sense in which interpretations do create new works. Did I then create *The Sun Also Rises* twice by offering the interpretations defended above? Did I collaborate with Hemingway, whom I never met, or did he fail to create any novel at all?

The answers to these now vexing puzzles lie, I believe, in a set of distinctions properly drawn between levels of text on the one hand and fictional worlds projected by those texts and acceptable interpretations of them on the other. If we want to begin at the most basic level, then we might mention the physical ink marks on the paper. But no reader sees these as such, and Hemingway inscribed similar ones, of course, only because he was choosing syntactic and semantic types. The reader need never interpret the ink marks (unless his or her copy is damaged), but reads them straight off as words with standard meanings. As mentioned above, the words and sentence meanings on the next level virtually never need interpretation in Hemingway either, although there may be a very occasional ambiguity that context does not immediately resolve. Irony, metaphor, and symbolism are different matters, but these are recognized via explanations of the language with its ordinary meanings read right off.

If the literal assertions made by the text Hemingway wrote are the second level, then what is fictionally true, what we are *required* to imagine as true, based on those assertions is the third. Here are included all those inferences from the literal assertions of the text upon which all competent readers would agree. It is undeniable, for example, that Brett makes her entrance into the story in the company of a group of homosexuals, although they are never explicitly identified as such. It is also undeniable that Jake suffered a genital injury in the war that has left him with sexual desire that he has no means to fulfill, although once more perhaps the last vestige of Victorian prudishness prevents Hemingway from explicitly saying so. These are interpretations based on the explicit assertions of the text, but they are epistemically unchallengeable. They therefore falsify the common assumption that interpretation is to be distinguished from description on epistemic grounds. What does distinguish it is that interpretations are inferred from the literal assertions of the text; they are inferred as explanations for what is literally asserted, explanations for the descriptions of characters and events that can be understood as such without interpretation.

What is fictionally true in a story, based both on the explicit assertions of the text and on those inferences on which all competent readers would agree, constitutes what can be called the narrow world of the work. The inferences in question include not all implications of what is explicitly asserted (if the latter contains a contradiction, for example, then everything would be implied), but only those statements that are uniquely related as parts of best explanations for or as best explained by what is literally asserted. The only fictionally true explanation for the way Jake's injury is explicitly referred to is that the injury is as I described it above; the only fictionally true explanation for the way Brett's escorts in her opening scene are described is that they are homosexual. This narrow world of the novel leaves indeterminate not only all those propositions that do not contribute one way or another to our understanding or appreciation of the novel, for example whether Jake has a sister, but also many propositions that do so contribute, answers to questions that naturally arise, such as whether he morally develops. These answers remain indeterminate in the narrow world because they are the subjects of interpretive disagreements.

Contestable interpretations, further explanatory inferences that fill out the world of the text in ways necessary to full appreciation, then constitute the fourth level. Here we begin to see multiple worlds of the novel (we might speak of a universe of worlds), and they begin to diverge: for example, one in which the characters develop and one in which they do not, one in which Romero remains an untarnished hero, having dodged a bullet in Brett, and another in which he ends up like Belmonte, his older, much maligned and disillusioned colleague, or like Vicente Girones, gored and dead "just for fun." While the third level, also in large part a product of interpretation, still contains only fictional truths that the text requires us to imagine as true, the fourth level is made up of propositions that the text *permits* us to imagine as true, although some such imagining is required for maximum appreciation. Here the reader does begin to collaborate with Hemingway in creating fictional worlds, to use the author's rich material for the much easier task of expansion. Here interpretation remains anchored to text by explanatory links, but there are several possible best explanations. The expanded worlds remain incomplete, in that there remain countless propositions—for example, that Jake has a sister—that are neither fictionally true nor false, but these worlds are richer to just the degree that there are contestable, that is, interesting, interpretations that add fictional truths to the work's narrow world.

We can see now that distinctions between texts, objects of interpretation, constraints on interpretations, interpretations themselves, and fictional worlds cut across one another. The text consists of what is explicitly asserted, as determined by the literal meanings of the words at the time of the writing. There is very little interpretation at the level of the text in *The Sun Also Rises* and most other novels. There are exceptions, such as *A Clockwork Orange,* in which one must often infer what the words of the futuristic language mean. But these are exceptions. There is much interpretation, though uncontestable, at the level of the narrow fictional world, which consists in those universally agreed upon fictional truths that the text requires us to imagine. The object of contestable interpretation is this narrow fictional world, as well as the text (especially its stylistic elements) that projects it. These constrain contestable interpretations, which must explain them in such a way as to enhance their values for readers.

IV

We may now return to our as-yet-unanswered questions. Whether we say that interpretations create works depends on where we locate the work in this scheme. If we locate it way out on the fourth level, identifying it with the complete story as supplemented by contestable interpretations, then *perhaps* interpretations do indeed create separate works, the author only supplying the raw material for them. The hedging word is included because, even on this very broad understanding of what the work is, we can still maintain that there is a single work with different relational properties, where these relations include responses of different readers or interpreters. There could be a parallel here to a work's aesthetic properties. Aesthetic properties, I have argued elsewhere, are relative to the tastes of different competent critics.[5] Thus, Hemingway's style, a feature of his text, might be terse and crisp to one critic and monotonous to another. The text would then have both these relational properties, which is not inconsistent, because it would have them relative to these different critics. Nor does this imply that the text is not an independent object, as long as it also has nonre-

---

5. Goldman, *Aesthetic Value,* chap. 2.

lational properties. My house has relational perceptual properties—for example, colors—but it remains an object independent of my perception. In like fashion, Jake might both develop and not develop in the same work, relative to different acceptable interpretations of it. His developing would then be a relational property, although, like terseness as a property of writing, it does not appear to be relational.

However, in the case of properties ascribed by contestable interpretations, as opposed to evaluational aesthetic properties, there is no good reason to make this relativizing move. The only reason to locate the work on the fourth level is the temptation to say that whatever properties the characters have, indeed whatever is fictionally true, must be fictionally true in the work. The characters must either develop or not develop in *The Sun Also Rises,* in that very work. But this is not a good reason. It is just as intuitive to say that the characters develop in the world of the work, more generally, that what is fictionally true is true in the world of the work.

The work itself is more intuitively identified with the text or, at the outside, with its narrow world. The text, remember, is what is literally asserted; the narrow world is what we are to imagine as true based on the text and incontestable inferences from it. What is literally asserted is not necessarily what we are to imagine as true, since there may be irony or fallible narrators involved. The work can then be the text or its fictional content, that is, what is fictionally true based only on what is asserted. Or it can be its narrow world, what is fictionally true based on what is asserted plus incontestable inferences from it, that is, what is universally agreed to be in the story, its universally accepted content.

Thinking of comparisons with other artistic media, perhaps the narrow world is most intuitively identified with the work as the object of interpretation. A painting, it seems, is not just pigments on a canvas, but a rural landscape, a still life, or portrait, its universally recognized representations. This suggests that a literary work too should be identified with its agreed content. There may seem to be a problem, however, with identifying a work with the narrow world that the text projects instead of with the text itself, at least if we want to claim that we do not create or change the work itself by interpreting it. If a work is identified with what is universally agreed to be true in the story, then it seems that as soon as someone disagrees, the scope of the work diminishes; hence the work changes. The way around this problem is to maintain that the disagreement must be reasonable, must be that of a fully competent critic. What can be a reasonable topic of disagreement is fixed before anyone actually disagrees. Hence the work can remain fixed as well.

Nevertheless, there is still something more to be said for identifying the work more narrowly with the text. Doing so maintains a clear distinction between the work and the world of the work, narrow or broad. Perhaps to maintain the parallel it would not be too counterintuitive to identify a painting with the colored shapes, what it represents being the world of the painting. Of course, the artist chooses the pigments and shapes partly in order to project a particular world. The decision between these two identifications in either medium is largely a verbal matter. The main point here is that on either of these construals, there is a single novel. There is a single text and a single narrow world. Opposing interpretations do not create separate works. What they do create or pick out are additional worlds of the work, broader worlds filled out in different ways. These broader worlds will be determinate in respects, such as the characters' developing, in which the work itself remains indeterminate.

I have already noted the answer to the third of our latest set of questions. Both the unambiguous text and its narrow world constrain acceptable interpretations that fill out this world by explaining or being explained by its contents. The practice of the community of interpreters is neither necessary nor sufficient as a constraint; indeed, it is largely irrelevant to the acceptability of new interpretations. The meaning of the text itself is, of course, determined by practice, but this is the practice of the linguistic community upon which the author draws at the time of writing, not the practice of interpreters later; and in any case we noted that such meaning is not normally what interpretations aim to reveal. The best interpretations at given times often contradict prevalent interpretive practice in order to generate fresh readings. Their acceptability does not await their influence on that practice. It is determined instead by their ability to enhance literary values only latent in the work previously.

Our last question was whether the equal acceptability of incompatible interpretations implies that there is no single overriding criterion of acceptability. The obvious answer as to implication seems to be no, since it certainly seems possible for the application of a single criterion to generate ties among different interpretations. But we need to show more concretely how this possibility is actualized. On my view the criterion for good interpretations, like many other criteria of goodness, follows from the function of the practice. If, for example, the function of interpretation were to allow the reader to take part in a conversation with the author, to understand what the author is trying to say, then correct interpretations would reveal authorial intentions. There would then be a single correct interpretation for each work, assuming a single consistent set of authorial intentions. Our initial interpretations could not then have been equally acceptable, except in a weak epistemic sense if we were not able to find out what Hemingway intended. In fact Hemingway did offer a few statements on the matter, the most relevant being his pronouncement that there are no human heroes in this novel.[6] This would support the thesis that the characters do not develop. But I do not take Hemingway's pronouncement to be definitive, indeed to be very strong evidence in favor of that interpretation. The reason is that the function of interpretation is broader—to guide the reader toward the fullest appreciation of the work and the values it can afford.

Seeing the world of the novel, and ultimately the real world, through the eyes of the narrator, and ultimately the author, is certainly one value that may be pursued in reading a novel. But it is not the only one, and it does not always override others, for example, in our case, appreciating the psychological complexity of characters who can take on a life of their own in the world of the novel. Given this broader goal of inferring explanations for the text or narrow world as presented that enhance the value of the work for the reader, it is clear why we can derive multiple interpretations from this single criterion. Different values that cannot be simultaneously realized, in our case psychological complexity versus consistent, building atmosphere, imply this possibility. New and different interpretations can lead us to see elements in a work that we had previously missed and to integrate them in aesthetically more fulfilling ways.

The intentionalist might respond that, if the constraint of author intention is dismissed as too restrictive of satisfying experiences of the work, there is similar reason to dismiss the work itself as a constraint, as more radical theorists do. Why should we not ignore or alter large sections of a work if a more interesting reading can be generated by doing so? The simplest answer is that rewriting the text in this way might be a valuable exercise for a clever writer if such improvement could be made, but the result would be a new, albeit largely plagiarized, novel, not a new interpretation. Most often, of course, plagiarizing authors such as Hemingway would not

6. Cited in Arnold E. Davidson and Cathy N. Davidson, "Decoding the Hemingway Hero in *The Sun Also Rises*," in *New Essays on "The Sun Also Rises*," ed. Linda Wagner-Martin, 104.

result in better works or more satisfying experiences for readers. It is generally more satisfying to try to understand Hemingway's works than to try to rewrite them. This does not mean, however, that we should be prohibited from finding motives in the characters, for example, that Hemingway did not explicitly intend when he brought them to (fictional) life. We find a similar mixture of constraint and freedom in interpreting other artistic media. Acceptable interpretations of a musical composition, critical or performative, cannot make major alterations in the notes as written, but neither are they limited to bringing out expressive qualities in the music explicitly intended by the composer.

V

I have spoken so far of interpretations that fill out the fictional world of the work, that create fictional truths suggested but neither stated nor implied by the text. There are also other sorts of explanations for why the text might be written as it is or why the narrow world of the work is as it is described by and inferred from the text, explanations that speak of the structure, style, or themes of the work without adding fictional truths to it. Thus, when Brett makes her entrance into the story in the company of a group of homosexuals to whom Jake reacts with hostility, this might be seen to introduce the fictional truth that they are both confused about their sexual identities. But it can also be explained as beginning to develop the theme of futility in sexual relations or as creating parallels or contrasts among the main characters, that is, as adding structure to the novel, and so on. These are all interpretations, albeit of different sorts, because they all explain why the episode might be described as it is, what literary value this adds to the text or its world. Furthermore, these different sorts of explanations or levels of interpretation can interact. What we take to be fictionally true obviously affects what we see as both the themes and the structure of the novel. I also noted above how an analysis of the style of the text can support an interpretation of what is fictionally true in its world.

In defending my own account of what the two initial interpretations of the Hemingway work show, I have along the way criticized the intentionalist view as too narrow and restrictive and the no-textual-constraint view as too permissive. There is another prominent compromise view that might be criticized briefly in closing. This account also aims at a position between the two extremes, although I believe it is less intuitively motivated and more ad hoc than the explanatory account that I have defended. I refer to hypothetical intentionalism. According to its criterion of correct interpretation, interpreters seek the intentions of the author that would be attributed to him or her by an ideal intended audience, whether or not the actual author had such intentions. This allows for richer readings than those foreseen by an author.

But what of the case in which there is good evidence that the author intended a reading different from and incompatible with the richer one being contemplated? In our example, for instance, we have Hemingway making a statement that indicates that he does not see Jake or Brett as the hero of this novel. That certainly indicates that he did not intend an optimistic conclusion to the novel,[7] in which their having developed sufficiently to have overcome their histories and the difficult times presages a better future for them. I have held nevertheless that the interpretation of them as developing remains a live option. This seems to make a perfect test case for differentiating the value-enhancing explanatory account from any intentionalist criterion, hypothetical or not.

Surprisingly, however, defenders of hypothetical intentionalism rule out authorial pronouncements as to their intentions as definitive, indeed as any evidence for the ideal audience.[8] The motive once more is the praiseworthy one of maintaining some autonomy for the work and its critics, presumably in order to allow more satisfying readings. But then how can this account be considered any form of intentionalism? According to what we ordinarily mean by "intention," a subject's sincere pronouncement as to a recent past intention, when this is not clearly overridden by a subsequent action inconsistent with it, is nearly definitive evidence for any audience, ideal or not.

We cannot any longer understand the concept of intention once conceptually linked kinds of evidence for it are ruled out by ad hoc barriers erected solely to allow particular interpretations that are attractive on wholly other grounds. An appeal to intentions that ignores subjects' sincere assertions as to what their intentions are is not really an appeal to intentions. We do want an account that allows for interpretations of a novel's episodes, characters,

---

7. Although at another time Hemingway is said to have commented that *The Sun Also Rises* is not a pessimistic novel. Cited in Frederick Svoboda, *Hemingway and "The Sun Also Rises"* (Lawrence, Kans.: University Press of Kansas, 1983), 108.

8. See, for example, Jerrold Levinson, "Intention and Interpretation in Literature," in *The Pleasures of Aesthetics* (Ithaca, N.Y.: Cornell University Press, 1996), 208. Levinson even allows the attribution of allusion when it is clear that the author never heard of its target (211).

and their motives that were unintended by their authors, that allows these events and characters to speak for themselves in their fictional worlds. We also want an account that is true to the text and the narrow world of the work. We can have the latter while allowing for the former without pretending that we are still bound by authorial intentions of any sort. The artificial notion of hypothetical intentions is entirely dispensable, and confusing at best.

Authors, like composers, ought to welcome the most rewarding interpretations of their works. Since they must accept that their works may fall short of their intentions, they should also accept that their works may exceed in value what they originally envisioned. Indeed, they should intend that this will happen. They should insist only that their texts be respected as they wrote them. Having created the single object that stands to be explained but that can afford multiple literary values under different and sometimes incompatible explanatory schemes, they can leave it to their readers and critics to provide such schemes in the service of their appreciation of the work. A single object of interpretation, such as *The Sun Also Rises,* under a single criterion of acceptable interpretation, which allows the author's work to stand on its own without disappearing, can provoke a rich variety of interpretations that reward the reader in different ways.

"One and Only One Correct Interpretation"

Joseph Margolis

I claim there are no principled grounds on which to demonstrate that the interpretation of artworks and histories and other cultural phenomena could not be coherent or objective if it were not committed to the regulative constraint that, for every suitably individuated artwork or other interpretable phenomenon, there is (must be) a unique interpretation; or that partial or incomplete interpretations could never be objectively validated if they were not demonstrably compatible with the single, ideally complete interpretation that fitted the artwork or referent in question.

A forthright version of the claim I oppose has been advanced by P. D. Juhl. It is in fact a version of the Romantic hermeneutic doctrine pressed as hard as possible. Juhl asserts: "[T]here is in principle one and only one correct interpretation of a work. . . . if a work has several correct interpretations, they must (if I am right) be logically compatible . . . [that is, they] can be combined into one (comprehensive) interpretation of the work."[1] Juhl's is a stronger version of a view earlier espoused by E. D. Hirsch, also a Romantic hermeneut.[2] But it is also a view advanced by

1. P. D. Juhl, *Interpretation: An Essay in the Philosophy of Literary Criticism* (Princeton: Princeton University Press, 1980), 199 and n. 11.
2. See E. D. Hirsch Jr., *Validity in Interpretation* (New Haven: Yale University Press, 1967).

Monroe Beardsley, an avowed opponent of hermeneutics and all reliance on authorial intent.[3]

All three insist on the necessary compatibility and convergence of all valid interpretations of a given work, no matter how "partial" or incomplete such interpretations may actually be. But if the very *nature* of interpretable properties cannot be shown to preclude incompatible interpretations for formal or ontic reasons, the unique-interpretation thesis will prove arbitrary or false. (I mean incompatible interpretations, of course, that are not rendered "compatible" merely by the formal tricks of disjunctive logic.) I claim that there is no convincing argument for the "one-interpretation" thesis. As far as I know, no one has ever offered a knock-down argument to show that its denial is contradictory or paradoxical—or arbitrary or anarchical or unworkable or implausible or not in accord with critical practice or chaotic. There's no convincing argument at all.

The counterthesis rests on a *faute de mieux* strategy, but it has no trouble mustering positive considerations. Fully developed, it demonstrates the coherence and viability—even the preferability—of one or another subset of the following claims: (i) that a given work of art (viewed as an exemplar of suitably interpretable *denotata*) can, consistently, have plural interpretations that are valid, objective, even if not mutually compatible; (ii) that, if we agree that pertinent *de re* and *de cogitatione* modal necessities cannot be confirmed, then no evidentiary resources offered by the partisans of the unique-interpretation thesis will be adequate to defeat thesis (i); (iii) that intrinsically interpretable properties lack the kind of determinacy the unique-interpretation thesis requires; (iv) that claims (i)–(iii) are compatible with any reasonable view of referential and predicative objectivity; (v) that the defense of objectivity in interpretive matters and that of objectivity in noninterpretive matters need not (do not) proceed in the same way; (vi) that the defense of thesis (i) need not depend on any equivocation regarding attributing incompatible interpretations to the same referent;[4] (vii) that there is no compelling reason to restrict evidentiary or interpretive sources in such a way that (i) could never be reasonably defended;[5] (viii) that inter-

---

3. See Monroe C. Beardsley, *The Possibility of Criticism* (Detroit: Wayne State University Press, 1970).

4. See, for instance, Robert Stecker, "The Constructivist's Dilemma," *Journal of Aesthetics and Art Criticism* IV (1997).

5. For a would-be example, which fails on internal grounds, see Antonin Scalia, "The Role of United States Federal Courts in Interpreting the Constitution and the Law," in *A Matter of Interpretation: Federal Laws and the Courts,* ed. Amy Gutmann, with commentaries by Amy Gutmann et al. (Princeton: Princeton University Press, 1997).

pretations defensible at time *t* may well alter the objective interpretability of a work at *t'* later than *t*, consistent with items (iii)–(vii); (ix) that (i) accords with actual critical practice; (x) that (i) is a realist claim; and (xi) that (i) does indeed allow for detecting the falsity, indefensibility, or defect of particular interpretations.

The validity of (i) is overdetermined. But its best defense favors what may be called an argument from "adequation": that is, (*a*) that the admissible range of interpretive claims must accord with the assigned nature of the interpretable things to which they answer, and (*b*) that the conceptual connection between the ontic and epistemic features of that adequation precludes any privilege or priority favoring either over the other. This is too compressed an argument to be helpful as it stands. I begin again, therefore, in a more discursive way.

I

I do not find it at all odd to concede that, say, Louis Leakey was drawn to *interpret* the stratification of the Olduvai Gorge, in northern Tanzania, when he and his wife attempted to date the Australopithecine fossils they first found at the gorge. I've seen the site: the layered sedimentations are perfectly visible, and on the strength of what I imagine are reasonable geological theories, Leakey was justified in claiming to have found the earliest remains (up to that date) of primeval man. In admitting that, however, one must take care to explain how it is that a natural formation—the gorge—is open to interpretation when, plainly, it lacks the kind of property that inherently invites interpretation: any of the usual expressive, representational, symbolic, semiotic, stylistic, traditional, historical, genre-bound, linguistic, purposive features of artworks and historical events.

The answer is that expressive and representational properties in paintings and sculptures are "intrinsically" interpretable and the gorge is interpretable "by courtesy" only, by being subsumed under an explanatory theory. Intrinsically interpretable properties I term "Intentional," meaning that they are properties of cultural origin, attributed to things that are the products, or entail the labor, of human artists or agents, and that they are interpretable for that reason. Aristotle, I note, nowhere addresses the possibility of a principled distinction between the natural and the cultural, which I view as decisive for the theory of interpretation, pretty well in accord with distinctions that have become unavoidable since the converging influence of the French and Industrial Revolutions.

I put the point this way because recent theories of art, of interpretation, of history, of the human condition itself, are still largely confined to the conceptual resources spanning no more than ancient and early-eighteenth-century philosophies. Theories of interpretation that fail to come to terms with the ontic difference between the natural and the cultural, or the historicity of the human world, or the intrinsically interpretable nature of the Intentional, are, I assume, simply defective.

Wherever, beyond the human or the encultured, we *interpret* what is before us—the behavior of animals or prelinguistic children, the causal processes and effects of the inanimate world—we speak by way of an obvious courtesy: in the first, we anthropomorphize animal and infant behavior in terms of human exemplars; in the second, we subsume what is "natural" under a theory that links a description of the phenomena in question to some scientific explanation we are trying to reach. (Explanations are, of course, themselves Intentional.) Here, we acknowledge a benign equivocation on the term "interpret."

All this is familiar enough. But the reminder confirms that there is little point in theorizing about the logic of interpretation without attending to *the nature of interpretable things*. The warning is resisted by those who assume the uniformity of the world—for instance, under the dubious belief that whatever is real is simply physical or must be modeled on the canonical description of physical phenomena.[6] Others profess to be able to choose a reasonable model of the logic of interpretation—under the uncertain scruple of remaining agnostic about the nature of interpretable things.[7] But how can we proceed if we neglect the "adequation" between *denotatum* and predicable?

By "adequation," I mean no more than the conceptual congruity between the supposed "nature" of certain *denotata* and whatever further attributes we ascribe to them as "objectively" theirs. The *Pietà*, we say, really represents the *pietà*: whatever counts as an objective interpretation of its actual representational features must surely be qualified by whatever may be

---

6. See, for instance, Beardsley, *The Possibility of Criticism,* and Robert Stecker, *Artworks: Definition, Meaning, Value* (University Park: Pennsylvania State University Press, 1997).

7. See, for instance, Michael Krausz, *Rightness and Reasons: Interpretation in Cultural Practices* (Ithaca, N.Y.: Cornell University Press, 1993), and the rather different account given by Paul Thom, *Making Sense: A Theory of Interpretation* (Lanham, Md.: Rowman & Littlefield, 2000).

rightly said of them. This seems beyond dispute, though it is disputed—or neglected—on its ontic side.[8]

II

The pivot of the argument rests with the analysis of Intentional properties. If I had more space, I would bring the analysis to bear on the conditions of the existence of cultural entities, on the *sui generis* emergence of the cultural from the natural, on the "second-natured" nature of human selves, on the fit between the cognizing competence of human selves and the cognizable things of the cultural world in which selves are first formed, on the historicity of the human world and the cognition of that world, on the very different ontologies of natural and cultural entities and the hybrid nature of the latter, on objective differences in reference and predication affecting entities of the two sorts, on the dependence of the cognition of natural entities on the reflexive cognition of the cultural world, on the constructive or constructivist nature of knowledge itself, on logical and technological constraints on interpretive relevance, on the analysis of linguistic meaning and its relation to meaningful structures that are not themselves linguistic.

But it would be a welcome economy that set all this aside, *if* the analysis of Intentional properties alone could rightly decide the issue posed by item (i) of the tally given above.[9] Consider, then, some specimen theories of interpretive work. Juhl himself has badgered the well-known disagreement between F. W. Bateson's and Cleanth Brooks's interpretations of Wordsworth's "A slumber did my spirit seal," but without providing compelling evidence for his own thesis. Many have worried these two readings, which, roughly, are said to mingle personal grief upon the loss of a loved one and

---

8. I regard this as the fatal weakness, for instance, of Danto's account of art and interpretation. See Arthur C. Danto, *The Transfiguration of the Commonplace: A Philosophy of Art* (Cambridge, Mass.: Harvard University Press, 1981). I don't deny that Danto *believes* that artworks are "real" and that interpretation is "objectively" constrained, but I see no basis for either claim in Danto's published work. See, further, Joseph Margolis, "Farewell to Danto and Goodman," *British Journal of Aesthetics* xxxviii (1998).

9. I have pursued these matters in some depth elsewhere, most recently in *Interpretation Radical but Not Unruly: The New Puzzle of the Arts and History* (Berkeley and Los Angeles: University of California Press, 1995); *Historied Thought, Constructed World* (Berkeley and Los Angeles: University of California Press, 1995); and *What, After All, Is a Work of Art?* (University Park: Pennsylvania State University Press, 1999).

either the affirmation of a kind of "pantheistic" reading of cosmic order or resignation in the face of a meaningless and ultimately dead world.[10] The critical stanza, following the speaker's realization of his beloved's death and the dawning of the thoughtful reflection it now occasions, runs this way:

> No motion has she now, no force;
> She neither hears nor sees:
> Rolled round in earth's diurnal course,
> With rocks, and stones, and trees.

I venture to say that one might reasonably find "in" the poem a distant echo, adjusted to Wordsworth's contemporary world, of John Donne's well-known divided reflections on the meaning of the then-contemporary eclipse of Ptolemaic astronomy, which is not actually mentioned in the Wordsworth poem.

The meaning of the poem's words is not ambiguous in the usual sense of ambiguity: Wordsworth is not often ambiguous in that way, and he is certainly not here. Yet, within a reasonable fit, the lines lend themselves to the two interpretations mentioned, which are indeed incompatible though textually inclusive: it is unlikely the poet "intended" both. Juhl confines himself (too much) to whether the phrase "Rolled round" signifies "gentle" or "violent" motion, in a sense suited to the rest of the line on either reading—hence, to affirming or denying a meaningful universe.[11] To me, Juhl's strategy obscures the option of reading the phrase "Rolled round" in a way that is *not* primarily occupied with its verbal congruity with specifically "gentle" or "violent" motion. (It seems plainly noncommittal.) The stanza does, however, raise the question whether the daily rotation of the earth signifies the one or the other cosmic conviction.

There is no satisfactory resolution of this matter on authorial or textual grounds (or on any other grounds): the two readings are palpably incompatible, and neither is demonstrably arbitrary or dependent on an obvious ambiguity. Other commentators—Torsten Pettersson, for instance, with regard

---

10. See F. W. Bateson, "Gray's *Elegy* Reconsidered," in *English Poetry: A Critical Introduction* (London: Longmans, Green, 1950), and Cleanth Brooks, "Irony as a Principle of Structure," in *Literary Opinion in America*, ed. Morton D. Zabel, 2d ed. (New York: Harper, 1951).

11. See Juhl, *Interpretation*, 70–89, 199–202. The dispute is also remarked in Beardsley, *The Possibility of Criticism*, and Hirsch, *Validity in Interpretation*.

to Gray's *Elegy*, Morris Weitz with regard to Shakespeare's *Hamlet*—have similarly collected diverging interpretations that yield at least a number of reasonably strong competing readings (by various hands) that cannot be dismissed or easily reconciled along the lines of a single valid interpretation and do not rest primarily on verbal ambiguities.[12]

Consider, also, some very well known interpretive specimens involving paintings, which require literary reference or historical context to establish their validity. I'm certain Leo Steinberg's celebrated lecture on the sexuality of Christ will be familiar to a large audience. What is most interesting about Steinberg's wide-ranging analysis is that it is, first of all, theologically well informed, even inventive in its detailed conjectures; that it is guided by a fresh authoritative disclosure of early-fifteenth-century papal sermons that identify the general "Incarnationist" theology of the time, which Steinberg learned from a certain J. W. O'Malley, S.J., and draws on;[13] and that O'Malley himself (who attended Steinberg's original lecture, on invitation) confirms the accuracy of Steinberg's grasp of the Incarnationist doctrine as well as the plausibility of his innovative conjectures about the significance of certain themes (for instance, the Infant's circumcision and erections).[14] Steinberg's work convincingly depends on the conceptual fashions of the period his specimens belong to. But notice: they do not rest on confirming artists' intentions in narrowly psychological or biographical terms.

I have two comments to offer, which are not meant to demean Steinberg's argument or his evidence. If I'm not mistaken, O'Malley was surprised by the fluency of Steinberg's account, drawn as it was from a detailed study of particular paintings and sculptures rather than imposed on them on the supposed authority of hitherto unknown or relatively unnoticed sermons, although, as I say, Steinberg relies on O'Malley's text in grasping the novelty of the Incarnationist doctrine. His interpretation would have been laughed out of court—even angrily contested—if we did not have something like O'Malley's new information about the actual texts of contemporary papal sermons (which Steinberg samples). The Incarnationist theology was in the air, but we cannot say with certainty that the artists of the period were

12. See Torsten Pettersson, *Literary Interpretation: Current Models and a New Departure* (Åbo: Åbo Academy Press, 1988), and Morris Weitz, *Hamlet and the Philosophy of Literary Criticism* (Chicago: University of Chicago Press, 1964).

13. J. W. O'Malley, *Praise and Blame in Renaissance Rome: Rhetoric, Doctrine, and Reform in the Second Oratory of the Papal Court, c. 1450–1521* (Durham, N.C.: Duke University Press, 1979), cited in Leo Steinberg, *The Sexuality of Christ in Renaissance Art and in Modern Oblivion* (New York: Pantheon, 1983).

14. These are remarked by John W. O'Malley in a postscript included in Steinberg's book.

pointedly occupied with its doctrinal distinctions. Accordingly, the interpretation cannot be more than plausible.

Thus it is that Steinberg contests interpretations of pertinent scenes—the "nursing Madonna," for instance, which was tactfully judged by Millard Meiss to signify "the Madonna's humility" but which Steinberg construes as attesting to "the truth of the Incarnation";[15] similarly, Steinberg reinterprets a woodcut by Hans Baldung Grien in which Saint Anne fondles the Infant's penis, against the judgment of "the foremost Baldung scholar Carl Koch," to the effect that Saint Anne's gesture should be interpreted in accord with "the artist's known interest in folk superstition."[16]

What is important for the theory of interpretation here is, first, that the relevant readings *cannot* be reliably recovered from the paintings alone—they depend on textual and historical information judged perceptually plausible, which, as far as one can see, overrides "authorial intent" in the narrow sense—and, second, that the interpretation of the perceptual features of particular paintings is brought into line with the *ethos* of the age, where we do not have sufficient grounds for singling out one painting or sculpture or woodcut or another from a *general* pattern of fifteenth- and sixteenth-century work.

You will find a similar interpretive strategy in Meyer Schapiro's well-known rejection of Freud's interpretation of Leonardo's treatment of Mary and Saint Anne as being more or less of the same age, "therefore" reflecting Leonardo's bastardy (that is, his having two mothers, his natural and his adoptive mother, which Freud draws inferentially from Leonardo's notebooks). Schapiro "defeats" the thesis by drawing attention to the then-current cult of Saint Anne, which favored depicting her in her prime—"hence" the parity of the represented ages of the two women.[17]

In these two cases, Schapiro's and Steinberg's, what we appreciate is the force of the *prior* question of the proper gauge within which we might hope to confirm one interpretation over another, among the works in question. Both Steinberg and Schapiro signify that, *under the circumstances,* it would be pointless to treat their interpretation biographically or psychologically

---

15. Steinberg, *The Sexuality of Christ*, 14.

16. Ibid., 6.

17. See Sigmund Freud, "Leonardo da Vinci and a Memory of His Childhood," in *The Standard Edition of the Complete Psychological Works of Sigmund Freud,* vol. xi, trans. and ed. James Strachey, with Anna Freud, Alix Strachey, and Alan Tyson (London: Hogarth Press and the Institute of Psycho-Analysis, 1957), and Meyer Schapiro, "Leonardo and Freud: An Art-Historical Study," *Journal of the History of Ideas* xvii (1956).

rather than in terms of the theological currents and the turn (in the period) toward naturalistic representation. There are very large alternative interpretive options here, large enough, I would say, to favor item (i) of my original tally.

Nevertheless, when we reach Michelangelo's *Risen Christ,* in the early sixteenth century, the older argument seems inadequate. Steinberg reports that "every 16th-century copy [of the sculpture] represents the figure as aproned." Michelangelo gives us a naturalistic nude Christ "complete [as the Incarnationist idiom has it] in all the parts of a man." But, says Steinberg, "[i]f Michelangelo denuded his *Risen Christ,* he must have sensed a rightness in his decision more compelling than inhibitions of modesty; must have seen that a loincloth would convict these genitalia of being 'pudenda,' thereby denying the very work of redemption which promised to free human nature from its Adamic contagion of shame."[18]

Pretty enough, but not compelling and certainly not decisive in the way of a unique right interpretation. Perhaps one cannot simply disconfirm Steinberg's conjecture. (I wouldn't dream of it.) But, by parity of reasoning (keeping Steinberg's larger argument in mind), it seems more reasonable to avoid psychologizing; it also seems much too specific to proffer a theologized conjecture in Michelangelo's behalf even when joined to the other evidence Steinberg adduces: he cites a remotely suggestive text from Saint Thomas. It seems better to refer the full naturalism of the sculptural figure to Michelangelo's general practice: perhaps the boldness of the nudity reflects stylistic consistency, given a wider *ethos.* There may be no doctrinal import of Steinberg's sort beyond the obvious convergence of the ancient and Renaissance preference for naturalism and the period's acceptance of the Incarnationist teaching. Here, we begin to see the limitations of moving toward a determinate or exclusionary interpretation: there seem to be no sufficient grounds for going beyond sheer plausibility—but not because of a "lack of evidence" centered in the paintings and sculptures themselves.

There is an instructive comparison that can be made out between Steinberg's treatment of the Michelangelo and Meyer Schapiro's treatment of Giotto's Arena fresco featuring the betrayal of Christ. Schapiro had also explored the connection between texts and pictorial images and had, by that device, developed an incipient semiotics of frontal and profile faces in religious paintings. But when he comes to Giotto's arresting treatment of Jesus and Judas, both of whose faces are in profile, Schapiro features "Giot-

18. Steinberg, *The Sexuality of Christ,* 18, 20.

to's originality of conception," which he could indeed confirm by way of Giotto's *oeuvre* and an earlier tradition of painting religious events, viewed against the import of the biblical text.

Schapiro contrasts the treatment of Giotto's paired faces with a painting of the same event that hangs in Assisi, produced a generation before (in which Christ's face and posture are frontal and Judas is in profile). As Schapiro says: "[T]he pair [in the Assisi painting] lack entirely the inwardness of Giotto's image of the fateful encounter of two men who look into each other's eyes and in that instant reveal their souls. The uncanny power of the glance in a strictly frontal head is transferred to the profile as an objective natural expression, fully motivated in the situation. It is perhaps the first example of a painting in which the reciprocal subjective relations of an I and a You have been made visible through the confrontation of two profiles."[19]

This is a bold conjecture, but it is not psychologized, or even, really, theologized. It is notably in accord with Giotto's transitional role and originality in the history of painting *and* almost entirely supported by visual and pictorial considerations. (I must ask you to keep Schapiro's interpretation in mind as suggesting the logical distinction of descriptions of specifically Intentional materials.) What is important is Schapiro's attempt to demarcate a visual clue to Giotto's decisive innovation. His interpretation becomes an unavoidable option in the gathering history of connoisseurship, but it cannot possibly preclude being contested by another strong interpretation, if there is one to be had, drawn from another selection of earlier paintings that might have suggested an alternative approach to Giotto's innovation. I find Schapiro's argument compelling, but it does not pretend to confirm any unique interpretation. None could be vouchsafed by Schapiro's methods.

III

I take these examples to confirm that there is no obvious way in which relying on authorial or artistic intent, textual meaning, historical ethos, genre, syntax, biography, context, rules or practices of interpretation, can-

19. Meyer Schapiro, *Words and Pictures: On the Literal and the Symbolic in the Illustration of a Text* (The Hague: Mouton, 1973), 46.

ons, or anything of the kind could possibly force us to accept the unique-interpretation thesis. It's quite possible that, in particular cases, the idea of exploring plural, nonconverging, or incompatible interpretations would prove pointless. But, on empirical grounds alone, it is surely the better part of good sense to leave the matter open-ended. It's the theoretical issue that's troublesome, and it's the pretense of having discovered a certain modal necessity binding on interpretation that poses the most insistent questions. Beardsley tells us:

> I hold that there are a great many interpretations that obey what might be called the principle of "the Intolerability of Incompatibles," i.e., if two of them are logically incompatible, they cannot both be true. Indeed, I hold that *all* of the literary interpretations that deserve the name obey this principle. But of course I do not wish to deny that there are cases of ambiguity where no interpretation can be established over its rivals, nor do I wish to deny that there are many cases where we cannot be sure that we have the correct interpretation.[20]

But in so doing he provides no more than an *obiter dictum*.

It's easy to see how, against Beardsley's view, we *could* still admit, *provisionally*, incompatible interpretations—on the expectation (Beardsley's perhaps) that, ideally, such conflicts cannot fail to be overcome as we approach the uniquely valid option. But why should Beardsley's dictum be honored at all? Well, you may argue—I agree Beardsley had something of this sort in mind—the interpretation of artworks (literature, paradigmatically) is very much like the description of physical objects; physical objects have determinate properties independently of any inquiry; hence, their right description accords with a strict bivalence, and interpretation accords with the same bivalence. But you may also argue *this* way: artworks possess Intentional properties, which physical objects do not; interpretation, therefore, addresses "meanings" and "meaningful" structures, and such structures do not, or cannot be shown to, behave in the same way (logically) that physical properties do; hence, Beardsley's argument fails.

How does the counterargument go? More or less as follows: first, by affirming that Intentional properties are not determinate in the same way physical properties are, and second, by conceding that, nevertheless, they

20. Beardsley, *The Possibility of Criticism*, 44.

remain sufficiently determinable to be open to their own kind of objective confirmation. The enabling notion holds that objectivity is itself a reasoned, or critical, construction fitted, reflexively, to different kinds of inquiries, that is, to inquiries about different kinds of things, involving different kinds of cognitive competence. The idea is simply that intrinsically interpretable properties—expressive, representational, symbolic properties, all Intentional, as I say—are *sui generis,* determinable enough to be confirmed but not determinate in the way physical exemplars are said to be. If so, then, contrary to Beardsley's view, they cannot be made to conform to a strict bivalent logic.

If this single concession could be won, it would prove impossible to vindicate the interpretive analogue of scientific objectivism: *some* reasonably strong form of relativism would have to be acknowledged,[21] for the determinacy/determinability problem would effectively preclude any principled victory for the unique-interpretation thesis. I don't suppose this can be fully demonstrated without bringing item (i) of my original tally into convincing alignment with the rest of the tally given; but any practitioner sympathetic with this line of challenge against the unique-interpretation thesis will find it easy to supply what's missing.

Let me mention another specimen view opposed to mine that converges somewhat with Beardsley's, though by way of artists' intentions. Arthur Danto straightforwardly declares:

> I believe we cannot be deeply wrong if we suppose that the correct interpretation of object-as-artwork is the one which coincides most closely with the artist's own interpretation. . . . My theory of interpretation is constitutive, for an object is an artwork *at all* only in relation to an interpretation. . . . If interpretations are what constitute works, there are no works without them and works are misconstituted when interpretation is wrong. And knowing the artist's interpretation is in effect what he or she has made. The interpretation is not something outside the work: work and interpretation arise together in aesthetic consciousness. As interpretation is inseparable from work, it is inseparable from the artist if it is the artist's work.[22]

21. On the meaning of "objectivism," see Richard J. Bernstein, *Beyond Objectivism and Relativism: Science, Hermeneutics, and Praxis* (Philadelphia: University of Pennsylvania Press, 1983).

22. Arthur C. Danto, *The Philosophical Disenfranchisement of Art* (New York: Columbia University Press, 1986), 44–45.

Now, I find this remarkably unguarded. It seems to mean, strictly speaking, that we don't have (or cannot discern) a *work* at all if we cannot know the artist's intention by way of something like the artist's say-so! Hence, too, if a would-be work is ambiguous (though that may not have been the artist's *intention*—Danto considers the possibility of ambiguity), then, once again, we will be unable to recover the work at all or recover any one work. And if the hermeneuts are right—even Romantic theorists like Hirsch, who introduce genre studies in order to override any narrowly biographical or psychological reading of intention[23]—then, once again, Danto will have put us at risk with regard to individuating and identifying particular works.[24] But what *is* Danto's philosophical argument or evidence?

What could possibly show that exploring an artist's intention *through* the enabling practices of the society in which he or she works (what Danto condemns as "deep interpretation") "always looks[s] past the work to something else"?[25] I don't find the supporting argument in Danto. I agree it would be nonsense to disregard the artist's intention altogether, though it may need to be reconstructed. But I don't see the force of any claim to the effect (1) that interpretations must accord with the original artist's intention; (2) that all departures from (1) are "wrong" or, worse, are about nothing at all or at least not about any one or the same thing; (3) that, wherever there is an "actual" work, there must be a determinate "constituting" interpretation in accord with the artist's intention; (4) that artists' intentions provide the only way artworks can be constituted; or, most important, (5) that intentional attributions drawn from examining the tradition (remember Steinberg and Schapiro) are (must be) "outside" the work ("always look past the work to something else"). *Where is the argument?*[26]

IV

It's unlikely that one could find a stronger set of opposing claims than those advanced by Juhl, Hirsch, Beardsley, and Danto. One way or another, they deny item (i) of my original tally and favor the unique-interpretation thesis.

23. See, for instance, Hirsch, *Validity in Interpretation,* chap. 3.
24. See Danto, *The Philosophical Disenfranchisement of Art,* chap. 3.
25. Ibid., 47.
26. See, further, Arthur C. Danto, "Responses and Replies," in *Danto and His Critics,* ed. Mark Rollins (Oxford: Blackwell, 1995), 201.

But none of them—and no one else, to my knowledge—has ever demonstrated the necessary falsity of item (i) or the greater viability, or even the independent adequacy, of the denial over the affirmation. Beardsley's account risks losing the distinctive nature of artworks; Juhl's founders on the supposed determinacy of artists' intentions in any psychological or biographical sense; Hirsch demonstrates the untenability of the psychologizing view but fails to see that genres are also open to plural interpretations; and Danto's account confirms the insuperable paradox of treating artists' original intentions as actually constituting artworks.

I have suggested another resource—item (iii) of my first tally—drawn from the inherent nature of culturally significant (Intentional) properties. This line of reasoning has the virtue of advancing beyond mere polemic. In any event, item (iii) puts the burden of proof squarely on those who, like Beardsley, believe we *can* arrive at the unique-interpretation thesis without bothering to address the matter of the inseparability of the epistemic and ontic aspects of interpretation.[27] I believe we cannot! The inseparability claim is nothing but the adequation thesis complicated by the distinctive features of cultural life and inquiry.

The deciding issue comes to this: non-Intentional properties (physical properties preeminently) can almost always be made extensionally more determinate in a "linear" way by simply adding more determinate intensional details to a given predicate—as if by selections made from an antecedently prepared vocabulary that is not tethered to controversial specimens. But that is normally not possible with Intentional properties in interpretive contexts. Among the latter, each interpretive ascription must be separately tailored and separately judged valid when applied to its appointed referent. Here, we lack the sense of any antecedently prepared vocabulary, from which we may make an apt selection that matches extensional and intensional determinacy in regularized ways.

Consider, for example, increasing intensional determinations of the predicate "red," that is, more and more precise determinations of a particular red before us. These can normally be arrayed in such a way that when extension decreases, it decreases inversely and linearly with increasing intension.

---

27. I have already mentioned Robert Stecker, who champions bivalence in interpretation without providing a convincing account of the nature of an artwork that would support the thesis; in a very different spirit, Michael Krausz professes to be open to competing conjectures regarding "singularism" and "multiplism," but he apparently believes the argument can be adequately pursued without reference to the nature of artworks themselves. That is precisely what I dispute.

But Intentional properties ("baroque") or interpretive descriptions (Schapiro's account of Giotto's treatment of the faces of Jesus and Judas) do not behave in the same way; each description or epithet must be judged apt or just as a singular attribution—*un mot juste*—not as a standard distinction in a more or less freestanding linear array of increasing intensions but as an attribution to a particular work. Intentional ascriptions do not behave like "red"; or when they do, marginally, they are usually modeled on the non-Intentional, as in restricting stylistic attributes to a certain historical interval or treating them as hardly more than physical distinctions ("early" or "high" baroque or gradations of *piano* and *lento*).

There is a grand puzzle here: it may be the single most important puzzle affecting the "logic" of interpretation. Let me put it in a full and proper setting. I hold that, among "natural" (or, better: physical) *denotata,* attributes are normally said to be *determinate* (though they remain, as they must be, general)—they are also *determinable* in a relatively linear way, matching intension and extension—whereas Intentional attributes are characteristically not determinate *in that way,* hence, also, *not* determinable in the related way. If so, then what count as objective interpretations of artworks and other cultural phenomena cannot be restricted to the strong bivalent logic said to be adequate for ascribing physical or non-Intentional natural attributes.

Physical properties are said to be determinate and linearly determinable in principle, without our ever reaching an infimate predicable. In that sense, Intentional properties are determinate and determinable in a very different way. They remain determinate of course, but only in the way of their relatively discrete fit to a given *denotatum.* That explains why we suppose that, ideally, physical but not Intentional predications cannot fail to conform to a bivalent logic. But even there, only if we can always be said to know what *is true* of independent nature. That also would fail if we could defend, objectively, incommensurable or incompatible descriptions of nature.[28] For then, even the ascription of physical properties would be constructive and

---

28. For example, in the manner advanced by Thomas S. Kuhn, *The Structure of Scientific Revolutions,* 2d ed., enl. (Chicago: University of Chicago Press, 1970), sec. x, and Paul K. Feyerabend, "Explanation, Reduction, and Empiricism," in *Scientific Explanation, Space, and Time,* Minnesota Studies in the Philosophy of Science, vol. 3, ed. Herbert Feigl and Grover Maxwell (Minneapolis: University of Minnesota Press, 1963). Interpretive ascriptions in the arts always, I suggest, involve the fitness of every single epithet addressed discretely to a particular work; whereas natural predicates tend to be regularized in intensionally linear ways *for* further contingent attribution.

conjectural and subject to the Intentional complexities of historical experience.

Where an interpretation is thought to be apt, we will not normally be able to make it more determinate by simply adding further, linearly linked intensional distinctions meant to pick out the same feature the first interpretation had identified. Intentional predicates are custom-made, heterogeneous, idiosyncratic, holist, "punctal" (to use an obsolete term), designed to fit individual *denotata* in such a way that they cannot be reliably disjoined from those *denotata*—so as to form an all-purpose extensional vocabulary similar to a system of physical predicates. Some marginal yielding is possible, but not much: even period styles tend to be holistic rather than extensional and require holistic adjustments when applied to strong new specimens beyond their first exemplars. It is notably difficult, for instance, to treat Rubens as a paradigm of early baroque and then fit the category to El Greco, or indeed to fail to bring El Greco into line with the phases of the Italian baroque and its variant forms in Spain and the Low Countries. This seems to be the rule rather than the exception.

V

I favor a strong distinction between the *linear* and *punctal* natures of non-Intentional and Intentional properties. But the significance of that difference gains its full force only when it is set in the larger context of a theory of physical and cultural phenomena. Let me add, without ceremony, therefore, a series of ordered distinctions to strengthen its intended lesson.

First of all, there is no algorithmic way (and no approximation to same) for confirming referential (or denotative) and predicative success with regard to either physical or cultural phenomena. Cultural phenomena are not poorer in this regard than physical phenomena. The best-known theories about reidentifying numerically distinct referents—from Frege to Kripke—fail to solve the epistemic question; it cannot be done predicatively, and every strategy (the causal strategy, for instance) depends on the predicative. Most discussants hardly make the effort.

There is also no algorithmic way to confirm predicative similarity (through whatever variant manifestations may arise: the ancient puzzle of the One and the Many). Only if some form of Platonism could be made operative in cognitive terms (which no one believes) could the predication of non-Intentional attributes provide a possible basis for an extensional treatment of Intentional attributes. The result is that we subordinate all confidence in an exceptionless, bivalent treatment of predication to the consensual tolerance of one or another viable society. This is close to Wittgenstein's master theme in *Philosophical Investigations,* except that Wittgenstein pretty well ignores the question of the historicized process of *lebensformlich* practices and the related problems of inter- and intrasocietal divergences that could never preclude the relevance of relativistic and incommensurabilist options.[29] But to admit any of these considerations would already defeat the unique-interpretation thesis—and obviously more.

Second, by distinguishing between "physical" and "cultural" entities, in the sense that the first lack and the second possess Intentional properties, we cannot fail to admit that artworks and histories are not "natural-kind" phenomena. But if that is so, and if cultural *denotata* can be individuated and reidentified with as much success as natural-kind entities, then, short of preserving coherence and discursive control, there is no reason to deny the distinction of intrinsically interpretable things—hence no reason to deny that such things *may be interpreted in incompatible ways though still objectively.*

We may say that cultural entities lack "natures" (natural-kind natures), have "histories" instead, or have natures that are no more than histories (on their Intentional side). But we must also bear in mind that cultural entities are, *qua* real, artifactually, indissolubly embodied in material entities: hybrid second-natured selves in the members of *Homo sapiens,* or Michelangelo's *Moses* in a block of cut marble. In saying that Intentionally qualified entities are "embodied," I mean (*a*) that, *qua* real, they are emergent in a cultural or *sui generis* way with respect to the merely physical or biological; (*b*) that they are inseparable from their particular *materiae;* and (*c*) that their real (Intentional) properties are also hybrid properties, indissolubly "incarnate" in material properties.[30]

The full significance of these distinctions may still elude you. What needs to be emphasized is that, contrary to what holds for physical entities, it *is* possible that the numerical identity of artworks can be fixed as effectively as the identity of physical objects, all the while we admit their labile *"nature."*

Number and nature need not move in tandem, despite what Aristotle

---

29. See Ludwig Wittgenstein, *Philosophical Investigations,* trans. G. E. M. Anscombe (Oxford: Basil Blackwell, 1953).

30. See further, on "embodied" and "incarnate," Margolis, *Historied Thought, Constructed World.*

says. It is generally assumed that a change in the "essential" nature of natural-kind entities logically precludes the possibility that a designated particular *of some kind* ("of that nature") could, consistently, remain one and the same thing through such a change. *That is not an operative constraint binding on cultural entities.* (Cultural entities are simply not natural-kind entities.) *Hamlet,* for instance, can be identified as one and the same play though its "nature" actually changes and evolves through such interpretation! Its properties remain determinable, without being determinate in the manner already sketched; and its properties may be subject to change in the manner characteristic of the historicized interpretation of the Intentional.

Taken together, the distinctive strands of the ontology of cultural things make it impossible to preclude the interpretive options afforded by relativism and allied policies. At any rate, the option is a coherent one and cannot be ruled out of bounds by objectivistic tastes. It is in this precise sense that the ontology of cultural entities affords a basis for defeating the unique-interpretation thesis.

Finally, if we take seriously the historicity of thought, we must accommodate the "constructed" nature of the cultural world itself, the constructed nature of Intentional properties within that world, *and* the constructed nature of the cognitive competence of interpreting selves. By "constructed" or "constructive" or "constructivist," I mean *here* what is (1) real in substantive or predicative respects, or both, (2) that results from distinctly cultural processes, (3) so that what rightly counts as objective in that world is *imputed* to be so by inquiring selves themselves constructed within the same world. (The "constructed" is not meant to entail any pernicious form of idealism.)

To admit the constructed and historicized nature of the Intentional world makes it impossible to view objectivity in cultural matters as anything but a constructed norm subject to indefinitely extended historicized revisions. Cultural understanding is essentially a society's self-understanding, formed under the conditions of radical history by creatures who are themselves the precipitates of that same process. It is impossible to draw from these conditions grounds for championing anything like the unique-interpretation thesis.

I have now identified four interlocking features of the cultural world on which interpretive objectivity depends: the constructed nature of referential and predicative success in general, the difference in the logical connection between "number" and "nature" as applied to natural and cultural *denotata,* the historicized conditions of a society's reflexive understanding of its own utterances, and the very different senses in which Intentional and non-Intentional properties may be said to be determinate and determinable. Two strong conclusions follow: one, that it is philosophically hopeless to venture an opinion on the logic of interpretive work without a reasonable sense of the ontology of the cultural world; the other, that all evidence bearing on the first conclusion confirms that there can be no convincing grounds for believing that the unique-interpretation thesis could possibly be true. I rest my case.

Rightness and Success in Interpretation

Paul Thom

This paper has three parts. In the first part I discuss a game, proposed by Wittgenstein, in which we are asked to complete each of Brahms's variations on the *Saint Antony Chorale,* in the appropriate style. I treat this as an exercise in interpretation. By imagining a couple of interpretive variants on Wittgenstein's game, I distinguish between success and rightness in interpretation and argue that there are four classes of interpretations—ones where there are many ways of succeeding but no right interpretation, ones where there is one way of succeeding (the right interpretation), ones where there are many ways of succeeding and many right interpretations, and ones where there is no way of succeeding and no way of being right. The general conclusion is that interpretation of itself is potentially plural.

In the second part I outline three related ways of articulating the structure of interpretation consistent with its potential plurality. These involve an external or internal object, an object-as-represented, and the resulting interpretation of it. An examination of the relation between internal and external objects leads to a distinction between two types of representation, only one of which involves intentionality. There follows a critical discussion of Michael Krausz's argument that the structure of interpretation, as proposed by me, includes a commitment to constructive realism.

In the third part I propose, by way of interpretation, an ontological analysis of the elements in the structure of interpretation, particularly "internal objects," which I take to be determined by sets of properties. In certain cases it is necessary to take these as fuzzy sets, and therefore as requiring a nonbivalent logic. Elaborating on Margolis's definition of artworks as physically embodied and culturally emergent entities, I construct an argument supporting Margolis's claim that the interpretation of artworks in general requires such a nonclassical logic.

I. Potential Plurality

There is no general answer to the question How many interpretations of a given object are there?—and this remains so even if we qualify the question with words like "ideally" or restrict consideration to "admissible" or "right" interpretations. You might as well ask how many ways there are of getting from one place to another. It depends on what the places are and on what counts as a way of getting from one to the other. In some cases there is only one way, in others many, and in some cases there is no way. Similarly with interpretation: you first need to specify what is being interpreted and what would count as an interpretation of it. Having done that, you find that in some cases there is only one right interpretation, in others there are many, and in yet others there are none.

Consider this game that Wittgenstein invites us to play:

> Take a theme like that of Haydn's (St. Antony Chorale), take the part of one of Brahms's variations corresponding to the first part of the theme, and set the task of constructing the second part of the variation in the style of its first part. That is a problem of the same kind as mathematical problems are. If the solution is found, say as Brahms gives it, then one has no doubt;—that is the solution.
>
> We are agreed on this route. And yet, it is obvious here that there may easily be different routes, on each of which we can be in agreement, each of which we might call consistent [*konsequent*].[1]

Playing this game can be seen as a form of interpretation, since it is akin to such paradigmatic cases as the interpretive completion of a damaged text or

---

1. Ludwig Wittgenstein, *Remarks on the Foundations of Mathematics,* ed. G. H. von Wright, R. Rhees, G. E. M. Anscombe; trans. G. E. M. Anscombe (Oxford: Basil Blackwell, 1964), V-8. It is of course *musical* consistency that Wittgenstein has in mind.

the elaboration of a text by a reader or a performer. Interpretations of this ilk are termed "elaborative" by David Novitz,[2] who contrasts them with "elucidatory" interpretations.[3]

Novitz takes elucidatory interpretations to be primary, since only they aim at achieving understanding.[4] According to him, provided that the interpreter wishes to understand, any interpretation that is not conducive to understanding is modified until it is so conducive. He states that elucidatory interpretation "can reflect on and modify" prior elaborations "if they impede a successful understanding."[5] He does not elucidate by way of an example; so let us elaborate.

Suppose there is a passage in *Pride and Prejudice* that implies that Elizabeth Bennett's hair is red. And suppose that someone, unaware of this passage, has by way of elaborative interpretation imagined Elizabeth Bennett's hair to be black. (So we have an elaborative interpretation that conflicts with a successful understanding of the text.) Suppose now that this interpreter is confronted with an elucidation of the text that draws out the implication that Elizabeth's hair is red. Novitz is presumably saying that this elucidation of the text in some way leads to the modification of the elaborative interpretation according to which Elizabeth's hair is red. But in what way? And does this show that elucidatory interpretation is prior to the elaborative variety?

Surely an imaginative interpreter may choose not to modify an elaboration in the light of a fuller understanding of the text. Such an interpreter may prefer to go on imagining Elizabeth with black hair, all the time knowing that the text has her with red hair. Doesn't this show that Novitz is wrong to insist that where elucidation conflicts with elaboration, the latter must be modified?

Well, Novitz might not think so. He might say that an imaginative interpreter who clings to an erroneous elaboration is no longer an interpreter of the text. Novitz's claim might be, not simply that imaginative interpreters

2. David Novitz, "Interpretation and Justification," *Metaphilosophy* 31, nos. 1/2 (2000) (special issue: *The Philosophy of Interpretation,* ed. Joseph Margolis and Tom Rockmore): 4–24.

3. This terminology is a little unfortunate. Elucidation is not repetition. To elucidate an object, you have to say something about it different from what you said in identifying it. So all interpretations—even elucidatory ones—elaborate on their intentional objects. Novitz explains that by elaborative interpretations he means ones that are consistent with the text but not specified by it.

4. Novitz, "Interpretation and Justification," 5–7.

5. Ibid., 7.

must modify their elaborations in the light of a fuller understanding of the text, but that they must do so if they are to be interpreters of that text. The point would be, not that they are no longer interpreting, but that they are no longer interpreting that text. In a strict sense this seems right. The willfully wayward reader of *Pride and Prejudice* is, strictly speaking, elaborating not on a text that implies red hair for Elizabeth, but on a version of the text in which the hair-color is not specified. Elaborating on a text one knows to be corrupt or otherwise erroneous cannot strictly be counted as elaborating on the (corrected) text, since the corrected text does not leave that particular elaboration open.

What this shows is that a correct understanding of certain things may be a precondition of elaborating on a text, and that such an understanding may in turn be the outcome of an elucidatory interpretation. Even so, this does not imply that elaborative interpretations in general are secondary to, or less valuable than, the elucidatory variety. So, if I adopt Novitz's terminology, I do so without the connotations that he attaches to it.

We are dealing, then, with a case of elaborative interpretation. Interpretations of this sort, because they aim to go beyond the work, do not have as their general aim getting the work right. Novitz thinks that elaborative interpretations have "no particular aim" and that there is no way of assessing them other than in terms of their virtuosity.[6] I disagree. All interpretations, including the elaborative variety, can be assessed at least for their coherence. (Recall Wittgenstein's reference to consistency.) Indeed, one of the standard traps in elaborative interpretation lies in the temptation to yield to a virtuosic elaboration of part of the work that cannot extend beyond that part and cannot be made to cohere with the rest of the work. Success and failure are categories that apply to all interpretation; but success does not always consist in rightness.

Notice that to play Wittgenstein's game successfully we have to get something right, namely Brahms's style. Our elaborations will not be successful unless we have a sound understanding of Brahms's style. But there are many different ways of achieving that: a style is not a formula. (Wittgenstein: "[T]here may easily be different routes, on each of which we can be in agreement.") If we continued one of the variations in a pseudo-Brahmsian style that was, say, a little too influenced by Schumann, then we wouldn't have got the style right. We can distinguish between this *preliminary* rightness and a true rightness of interpretation. Players of the game, after all, are

6. Ibid.

subject to two constraints—getting Brahms's style right and producing *variations* on the Haydn theme. Satisfaction of the first condition doesn't guarantee satisfaction of the second. In fact there is no *right* way of constructing the interpretations that Wittgenstein's game invites, since among the constructions that satisfy the preliminary condition of being in Brahms's style there is no way of singling out a subclass of the "right" elaborations. (Maybe it was a recognition of this that led Novitz to think that elaborative interpretations have no particular aim.) On the other hand, there are many ways of *succeeding* in Wittgenstein's game. The rule of the game is "Continue each of the variations in Brahms's style," and there are many ways of doing that.

But (you might say) surely not all ways of succeeding in the game are equally good; surely someone who managed to produce exactly Brahms's own way of continuing a particular variation would have done better than anyone else! (Wittgenstein says "that is the solution.") Well, not necessarily. Remember that the point of the game is not to guess the way Brahms wrote the variations. (We are meant to suppose that players are familiar with Brahms's style but not with his finished variations.) Given the rule of the game, the best game is played by someone who produces the best Brahms-style variation on Haydn's theme; and this might not be identical with Brahms's own variations. Of course, someone who independently came up with exactly what Brahms wrote would have every right to feel pleased with this achievement. But that is different from having done the best. After all, Brahms himself may not have done the best possible job of finishing a variation in the same style.

Well, if Brahms's own completions of the variations play no "official" role in the game, let's eliminate them by imagining a second scenario: Brahms wrote only the first half of each variation, the whole set having been composed as an exercise ("the BH Game") for young composers. The players of the BH Game are required to continue the unfinished variations in Brahms's style. Again, interpretive success can be achieved in many distinct ways, and again, there is no right way of completing each variation in the same style. But now there is no temptation to think that there is one best (Brahms-blest) way to play the BH Game.

Now imagine a third scenario. Brahms wrote the set of variations as we know them, but *published* only the first half of each variation, keeping the unpublished second halves in his bottom drawer. What he wrote was the complete set of variations; but what he published was a BH Guessing Game whose rule is not "Complete each variation in the style of Brahms" but

"Guess how Brahms completed each variation."[7] Only one way of constructing the variations is right: it is to be found in Brahms's bottom drawer. When young composers play the BH Guessing Game, coming up with completed variations that differ from the score in Brahms's bottom drawer, they are getting it wrong (even if they are writing better music than Brahms did).

We could also imagine a fourth scenario: Brahms composed several alternative completions of each variation, keeping these secret but publishing the BH Guessing Game. Interpretive success would again be a matter of rightness; it's just that there would be *several* right interpretations.

Finally we could imagine a fifth scenario in which Brahms published the BH Guessing Game, pretending that he had kept copies of the completed variations, when in fact he had not done so. Here, players of the game would be deceived into believing that there was a criterion of rightness when in fact there was no such thing. As in the first scenario, there would be no right interpretation; but, in contrast to the first scenario, no interpretation would be successful, since the game's rule has the effect of limiting success to rightness.

Thus far we have seen that there are four different types of elaborative interpretations where respectively

1. no interpretation is right but many are successful;
2. only one interpretation is right;
3. many interpretations are right;
4. no interpretation is right and none is successful.

In all cases where there are right interpretations, the reason is that there exists something that determines the interpretation—something already present in the phenomenon—even if this determining element is unknown to the interpreter.

These results may be summed up by saying that while there are cases (case 2) where an object has just one right interpretation, interpretation does not of its nature require that each object have a right interpretation (as cases 1 and 4 demonstrate) or have only one right interpretation (as case 3 demonstrates) or have only one successful interpretation (as case 1 demon-

---

7. We might say that, though the result of a guessing game (the answer) has the status of an interpretation, not all ways of arriving at that result deserve the name "interpreting." For example, if we arrive at a solution to the BH Guessing Game by interrogating Brahms or by breaking into his house and opening the secret drawer, then though our answer is the correct interpretation, it was not by a process of interpretation that we arrived at it. We cheated.

strates). In general, interpretation is potentially plural (though this doesn't imply that any given object of interpretation has many ideally admissible interpretations). Let's call this the thesis of Potential Plurality.

II. The Structure of Interpretation

It seems at first sight that interpretation is a two-place relation whose first term is an output (also commonly called the "interpretation") and whose second is an input (the "object of interpretation"). Such a dyadic structure would be consistent with Potential Plurality. To accommodate Potential Plurality, interpretation merely needs to be a many-one relation.

However, there is a difficulty in regarding interpretation as a two-term relation. The difficulty can be illustrated by Michael Krausz's discussion of a line drawing that can be seen either as two faces or as a vase. Discussing the interpretation of this drawing, Krausz says "the object-of-interpretation is understood in terms of its imputed properties,"[8] and in one sense this is perfectly correct; but that sense cannot, consistently with the thesis of Potential Plurality, be allowed to imply that in this case there are two distinct objects-of-interpretation. For if that were allowed, then we would have no way of stating—what must be stated in this case—that there is a single object (the line drawing) that admits two distinct interpretations. The most that Krausz's formulation can be allowed to imply is that interpreters *represent* this single object-of-interpretation *differently* when they interpret it as faces and when they interpret it as a vase. For this reason I suggested in a review of Krausz's book that interpretation should be understood as a three-term relation, linking an interpretation, an object-as-represented, and a "further object."[9] On this analysis, there could be many interpretations of a single "further object" even if there were a one-one relation between interpretations and objects-as-represented, provided that the representation relation was many-one. The representations in question would have to be representations-for-interpretation, and their success or failure would have

8. Michael Krausz, *Rightness and Reasons: Interpretation in Cultural Practices* (Ithaca, N.Y.: Cornell University Press, 1993), 68.

9. Paul Thom, review of *Rightness and Reasons*, by Michael Krausz, *Interpretation Radical but Not Unruly*, by Joseph Margolis, and "The Constructivist's Dilemma," by Robert Stecker, in *Literature and Aesthetics: The Journal of the Sydney Society of Literature and Aesthetics* 7 (1997): 181–85.

to be judged by their suitability for the proposed interpretation and not necessarily by their fidelity to the further object. Nonetheless, one subclass of interpretations could be distinguished by the fact that they require the object-as-represented to represent the further object faithfully: these would include Novitz's elucidatory interpretations.

The "further object" could be read as a real object—the lines in the face/vase drawing, the paint and canvas that embody *The Potato Eaters*. Elsewhere I use slightly different terms[10]—"interpretation," "object-as-represented," and "object"—and I specify that the object is an intentional object (which I had not done in my review of Krausz's book). The difference in question is that between internal and external objects of an intentional act.[11] An internal object is what the act is directed at, conceived from the agent's point of view; an external object is a really existing thing that happens to fit the specification contained in the internal object. Such an external object may in addition possess features that are not contained in the internal object. The first (externalist) approach envisages a realist answer to the question When are two interpretations about the same thing?—namely, by requiring that there be a real thing, independent of the two contesting interpretations, that is the object of both.

The second (internalist) approach does not require that there be any such real object, nor does it make sameness of object an all-or-nothing affair. Instead, it acknowledges that we can at best be *reasonably* confident that two interpretations are about *pretty much* the same object, provided that their (internal) objects are sufficiently similar.

We could also consider a third approach, one that combines these two by requiring both an external and an internal object; here there are four elements: "interpretation," "object-as-represented," "internal object," and "external object." On this third approach we will hold that two interpretations are about the same thing when their internal objects both correspond to some common external object.

At first glance, it seems that the internal object is some sort of representation of the external. In that case, representation would enter into this structure twice, the object-as-represented representing the internal object and the latter representing the external object. But we must be wary of viewing the

10. Paul Thom, *Making Sense: A Theory of Interpretation* (Lanham, Md.: Rowman & Littlefield, 2000), chap. 2.

11. For the distinction between internal and external objects, see Paul Thom, *For An Audience: A Philosophy of the Performing Arts* (Philadelphia: Temple University Press, 1993), 116–18.

matter thus. The way the internal object represents the external object is different from the way the object-as-represented represents the internal object. The former representation aims at a faithful identification of the external object; the latter aims to represent the output of the former representation—namely, the internal object—in a way suitable to the contemplated interpretation. Here fidelity is not of the essence; rather, we find representational techniques such as selective foregrounding, cutting, and so on. The two types of representation might be compared to two stages in the making of a movie: at the shooting stage we want the camera to represent faithfully what is visible before it, but at the editing stage what the camera has recorded needs to be cut or otherwise treated in ways that adapt it to suit the film's overall point. Analogously, in interpreting a play for the stage, we begin with a representation of what the play contains (e.g., we assume a definitive text) and then subject that representation to a further representation by processes of cutting, stylization, and so on.

However, there is a deeper reason for resisting the idea that in the third approach we have a duple occurrence of a relation of representation. If the relation between internal and external object were one of representation, like the relation of object-as-represented to internal object, then there would be an infinite regress of representations, given that representation is itself a relation admitting both internal and external objects. So the internal and external objects cannot be related by a relation of representation, if representation is itself a relation admitting both internal and external objects distinct from those that we already recognize in the act of interpretation. This is not to deny that there is a question whether a *correspondence* pertains between the internal and external objects. It is to deny that in order to perform an act of interpretation a person must perform a prior act, one of representation, requiring its own internal and external objects distinct from those that we already recognize in the act of interpretation.[12]

The relation between internal and external objects may be described as a form of representation, but only if representation is seen as a nonintentional relation, and a purely dyadic one, that does not tacitly involve a person in addition to those two objects. But then, this is not representation in the same sense as in the relation between object-as-represented and internal object; so the threat of an infinite regress of representations is defused.

12. The external and internal objects of the interpretation must be the same as the external and internal objects of the representation. Since the representation's function is to adapt the interpretation's object to fit the proposed interpretation, it must have the same object as the interpretation has; and this applies to external as well as internal objects.

There is no personal perspective involved in the gap between internal and external object, over and above what is already involved in the act of interpretation. The internal object is just the external object as the interpreter believes it to be. All there is, is one act of interpretation with an internal and an external object. The interpreter is not free to say, "I know *this* is the internal object and *that* is the external object, and I choose to take *that* as *this*"—just as (in Moore's paradox) the believer is not free to say, "Things are like *that,* but I believe they are like *this.*" Of course, interpreters can and do take things to be otherwise than they believe them to be; my point is that they can't do this at the level of the internal object. The internal object is just what you would say you are interpreting.

The structure of the third approach can be illustrated by reference to Brahms's Haydn Variations. As a whole, these can be seen as an interpretation of their theme.[13] In the present case the internal object as Brahms saw it is a theme entitled *Saint Antony Chorale,* written by Joseph Haydn. In reality there is no such thing, since the theme that is the basis of the variations, though titled *Saint Antony Chorale,* was not written by Haydn. So there is no external object, in the sense that there is no really existing object that perfectly fits the specification in the internal object, though there does exist an object—the *Saint Antony Chorale*—that fits that specification imperfectly. The internal object is represented in a succession of ways in the course of the variations: these modes of representation include a variety of contrapuntal and rhythmic techniques.[14] For example, the sixth variation

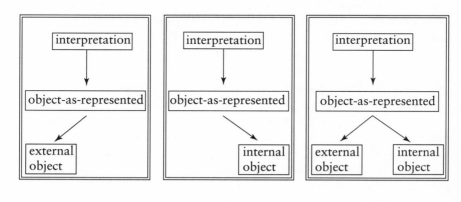

APPROACH 1   APPROACH 2   APPROACH 3

13. For variations as a type of interpretation, see Thom, *Making Sense,* 66.
14. See Roger Norrington and Michael Musgrave, "Conducting Brahms," in *The Cam-*

passes the theme through a representational filter that includes a trochaic rhythmic organization.[15]

Michael Krausz reads the structure of the first approach as requiring a "constructive realism." He defines realism and constructivism: "roughly, realism holds that that which is interpreted is fully constituted independently of interpretive practices, and constructivism holds that at least some of its defining properties are dependent upon such practices."[16] Krausz sees this first structure as constructivist to the extent that "there is a symbiotic or hermeneutic relation between objects-as-represented and interpretations."[17] On the other hand, he finds a strain of realism in this structure because the "further object" (the external object) "precedes interpretive activity" and is "representation-independent."[18] He states that "an object as such would be an object whose properties are independent of any representation of it."[19] I think Krausz reads too much into the first structure. An external object of interpretation in my sense does not have to be independent of all representation. My distinction between external objects and objects-as-represented carries no implications about whether there is or could be an object that is independent of all representation. All that my distinction between object and object-as-represented requires is that, when a given object is the subject of a given interpretation, the object undergoes a representation that is not the same as the interpretation and that is not already implicit in the specification of the object. Thus, in order to sustain the distinction, I do not have to believe in "most basic" objects;[20] on the contrary, I could, consistently with the distinction between objects and objects-as-represented, believe that objects of interpretation are always or sometimes themselves representations of something prior. All I would need to maintain is that, even though this prior representation is already implicit in the specification of the object, the object's representation for the purposes of the given act of interpretation is not so implicit.

I agree with Krausz that realists should provide some way of individuat-

---

bridge Companion to Brahms, ed. Michael Musgrave (Cambridge: Cambridge University Press, 1999), 240.

15. Grosvenor Cooper and Leonard B. Meyer, The Rhythmic Structure of Music (Chicago: University of Chicago Press, 1960), 39.

16. Michael Krausz, "Interpretation and Its 'Metaphysical' Entanglements," Metaphilosophy 31, nos. 1/2 (2000): 126.

17. Ibid., 139.

18. Ibid., 137.

19. Ibid., 127.

20. The phrase is Krausz's; see ibid., 127.

ing any objects they take to precede all interpretation and to be independent of representation. Where I disagree with him is in the assessment of my first structure as including a commitment to realism. Krausz's formulation of realism refers to an object of interpretation that is tacitly indexed to a particular operation of interpretation. In saying that this object is fully constituted independently of interpretive practices, Krausz must mean *all* interpretive practices. However, the first structure need not suppose that there are any such objects. Krausz's sense of "independence" is global, but the relevant sense for this structure is purely relative; and there is therefore no commitment to realism in it.

Krausz himself forswears a staunchly nonmetaphysical position in the philosophy of interpretation.[21] However, philosophers with minimalist inclinations might be attracted to just such a position. I believe that any of the three structures I have proposed can be defended while avoiding a metaphysical commitment to realism. The question I now wish to put is whether further reflection on the aspects of interpretation that we have thus far noticed might force a metaphysical commitment on us.

III. An Ontology of Interpretation and Art

I have spoken about internal objects of interpretation. What *are* these objects? The word "object" here must not be allowed to mislead us into thinking that internal objects of interpretation are a species of real particulars. After all, the description that defines the internal object of a given interpretation may not describe any real particular. Brahms's Haydn Variations are a case in point. As I mentioned earlier, the work is an interpretation of its theme, and the internal object is identified by the description "St. Antony Chorale by Joseph Haydn"; but this description does not apply to any really existing particular. Real particulars possess their properties whether or not we are aware of the fact, whereas internal objects of representation are defined from a person's perspective, and they are necessarily as that person takes them to be. Moreover, real particulars are determinate in ways that internal objects of interpretation need not be. There are property ranges so constituted that a real particular must possess some property in the range, whereas an internal object of interpretation may possess none of the properties in the range. For example, an actual performance of Brahms's piece

21. Ibid., 125.

must be fully determinate with respect to tempo in every bar, even if the work itself is not so determinate.

Internal objects of interpretation are better understood as determined by properties, or rather sets of properties. Understanding them this way is consistent with our taking these objects to be specified by a thing's aspects, for aspects are nothing other than properties. Given this general understanding of internal objects, there will be the further question what ontological standing properties have—Platonist, nominalist, and so forth. I do not address that further question in this paper.

In some instances the proper sets that determine internal objects of interpretation are fuzzy. Let me explain.

Simon Blackburn notes that fuzzy-set theory "recognizes degrees of applicability of predicates": "Thus although classical logic regards 'this room is hot' as either true or false, it may better represent the way we actually reason (or the way we ought to reason) to say that it is pretty much true, or truer than saying that the room is cold."[22] It is clear from this description that a logic recognizing fuzzy sets needs to allow for propositional semantic values other than truth and falsity (such as Blackburn's "pretty much true"). To put the same point in ontic, rather than semantic, terms: a logic recognizing fuzzy sets needs to allow for *tertia* between what is simply so and what is simply not so. It needs to be a many-valued logic. Maciej Wygralak describes one motivation that leads to the construction of such logics: "To avoid misunderstandings, . . . sharp two-valued interpretations of terms like 'adult,' 'middle-aged' and 'densely populated' are . . . required. . . . for instance, in many law systems, [where] the term 'adult' is defined as '18 years old or over.' Understanding this necessity, one should mention that such interpretations are always deforming."[23] In categorizing these interpretations as "deforming," Wygralak assumes (correctly) that terms like "adult" in their ordinary usage do not behave bivalently, so that if we want to capture the semantic behavior of such ordinary concepts (rather than the precising interpretations of them that are tailored to fit classical semantics), then we need to develop many-valued logics.

There is a class of interpretations whose internal objects are fuzzy, namely, those very "deforming" interpretations of which Wygralak speaks. We might call these *precising* interpretations, and their internal objects are

---

22. Simon Blackburn, *The Oxford Dictionary of Philosophy* (Oxford: Oxford University Press, 1994), 151.

23. Maciej Wygralak, *Vaguely Defined Objects* (Dordrecht: Kluwer, 1996), 6.

necessarily fuzzy. It is the very fuzziness of these objects that such interpretations aim to remedy, by subjecting them to a suitable deformation—one that brings them within the ambit of a bivalent semantics. Some philosophers detect a similar fuzziness in a wide range of internal objects of interpretation. Joseph Margolis is one such. He thinks this is true of interpretations involving what he calls "Intentional" (with a capital *I*) properties: "[W]orks of art (I would now say all Intentionally qualified 'things') lack determinate boundaries or assignable natures, in virtue of which we can say what is 'in' a work and what is merely 'imputed' to it."[24] If this is right, then it follows that all internal objects of cultural interpretation are vague, on the assumption that the internal objects of cultural interpretation are always already Intentionally qualified. But is this assumption true? By way of answering that question, I will sketch an ontology of those objects that are the objects of cultural interpretation.

Preeminently these include what philosophers call "artworks." I will follow this usage, with the caveat that it should not be understood as implying that these objects of interpretation are enduring particulars. Artistic performances, ephemeral though they are, are just as much objects of cultural interpretation as are the enduring works that constitute their content. We interpret the dancing as well as the dance.

It will be useful for present purposes if we understand artworks in a manner broadly in tune with Margolis's formula: "physically embodied and culturally emergent entities."[25] We can elaborate this formula in the framework of the present paper by saying (i) that an artwork is embodied in a particular, (ii) that the artwork presents an intentional object, (iii) that that intentional object is presented in ways that invite interpretation, (iv) that an interpretation of an artwork has for its external object the ordered pair comprising the embodying particular and the presented intentional object, and (v) that an interpretation of a work has for its internal object the interpreter's understanding of that external object. Further elaborations follow.

(i) While there could be a content that was not embodied, it would be merely "ideal" or abstract and would thus lack the concrete form that is a hallmark of artworks. Embodiment can take various forms. In traditional visual arts, the work is embodied in a comparatively stable material object.

24. Joseph Margolis, "Replies in Search of Self-Discovery," in *Interpretation, Relativism, and the Metaphysics of Culture: Themes in the Philosophy of Joseph Margolis*, ed. Michael Krausz and Richard Shusterman (Amherst, N.Y.: Humanity Books, 1999), 372.

25. Joseph Margolis, *What, After All, Is a Work of Art? Lectures in the Philosophy of Art* (University Park: Pennsylvania State University Press, 1999), 68–71.

In the performing arts, works should be said to be embodied (multiply) in performances rather than in the scores or scripts with which such performances aim to comply, even though scores and scripts (and their contents) endure in a way that performances do not. The scores or scripts are best said to embody not the works but directives for producing those works. Alternatively, we could distinguish between works-for-musical-performance and musical-works, the former being embodied in scores, the latter in performances. Works-for-performance would then be directives for producing artworks in various media and would be conceptually posterior (even if temporally prior) to such works. An analogous distinction might be applied in the field of literature, where literary works could be understood as works-for-reading and as embodied in the "script" of the novel or poem. The artwork, for the sake of which the work-for-reading exists, would then be embodied not in that script but in acts of reading.

(ii) Artworks are not simply there; they *present* something for beholding. Thus there is a distinction in principle between what is in the work and what it presents to its beholders. Nikolaus Harnoncourt touches on this point in relation to Brahms's Haydn Variations: "Music often draws for its inspiration on literary or pictorial sources. . . . But composers are not interested in conveying this to their listeners. . . . I respect the composer's desire to keep things hidden and do not think that I would conduct the Haydn Variations any differently if I knew that the piece was about the temptations of St Anthony. For me, these variations are in themselves a temptation, I don't need St Anthony as well."[26] Harnoncourt can be understood as saying that he cannot see how a performance of the Haydn Variations could *present* the work as depicting the temptations of Saint Anthony, even if Brahms had somehow drawn inspiration from those temptations. The manner in which artworks present their content varies according to art form: there are characteristic visual, auditory, literary, filmic, and performative techniques of presenting content and focusing the beholder's attention on it. Ontologically, what is presented is an intentional object of an anticipated act of interpretation on the part of someone who beholds the embodied work. It consists in a set of aspects, or properties, of the embodying particular. These properties of the embodying particular are, in Goodman's word, *exemplified* by that particular: it simultaneously possesses them and refers to them.[27]

26. Walter Dobner and Nikolaus Harnoncourt, liner notes to Johannes Brahms, *The Symphonies, Haydn Variations, Academic Festival Overture, Tragic Overture,* Berliner Philharmoniker, Nikolaus Harnoncourt Teldec 0630–13136–2.

27. Nelson Goodman, *Of Mind and Other Matters* (Cambridge, Mass.: Harvard University Press, 1984), 59.

(iii) As just mentioned, the artwork presents something as an intentional object of an anticipated act of interpretation, and to that extent *invites* interpretation. Works in different art forms use a variety of techniques in extending this invitation. These include ambiguities, the creation and frustration of a beholder's expectations, and other pertinent indeterminacies in the work's content. However, artworks are not indeterminate with respect to *every* property (Peter Lamarque reminds us that *The Potato Eaters* determinately depicts human beings sitting around a table),[28] to which it should be added that what the work presents as already determinate is not included in what it presents for interpretation.

(iv) The dual nature of artworks as sets of properties exemplified in embodying particulars implies that, as objects of interpretation, they always include a referential element, by virtue of the embodying particular's exemplification of a set of properties. The exemplifying particular refers to the exemplified properties, just as the tailor's swatch refers to a color or a fabric and so on. This is not just a matter of there being a correspondence between properties of the exemplifying particular and the exemplified properties in the work's content; rather, for us to understand the artwork as an artwork, we must consider the relation between exemplifying particular and exemplified properties as an intentional relation. If it were just a matter of correspondence, we would have to conclude that the embodying particular exemplifies *all* of its properties.

(v) When an artwork is interpreted, certain aspects of the external object are mirrored (though not represented—at least, not intentionally) in the internal object of interpretation. Since the external object has a dual nature whereby one of its parts exemplifies the other, the question arises whether the internal object of interpretation must share this dual nature. I believe that—at least for successful interpretations—the answer should be affirmative. Any interpretation of an artwork that failed to understand its dual nature would be flawed. To understand the work merely as a physical particular would be to omit the work's content. To understand the work without reference to the way that content is embodied would be to overlook the achievement of the artist in making such a content concrete.

We can now return to the question whether the interpretation of artworks requires a nonbivalent logic. On the analysis I have proposed, artworks are indeed, and are construed by successful interpreters, as involving

---

28. Peter Lamarque, "Objects of interpretation," *Metaphilosophy* 31, nos. 1/2 (2000): 117.

exemplification. Now, exemplification must be Intentional for Margolis, since he applies that label to all "expressive, representational, stylistic, rhetorical, symbolic, semiotic, linguistic, traditional, institutional, and otherwise significative features of artworks."[29] If that is so, then he is right to treat artworks, and objects of cultural interpretation in general, as already charged with Intentionality.

But is he right in thinking that where you have Intentionality, you have the sort of nebulousness that requires a nonbivalent logic? Arguably so. Even given that artworks have the dual exemplificatory nature I have outlined, there is never a cut-and-dried answer to the question What properties is the embodying particular supposed to exemplify? As Peter Lamarque observes in relation to an interpretation of *Crime and Punishment:* "Every element in a work, given the kind of work it is, has potential saliency, but the aesthetic function of elements like the time-sequences and flashbacks is determinable only relative to an interpretation. Margolis is right that at this level the insistence on bivalent truth-values—either truth or falsity of interpretive statements—is gratuitous."[30] Just as it is neither *simply so* that the swatch exemplifies a color nor simply so that it exemplifies a fabric, in general it is never simply so that an artwork exemplifies any particular content.

It does seem then that for artworks considered as objects of cultural interpretation there is no determinate boundary in virtue of which we can say what is in the work and what is merely imputed to it. Because of their exemplificatory nature such objects seem to be inherently vague. They do indeed "lack determinate boundaries" and are indeed "nebulous"; consequently any attempt to straitjacket them into bivalent conformity will indeed be "deforming."

I have sketched but one among a plurality of possible ontologies for objects of interpretation and for artworks. Instead of taking interpretation to be a relation, we might have understood interpretation-sentences as being monadic, in the way that Margolis understands representation-sentences: "[W]hen we begin with *representations,* as in paintings, then, I say . . . that they are monadic in their representational capacity. . . . [W]hen I see a Cézanne painting of a woodstove, I see a (monadic) woodstove-representation."[31] Accordingly, I do not claim that the ontology sketched here is the right one: I put it forward as having the standing of an interpretation whose success need not imply rightness.

29. Margolis, *What, After All, Is a Work of Art?* 55.
30. Lamarque, "Objects of interpretation," 119.
31. Margolis, "Replies in Search of Self-Discovery," 401.

Works Cited

Blackburn, Simon. *The Oxford Dictionary of Philosophy*. Oxford: Oxford University Press, 1994.

Cooper, Grosvenor, and Leonard B. Meyer. *The Rhythmic Structure of Music*. Chicago: University of Chicago Press, 1960.

Dobner, Walter, and Nikolaus Harnoncourt. Liner notes to Johannes Brahms, *The Symphonies, Haydn Variations, Academic Festival Overture, Tragic Overture*. Berliner Philharmoniker, Nikolaus Harnoncourt Teldec 0630–13136–2.

Goodman, Nelson. *Of Mind and Other Matters*. Cambridge, Mass.: Harvard University Press, 1984.

Krausz, Michael. "Interpretation and Its 'Metaphysical' Entanglements." *Metaphilosophy* 31, nos. 1/2 (2000) (special issue: *The Philosophy of Interpretation*, edited by Joseph Margolis and Tom Rockmore): 125–47.

———. *Rightness and Reasons: Interpretation in Cultural Practices*. Ithaca, N.Y.: Cornell University Press, 1993.

Krausz, Michael, and Richard Shusterman, eds. *Interpretation, Relativism, and the Metaphysics of Culture: Themes in the Philosophy of Joseph Margolis*. New York: Humanity Books, 1999.

Lamarque, Peter. "Objects of Interpretation." *Metaphilosophy* 31, nos. 1/2 (2000) (special issue: *The Philosophy of Interpretation*, edited by Joseph Margolis and Tom Rockmore): 96–124.

Margolis, Joseph. "Replies in Search of Self-Discovery." In *Interpretation, Relativism, and the Metaphysics of Culture: Themes in the Philosophy of Joseph Margolis*, edited by Michael Krausz and Richard Shusterman, 337–408. Amherst, N.Y.: Humanity Books, 1999.

———. *What, After All, Is a Work of Art? Lectures in the Philosophy of Art*. University Park: Pennsylvania State University Press, 1999.

Margolis, Joseph, and Tom Rockmore, eds. *The Philosophy of Interpretation*. A special issue of *Metaphilosophy* (vol. 31, nos. 1/2 [2000]).

Norrington, Roger, and Michael Musgrave. "Conducting Brahms." In *The Cambridge Companion to Brahms*, edited by Michael Musgrave, 231–49. Cambridge: Cambridge University Press, 1999.

Novitz, David. "Interpretation and Justification." *Metaphilosophy* 31, nos. 1/2 (2000) (special issue: *The Philosophy of Interpretation*, edited by Joseph Margolis and Tom Rockmore): 4–24.

Thom, Paul. *For an Audience: A Philosophy of the Performing Arts*. Philadelphia: Temple University Press, 1993.

———. *Making Sense: A Theory of Interpretation*. Lanham, Md.: Rowman & Littlefield, 2000.

———. Review of *Rightness and Reasons*, by Michael Krausz, *Interpretation Radical but Not Unruly*, by Joseph Margolis, and "The Constructivist's Dilemma," by Robert Stecker. *Literature and Aesthetics: The Journal of the Sydney Society of Literature and Aesthetics* 7 (1997).

Wittgenstein, Ludwig. *Remarks on the Foundations of Mathematics*. Edited by G. H. von Wright, R. Rhees, G. E. M. Anscombe; translated by G. E. M. Anscombe. Oxford: Basil Blackwell, 1964.

Wygralak, Maciej. *Vaguely Defined Objects*. Dordrecht: Kluwer, 1996.

Intentionality, Meaning, and Open-Endedness of Interpretation

Jitendranath Mohanty

I

A theory of interpretation should begin with a minimal account of the interpretive *act* as well as of the *object* of interpretation. And, yet, in attempting to do this, one should also avoid a full-fledged metaphysics of the act and the object—not because such a metaphysics is impossible, but because it is just uncalled-for. The minimal account should restrict itself to what is needed for theorizing about interpretation. Such an account may be called "phenomenology." This phenomenology should be developed *from within* the phenomenon or experience of interpretation. So we need to introduce ideas of the act and the object that are relevant for interpretation.

From the side of the subject, one may insist that the interpretive act is the act of a person, the interpreter, and so we cannot dispense with an account of the nature of the interpreter. For how one understands the nature of the interpretive act will depend upon how one understands this being. It is possible to conceive of this being as having direct, unmediated access to the object, in which case interpretation is uncalled-for. In the same way, a certain ontology of the object of interpretation may so construe the nature of that object that interpretation would lose its ontological access and would be reduced to a mere subjective intervention with no cognitive dignity. What this would imply is that when one achieves genuine cognitive access to the object, one no longer needs to interpret, and that as long as one is interpreting, one is not knowing the object.

From within the phenomenon of interpretation, our phenomenology requires that we avoid such metaphysical theories. At the same time, we cannot but recognize the truth of Heidegger's claim that at its most basic level, the very mode of being of humans is interpretive. In Heidegger's technical locution, Dasein is *verstehend-auslegend*. Only a being whose very mode of being consists in understanding itself and its world, such that it is concerned with its own possibilities of being in a situation and from within a tradition it inherits—only such a being is a genuine interpreter. Following Heidegger, one may call this "ontological interpretation," and may distinguish it from the higher level of interpretation, which is interpretation of texts and works of art. In this essay we will be concerned with the latter.

There is, however, another stratum of interpretive activity that mediates between the basic ontological and the higher-level—I should add, methodological—interpretation. While every Dasein is *verstehend-auslegend,* not everyone interprets texts and artworks. But everyone does participate in the mediating, middle-level interpretive work, which characterizes our everyday experience of things in the world as well as of other persons we encounter. It is here that the phenomenological concept of intentionality plays a central role. Intentionality may be implicated—contrary to Heidegger's thesis—in the mode of being of Dasein, but it is in the domain of perceptual experience that its operation is first to be determined.

To determine the operation of intentionality in perception, let me briefly recall Brentano's account of it in terms of being-directed-toward an object (without pausing to consider the problems connected with Brentano's locution "intentional inexistence" of the object in the mind). Perception is always of an object. This is its essence. However, there are cases where the object of perception does not exist, as with hallucinations. There are also cases where a single object is perceived differently, now as a duck and now as a rabbit (as in he case of the following figure).

It follows then that whether or not the perceived object truly exists, what belongs essentially to the structure of a perception is the perceived object precisely as it is being perceived, that is to say, a perceptual meaning, or *noema*. In perception, its object is presented as being such and such, as having a certain meaning, as an X that satisfies a certain description. In the duck-rabbit case, whether one sees a rabbit or a duck, the sensory input,

one may presume, is the same. In one case, those data are interpreted as rabbit, in the other case as a duck. This leads to the thesis:

(1) Intentionality confers meaning upon the given datum. To confer meaning is to interpret. Intentionality interprets the given datum.

We find the same structure in the case of hearing a meaningful utterance and understanding its meaning. Here too the speaker both utters a sentence and intends to convey a certain thought by means of that utterance. Another speaker of the same language, the auditor, hears the utterance and interprets the utterance as having a certain meaning. If the auditor's meaning coincides with that intended by the speaker, then the former understands the latter; if they are different, he misunderstands. In any case, both interpret the utterance by conferring meaning upon the utterance. We can then say:

(2) When understanding an utterance, one interprets the sound emitted by the speaker.

It is no different in the case of encountering another person and determining on the basis of that person's nonverbal behavior that he or she is in pain or is sad. In this case, too,

(3) one interprets the other's behavior when ascribing to him or her certain mental states.

It should be noted that in all these cases, (1)–(3), it is perfectly legitimate, possibly in a slightly different but nonetheless analogous sense, that one *sees* a rabbit (or a duck, as the case may be), that one *grasps* the meaning of an utterance one understands, and that one *sees that* the other is in pain or is sad. The point of insisting on this is that perceptual consciousness, in (1), despite its interpretive function, is still perceptual. Likewise, in (2) and (3), the presence of "giving meaning" is not inconsistent with directly experiencing the object as having that meaning. Although, in these cases, perceptual intentionality interprets, what meaning one's intentionality confers is neither totally determined nor totally free, but has a status that is midway between the two extremes. The perceptual meaning that, as it were, clothes the object and gives it its appearances, is determined by the appropriate system of concepts the community's culture provides. It is conceivable, and often observed, that members of different cultural groups interpret the same sensory input very differently: what is a tool for construction for one may be a religious artifact for another; what is perceived by one as a rock with interesting geological properties may be perceived by another as a holy object. That there is a certain freedom—not reducible to causal determination—at play here is borne out by the fact that one can overcome, with effort, this cultural determinism and replace one way of seeing with another—the religious, for example, with the so-called scientific. The cultural context does not make you see as something rather than as something else, but motivates the presentation of one meaning as though it were not a matter of choosing from among alternatives but of bringing into clear relief a mode of presentation. The duck-rabbit case is interesting insofar as there is a sudden switch from one percept to another, a Gestalt-switch that resists any deterministic explanation, or even an indeterministic one, although the total concept "duck-or-rabbit" is made available within the cultural horizon of the perceiver.

To render this account comprehensive, it needs to be added that conferring meaning is a function not merely of cognitive intentionality but also of the practical and affective. Actions and emotions also confer appropriate significance on their objects, as things to be acted upon or as things (or persons) that are lovable or despicable. Here too what one agent finds useful, deserving to be acted upon, another may find useless. It should also be pointed out that cognitive, perceptual meaning and actional-emotional meaning are not entirely separate and disconnected, but rather thoroughly interpenetrate. Perceptual meaning may be shot through with actional and affective significances of various sorts. Consider this as thesis (4).

In none of these cases ([1] through [4]) is there a conscious adoption of a position. One does not, after careful deliberation, decide to interpret the datum in a certain way, in this, rather than that, manner. One decides, for example, to act, to undertake a certain project, but one does not decide to confer on the object or situation that is acted upon a certain actional meaning. That meaning comes with the action and the agent's (and the action's) intellectual and valuational background. The meaning is thus a necessary correlate of that particular intentional act. There is not a bare perceptual act that by interpreting its object becomes perception of that object qua such and such. To the contrary, the perception is perception of that object qua such and such. That perceptual meaning belongs essentially to this perception. The same is true in other kinds of intentionalities. In brief:

(5) There is a correlation between noesis and noema.

We should now bring this story to an end. The point of the story is that one and the same object may be perceived differently, in one case as a duck, in another case as a rabbit. Likewise with variations in actional-emotional significance. At this point one may introduce a rather generalized idea of "perspective" and say that an intentional act is directed toward its object always from a certain perspective. To the change of meaning there corresponds a change of perspective. We can then say:

(6) An act I_1 presents an object as having the meaning M_1 from a perspective P_1.

This suggests that while the object O remains fixed, I_2 may present the same O as having the meaning M_2 from a perspective P_2. In that case the same O may have different meanings from different perspectives. But since, as Frege emphasized, there is no route from O to M, but always from M to O, we can say:

(7) The identity of O must be a function of the series of Ms.

In other words, as one shifts perspectives and runs through the various Ms, one begins to recognize that one and the same object is being presented through the Ms. Here are two metaphysical theses that need to be avoided: On the one hand, one may contend that there is no identity that the Ms represent, that there are always differences. On the other hand, one may take the Ms to be parts/aspects of O, and therewith dismiss the concept of meaning as being extrinsic to the situation. Following the guideline of phenomenology that restricts itself to the way things are presented, we may insist that in some cases at least

(8) the sense of identity is carried over from one M to another (while in other cases, to be sure, the identity of the object has to be established).

The identity of O is a presupposition of the idea of varying perspectives and the meanings they yield. But again, to be sure, in no case can this identity be *a priori* and apodictically established. An identity claim is defeasible. A standard way of recovering identity is to ask: do the Ms have a common, shared content or not? One may then proceed to assert:

(9) The identity of O is constituted by the overlapping synthesis of contents of $M_1 \ldots M_n$.

II

What I have outlined above is intended to form the basis of a satisfactory theory of interpretation, especially of the higher modes of interpretation that apply to texts and works of art. If interpretation were suddenly to begin at the higher level, its very possibility would be questionable. If the activity of conferring meaning were foreign to the human mode of being, and if no such activity characterized our everyday experience, it would be surprising if, suddenly confronted with texts and works of art, we would begin to interpret them. It is not surprising that when human existence is conceived as nonintentional and as just world disclosing, that is, as disclosing things as they are, understanding a text is not understood as interpreting but rather as discovering its meaning. As intentional and meaning conferring, human consciousness finds a text appropriate material for its interpretive adventures. It looks for meaning and in this process finds what has been put there, either by its predecessors or by itself. One does not always initiate an interpretation, but more often than not takes up already available interpretations.

At this point I will introduce a distinction that was made by Indian philosophers of language. This is the distinction between literal meaning (*abhidheya*), secondary meaning (*lakṣaṇā*), and the poetic meaning (*vyan-janā*). The literal meaning of "cow" is cow (either a cow or the class of cows or the universal "cowness" or a cow qua possessing cowness—depending on which school of Indian philosophy performs the definition). The second-ary meaning is one that, though not the literal meaning, is related to the literal meaning. Thus in "village on the Ganges," "Ganges" signifies not the river but the bank of the river (for, in this case, there could not literally be a village on the river itself). Poetic meaning (*vyanjanā*, or also called *dhvani*) is what is suggested without being said, as in the expressions "a human lion" and "a face like the moon," the former suggesting courage and strength, the latter suggesting beauty. I shall quickly trace the role and scope of interpretation in each of these three cases.

First, with regard to literal meaning. This is one area in which the scope for interpretation would seem to be at a minimum, if it is there at all. To understand a word is to know its meaning; to understand a sentence is to know the meanings of the constituent words. Who assigns the meanings to words is a question we need not pursue in our present context. Certainly, the speaker or the hearer does not. They both learn the meanings and are able to assign them to appropriate words in appropriate contexts. However, I will here make a few remarks that open the door for interpretation at this level. Only if one subscribes to meaning atomism (according to which word meanings are prior to, and independent of, sentence meaning) can one elimi-nate the role of interpretation from literal understanding of sentences. How-ever, if one advocates a meaning holism according to which the meanings of words are the roles they play in sentence meanings, on the ground that the original home of words is in the sentences, then the role of interpretation opens up even in understanding the literal meanings of sentences. A sentence has to be interpreted *in toto* and in context, not only when it contains index-icals and other context-sensitive words, but also when a component word has a specific meaning only in a specific context—cultural, social, and prag-matic. One needs, in such interpretation, also to take into account the speaker's intention, where necessary, to remove ambiguities and inconsist-encies.

Moving on now from sentences in ordinary discourse to sentences in an-cient texts, the Upanisads, for example, the need for interpretation and the unavoidability of multiple interpretations becomes more pressing. I will show this by recalling some texts and the ways they were interpreted.

First of all, the Upanisads contain such sentences as "sarvam khalu idam brahman" (literally meaning "all this is indeed *brahman*") and also such sentences as "neti neti" (not this, not this). Every commentator on the Upanisads had to reconcile these opposite texts, one group affirming the ubiquitousness of *brahman,* the other group affirming the transcendence of *brahman* with regard to every mundane entity. All interpreters had to proceed on the assumption that the Upaniṣads, sacred texts as they are, could not contain any self-contradiction. There are at least two hermeneutic principles that were used to reconcile: one gives priority (or "strength," as it was called) to affirmative texts, the other to the negative texts. Using the first principle, some interpreters contended that in "not this, not this," the "this" refers to each mundane entity separately, the "not" negates identifying *brahman* with any of them separately. However, after the negation achieves its purpose, then the affirmative texts prevail—asserting that *brahman* is the totality (*sarvam*). Other interpreters, notable Samkara, proceed with the principle that negations must supersede affirmations, that only after an affirmation has been made can it be negated, so that, logically, negation is stronger than affirmation. Applying this principle, they contend that the positive identification of *brahman* with "all this" (*idam sarvam*) is only provisional, intended to be subsequently negated by statements such as "not this, not this." These are only two among myriad possibilities.

One may, in such cases, insist that the differences between these interpreters can be traced to differences in their interpretation of the crucial words such as *brahman.* But the word *brahman* derives its meaning from the sentences in which it is used in the Upaniṣads, and it is more plausible that interpretations of those sentences determine the meaning assigned to the word by itself. The sentences again play their role in the entire discourse. *The larger the context, the more scope and need, the greater the possibility, for range of interpretive variations.* Let me call this my thesis (9).

What is the role of authorial intention? Should the interpreter not aim at capturing the original intention of the author? Would there then be scope for different interpretations only as long as the intention of the author was not ascertained? Once that is ascertained, you know what is *the* meaning of the text—which then rules out all other interpretations. However, this is a misleading thought. For one thing, there is a circularity involved: You know *the* meaning when you ascertain what the author intended to mean, and you determine, or claim to have determined, the author's intention when you are satisfied that you have grasped *the* meaning of the text. For another, how do you ascertain the author's intention except by interpreting other speeches and documents—if you have such access to the author's mind at all. For theory, intention is a correlate of meaning. But, in practice, you have no independent access to intentions save by way of meanings.

Here I will introduce the concept of *apauruṣeyatva* (or "not authored by a human being"), which has played an interesting role in the Indian understanding of the nature of sacred truth. The significance of this concept is lost if one understands by it "revealed by God or gods." As a matter of fact, many of the overzealous defenders of the thesis of *apauruṣeyatva* of the Vedas rejected the idea that these texts are "revealed." How are we to make sense of this claim?

Some years ago, I interpreted *apauruṣeyatva* to mean the primacy and autonomy of the texts (of the *Śruti*, that is, the "heard" texts) over the subjective intentions of their authors. More so in these texts than elsewhere, the authorial intention completely "recedes into the background, and remains anonymous, pushing the text and its possible interpretations to the front."[1] And then I went on to recommend a theoretical principle: "The more we need to know the author to understand or interpret a text, the less fundamental it is. The less we need to know the author in order to understand or interpret a text, the more fundamental it is."[2] I will now mark this as my thesis (10).

Once authorial intention is pushed aside, the door opens for as many interpretations as are possible. Interpretation of the texts has remained a historical process by which the efficacy of the texts grows. A text of that foundational eminence of the Vedas "stands on its own, inviting us to interpret it, converse with it, and make it efficacious in shaping our thoughts."[3] Here is a difference between texts such as the Vedas and the Upaniṣads and texts such as Manu's Law Book. The words of the latter, not entirely devoid of hermeneutical possibilities, are more rigid and ask you more to obey them than to understand them, while the words of the former group of texts have a plasticity, a reservoir of meaning, a power to challenge thought, that does not ever close the door on new ways of understanding. Such are the words *brahman, māyā, ātman, mokṣa,* and *ānanda.*

The same plasticity of meaning and reservoir of meaning possibilities are to be found in the *sūtra* texts, such as the *Brahmasūtras* of *Bādarāyaṇa.* Witness the numerous *bhāṣyas,* or interpretive explanations written on the

---

1. J. N. Mohanty, *Reason and Tradition in Indian Thought* (Oxford: Clarendon Press, 1992), 257–59.
2. Ibid., 259.
3. Ibid., 273.

sûtras, which differ not only with regard to the meanings of the key words but also with regard to the meanings of such common words as "now," "then," and "this." The indexicals point to contexts that remain "unsaid," which the commentaries spell out in different ways.

One might wonder about the source of such different interpretations. One might speculate, for example, that differences in interpretation may be traced to different religious and philosophical positions of the commentators. This explanation, however, may be questioned on the ground that these latter differences are themselves founded on the very seminal texts in question. It is possible to argue—and I am willing to press this point in this essay—that the different interpretations are just that, namely, different interpretations of the texts themselves. The texts themselves contain possibilities of such different readings.

Sanskrit is a language that is eminently open to such differences. I will illustrate this with examples from the Vedic hymns, with special reference to Sri Aurobindo's *On the Veda.*[4] The principle "one word, one meaning" is simply not true of Sanskrit, indeed is not true of many ancient languages. A look at the Sanskrit compendium of words for the same meanings, *Amarakoṣa,* illustrates this. Since Sanskrit words are formed out of verbal roots and these roots have multiple significance (as do the prefixes and suffixes), the resulting words have many different meanings. However, there is generally no equivocation in such cases; there is rather a family of meanings. The Vedic word *Agni* means, in Vedic discourse, "fire" as well as "that which purifies," among other meanings; it also means, by implication, "the purified will." Both the physical and the psychological meanings ("fire" and "purified will") were intended—not in their clear Cartesian distinction but more likely in their nondistinction (the concept of the purely physical not being available). The other characteristic of the Sanskrit of Vedic discourse has been that the same word can do the work of different parts of speech—for example, noun as well as verb. Thus the word *cit* may equally well mean "consciousness," "to know," "knowing," "knower," "knowledge," and "knowingly." Given these two principles, as Sri Aurobindo insists, the Vedic hymns always have at least two meanings: one referring to deities, the Vedic *devas,* who are symbolized by natural "powers" (sun, cloud, rain, water, air, sky, etc.); the other profoundly psychological, referring to different inner mental powers and their subtle modulations and modes of functioning. The former—in principle championed by the *Brāhmaṇas,* by Sāyaṇa,

---

4. Sri Aurobindo, *On the Veda* (Pondicherry: Sri Aurobindo Ashram, 1964).

and by most Western Vedic scholars—may be called *ādhidaivika* (i.e., "pertaining to the gods"); the latter—in principle developed in some of the Upaniṣadic texts—may be called *ādhyātmika* (i.e., "pertaining to the inner spiritual life"). When I asked Vinoba Bhave what he thought of Sri Aurobindo's Vedic interpretation, he not only agreed with it in principle but added a third possibility, namely, the purely naturalist-cum-social interpretation, or what may be called the *ādhibhautika*. Purely from the standpoint of interpretation, all three of these different possibilities are valid; there is no one right interpretation.

It is, however, possible to accord to any one of these a more fundamental status. Sri Aurobindo himself, for example, regards the psychological meaning of the Vedic hymns more fundamental, the "true" meaning, and then, in somewhat Straussian manner, proposes that the ritualistic, *ādhidaivika* meaning is intended for people who are not "qualified" to grasp the deeper meaning. I would not go ahead with him in this part of his account. To the contrary, from the purely hermeneutic point of view, the two are equally valid possibilities. If any of them is to be ruled out, that must be on textual grounds. A similar story is told by the Marxists, who regard the *ādhibhautika* reading to be more fundamental and the other two to be superstructures. I reject this too, on similar grounds, and regard multiple interpretive possibilities to be basic to the ancient texts.

Similar hermeneutical strategies were adopted by Buddhists who sought to harmonize the various teachings of the Buddha, to remove seeming inconsistencies by following two principles: one, that the Buddha taught according to the qualifications of those to whom he spoke; the other, that the Buddha's words have been understood differently in different ages. Thus, according to a well-known hermeneutical principle, there have been at least three major "turns" in the understanding of his words, one at the beginning, a second after the first five hundred years, a third after another five hundred years—corresponding to three revolutions of the wheel of *dharma*. Buddhist hermeneutics thus introduced a historical point of view that was lacking in the Hindu hermeneutical practices.

A striking example of multiple interpretations of the same text is to be found in Abhinavagupta's commentary on *Parātriśikā*.[5] Of verse 9, Abhinavagupta gives sixteen interpretations and does not tell us which one he prefers. One is left with the impression that he finds all sixteen equally acceptable, though from different points of view.

5. Abhinavagupta, *Parātriśikā Vivarana*, translated, with notes, by Jaidev Singh, ed. Bettina Bäumer (Delhi: Motilal Barnarasidass, 1988), 210–18.

There are still other texts that demand this openness. Many passages in the Upanisads fall into this category. I have in mind especially verses 9–11 of the Isa Upanisad. If I had more time at my disposal, I would go through various readings of these verses and argue for the same overall thesis. But I do not want to maintain that this plasticity of meaning is true only of Sanskrit texts. I believe the thesis is true of many texts in ancient languages, though less so of modern texts. Among modern texts, an exemplary piece is the chapter "Lordship and Bondage" in Hegel's 1807 *Phenomenology of the Mind*—a text that allows of a historical-economic, an inner-psychological, and a metaphysical reading, and maybe all three are "valid."

III

A remark is called for to alleviate one anxiety in the face of the thesis I have advanced. An interpreter generally proposes an interpretation and defends it against other rival interpretations. Thus Rāmānuja, while interpreting the *Brahmasūtras*, vehemently opposes Śamkara's interpretation. How is this phenomenon compatible with the thesis advanced here? In response, I would press several points. An interpreter may consider his or her interpretation to be the best, sometimes as the only plausible one, but it is not necessary for the interpreter to do so, for a person may uphold the possibility of two or more interpretations without making a choice from among them. This commitment to one allegedly right interpretation is not uncommon on the part of an interpreter. But a dispassionate approach "from above," as it were, would show that none of the interpretations proposed is *the* right one (though some may clearly be "irrelevant," having nothing to do with the text).

We can, I believe, rank texts in an order, at the top of which are the ancient "wisdom" texts, whose plasticity of meaning—or reservoir of meaning—will always exceed any particular effort to make sense of them, and at the bottom of which would be the ordinary matter-of-fact sentences that clearly describe a well-defined state of affairs, such as "It is raining now in Philadelphia." In between stand texts embodying theories and thoughts, and works of literature. In the former, a complex web of ideas and propositions offers the context against which texts have to be interpreted, allowing for possibilities that cannot be captured as a whole by any interpreter— more so since historically processed thoughts necessarily enter into the interstices of the text. In the latter case, that of a poem, for example, literal meaning yields place to "secondary meaning" (*lakṣaṇā*) and "suggested meaning" (*vyanjanā* or *dhvani*), but these latter have no immediate "resting place." The implications that *lakṣaṇā* unravels are varied and belong to different levels of discourse. The "suggested" meanings likewise are not exhausted by "beauty," "elegance," and "style," but penetrate into the emotional responses of the reader and, in the long run, into the deeper recesses of the reader's psyche. Interpreting poetry therefore is a never-ending process, as is making sense of a text like Hegel's *Phenomenology*.

A reason why in these cases there is no final interpretation is that while the text as printed matter (e.g., Shakespeare's First Folio) is a work complete in itself, as an aesthetic object it is constituted by the printed text and the responses of the reader (or actor, as the case may be),[6] who "fills gaps," "removes indeterminacies," "supplies needed overtones," and so forth. The total aesthetic object, growing as it does through time and history,[7] demands ever new interpretations. The same may be said of Hegel's *Phenomenology* as well.

How are theses (1) through (8) regarding intentionality, stated in the first part of this essay, related to the thesis about interpretation formulated in the second part? In the second part intentionality recedes to the background, remains, as it were, anonymous, and allows the text itself to demand interpretation. The two are parts of a seamless whole. The first part sets aside the picture of the text as having a right meaning and instead traces meanings to intentional acts of an interpreter. Moreover, some texts clearly announce their author's intention, while others conceal it. But even in the former case, the interpreter has no direct access to that intention save by interpreting that text (or some other text, such as the author's correspondence). The latter are more radical. The anonymity of authorship puts the whole weight upon the text itself. To say that the text has an inexhaustible reservoir of meanings is to say that it can always be interpreted anew and that neither authorial intention nor the text's literal meaning constrains us to accept a final closure.

---

6. For this distinction, see Roman Ingarden, *Das literarische Kunstwerk* (Halle: Max Niemeyer), 1931.

7. Cp. Hans-Georg Gadamer, *Wahrheit und Methode: Grundzüge einer philosophischen Hermeneutik,* vol. 2 of *Gesammelte Werke* (Tübingen: J. C. B. Mohr, 1986).

Are There Definitive Interpretations?

Laurent Stern

Useful strategies for proving other universal negative claims are futile in defending the thesis that there are no definitive interpretations. We cannot point to the best available candidates for a single right interpretation and show that they do not satisfy the conditions for being definitive interpretations. Nor can we provide an indirect proof that there are no definitive interpretations by assuming that there are such interpretations and showing that all arguments on behalf of a single right interpretation are unsound. These strategies are successful in other contexts, but in discussing claims about interpretations, they easily become self-defeating. Overarching claims about interpretations are conclusions from interpretive premises. Many of these claims are self-referential. We want to reach the conclusion that there is no single right interpretation, but isn't that conclusion an interpretive claim about interpretations? If it is, then the conclusion exemplifies a single right interpretation showing that there are no such interpretations. If it is not, then the conclusion is a factual claim about interpretations; but how did we squeeze out a single factual claim from many interpretive claims about interpretations? One answer is that if the

I am grateful to Ferenc Altrichter, John Boler, Garry Hagberg, Elizabeth Huffer, Peter Kivy, and Sándor Radnóti for advice about this paper.

conclusion is considered a factual claim, we did not squeeze it out from interpretive claims about interpretations. At issue is our concept of interpreting: our concept of interpreting is such that single right interpretations are defined out of existence.

There are other answers to these questions. The reader will object that the answer here provided is begging the question. If the views presented here about our concepts of interpreting, translating, and understanding were uncontroversial, this would be a very short paper. Since they are controversial, my conceptions of these concepts must be defended. Meanwhile, prudence requires that we refrain from universal claims about these concepts. But it will be useful to examine and preserve the intuition behind such claims.

1. Constraints

The notions of interpretation, translation, and understanding are quite close. For some purposes they are discussed separately; for others these expressions are used interchangeably. To be sure, we can always differentiate between understanding and interpretation or translation: understanding is a state, while interpreting and translating are activities. We can also differentiate between translation and interpretation, even if translators of spoken words are called interpreters: interpreters at the United Nations are expected to translate rather than interpret the delegates' speeches. At the same time, it is sometimes useful to think about understanding of what was said or done not only as a result but also as a counterpart of interpreting or translating. Or the other way around, it is sometimes helpful to consider interpreting or translating not only as a precondition for understanding but also as continuous with understanding.

In interpreting and translating we start from the viewpoint of the interpreter or translator. Her goal is to understand what was said or done. Very roughly, she reaches her goal—refinements will be added later—when she can claim that if she were in the speaker's or agent's place, she would have said or done what the speaker or agent has said or done. For all that we know, her claim may be mistaken or insincere; but a mistake is only possible if she is sometimes right. Actually, she is right most of the time. There are telltale signs for being mistaken: among others, the speaker's or agent's protests that he has been misunderstood. But ordinarily, she has been so often successful in understanding others that she can rely on her past experiences when the same words are spoken or the same action performed: she understands immediately what is said or done without going through the interpreting or translating activity. In other cases she is only half conscious of these activities. In the large majority of cases she understands the speaker or agent as he understands himself.

In interpreting we steer by what we accept as facts. Others may consider interpretations what we accept as facts. Nevertheless, as soon as what was said seems to be incompatible with what we accept as facts, we ask: what was the speaker or agent trying to say or do? The incompatibility triggers the interpreting activity, which does not have theoretically satisfying beginning and end points. When an incompatibility with what we accept as facts triggers our interpreting, we can always ask whether our interpreting could have or should have started at a much earlier stage. Similarly, there is no theoretically satisfying end point to our interpreting. We could always go on and raise further questions about what others have said or done. If we stop at one point, this merely means either that we claim to have reached an understanding of what was said or done or that we have given up on trying to understand it or that we have reached some intermediate point on the continuum between the two previously mentioned extremes.

The connection between facts and interpretations yields one constraint on interpreting. Interpretations must be compatible with what we accept as facts. If the reader wishes to claim that there are no facts, that there are only interpretations, then he must decide what interpretations he accepts as secured, while attending to more contentious interpretations. An example will be helpful here. One reader believes that she is reading words, whose succession she interprets as sentences, leading to the understanding of paragraphs, and finally of the whole text that is presented for interpretation and understanding. Another reader believes that he is reading, against a contrasting background, marks that he interprets as letters, whose succession he interprets as words—from this point he continues as the first reader. A critic of both readers may argue that the starting point of their interpreting is arbitrary; but it is not arbitrary that both must start the interpreting activity somewhere. Philosophers of nominalist persuasion will accept letters, punctuation marks, and spaces as facts or basic interpretations on which further interpretations are built to reach understanding of a given text. Medieval scribes copying the Hebrew Bible were unconcerned about nominalism, but they only accepted letters and spaces as facts in copying the text; they knew the number of letters in each book, and they recorded which letter in a sequence of letters marked the middle of each book.

A second constraint on interpreting is normative. In interpreting we try to bring out from what is being interpreted its value for our purposes. Religious interpreters of different denominations may agree on wanting to provide the best interpretation of a biblical verse, and they may also agree on applying in their religious practices what is considered within each denomination the best interpretation. But given some beliefs that are different for each denomination, they may not agree on one interpretation as the best interpretation. However, interpreters of each denomination must argue that they have provided the best available interpretation. Interpretations are always offered and accepted as the best available for a given purpose. The reader may object: sometimes we accept what we believe to be the second-best interpretation.

This is indeed true, but in each of these cases, when we accept the second-best interpretation, we do so because what is the best interpretation from the viewpoint of our purposes is unavailable within the limits of our understanding. The educated layperson may be convinced that the expert's interpretation of what is at issue is considerably better than another available interpretation. Yet he must choose the second best, for given his lack of background knowledge or limited understanding, he cannot accept the best interpretation for his own purposes. Given the factual and normative constraints on interpreting, it would seem that we are well on the way to showing that there is a convergence to the best interpretation. It remains to be seen why this is false.

2. Persuaders

Ordinarily we understand immediately what was said or done; when we raise questions about it and an iteration of what was said is insufficient for our understanding, we are provided with an interpretation. The interpretation is offered to tell us in indirect speech what was said. Again, in the majority of cases we understand the interpretation and go on to other matters of our concern. If we do not understand or cannot agree with the interpretation, we raise further questions. We ask only in exceptional cases for reasons or arguments in support of an interpretation. But if we ask for such support, we expect to be persuaded either by the speaker—who acts as his own interpreter—or by another interpreter who claims to know what the speaker has said or done. Interpreters' efforts to persuade us are successful if we come to see or understand what is at issue as they do. We agree with them if they succeed in persuading us.

Let us assume that an interpreter offers to others the same interpretation about a given issue that she accepts—in other words, she is sincere and she does not wish to mislead her audience. When asked to support her interpretation, she will first claim that her interpretation satisfies both the factual and the normative constraints on interpreting. When pressed further, she will be aware of the need to persuade her audience to see or understand what is at issue as she does. She will achieve her goal if she can show (i) that her interpretation is not just a story that has a rather tenuous connection with what is being interpreted, and (ii) that from a range of plausible interpretations hers is the best available for a given purpose. The reader will note that if she satisfies the second condition, she will have satisfied the first. Both must be mentioned, for they exclude different kinds of interpretations. (As we shall see later, the first condition excludes off-the-wall interpretations, while the second condition excludes misinterpretations.)

In trying to persuade her audience about the correctness of her interpretation, the interpreter must rely on a principle that I have called elsewhere the

Universalizability Principle: Every reasonable person who is familiar with the circumstances understands what is at issue the way I do.

Sometimes it is useful to inquire how others understand what is at issue. But even if the interpreter never engages in such an inquiry, she is entitled to rely on the Universalizability Principle to demand agreement with her view. Her demand is justified if she has satisfied both the factual and the normative constraints on interpreting. It will be insufficient to invoke a much weaker—maybe even defective—principle that I have called the

Restrictive Principle: Only reasonable persons who are familiar with the circumstances understand what is at issue the way I do.

This principle is equivalent with "All persons who understand what is at issue the way I do are reasonable and familiar with the circumstances." For dogmatists or authoritarians the difference between the two principles is negligible. Confronted with disagreement, they can adopt either one of the two principles and argue that their opponents are either not reasonable or not familiar with what is at issue.

The difference between the two principles is of crucial importance only for the opponents of dogmatism. They can rely only on reasons and arguments in support of their interpretive choices. They must derive their choices from the conclusions of such arguments if they wish to remain dogmatism's opponents. In presenting reasons and arguments, they must solicit the agreement of all reasonable persons; hence, they are bound to prefer the Universalizability to the Restrictive Principle. Even a temporary retreat to the Restrictive Principle suggests that they could not abandon their interpretive choices, although they failed to convince some reasonable persons. How long can they maintain that those they could not convince are not familiar with what is at issue? It is conceivable, for example, that such a temporary retreat is necessary when an interpreter tries to establish a foothold for a new interpretive choice. But when a temporary retreat to the Restrictive Principle becomes a permanent feature of a given interpretive choice, then that choice becomes unacceptable for dogmatism's opponents. For in accepting the Restrictive Principle, we imply that we do not and need not take seriously the disagreement of at least some reasonable persons. The blanket claim that reasonable persons who disagree with our interpretive choices are unfamiliar with what is at issue loses its credibility the longer our choices remain available for public scrutiny.

Two cases must be distinguished. The interpreter is successful in persuading her audience that she has satisfied the factual and normative constraints on interpreting. In this case her audience will accept the interpretation presented and, if the need arises, pass on the interpretation to their audiences. The interpretation so transmitted, from one interpreter to an audience and from there to other audiences, creates an unbroken interpretive chain that occasionally leads from a speaker or agent—who happens to act as his own interpreter—to an audience that is far removed from the original interpreter. Within this chain the interpretation becomes a hereditary property of what is being interpreted.

In the second case, the interpreter relying only on reasons and arguments in persuading her audience is not successful. Of course, the interpreter and her audience can continue their conversation indefinitely, or due to exhaustion one side or the other may no longer find the continuation of the conversation rewarding. Occasionally, the interpreter will end the conversation with a conversation terminator. Such terminators are often heard when parents, teachers, experts, or self-appointed gurus fail to persuade their audiences. As long as the interpreter is convinced that she has satisfied both the factual and normative constraints on interpreting and that she has relied only on the Universalizability Principle, she may say

"When you become an adult, you will understand this as I do!" or
"When you are an expert in this field, you will understand this as I do!" or
"When you are rid of your neurosis, you will understand your story as I do!" or
"When the workers become class-conscious, they will understand their own situation as I do!"

Provided that the interpreter is sincere—this condition was stipulated before, but here we must exclude even cases where charges of self-deception arise—she is entitled to this conversation terminator. In fact, this terminator can be derived from the Universalizability Principle. If the adult, the teacher, the expert, and the guru have satisfied the factual and normative constraints on interpreting, and if they support their interpretations by appealing to the Universalizability Principle, then they are entitled to expect the agreement of the child, the student, the novice, and the newly initiated. Even if such an agreement cannot be established at this time, it will be forthcoming when their audiences take their places among the reasonable persons who are knowledgeable about what is at issue. For this reason, the agreement can be attributed to their audiences in the subjunctive mood: if they were reasonable and knowledgeable about what is at issue, they would agree with the interpretation.

Of course, the world does not always cooperate with the interpreters' wishful thinking. The child becomes an adult, the student becomes an expert, and the novice takes his place among the gurus—yet in some cases they still do not agree with the interpretations offered by their parents, teachers, or illustrious predecessors. In the long run in this debate, neither side can withdraw from an appeal to the Universalizability Principle to an appeal to the Restrictive Principle. For, if either interpreter withdraws to the Restrictive Principle, she can support her interpretive claims only by a weak principle: all persons who understand what is at issue the way she does are reasonable and knowledgeable about what is at issue. Sectarians of any persuasion will notice that even a minority of one is sufficient for satisfying this principle. Moreover, the conversation terminator that can be derived from the Restrictive Principle contains a promissory note. From "All persons who understand this as I do are reasonable and knowledgeable about what is at issue" we can derive

> "When you understand this as I do, you will be reasonable and knowledgeable about what is at issue!" or
> "When you understand this the way I do, you will become an expert in this field!"

Such promissory notes are empty. Finally, the Restrictive Principle is deficient: in some cases it can be shown to be false. Another person may agree with the interpreter in understanding a given issue, although that person is neither reasonable nor knowledgeable about that issue. Or two sectarians may have the same understanding of a given issue, although in the judgment of a third interpreter neither is reasonable or knowledgeable about that issue. If the terminator we derived from the Restrictive Principle is defective, then the principle itself is deficient. To be sure, the support of an interpretive choice by the Restrictive Principle is warranted in some cases, and the terminator that can be derived from it is appropriate. Insisting that she belongs among the reasonable persons who are knowledgeable about a given issue may be sufficient for a sectarian, but with the exception of cases of deep-level interpretation, reliance on the Restrictive Principle will be insufficiently persuasive.

Interpretations in both the indicative and subjunctive moods are natural, or surface-level, interpretations. On this level the interpreter tries to understand the speaker's words as he understands them or as he would understand them if he were in the interpreter's place. Disregarding the case where both of their interpretations are mistaken, a surface-level interpretation is considered successful and yields understanding of the speaker's words if it agrees with the speaker's self-interpretation, either in the indicative or the subjunctive mood. The interpreter leaves the limits of surface-level interpretation and takes a step toward deep-level interpretation as soon as she substitutes an alternative to the speaker's self-interpretation that is no longer warranted by the Universalizability Principle. By substituting for the speaker's self-interpretation an alternative, she enters the claim that she knows what the speaker means better than does the speaker himself. For example, the speaker believes that every reasonable person who is familiar with the circumstances agrees with his understanding of what is at issue. Accordingly, he believes that he is entitled to the observation "When you become an expert in this field, you will understand this the way I do!" His interpreter may concede only that every person who understands what is at issue the way the speaker does is reasonable and familiar with the circumstances. Hence, the speaker is entitled only to the statement "When you understand this the way I do, you will be an expert in this field!" The speaker believes that the facts of what is at issue support his reliance on the Universalizability Principle; his interpreter believes that the facts support the speaker's reliance only on the Restrictive Principle and not on the Universalizability Principle. Since we disregarded the case that both of them are mistaken, we can conclude that in such a debate the speaker's view that he is relying on the Universalizability Principle is mistaken. Why is this so?

The speaker's belief about his reliance on the Universalizability Principle in support of his views can be easily falsified by his interpreter. After all, the mere fact that a qualified interpreter—that is, a reasonable person who is familiar with what is at issue—believes that the speaker's understanding of the issues is mistaken is sufficient for defeating the speaker's contradictory claim, that every reasonable person who is familiar with the circumstances agrees with his understanding. Moreover, there is no need for the interpreter to rely on the Universalizability Principle in support of the claim that the speaker's understanding is mistaken; in her debate with the speaker it is sufficient for the interpreter to rely on the Restrictive Principle. Hence it is easier to defeat than to establish the claim that a given interpretive choice can be derived from the Universalizability Principle. An example—it is not purely fictional—will illustrate the contrast between natural and deep-level interpretation.

3. An Example

An art historian–connoisseur of established reputation attributes a certain painting to X; his younger colleagues and admirers doubt the attribution and are willing to concede only that the painting may have been produced in X's studio. When the older connoisseur wishes to terminate the discussion by reference to the Universalizability Principle and tries to silence his younger colleagues with the line "When you are an expert in this field, you will understand this the way I do!" the latter insist on continuing the discussion. The younger colleagues doubt neither the expertise nor the sincerity of the older connoisseur; in fact, they would not want to continue the conversation if they doubted one or the other. But they know that the older connoisseur routinely receives a percentage of the price of the paintings sold with his attributions. Could it not be that the older connoisseur's self-interest has played an intangible role in the attribution? So they tell their older colleague: "We don't believe this painting can be attributed to X; of course, you may continue to believe that your attribution is supported by the Universalizability Principle; but if you continue in holding that belief, you can count neither us nor anyone who disagrees with you among the reasonable persons who are familiar with the circumstances; hence, unless you are willing to consider all those who disagree with you either unreasonable or unfamiliar with the circumstances, you can only believe that your attribution is supported by the Restrictive Principle; finally, we would be glad to agree that your attribution is supported by the Restrictive Principle, for this only commits us to the claim that all those who agree with you are reasonable and familiar with the circumstances."

Deep-level interpretation is at work in this story. Prompted by self-interest, the older connoisseur could be lying; or his attribution could be based on an honest mistake. In these cases there is no need for deep-level interpretation. Natural, or surface-level, interpretation is sufficient for the understanding of lies and honest mistakes. Deep-level interpretation is needed only if all of the following conditions obtain:

(i)   In the interpreter's judgment it is at least questionable whether the facts or the speaker's understanding of the facts supports what the speaker believes.

(ii) The interpreter is convinced that the speaker sincerely believes what he claims to believe.

(iii) The speaker's knowledge of the facts—in our example: his expertise—is incompatible with any claim that his belief could be based on an honest mistake. Of course, the younger art historians could avoid all complications connected with discussions of self-deception by claiming that the older expert was mistaken. No doubt he was mistaken—but we would seriously underdescribe the example if we merely said he was mistaken. It is important to add that he was not entitled to this mistake. Given the speaker's level of knowledge or expertise, the mistake could have been avoided.

(iv) The speaker can be blamed for failing to avoid the mistake.

(v)   By failing to avoid the mistake, the speaker prepared the ground for his interpreter's substitution of an alternative to his self-interpretation.

(vi) By substituting an alternative for the speaker's self-interpretation, the interpreter enters the claim that she knows what the speaker meant better than does the speaker himself.

(vii) The interpreter relies on a set of interconnected beliefs about human nature—an overt or covert rudimentary theory—supporting the claim that she knows what the speaker meant better than does the speaker himself.

4. Natural and Deep-Level Interpretation

In offering a natural, or surface-level, interpretation, we expect the agreement of the speaker, writer, or agent whose words or deeds we are interpreting. Such an agreement confirms the interpretation. The agreement is only virtual if the speaker is not available to confirm the interpretation or if we attribute agreement to him in the subjunctive mood. Since we can support a natural, or surface-level, interpretation only by the Universalizability Principle, our interpretation must be reconsidered if not even a virtual agreement can be attributed to the speaker. In invoking Universalizability, we claim that all reasonable persons who are knowledgeable about the issues agree with our interpretation (alternatively: would agree with our interpretation if they were in the position to do so). If the speaker disagrees, and if it seems insufficient to claim that, were he in our position, he would understand his own words and deeds as we understand him, then we must reconsider supporting our interpretation by the Universalizability Principle. Why is this so?

We take it for granted that most of the time—but not always—a speaker, writer, or agent understands what he says or does and what he has meant to say or do. He is in a position of authority regarding what he says and does; he has *interpretive authority* over his own words and deeds. If he disagrees with our understanding of what he has said or done and we cannot be persuaded by his disagreement, then we must either dismiss his disagreement and continue our reliance on Universalizability or support our interpretation by the Restrictive Principle. We can dismiss his disagreement if we can show that the speaker is either insincere or not reasonable or not knowledgeable about the issues. If he were sincere, reasonable, and knowledgeable, he would agree with our understanding of his words and deeds. Our continued reliance on Universalizability requires that we claim his agreement with our understanding in the subjunctive mood.

If we support our understanding by the Restrictive Principle, then we fault him in rather subtle ways for being insincere, unreasonable, and insufficiently informed about what is at issue. He is insincere, not because he is trying to deceive others, but because he has allowed himself to become self-deceived. It is his self-deception that raises doubts about his reasonableness and his knowledge of what is at issue.

It may be objected that in speaking about self-deception we merely use a *façon de parler,* but this phenomenon is not exemplified. In fact, even if there is no such phenomenon, this way of speaking is useful whether or not we speak with the vulgar or the learned. We can avoid speaking about self-deception if we focus on the notion of right understanding. This notion must not be confused with interpretive authority. In fact, right understanding presupposes interpretive authority. For example, a Serbian engaged in ethnic cleansing against the Albanian Kosovars understands his own words and what he means to say when he says that the Albanian Kosovars do not deserve to survive. His saying what he says and his acting on his words prove both that he understands what he says and that he does not have a right understanding of what he says. He has interpretive authority concerning what he says, but interpretive authority does not yield authority concerning a right understanding of what he says.[1] There is no authority about right understanding. To be sure, his interpreter or critic may have a right understanding of this matter, but that understanding does not depend on any authority.

We can avoid speaking about self-deception and rely on the notion of a right understanding when we blame the Serbian engaged in ethnic cleansing. In this case we must be prepared to admit that he fully believes what he is saying. Our understanding of his words and deeds is supported by the Universalizability Principle. We accept his interpretive authority about his own words and deeds and blame him for not having a right belief and a right understanding. Alternatively, we can rely on the notion of self-deception in blaming him for failing to have a right understanding. We need not

---

1. For an alternative view, see Joseph Margolis, "Replies in Search of Self-Discovery," in *Interpretation, Relativism, and the Metaphysics of Culture: Themes in the Philosophy of Joseph Margolis,* ed. Michael Krausz and Richard Shusterman (Amherst, N.Y.: Humanity Books, 1999), 356. In a response to my views, Margolis writes: "I see no reason—certainly, no reason is given—to think that any form of 'authority' is 'constitutive of interpretation.' " His readers will surely concede that he understands what he says and what he meant to say in the quoted sentence, and in this sense he has *interpretive authority* over his own words. The denial that there is such an authority is seriously mistaken. Is it due to a confusion between interpretive authority and right understanding?

admit that he fully believes what he is saying; he merely deceives himself into believing what he is saying. At the same time, we question whether he is reasonable and knowledgeable about what is at issue. The price we must pay for choosing to rely on the notion of self-deception in blaming him is that we can no longer support our claims by the Universalizability Principle. The very notion of self-deception is controversial, and we can be certain that anyone we claim is deceiving himself will disagree with our claim. After all, it would be self-defeating for him to admit that he is here and now deceiving himself. Accordingly, we can support our claims only by relying on the Restrictive Principle.

Why should we rely on the admittedly deficient Restrictive Principle when we can rely on the Universalizability Principle in the subjunctive mood? If our choice were merely between two ways of understanding others, then reliance on Universalizability would always be preferable to reliance on the Restrictive Principle. We rely on the Restrictive Principle only if our understanding others has an additional therapeutic point. In relying on the Restrictive Principle, we urge them to change their lives. Rilke's line, "You must change your life!" is the shortest expression of this therapeutic point. The great nineteenth- and twentieth-century deep-interpretation theories of Marx, Nietzsche, and Freud were infused with their authors' awareness of the therapeutic point of deep-level interpretation. In supporting deep-level interpretation by the Universalizability Principle in the subjunctive mood, we invite charges of dogmatism. In supporting it by the deficient Restrictive Principle, we avoid the charge of dogmatism. At the same time, we offer those we are interpreting a way of speaking about what we have discovered to be their predicament. Reliance on Universalizability is sufficient only for blaming them for failing to have a right belief and right understanding. Reliance on the Restrictive Principle permits us to blame them for allowing themselves to be self-deceived and, as by-products of that self-deception, for being insufficiently reasonable and knowledgeable about what is at issue.

The change demanded by Marx's, Nietzsche's, and Freud's theories can be brought about only by those who are targeted by deep-level interpretation. If they change their lives, the deep-level interpretation will be successful, and they will agree with their interpreters. In case of success, what once was deep-level interpretation becomes natural, or surface-level, interpretation, supported by the Universalizability Principle. While they were unsuccessful, deep-level interpretations were supported by sets of interconnected beliefs about human nature. Once they are successful, these interconnected beliefs become either commonsense generalizations or theories about human nature. Deep-level interpretations, supported by theories of deep interpretation and the Restrictive Principle, thrive only as long as their targets fail to bring about the demanded changes.

As mentioned before, the Restrictive Principle is deficient. Since it can be easily falsified, it is a principle only in scare quotes. When falsified by those who are neither reasonable nor knowledgeable, it must be replaced by an even weaker principle—"Some persons who understand this as I do are reasonable and knowledgeable about what is at issue"—yet it is indispensable. For how long? As long as deep-level interpretations, supported by theories of deep interpretation, fail to be successful.

5. Conflicts

Deep-level interpretation is available only if we shift the focus of interpreting, from what has been said or done, to the speaker or agent whose words or deeds are interpreted. In interpreting a work of art, a legal or a religious document, our concern is the discovery of evidence internal to that work or document. The internal evidence provides us with a first approximation of the realized intentions of the speaker, writer, or agent. These first approximations are subjected to critical judgment before they are accepted as a speaker's or agent's realized intentions. Editors routinely correct the typing, spelling, and punctuation mistakes of poets; according to Old Testament scholars, even the Hebrew Bible was subjected to correction by medieval scribes at about twenty different places.[2]

Some readers will argue that we must also account for external evidence, that is, evidence that cannot be discovered by inspecting a given artwork, legal or religious document. They are right if the speakers, writers, or agents, and not what they have said or done, are the primary targets of our interpreting. In these cases we can raise questions about the intentions of the speakers or agents whose words and deeds we are interpreting. Occasionally we may even ask whether they were fully aware of their own intentions or whether they were mistaken or self-deceived about them. Deep-level interpretation may be in order, as long as the focus of interpretation is

2. Otto Eisfeldt, *The Old Testament: An Introduction*, trans. Peter R. Ackroyd (New York: Harper & Row, 1965), 686.

the biography or history of speakers and agents rather than what they have said, written, or created. For example, when Jefferson wrote that "all men are created equal," he did not have the same understanding of "men" as today's readers. What today's readers perceive as a tension between his words and his understanding of these words may call for deep-level interpretation, but the target of such interpretation is Jefferson, not his words.

If we avoid deep-level interpretation, then we can rely only on the Universalizability Principle in support of our natural, or surface-level, interpretations. Natural interpretations in either the indicative or the subjunctive mood are expected to satisfy both the factual and normative constraints on interpreting; their support by the Universalizability Principle implies that they are believed to be true at least by the interpreters who proposed them. Since there are incompatible interpretations, questions about their truth or falsity must be raised. To be sure, these questions can be avoided as long as we can show that incompatible interpretations have different purposes or fit into different contexts or are addressed to different audiences. Interpretive conflicts that prompt a choice between incompatible interpretations occur seldom, but there are no good reasons for believing that they can always be avoided or that the choice between them can always be deferred. Such conflicts must be understood from two different perspectives: our disagreement with one interpretation and our agreement with another.

Concerning a disagreement with a given interpretation, it must be mentioned that not every interpretation deserves to be taken seriously as an interpretation of its purported object. If an interpreter seems to be looking at a painting but her description of what she sees provides evidence that she in fact has looked away from that painting and superimposed on it her own fantasies, then her interpretation need not be taken seriously. Such interpretations are off-the-wall interpretations or no interpretations at all of that painting. At best they are stories that have only a tenuous connection with the purported objects of the interpretation. On the other hand, mistaken interpretations or misinterpretations are at least on the wall: they deserve to be taken seriously. They are within the range of possible interpretations of their purported objects. We fault them only for failing to satisfy the normative constraints on interpreting. We judge them to be misinterpretations, since there are better interpretations from the viewpoint of our purposes.

If we agree with a given interpretation, and especially if we pass it on to others, we must be persuaded that the interpretation satisfies the factual and normative constraints on interpreting. We are entitled to support the interpretation by the Universalizability Principle if we are persuaded that both constraints have been satisfied. No doubt we may be mistaken; in this case the interpretation we agree with will be discredited, and it will turn out to be a misinterpretation. We may be right; in that case the interpretation deserves to be accepted and considered to be the best available until it is defeated by a better interpretation.

6. Hedging

If we defend an interpretation or agree with it, then we hold it to be true. But are there true interpretations? Are misinterpretations false interpretations? The answers to these questions are controversial. Moreover, it is unclear what can be gained by supporting either side in this controversy. Some readers will argue that interpretations are neither true nor false; they are recommendations that are more or less plausible. Others will argue that they are indeed true or false. No matter what arguments we accept and what views we hold, we cannot avoid believing, as long as we are sincere, interpretations that we defend. Neither passionate crusaders nor tolerant interpreters would admit that an interpretation they defend is merely plausible. In supporting their interpretations by the Universalizability Principle, they demand agreement with their interpretations. If they cannot persuade others, their choices are limited. They can (i) attribute agreement to them in the subjunctive mood; (ii) exclude them from the ranks of those who are considered reasonable and knowledgeable about the issues; (iii) support their interpretation by the Restrictive Principle and claim that the unpersuaded are victims of self-deception; (iv) withdraw their interpretations.

For the sake of this argument let us suppose there are two interpretations that seem to be incompatible while serving the same purpose, such that there is no consistent third interpretation containing both. As long as we are indifferent to both interpretations or their target, we will find it easy to judge both plausible or both false. Interpreters are quite tolerant whenever they don't care about the topic being interpreted. Toleration gives way to contentiousness when we start to care about what is being interpreted. We will find it more difficult to practice relativism's preaching when we focus on agreeing with or defending an interpretation than when we are engaged in abstract reflections on interpreting.[3]

3. For an alternative view on this matter, see Michael Krausz, *Rightness and Reasons: Interpretation in Cultural Practices* (Ithaca, N.Y.: Cornell University Press, 1993).

It can be objected—and it has been objected—that acceptance of my views entails acceptance of bivalence.[4] Can we avoid intolerance, even when we care about an interpretation and its target, if we accept a many-valued logic? The answer is that the existence of many-valued logics is irrelevant to this topic. Every informed defender of bivalence would agree that there are many-valued logics. They can even provide various matrices for the different many-valued logics and show how such logics can be extended to the logic of predicates and quantifiers. But the reference to such logics is merely an exercise in hand-waving if we are not provided with instruction in applying them in the context of agreeing with or defending interpretations. Until I am provided with acceptable instruction on this topic, I am prepared to dig in my heels, while—for reasons independent of this discussion—I remain an unrepentant defender of bivalence.

We agree with or defend interpretations we happen to believe or hold to be true. This does not imply that what we happen to believe is true, but it does imply that we believe that it is at least possible for some interpretations to be true. True interpretations are ordinarily called statements of facts and not interpretations. Statements corresponding to facts are true, and they are true not because they can be supported by the Universalizability Principle but because they state what happens to be the case in the world in which we live. Unscrupulous interpreters—aware of the falsity of their claims—use the transformation of successful interpretations into factual descriptions for their own purposes. They save themselves the effort of providing reasons and arguments for their interpretations: they gain all the advantages of theft over honest toil by presenting their interpretations as if they were factual descriptions. Partially insincere interpreters, interpreters whose beliefs or understanding is deficient, or the self-deceived succeed in convincing themselves that instead of interpretations they argue for descriptions. Finally, mistaken interpreters falsely claim that they have discovered facts about what they have interpreted. Sincere interpreters will rest their case on the Universalizability or Restrictive Principle, while holding their interpretations to be true without making premature claims that they are true. For how long? As long as their interpretations are confirmed as factual claims or until they are discredited by better interpretations.

---

4. Margolis, "Replies in Search of Self-Discovery," 356. For an excellent review of *Interpretation, Relativism, and the Metaphysics of Culture,* see Robert Stecker, *Journal of Aesthetics and Art Criticism,* 60, no. 1 (Winter 2002).

7. Translations

Two patterns emerge: the instability of interpretations and the transformation of successful interpretations. Interpretations are unstable, for they thrive as interpretations only as long as they are not considered to be factual descriptions. If they gain in stability, they are transformed from deep-level to surface-level interpretations, and from surface-level interpretations to what are considered factual descriptions. As we have seen, deep-level interpretations are contested, and the theories supporting them are controversial. Successful deep-level interpretations become natural, or surface-level, interpretations supported by the Universalizability Principle. Successful deep-interpretation theories are upgraded and become either commonsense generalizations or theories about human nature. Successful natural, or surface-level, interpretations become factual descriptions. The very notion of a definitive interpretation implies success. But if interpretations are successful, accepted, and considered to be incontestable, they are transformed into true descriptions. Could we find definitive interpretations among the less-than-completely-successful interpretations? A brief comparison between interpreting and translating will suggest a negative answer to our question.

It is trivially true and always in the foreground in the context of translating that the primary goal in translating is to make a text available in a target language for those who are unfamiliar with that text's source language. The translator—ordinarily a native speaker of the target language—provides understanding of a text or what is said in that text for those who could not understand it without such mediation. Translations are always for a given audience, and the translator often includes herself within that audience. The need for a new translation arises if the language of the translation's audience or the knowledge of the translated text's subject matter radically changes. For example, in the last seventy years of the twentieth century three complete and two abridged English translations of Kant's first *Critique* were published. Texts are retranslated if the audience of that text changes. The older translations are discarded not because they are mistaken—although the mistakes are ordinarily pointed out by the more recent translators—but because the older translations are themselves in need of what could be called a "translation"—translation in scare quotes. (Teachers of philosophy often suggest such "translations" from the language of Locke or Hume to the vocabulary currently used among philosophers or to their students' vernacular.) The older translations are not necessarily discredited, but due to changes in their audience, they are considered to be old-fashioned or quaint. Texts are retranslated, not because the texts change, but because their audiences change.

Translations with or without scare quotes are dependent on the needs of their audience. The audience's needs are also decisive in the context of interpreting. What was once an interpretation may be either accepted as a factual description or discredited as no longer satisfying the factual or normative constraints on interpreting. As long as a discredited interpretation is understood to be a misinterpretation—and not an off-the-wall interpretation—it will be seen as quaint as soon as it is replaced by another interpretation. Our judgment about the quaintness of discredited interpretations suggests that, at least in part, reinterpretations are motivated by the changing needs of the interpretation's audience. So, is there a convergence to the best available interpretation? Can there be a definitive interpretation?

8. Understanding

If there is a convergence to the best available interpretation or if there is a definitive interpretation, it will be found among the successful interpretations. Yesteryear's successful interpretation can easily become either a misinterpretation or a factual description. Successful interpretations occupy a segment of the line leading from misinterpretations to successful interpretations and from there to factual descriptions. How wide or how narrow is that segment? The answer to this question will be different for each interpreter; to show this we must first explain what determines the width of that segment for each interpreter.

For ease of exposition, I shall speak in the first person singular. I shall call a "privileged fact" whatever a given interpreter is unwilling to doubt, except in the context of discussing the merits of radical skepticism. For example, I have a brain, I am now looking at a computer screen, I am now in a book-lined study, some words in my native language hook up with some items in the world in which we live, I knew my biological parents.

I also have firmly held beliefs that I hold to be true, but about these I can merely say that I will reexamine them if some reasonable persons who are familiar with the circumstances disagree with me. In the past, I have been mistaken, and it would be welcome if others would show me the error of my ways. Beliefs function as intermediaries between me and the facts: I hold them to be true as long as they are representative of the facts; I reject them as soon as they are discredited by the facts. Concerning the privileged facts, I have no need of such intermediaries. I understand these facts immediately and directly, and as long as I am the same person I am now, I will not even entertain the possibility of error—provided that no philosophical considerations concerning these privileged facts are at issue.

Now, it would be easy to bury the distinction between privileged facts and firmly held beliefs underneath an avalanche of objections drawn from the current philosophical literature. After all, it has been claimed that there are no facts, that there are only beliefs, that there are neither facts nor beliefs, that there are only propositions we hold to be true, that the very notion of a proposition is unclear, and so forth. These views are not incompatible with the distinction between privileged facts and firmly held beliefs. Those who hold some of these views will be able to translate what I have said into their preferred idiom. The following may be useful for facilitating such a translation.

Let us dispense with the talk about facts and suggest instead a distinction between two kinds of beliefs. Let us assume that belief box #1 contains all my beliefs that are so deeply entrenched and so compelling that I am prepared to hold on to them no matter what happens. Should I ever abandon them, I would no longer be the same person I am now. Belief box #2 contains all my beliefs that I am willing to revise.[5] I would dismiss objections raised on the grounds of the Universalizability Principle against the content of my box #1. Since I am prepared to hold on to these beliefs against any majority, no matter how compact or how large, I cannot defend them by relying on the Universalizability Principle. I can defend them only in one of two ways. I can argue that anything said in support of the contents of my belief box #1 is less certain than what is in that box. Or I can support these beliefs by relying on the admittedly weak Restrictive Principle. On the other hand, objections raised on the grounds of the Universalizability Principle against the contents of my box #2 are highly effective. The contents of both boxes will vary from one person to the next. Some prefer desert landscapes to oriental bazaars, others jungles to formal gardens. Similarly, some will keep in belief box #1 very few items and argue for placing what others keep in that box in belief box #2. Some will keep in belief box #1 what they

---

5. I assume that everyone who has beliefs has at least one belief box in his head. The heuristic device of a belief box has been invented by Stephen Schiffer, "Truth and the Theory of Content," in *Meaning and Understanding*, ed. H. H. Parret and Jacques Bouveresse (Berlin: Walter de Gruyter, 1981).

know about physics; others will keep in that box what they have learned in the course of their religious instruction. Some will claim that they keep their religious—or antireligious—beliefs in box #2, but after some probing it may turn out that in fact they keep them in box #1, or the other way around.

Our judgments about interpretations of what has been said or done are dependent on the content of our two belief boxes. The more certainties we carry in our belief box #1, the narrower will be the segment of successful interpretations that we are willing to recognize. What others, with fewer certainties in their belief box #1, recognize as successful interpretations, we would characterize as factual descriptions or as misinterpretations. The fewer certainties our belief box #1 contains, the wider will be the segment of successful interpretations that we are willing to entertain. So we shouldn't be surprised to find that the segment of successful interpretations will be different for each interpreter and that parts of that segment will be the same for many interpreters.

We must face an additional problem. Contrary to all protestations and assurances that we will unconditionally hold on to the contents of our belief box #1, we do in fact abandon some beliefs that are found in that box. In the course of a lifetime some skeptics become dogmatists, and some dogmatist lose their most firmly held convictions. Some lose their religious faith, while others become born-again Christians. Such fundamental changes in the content of our belief box #1 may prompt us to claim that we are no longer the same persons as we were before. We make good use of the admittedly weak Restrictive Principle in explaining to ourselves and to others the sudden changes in our fundamental beliefs. This principle just says more ponderously what popular wisdom teaches a religious person to say after he has lost his faith: "I only lost my faith, not my mind." The Restrictive Principle is sufficient, even in its most weakened form—"Some persons who understand this as I do are reasonable and knowledgeable about what is at issue"—when we need to support the content of our belief box #1.

9. Alternatives

The result of our inquiry was not in doubt. We have not found a definitive interpretation or a convergence to the best available interpretation. What has emerged is the reason for our failure. Definitive or best available interpretations are among the successful interpretations. Successful interpretations can be found in the segment of the line between misinterpretations and factual descriptions. The width or narrowness of that segment depends upon the content of our two belief boxes. To the extent that parts of the segment of successful interpretations is the same for many interpreters, we may come to believe that there is a convergence to the best available interpretation. But such a convergence is quite unstable, since different interpreters change their minds about what they accept within the segment of successful interpretations; also, one and the same interpreter may in the course of a lifetime change her mind about this matter.

Three objections may be raised. The first suggests an escape from our conception of successful interpretations as a segment between misinterpretations and factual descriptions. One objector may stipulate that there are only interpretations and that whatever is not a misinterpretation is a more or less successful interpretation. Accordingly, there are no factual descriptions. Among the more successful interpretations there may be a convergence to the best interpretation and even a definitive interpretation. The answer to this objection is that this view changes only the terms of the debate, but not the underlying conception of interpretations. If we stipulate that there are no factual descriptions, we will find the field of successful interpretations quite crowded. In that crowded field we must find order by distinguishing between the more and the less successful interpretations. Once we introduce this ordering principle, we will find that we call factual descriptions what the objector calls the more successful interpretations. What the objector wants to discard returns under a different name.

Another objector suggests that we erase the demarcation line between misinterpretations and successful interpretations. According to this view there are only interpretations—containing both misinterpretations and what we would call successful interpretations—and factual descriptions. The interpretations can be more or less fitting, to the point, relevant, appropriate, and so forth. Interpreters of relativist persuasion may welcome this suggestion. But if we accept this suggestion, we must still argue for our interpretive choices. In a crowded field, when arguing for our choices or agreeing with the choices of others, we must show why some choices deserve to be discredited. Again, the demarcation line between misinterpretations and successful interpretations that the objector wants to discard will be reestablished.

Finally, a third objector adverts to the fundamental difference between facts and interpretations. To be sure, interpretive claims may approach factual statements asymptotically, but they cannot become factual statements. Even if interpreters believe, while recommending their interpretations, that they are true, it does not follow that they are indeed true. If we believe that interpretations are more or less plausible—and not either true or false—we must hold that interpretive claims cannot become factual statements. But even if we admit the fundamental difference between facts and interpretations, we must decide whether a given claim is interpretive or factual. Yesterday's fact is today seen as an interpretation, just as what was at one time an interpretation is now understood as a fact. The distinction between what is a fact and what is merely seen as a fact, or what is an interpretation and what is merely understood as an interpretation, depends upon what appear to us as other facts and other interpretations. Ultimately, it depends on the content of our two belief boxes. If we were endowed with intellectual vision enabling us to distinguish between facts and what merely appear to be facts, we could do without beliefs and interpretations. When confronting problems of skepticism, we would welcome such a dispensation. In other contexts we would deplore it as an unhappy arrangement, for it would harm our powers of imagination and impoverish our lives.

10. Envoy

Practical needs dictate the beginning and end points of interpreting. While pursuing our practical needs, we hope for definitive interpretations. The hope is salutary: it motivates the search for its realization. It can be realized when an interpretation is understood as a factual description, but then it is no longer seen as an interpretation. The burden of proof that there are definitive interpretations that do not appear to us as factual descriptions is on those who happen to make such claims. Meanwhile, prudence requires that we withhold judgment on the matter of definitive interpretations but issue a challenge: show us a definitive interpretation. If presented with one such case, we will have to be persuaded that it is not a factual description or a scientific explanation that is independent of the interpreter's two belief boxes.

PART II

Against Critical Pluralism

David Novitz

Art critics frequently argue about the correctness or validity of the interpretations that they and others offer of particular works of art. More often than not, they are convinced that their own interpretations are exclusively correct and that the rival interpretations of their opponents are wayward and mistaken. This requires, of course, that they should assume as a regulative ideal that, for any work of art, there is only one correct, right, valid, or true interpretation. Increasingly, though, such a "singularist" ideal is held to be groundless. It is an ideal, we are told, that does violence to the nature of art—indeed to the nature of any cultural object.[1] One reason often advanced for this view is that cultural objects are historically constituted and cannot themselves be properly discerned or individuated independently of a range of variable cultural practices, including, of course, the cultural practice of interpretation. It follows that there may often be more than one acceptable way of interpreting a cultural object.

On some versions of this view, interpretation involves imputing properties to cultural objects—properties, it turns out, that are partially constitu-

---

1. Michael Krausz, *Rightness and Reasons: Interpretation in Cultural Practices* (Ithaca, N.Y.: Cornell University Press, 1993), 1. Where possible, all futures references to this work will be given as RR in the text.

tive of them. Moreover, since the cultural beliefs and principles that mediate interpretation are unstable, so too are the properties of these objects. It follows, on this view, that there are and can be no interpretatively neutral properties internal to a cultural object that can be objectively singled out and correctly described in order to show that an interpretation is exclusively correct. Hence it is concluded that the regulative ideal of a single right interpretation for a cultural object must be misplaced. When once this is understood, any pretence to critical singularism—to the claim, that is, that one has produced, or that it is possible to produce, the single correct interpretation of a work of art—is and has to be insincere.

1. Critical Pluralism

This is where the most persuasive form of critical pluralism begins. In developing his version of it, Michael Krausz speaks of, and attempts to defend, what he calls multiplism—a variety of critical pluralism that holds that while "there may be reasoned critical comparison between contending interpretations, . . . such critical comparison would not show that a preferred interpretation was strong enough to unseat its rivals conclusively and render them inadmissible" (RR, 2). It is not that pluralists do not hold their preferred interpretations to be right; rather, they hold them "to be inconclusively so" (RR, 2). On this view, there is room for rational disputation about interpretations, but such disputes are about the plausibility or adequacy of a particular interpretation, about whether it should be adjudged acceptable, not about whether it, and it alone, is the single right interpretation.

Crucially, then, the critical pluralist challenges the view that the singularist ideal is essential to rational criticism (RR, 4). On the contrary, the pluralist maintains that one can rationally compare interpretations and, moreover, that one can have sound reasons for arriving at the view that two incongruent (that is, contrary rather than contradictory) interpretations can both be regarded as admissible accounts of the work in question—in the sense that neither can be shown to unseat the other.

According to Krausz, the range of "ideally admissible interpretations" is something that is itself socially constituted (RR, 39), while questions about "how they relate to their objects-of-interpretation, and how interpretations may be rationally compared," are never properly decided by appeal to the actual inherent features of the object of interpretation. To some critical singularists this latter claim will appear particularly odd, for to them it seems obvious that an interpretation will be true if the object of interpretation actually has the properties that are interpretatively attributed to it. But according to Krausz, "practice-independent objects" need not be assumed, and certainly need not be assumed to be completely determinate, "for either singularist or multiplist conditions to obtain" (RR, 146). One reason for this is that, on his view, we cannot have epistemic access to a practice-independent object (RR, 33), so that even if the notion of such an object is coherent, such objects cannot play any role in determining the truth or otherwise of an interpretation (RR, chaps. 5–7).

2. Points of Agreement and Disagreement

The variety of critical singularism that I wish to defend does not deny, indeed insists, that works of art are cultural objects and that the properties that properly belong to them are themselves dependent on the culture within which the work is located. Like Krausz, I also argue that "no cultural entity can be understood as such independently of the practices in which it is found and fostered" (RR, 13).[2] Furthermore, I allow, together with him, that some of the properties that works of art are taken to have are imputed to it through a particular variety of interpretation. But here all agreement ends. My claim is that Krausz's multiplism can only get going because it conflates varieties of interpretation that need to be distinguished and treated separately. In particular, I argue that the variety of interpretation that involves the imputation of properties to works of art has to be distinguished from that which seeks self-consciously to fill gaps in our understanding by explaining particular problems or puzzles in the work. Inquiry is, as Krausz maintains, a cultural practice, but there are significantly different modes of inquiry. When once this is understood, it becomes a relatively easy matter to show, first, that certain sorts of inquiry, namely those that seek to elucidate and explain and thereby to uncover the properties of the work, are either false or true and, second, that it is not reasonable to seek to elucidate

2. At least, I agree on one reading of this quotation. See my "Interpretation and Justification," *Metaphilosophy* 31, nos. 1/2 (2000) (special issue: *The Philosophy of Interpretation*, ed. Joseph Margolis and Tom Rockmore): 4–24, as well as *Knowledge, Fiction, and Imagination* (Philadelphia: Temple University Press, 1987), chap. 5, hereafter referred to as KFI in the text. The arguments that follow attempt to strengthen the position found in these works.

or explain on any other assumption. This, of course, is not to deny that there are varieties of interpretation that are not amenable to singularist assumptions, but these, I argue, play a relatively minor role in the criticism of art. To overemphasize them is to banish art criticism to the wastelands of irrationalism.

More emphatically, I argue that unless we can have epistemic access to works of art—as they are in themselves—there just is no point in trying to understand them. The precise properties that works possess independently of specific interpretations are, I argue, what interpretation in its primary and central sense seeks to uncover, and in this sense it is always the case that interpretations are either true or false and that there always is a single right interpretation.

Certainly we can interpret in a different sense and so weave webs of impressive words around each (assumed) work, but, if we have no epistemic access to the work itself, I argue that there can be no nonarbitrary constraints on this activity—nothing, that is, that we could know about the work that could put brakes on our claims about it. And this, of course, leads ineluctably to the interpretative anarchy that Krausz seeks valiantly but vainly to avoid (RR, 49–53).

3. Talking About Interpretation

In the early parts of his book, Krausz attempts to establish his variety of critical pluralism by looking to musical performance, telling us there that "in this discussion I shall be using 'interpretation' in music more or less synonymously with 'performance' " (RR, 18). This embodies an odd and a controversial assumption, for while musical performances may presuppose certain critical interpretations of the score and the work, the two are so dissimilar that it is at best problematic to make inferences from the one to the other.[3] Krausz does concede that "for certain purposes we may note some differences between them," but not, he thinks, for the purpose of establishing his multiplism (RR, 18). Let us suppose for the moment that he is right about this. On his view, then, because performances are underdetermined by scores, so too are critical interpretations, and this, he thinks, is

---

3. For more on this, see Jerrold Levinson, "Performative Versus Critical Interpretation in Music," in *The Pleasures of Aesthetics* (Ithaca, N.Y.: Cornell University Press, 1996), 60–89.

sufficient to establish that interpretative inquiry into the nature of any musical work is not amenable to the singularist ideal: that there is more than one
admissible critical interpretation of the score and hence of the work. But
this plainly need not follow. What does follow—or so I argue in this
paper—is that if it is true that the score and the work are indeterminate in
certain respects, this fact must be captured and relayed in the single right
critical interpretation of the score and the work. Of course, a musical performance is always determinate; it has to be a particular rendering of an
indeterminate score and work. Performances, then, cannot capture indeterminacies, but critical interpretations can and do. Only by overlooking this
(and other salient differences between the two) is it possible to regard performances as critical interpretations.

In supposing that musical performance is in all salient respects the same
as critical interpretation, we conflate at least two kinds of interpretation
that need to be considered separately. In one fundamental and primary sense
of this word, "interpretation" mentions an activity that we self-consciously
perform in order to promote understanding. In this sense, interpretation is
elucidatory and is called for only when we recognize that we have run out
of knowledge and established belief in terms of which to banish our ignorance or our confusion (KFI, 91–93). Put differently, interpretation (in the
primary, or elucidatory, sense) always requires knowledge of one's own lack
of understanding—of the fact that one is unable to grasp whatever it is
that one wishes to understand. And the subsequent process of coming to
understand (assuming that there is no extant body of knowledge or belief
that one can easily consult) involves the deliberate formulation of hypotheses that are meant to dispel one's ignorance and incomprehension. A pianist,
then, might seek the right way of rendering a score, and might find that
some aspects of it are more easily grasped than others. Those that are puzzling or confusing stand in need of elucidation, and it is here that elucidatory interpretation is called for.

There is, though, a second and a different sense of "interpretation" that
also enters into musical performance and that needs to be distinguished
from the first. In this sense of the word—what I have elsewhere called "elaborative interpretation" and which is similar to aspects of what Krausz refers
to as "imputational interpretation"—interpretation does not involve a self-
conscious quest for understanding. A pianist's performance of a musical
work, or aspects of that performance, can be elaborative, and will be if the
pianist subjectively and imaginatively elaborates on the score by "filling in"
its indeterminacies without attempting to solve particular puzzles—

believing, on occasion, that his or her performance is obvious or else un-problematic. Here the elaboration is not prompted by an awareness of ignorance on the part of the pianist; nor, from the pianist's point of view, is the elaboration demanded by the score. He or she elaborates on the score, imaginatively completing it in ways that are considered natural, obvious, or unproblematic.

The subjective, largely gratuitous nature of elaborative interpretation be-comes more obvious when we consider the ways in which we read and un-derstand novels. When, for instance, we read the opening sentence of Jane Austen's *Emma*, we learn only that Emma Woodhouse was "handsome, clever, and rich, with a comfortable home and happy disposition," and that she "seemed to unite some of the best blessings of existence; and had lived nearly twenty-one years in the world with very little to distress or vex her."[4] What we do not learn is how rich or handsome she was; nor do we learn anything about her facial features, her hair color, her height, and much besides. And yet, without pausing to think about, or to recognize their igno-rance, readers will readily supply these missing details.

Although elaborative interpretations of this sort can affect one's under-standing of cultural objects, they are not designed to secure understanding. They sometimes seem obvious to the interpreter, and there need be no awareness of having imaginatively imputed properties to a fictional charac-ter or a score, still less of having done so without obvious warrant. Even when elaborative interpretation is deliberate, it still is not designed to secure understanding. Usually, when deliberately performed, it becomes a kind of play involving the imaginative imputation of properties to a work—what is sometimes referred to as "ludic" interpretation.

Whether deliberate or not, it is vital to distinguish elaborative interpreta-tion from its elucidatory counterpart. Questions regarding the correctness or validity of interpretation belong for the most part to those interpretations that seek specifically to understand and to explain—that is, to elucidatory interpretations—not to those that gratuitously elaborate by "filling in" the indeterminacies of a work. Since such indeterminacies can be resolved in many different ways, there is a large range of possible elaborations, all equally plausible, but not always compatible with one another. The inhabi-tant of Los Angeles, for instance, who thinks of Emma Woodhouse as slightly brash in conveying her firmly held opinions is not mistaken, but nor is the Englishman who imagines her to be self-effacing, yet quietly confident

4. Jane Austen, *Emma*, ed. James Kinsley (Oxford: Oxford University Press, 1995), 3.

in manner. Nor are either of them correct about this if it is also the case that Jane Austen nowhere describes Emma's manner. Of course, if the text tells us that she was mousy and shy, both elaborations (or imputations) would be false, but false only because they transgress the authorial prescriptions that help constitute the character. Plainly, then, questions about the truth of elaborative interpretations do not usually arise, and will do so only if an elaboration of one sort or another contradicts or gainsays certain other beliefs that are held about the object of interpretation.

What I call elaborative interpretation has a good deal in common with what Roland Barthes calls a "writerly" response to a cultural object.[5] Barthes, it is well known, maintains that our "writerly" interpretations help constitute what we regard as the object of interpretation. This same view occurs in Krausz, for he maintains that "imputational interpretation involves imputing properties which, in being imputed, actually become intrinsically part of the work" (RR, 67). Of course, since cultural objects are largely identified and reidentified in terms of their intentional properties, and certainly not just in terms of the spatio-temporal location of the physical object that embodies them, there do need to be constraints on the properties that can properly be imputed to such objects—constraints, that is, on the ways in which readers construe texts and other cultural objects.[6] These constraints are necessary just in order to permit the reidentification of cultural objects across time and to ensure that those who speak of what they take to be the same work of art remain part of the same conversation. Krausz agrees. "From the thesis of imputational interpretation," he writes, "it does not follow that anything one imputes is admissible. . . . While there are no general criteria for separating admissible from inadmissible interpretations, there are general considerations—such as sufficient correspondence—which pertain to appropriate local constraints" (RR, 70). But contrary to what Krausz asserts here, there most certainly are general criteria that can be appealed to in order to determine whether the attribution of properties to a work of art is admissible—constraints that include particular inscriptions on paper, in paint, specific images on the moving screen, and, of course, the cultural conventions that mediate these within a society at a

5. Roland Barthes, *S/Z*, trans. Richard Miller (New York: Hill & Wang, 1974), 4.
6. Joseph Margolis, *Interpretation Radical but Not Unruly: The New Puzzle of the Arts and History* (Berkeley and Los Angeles: University of California Press, 1995), 36 and 39. Margolis supposes that because the work of art is an enduring physical object, reference is secured. But reference is secured only to the physical object that embodies the work, not to the work itself.

given point in time. How precisely such constraints operate, as well as how we have epistemic access to them, is something that I return to presently.

Elaborative interpretations, I have said, need to be distinguished from those that seek, self-consciously, to add to our understanding, and Krausz plainly fails or else declines to do so. While his imputational interpretation includes what I have called elaborative interpretation, it also goes beyond it to include deliberate explanation and puzzle solving, since, as he says, "imputational interpretation may or may not be solving a puzzle" (RR, 99). Later on in his book, he claims that in imputational interpretation we assign salience to aspects of the work, from which we derive particular explanations and understandings of its meaning (RR, 123). But this is ambiguous. It is true that one may unreflectively assume the salience, relevance, or importance of one or another aspect of a work and that to do so in this way forms part of elaborative interpretation. This, however, has to be distinguished from the self-conscious yet tentative attribution of salience to an aspect of a work in order deliberately to solve a puzzle, for this process is part of the hypothesis-formation involved in elucidating that work. In any event, and contrary to what Krausz tells us, the fact that different interpreters assign or impute differing saliences to the same aspect of a work does nothing to show that there is not a single and a true interpretation of that work. It establishes only that there are interpretative disagreements about salience. As we will see, either an aspect is or is not salient to a work of art, and this, I argue, is not something that is determined either by the individual or by variable cultural influences.

Where elucidatory interpretation is concerned, there is, and there has to be, just one right answer to this and other puzzles about the work. It is not just that the goal of elucidation is and has to be to find out how things are; it is that things, so to speak, can only be one way at one time, have one set of cultural or physical properties, so that a genuinely elucidatory interpretation must capture the one way that a cultural (or a natural) object is at a particular time.

4. Epistemic Access and Interpretation

Krausz's argument against this claim is based on two grounds, the second of which is taken to establish the first. The actual nature of the object of interpretation, so he tells us, is simply irrelevant when it comes to establishing that any particular interpretation is exclusively right. This is so because, even if there are objects that exist independently of interpretative practices, they are not epistemically available to us. Coming to know, on his view, is itself an interpretative practice, and there can be no question, therefore, of epistemic access to what he calls practice-independent objects (RR, 150). It follows, of course, that interpretations cannot be shown to be true by our coming to know the properties that their objects possess. There just is no interpretatively neutral way of doing so.

Let us begin with the claim that there can be no epistemic access to practice-independent objects. As Krausz defends the claim, it turns out to be trivially true. The process of inquiry, of coming to know, is, on his view, an interpretative practice. It follows that we cannot come to know practice-independent objects. Put differently, this time in the words of Leon Goldstein, we cannot know objects that exist beyond the framework of knowing (RR, 132).[7]

It is not my purpose to argue against tautologies, although it is worth reminding ourselves that logical truths cannot limit our powers of knowing and place no constraints at all on what we are capable of observing (KFI, 55–72). A realist will not deny that one cannot know the things that one cannot know, but may nonetheless insist that one can observe and know the properties that objects actually possess. The problem is to explain how.

Even if it is true, as Krausz supposes, that the process of inquiry crucially involves interpretative practices, it does not follow from this that there is no firm distinction to be drawn between interpretations, on the one hand, and what we claim as knowledge, on the other. Nor does it follow that our interpretations somehow prevent us from having real cognitive access to things themselves. For suppose that certain interpretations about the nature of the physical and social environment serve us well, enable us to cope in the world, and continue to do so over a protracted period of time. As a result, and not unreasonably, we rely on these interpretations, assent to and so believe them, and, provided that they continue to work, we will not just assert their truth but will claim to know the propositions that they embody. We do so on pragmatic grounds: the interpretations work, they enable us to make sense, to explain, to predict, navigate, control, and manipulate.

In light of this, it would be seriously misleading to entertain the meta-interpretation that successful first-order interpretations about our world

<hr />

7. Leon Goldstein, *Historical Knowing* (Austin: University of Texas Press, 1976), 40. See, as well, Margolis, *Interpretation Radical but Not Unruly*, 2.

somehow prevent cognitive access to the furniture and the properties of the world. To assent to this meta-interpretation would not just undermine our initially successful first-order interpretation but, if sincerely entertained and relied upon, would starkly limit our capacity to act in the world around us. Such a meta-interpretation (which is what Krausz's claims about epistemic inaccessibility amount to) would not place us in an epistemically stronger position regarding our physical or social environment; it would not facilitate understanding, and for this reason—and reverting once again to pragmatist criteria—it would be a wholly unsuccessful interpretation.

We would do better, therefore, to construe those interpretations that serve us well as revealing, in all salient respects, the way an object is. In other words, where we successfully interpret the object as having certain properties—"successful" in the sense that the interpretation enables us to negotiate the object—the best meta-interpretation concerning our original is that it successfully isolates those very properties in the object. But since this is the meta-interpretation that works best, and since it withstands the tests of experience and time, there is good reason to assent to it, hence to say that we *know* and have access to the fact that the object has a particular set of properties.

Certainly our knowledge of the world in this case is a function of interpretative discourse and does not leap into our minds independently of some or other discursive means of discovering it. But this does not entail that the world as it is, is cognitively unavailable to us. On the contrary, interpretation is the very process that makes the world epistemically accessible and, when successful, renders the world cognitively transparent—not in the sense that it affords direct, unmediated access to it, but in the sense that, when once the interpretation works, and for so long as it continues to work, there is no good reason to doubt and considerable reason to maintain that one does have cognitive access to those aspects of the world that it purports to reveal.

Certainly our empirical knowledge-claims are fallible, so that it may indeed turn out that experience shows our knowledge-claims to be mistaken, hence that the interpretation on which a particular claim to knowledge is based was inadequate from the start. But so long as we have no reason to suppose this, and as long as there is reason to suppose the contrary, we remain justified in believing it and in basing claims to knowledge on it. We are justified, that is, in claiming to know how the world is. Any future interpretation will have to be consistent with this claim to knowledge, and in some cases conform to it, before we will be in a position to rely on it, believe it, and eventually treat it as knowledge.

The claim that the objects of interpretation are epistemically unavailable to us is not just misleading, it is also unacceptably paradoxical. For the assertion that our so-called knowledge of the world is an interpretative construct that cannot be known to correspond to how things really are prompts the question "Is this something that can be known by those who assert it, or is it similarly a construct?" If it is just an interpretative construct, why should we take it as revealing how things are with respect to knowledge and the world? For anything that would count as a reason for believing it would also count as a reason for saying that it is something about the world that is epistemically accessible to us. If, on the other hand, the doctrine of epistemic inaccessibility is not just a construct but is a known fact about our cognitive capacities, then at least one aspect of the world—that which has to do with human cognition—is epistemically available to us. But if *it* is epistemically available, why should other aspects of the world remain cognitively occluded? Until this question is answered, there is no reason to believe the claim that the world is epistemically inaccessible and considerable reason to believe otherwise.

Since there is, as I have argued, good reason to believe that we can have knowledge of how things are in the world, there is also good reason to believe that those speech acts which involve the linguistic application of such knowledge, namely descriptions, can be distinguished from and can serve rationally to confirm and so justify particular interpretations (KFI, 90–97).[8] In the elucidatory sense that concerns us here, we interpret precisely when we are confused or puzzled and do not have the requisite knowledge or beliefs with which to resolve our confusion or ignorance. Interpretation, then, has an epistemic structure different from that of description, for, as is now clear, we describe something when we either know or believe that we know what it is or what properties it has—and we do so by applying such knowledge or beliefs linguistically.

My claim, then, is that the properties actually possessed by objects of interpretation may indeed be known. Since what I seek to interpret in the elucidatory sense is always a function of my own ignorance, it is often possible to verify my interpretation by reverting to what other reliable authorities

8. See, as well, Robert Matthews, "Describing and Interpreting Works of Art," *Journal of Aesthetics and Art Criticism* 36 (1977): 5–14.

know—hence to their descriptions of the world. It is also possible to verify my interpretations through my own endeavors, by subsequently discovering through my own research what properties a cultural or a natural object actually possesses. The properties, for instance, that I interpretatively attribute to *Hamlet* on my first reading of it may stand confirmed by the independent research that I do into the cultural conventions of the Elizabethan Age. The fact, if it is one, that such learning, at some stage or another, itself involves interpretations does not entail that all of what passes as knowledge is in fact interpretation. Quite the contrary, for as we have now seen, we do distinguish what we know from what is merely an interpretative hypothesis, and there are good pragmatic grounds for doing so.

5. Interpretation and History

Some critical pluralists will doubtlessly object to the claim that we can rely on past successful interpretations and so on our knowledge of the way the world is, in order to justify a particular interpretation. On their view, it is a claim that ignores the extent to which each particular interpretation is shaped by historical and social circumstance.[9] We are all reared within cultures, the argument goes, and we adopt specific sets of beliefs, worldviews, myths, and values on account of our cultural location. These influence or else determine the way in which we interpret or construe the world, and this is why two people from different cultures may very well construe cultural and natural objects differently.

More important, since two incompatible interpretations can both enable us to negotiate the world or certain of its objects satisfactorily, it is always possible (so the argument goes) that there should be two or more interpretations that impute different and exclusive properties to the same object—interpretations, moreover, that both work, that both facilitate our understanding, and that both enable us to cope in the world. Since this is so, it is argued, the fact that any particular interpretation is adjudged successful in pragmatist terms cannot ensure that it reveals the world to us as

9. This rejoinder is defended, inter alia, by Goldstein, *Historical Knowing;* Joseph Margolis, "Robust Relativism," *Journal of Aesthetics and Art Criticism* (1976): 37–46; idem, *Art and Philosophy* (Atlantic Highlands, N.J.: Humanities Press, 1980), 156–64; idem, *Interpretation Radical but Not Unruly,* chap. 1; and Richard Rorty, *Contingency, Irony, and Solidarity* (Cambridge: Cambridge University Press, 1989), esp. pt. i.

it is. This is why there can be no grounds for saying of an interpretation that it is the one true interpretation of a work of art, for this would require some culturally neutral terrain from which to tell how things really are (RR, 1).[10] But, we are told, there is no such terrain. We are the contingent products of our respective cultures, and the culturally instilled systems of belief that shape our respective worlds determine our interpretations, which, in their turn, partially create not just our experience but the very properties of the objects that we interpret. They are "writerly" or "imputational" or "elaborative" interpretations that ensure that there is no neutral ground, no Archimedean point, from which they can conclusively be verified.[11]

I do not, of course, wish to dispute that we are all historically located and, in some measure, historically shaped beings—reared within cultures that impart particular beliefs, values, and worldviews at particular times. Nor would I deny that our cultural inheritance is, and has to be, a primary resource whenever we try to understand something that puzzles and bemuses us. But it does not follow from this that interpretations cannot be true and known to be true.

In particular, it is wrong to maintain that because our thinking is historically shaped, it must also be decisively constrained by history in a way that prevents us from adopting different ways of construing the world. Certainly our attempts to understand through interpretation are initially framed in terms of current cultural beliefs and values, but it is also the case that only those who are closed in their thinking, who believe that their cultural beliefs are either sacrosanct or else natural and invariably correct, will be limited in the way that a strong historicist thinks we all are.

If an interpretation that is couched in terms of our cultural beliefs and values fails to promote an adequate understanding, we can construe its failure in one of two ways. Either we can regard our beliefs as unquestionably correct, so that the source of our failure to comprehend is identified as residing in the nature of whatever it is that puzzles us, which is then considered to be at fault—as "irrational," "stupid," "unnatural," or whatever. Alternatively, if we really wish to understand, we can treat our failure as the result

10. See, as well, Margolis, "Robust Relativism," 37 and 44, and his more recent "Plain Talk About Interpretation on a Relativistic Model," *Journal of Aesthetics and Art Criticism* (1995): 1–7, esp. 2.

11. For a recent defense of a related view, see John McDowell, *Mind and World* (Cambridge, Mass.: Harvard University Press, 1994), who regards experience as inherently conceptual. For a critique of this view, see Robert Brandom, "Perception and Rational Constraint," *Philosophy and Phenomenological Research* LVIII (1998): 369–74.

of the limitations of our own perspective, and if we do, we will seek tenta-
tively to modify certain of the beliefs in terms of which we normally seek to
understand.[12] These are the beliefs, in Hans-Georg Gadamer's words, that
help constitute our "horizons," that in some sense make us the people we
are and afford us our greatest certainty. We modify them through trial and
error, through "play" or a "to-and-fro movement" of successive cognitive
adjustments, until we secure what Donald Davidson would call the best
"holistic fit"—thereby securing an adequate understanding of whatever it is
that puzzles us.[13]

6. Incompatible Interpretations

All that the argument of the previous section shows, however, is that our
interpretations and our thinking are not strongly determined by our cultural
affiliations. What it does not show is that we cannot have two competing
interpretations that both promote an adequate understanding—in the sense
that both enable us to predict, manipulate, control, and negotiate the world
and its objects with a high degree of success. Interpretation does not have
to be strongly determined by history and culture for this to be the case. And
if it is the case, then it is simply wrong to maintain that there is such a thing
as the single right interpretation of a work of art.

In what follows, I assume that there are genuinely incompatible interpretations that one and the same person may find acceptable.[14] This, of course,
is hardly surprising, for it only requires the capacity on the part of a person
to be inconsistent. What I deny is what the critical pluralist affirms, namely,
that incompatible interpretations can be jointly admissible, where this is
taken to entail that there are occasions when it is in principle impossible to
resolve the incompatible claims of competing interpretations about one and
the same cultural or natural object, and so for one interpretation to be seen

12. This same point is nicely made by Hans-Georg Gadamer, *Truth and Method* (New
York: Crossroad, 1988), 239ff.; idem, *Philosophical Hermeneutics* (Berkeley and Los Angeles:
University of California Press, 1976), 9. See, as well, Richard Bernstein, *Beyond Objectivism
and Relativism* (Philadelphia: University of Pennsylvania Press, 1983), 129.

13. Donald Davidson, "Radical Interpretation," *Dialectica* 27 (1973): 313–27, esp. 315.

14. Here I would seem to differ with Robert Stecker, *Artworks: Definition, Meaning, Value*
(University Park: Pennsylvania State University Press, 1997), chap. 7, who argues that "many
of the most likely candidates for incompatible acceptable interpretations turn out to be compatible when we carefully attend to what they each are *asserting*" (121).

to unseat the other (RR, 2).[15] I concede, of course, that there may be contingent difficulties that prevent such resolutions; what I deny is that such a resolution is ever impossible.[16] Rather, on the view that I defend, it is always possible to show of two apparently competing interpretations either that they do not really compete or that, if they do, both are false or that the one is true, the other false. Where interpretation is concerned, I argue, bivalence rules; there is and can be only one true interpretation.

This is an indispensable assumption of rational critical inquiry. For as I have explained it, the aim of elucidatory interpretation is to secure an adequate understanding of whatever it is that confuses or puzzles us. An understanding, I have said, will be adequate if and only if it enables one to negotiate the world successfully, where this includes both its natural and cultural objects, events, relations, and states of affairs. Since it is reasonable to assume that there is only one way in which the world and its objects can be at any one time (elsewhere I have called this the singularity constraint), one normally concedes that one has not finally understood an object or state of affairs if one also recognizes that the object or state of affairs is amenable to two conflicting interpretations: interpretations that impute different and exclusive properties to the phenomenon in question. For if there is only one way that the world is at any one time—one shape to an object, one set of semantic properties to a text, or one set of pictorial properties to a painting—this suggests that an adequate understanding has not been reached, that there is work to be done and a convergence to be sought. Of course, it may be the case that two different people are each satisfied with interpretations that exclude one another. This happens often enough. But, given the singularity constraint, one and the same person will not consider herself to have understood, so long as she subscribes to, and cannot decide between, two interpretations that are recognized by her to conflict with each other.

It might be objected, though, that the singularity constraint begs the question against the critical pluralist. For it assumes what the pluralist explicitly denies, namely, that there is just one set of properties that a work of art has at one time. But notice the implausibility of denying this constraint. It straightaway commits the pluralist to the view that one and the same

15. See, as well, Margolis, "Plain Talk About Interpretation," 2–3.
16. Cf. Annette Barnes, *On Interpretation* (Oxford: Basil Blackwell, 1988), 2, who maintains that "it is possible for criticism to legitimately tolerate incompatible (*genuinely* and not seemingly incompatible) interpretations for a single work." See, as well, Alan Goldman, "Interpreting Art and Literature," *Journal of Aesthetics and Art Criticism* 48 (1990): 205–14, esp. 207, where he maintains that "incompatible interpretations may be equally acceptable."

cultural object both has and does not have a particular property at a given time, and to affirm this is, of course, to contradict oneself.[17]

Furthermore, since we do identify works of art in terms of their properties, any denial of the singularity constraint makes it very difficult to know that we are speaking about the same work. It does not help to maintain, as Krausz does (RR, 121), that we identify works in terms of our shared imputation of properties to them. This merely postpones the more basic problem of explaining how these verbal imputations come to be shared and, embarrassingly for Krausz's variety of pluralism, how we know that they are shared—that is, how the semantic properties of the imputational sentences can be known in a way that allows two people from different cultural backgrounds to agree that they describe the work in the same way. Much worse, since Krausz also holds that we can have no epistemic access to the work of art itself, the fact that we both impute the same properties to it, and do so without even discussing the work, must be the result of chance and cannot be based on our knowledge of these properties. So either we just come, for no apparent reason, to hold the same descriptions of a particular cultural object (which seems plainly absurd), or there are certain properties inherent in the object itself that are the source of, and in some way constrain, these descriptions. But if the latter is true, it is not the shared imputations that enable people from different cultures to identify something as an enduring work of art; it is the properties inherent in it, to which we must, after all, have epistemic access (cf. RR, 120–23).

It is important to understand what exactly the singularity constraint commits us to. In particular, just by saying that there must be some one way that something is at a particular time, we do not commit ourselves to the view that cultural objects cannot be vague, confused, nonsensical, ambiguous, or else indeterminate in their meaning or their properties. What it commits us to is a realism about cultural properties such that if a work really is vague at a certain time, then it cannot also have a precise and determinate meaning; that if it is ambiguous at that time, it cannot also have a single meaning at that time. This, of course, entails that the single right interpretation of an ambiguous work will reveal that ambiguity in more or less detail, and just the same for vague or semantically confused or nonsensical works.

---

17. I take this to follow from Krausz's support for that variety of pluralism according to which the properties imputed in interpretation "actually become intrinsically part of the work" (RR, 67). Since people from different cultures impute different properties to one and the same work, it must be possible, on this view, for one work both to have and not have a particular property at the same time.

Nor is the singularity constraint unwarranted. Any conjunction of two contrary or contradictory, hence conflicting, propositions about the same object or state of affairs fails to inform and so cannot ensure an adequate understanding of whatever it is that one seeks to understand. Hence, to accept as jointly admissible two conflicting interpretations that attribute different and exclusive properties to one and the same object is effectively to concede that one does not properly understand. But elucidatory interpretations, I have said, are intended to promote understanding—and are meant to do so by placing people in an epistemically stronger position regarding whatever it is that puzzles them. In order to achieve this end, though, it is always necessary to resolve any incompatibility between two interpretations, for failing this, they cannot promote any clear understanding of the way things are.

The singularity constraint is warranted for another, related reason. For in order to judge and sincerely assert something to be the case at a certain time, one has to assume that there is some one (albeit complex) way that it is at that time; failing this, there could be no point to informative discourse about the way the world is.[18] Nor would there be any point to elucidatory interpretations that prepare the ground, as it were, for such discourse.

To all of this it might be objected that whereas the singularity constraint might apply to all natural objects, it cannot be assumed to apply to cultural ones. But it is difficult to see why not. For elucidatory interpretation, as we have seen, is an activity that involves the imaginative formulation and application of hypotheses in an attempt to dispel ignorance. That there is no good reason to confine this activity to cultural objects is clear from the fact that there are occasions when we do not even know whether the phenomenon that we seek to understand is natural or cultural—and it is, of course, entirely arbitrary to suggest of such situations that whether we are engaged in the activity of interpreting depends on whether the object of our bemusement turns out to be cultural in origin. The character of our activity remains constant no matter the origins of its object.

Since we may interpret both cultural and natural objects, it is not obvious why the criteria for success in interpretation should differ as between the two. Coming to understand a phenomenon, whether cultural or natural, requires that we somehow manage to fathom the set of properties that it possesses at any given time. To arrive at the conclusion that it is amenable

18. Cf. John McDowell, "Précis of Mind and World," Philosophy and Phenomenological Research LVIII (1998): 365–68, esp. 365.

to two exclusive interpretations at one and the same time is effectively to concede that one has not properly understood it.

7. The Properties of Cultural Objects

Whereas natural objects enjoy the material instantiation of their properties, many of the properties of cultural objects, and certainly those that identify them *as* cultural objects, are intentional and emerge only against the background of our knowledge of specific conventions. Here I am in agreement with Joseph Margolis, who construes cultural objects as physically embodied and culturally emergent entities.[19] Their physical embodiment permits us to locate them in space and time, while their remaining properties depend for their existence on the cultural background against which they emerge.

Since these properties are discerned only in terms of certain historically located cultural principles, both Krausz and Margolis believe that there can be no neutral way of deciding between competing interpretations of a cultural object. On their view, there are as many admissible interpretations as there are "preferred" (Margolis) or "pertinent" (Krausz) cultural principles in terms of which the work may be interpreted (RR, 93–94).[20] And since there may be different yet undeniably pertinent or preferred cultural principles, it follows that there is no single right interpretation of a cultural object.

These claims, however, are misleading. Although we do discern cultural properties in terms of our knowledge of prevailing cultural conventions, this does not involve imputing such properties interpretatively in terms of just any pertinent or preferred cultural principle, since some such principles can actually be misleading. There are, in other words, important, epistemically based constraints on this activity that reach beyond mere pertinence or our cultural preferences.

Consider this example: the sound made by uttering the word "bid." When this sound is taken in conjunction with the conventions of Afrikaans that are undoubtedly pertinent to it, the semantic property that emerges in

19. Joseph Margolis, "Works of Art as Physically Embodied and Culturally Emergent Entities," *British Journal of Aesthetics* 14 (1974): 187–96.

20. Krausz contends that "the imputationalist view holds that cultural entities are capable of being transformed through history" and that the only constraints on this are furnished by the "context of a pertinent practice." See, as well, Margolis, "Robust Relativism," 37 and 44, and his more recent "Plain Talk About Interpretation," 1–7, esp. 2.

standard contexts is the verb *to pray*. Taken against the conventions of English, however, the semantic property that emerges is *an offer of money*. Importantly, when once we know from the speaker or the context that the proper conventions in terms of which to construe the sound are the conventions of English, it is exclusively true to say that (in a standard context) the word means *an offer of money*, not *to pray*. It follows that it is not as if one is free, when responding to cultural objects, to impose one's own cultural understandings or preferred systems of explanation on the object, no matter how pertinent we take them to be. One is bound by those conventions that actually apply to it. And it is our sometimes hard-won knowledge of these conventions that allows us to say of anyone interpreting the object *ab initio* that their interpretation is either true or false, right or wrong.

Languages, like words and utterances in a language, are paradigmatic examples of cultural objects; what applies to them applies to cultural objects in general. One might, for instance, construe the fate of King Lear in terms of a range of twentieth-century ideas that are undoubtedly pertinent to the play, and so see him as a person of liberal temperament who is cruelly treated for that reason. But even a passing acquaintance with Elizabethan culture tells us that this is wrong, that Lear has upset the divine order and so is reaping the chaos that he has sown and in some sense deserves.

Of course, we appeal to more than knowledge of cultural conventions when seeking to establish an interpretation as exclusively correct. We appeal, as well, to a range of genetic factors—most especially to an agent's intentions in producing the artifact. Here we can, and in academic art criticism we sometimes do, turn to biographical accounts of authors' personal histories, events that occurred in their lives, their diaries, speeches, and so on. And where this is not available to us, we look to generic factors: to our knowledge of particular art forms, categories of art, or kinds of cultural objects. All can be, and often are, appealed to in our various attempts to justify an interpretation and establish it as uncontestably correct (KFI, 108–9). In the end, an interpretation of a cultural object will be pronounced correct if it can be shown to cohere maximally with other propositions that we claim to know about the object and its cultural setting, and so allows us to negotiate (explain, predict) other aspects of the cultural object and of the world that it inhabits.

There are, though, very many different sorts of things that we may not understand about a cultural object. In the case of a novel, for instance, the motives of a character, the meaning of a sentence, the theme of a work, the structure of its plot, its origins, or its relevance to particular cultures at particular times may all be considered legitimate objects of inquiry. It follows that the adequacy of any interpretation can properly be assessed only with reference to the particular problem that it seeks to solve. If one is puzzled by Willoughby's strange behavior towards Marianne when they meet in London (in Jane Austen's *Sense and Sensibility*), one's interpretation must solve *this* problem, not some other. Relative to it, it is *true* that Willoughby wishes to avoid her in order to court a richer woman, and it is false that he wishes to hurt her feelings.

Understood against the background of the cultural and linguistic conventions appropriate to the work, this is the one true interpretation of this event in the novel; it coheres with our knowledge of other aspects of the work and so corresponds to its describable features; it allows us, furthermore, to understand the rest of the novel—to negotiate it successfully, in the sense that it coheres with all of our other understandings of sequences within the novel. This is not to say that there is not more that can correctly be said of this incident. There undoubtedly is. The important point is that what is said is true, not false—and that this is quite easily ascertained.

All of this supports my contention that the interpretation of cultural objects, as with natural objects, observes the singularity constraint, for part of what is here entailed is that it is not *also* the case that some contrary interpretation applies to this incident in *Sense and Sensibility*: say, that Willoughby is infatuated with Elinor and so seeks to avoid Marianne. For even if there are, or should one day be, cultural conventions relative to which the latter interpretation can be derived, these conventions would simply not apply to this work or the period and culture in which it was produced.

This, I have already said, is not to deny that a novel, like any other cultural product, can be deeply and pervasively ambiguous relative to an appropriate set of cultural conventions; but if it is ambiguous, the singularity constraint requires that this ambiguity stand revealed in any true interpretation of the work. So while it may often be the case that a work can support what appear to be two incompatible interpretations, this entails that the work, if it really does support them within the framework of the same set of cultural conventions, is ambiguous—and that a true interpretation will find it so.

7. Conclusion

The claims of the critical pluralist depend crucially on a failure to distinguish elucidatory interpretation from its "imputational," "elaborative," or "writerly" counterpart. While it is true that writerly elaborations or imputations can affect the elucidatory interpretations that we offer, it does not follow from this that elucidatory interpretation imputes to the object it wishes to understand properties that then become a part of it; nor, we have seen, does it follow that elucidatory interpretations cannot be true. For if, as I have shown, our aim in interpretation is to understand whatever it is that puzzles us, elaborative or imputational interpretations can be admitted only for so long as they actually facilitate understanding, and they cease to do this whenever they fail to take due account of the physical properties that are part of, or the conventions that properly mediate, the cultural object.

Nor is it the case, I have shown, that we become acquainted with these cultural conventions only through further interpretive acts, which are themselves the product of our historical and cultural location. To say this is either to relativize knowledge of other cultures or to insist that such knowledge is unavailable to us. Either option is unsatisfactory; both make it impossible to know other cultures or to know even that their interpretations differ from ours. Yet knowledge, I have argued, is to be accounted for and identified pragmatically: those conjectures, hypotheses, and beliefs that work and that enable us to negotiate the world successfully count as knowledge. Thus explained, there certainly is knowledge of other cultures—much of which is derived from the interpretative endeavors of others.

Since, as the singularity constraint tells us, there is only one way that any object can be at one time, and since it is possible to verify our interpretations of cultural objects in terms of existing or yet to be discovered bodies of knowledge, it is possible to establish not just that an interpretation is admissible but that it is, in fact, the single right interpretation of the work in question. To deny the possibility of this, I have argued, and to ignore the singularity constraint is to strike at the heart of rational discourse about the arts.

Interpretation and Its Objects

Michael Krausz

This paper discusses two themes. The first theme concerns ideals of interpretation. It addresses the question whether for any object of interpretation there must be only one ideally admissible interpretation ("singularism"), or whether for some objects of interpretation there may be more than one ideally admissible interpretation ("multiplism"). The second theme concerns certain ontologies of objects of interpretation, namely, realism, constructivism, and constructive realism.

Singularism is often associated with realism, and multiplism is often associated with constructivism. But, as I have argued elsewhere, these associations are not logically necessary.[1] So, the question whether there must be one or whether there may be more than one admissible interpretation is logically detachable from realism and constructivism. In addition to realism and constructivism, I develop a third type of ontology, namely constructive realism. It is something of a compromise between realism and constructivism. And I argue that constructive realism is also detachable from singular-

For their helpful suggestions, thanks are due to Andrew Brook, Michael McKenna, and Christine Koggel.

1. See Michael Krausz, *Rightness and Reasons: Interpretation in Cultural Practices* (Ithaca, N.Y.: Cornell University Press, 1993), and idem, *Limits of Rightness* (Lanham, Md.: Rowman & Littlefield, 2000).

ism and multiplism. One of its versions is detachable because it is consistent with either singularism or multiplism. The other version is detachable because it could answer to neither singularism nor multiplism. But, as we shall see, the detachability of singularism and multiplism from the enumerated ontological theories does not preclude the fact that ontological considerations in a wider sense are relevant to interpretive concerns.

(I)

More fully, singularism is the view that an interpretandum should *always* answer to one and only one ideally admissible interpretation. It holds that there should always be a one-one relation between an interpretandum and its interpretation. In contrast, multiplism is the view that an interpretandum need not always answer to one and only one ideally admissible interpretation. It may answer to more than one interpretation. That is, there may be a one-many relation between an interpretandum and its interpretations. But, for the multiplist, in order that a multiplicity of admissible interpretations not be combinable into one more comprehensive "seamless" interpretation, they should be incongruent. That is, multiplism requires that its incongruent interpretations should be *opposed* in a soft sense. Otherwise, they could, conjoined, count as one interpretation. Yet incongruent interpretations should *not be exclusive*. Otherwise, at most one would be admissible. Thus, incongruent interpretations should exhibit *opposition-without-exclusivity*. Notice further that singularism is asymmetrical with multiplism in the sense that singularism allows no multiplist cases, but multiplism allows some singularist cases. Singularism is universal and multiplism is not.

I have adopted the nomenclature of "singularism versus multiplism" rather than an older nomenclature of "critical monism versus critical pluralism" for two reasons. First, critical pluralism holds that two or more interpretations are *equally* admissible. In contrast, while multiplism holds that more than one interpretation is ideally admissible, it does not hold that all admissible interpretations are equally preferable. Multiplism allows that one may have good, though nonconclusive, reasons for preferring one admissible interpretation over another.[2] Second, I reserve the word "plural-

---

2. For illustrations of this point, though the author does not put it in these terms, see Alan Goldman, "*The Sun Also Rises:* Incompatible Interpretations," in this volume.

ism" (or "pluralizing") to designate a strategy that transforms a multiplist condition into a singularist condition. That is, the one interpretandum that initially answers to more than one interpretation is pluralized into several interpretanda each answering to its own single interpretation. The result would be several pairs of one-one relations, each between an interpretandum and an interpretation. And this would satisfy the singularist condition.

Now consider singularism as propounded by one of its chief advocates, David Novitz. He says,

> What I deny is what the critical pluralist [multiplist] affirms, namely, that incompatible interpretations can be jointly admissible, where this is taken to entail that there are occasions when it is in principle impossible to resolve the incompatible claims of competing interpretations about one and the same cultural or natural object, and so for one interpretation to be seen to unseat the other. . . . it is always possible to show of two apparently competing interpretations either that they do not really compete or that, if they do, both are false or that the one is true, the other false. Where interpretation is concerned, I argue, bivalence rules; there is and can be only one true interpretation.[3]

Notice that Novitz runs together two issues that multiplists seek to distinguish. The first issue concerns *incompatibility,* which Novitz rightly construes in terms of a bivalent logic. The second issue concerns *incongruence,* or a softer form of *opposition,* which the multiplist construes in terms of a many-valued logic. The multiplist agrees with Novitz that incompatible interpretations are inadmissible. *But incompatible interpretations do not exhaust the class of interpretations that are opposed.* Novitz's rejection of multiplism is predicated on conflating these issues. The notion of incongruence—which is central to the multiplist program—should be understood in

---

3. David Novitz, "Against Critical Pluralism," in this volume, pages 114–15. Novitz discusses my *Rightness and Reasons: Interpretation in Cultural Practices* (1993). He does not discuss my more recent *Limits of Rightness* (2000). Note that in the very first paragraph of his article (101), Novitz reports that I hold that singularism does violence to the nature of *any* cultural object. This mischaracterizes my view. Both RR and LR emphasize that some cultural entities answer to the multiplist condition, and other cultural entities answer to the singularist condition. Further, while these works rehearse the imputationist arguments for multiplism, they do not propound them. Finally, they do not argue that the nature of the object of interpretation is irrelevant "when it comes to establishing that any particular interpretation is exclusively right . . . because . . . they are not epistemically available to us" (108–9). Rather, they argue that even if they were epistemically available to us they would mandate neither singularism nor multiplism.

terms of *opposition-without-exclusivity,* rather than opposition-with-exclusivity. Novitz mistakenly assumes that opposition must be defined in terms of exclusivity. Novitz says, "to accept as jointly admissible two conflicting interpretations that attribute different and exclusive properties to one and the same object is effectively to concede that one does not properly understand."[4]

Novitz mistakenly thinks that multiplism must affirm that two opposing or conflicting interpretations must attribute *exclusive* properties to one and the same object. But without considering a more nuanced notion of incongruence, one that is central to multiplism, it won't do for Novitz to *define* "understanding" in terms of singularism.[5]

So let us now consider the notion of incongruence in terms of opposition-without-exclusivity. This notion motivates Joseph Margolis's "relativistic" formula that holds that two interpretations are incongruent if on a bivalent logic they *would be* contradictory but on a many-valued logic they *are not.* Typically, Margolis says that incongruent "claims and judgments that on a bivalent logic would be or would yield incompatibles can be shown to be (formally) consistent by suitably replacing or supplementing bivalence, in context, with a many-valued logic."[6]

Margolis's effort is "cognitivist" in the sense that it addresses claims or judgments that carry truthlike values. Retiring bivalence in pertinent cases, he unpacks incongruence in terms of a many-valued logic, invoking such "truthlike" values as reasonableness, aptness, and appropriateness. Margolis's formula points the way toward articulating the "nonexclusive" part of the opposition-without-exclusivity condition.[7] But the demonstration that otherwise contradictory interpretations are not so on a many-valued logic does not show that the interpretations in question remain *opposed* in a pertinent sense. And without such opposition multiple interpretations *could be* conjoined, thus installing a singularist condition. How then should one understand opposition-without-exclusivity?

Consider the thought that interpretations might be regarded noncognitively rather than cognitively, that is, as carrying neither bivalent nor multivalent values. Accordingly, interpretations would not be regarded as claims

4. Novitz, "Against Critical Pluralism," in this volume, page 117.

5. Ibid. See pages 115 and 117.

6. Joseph Margolis, "Relativism and Interpretive Objectivity," *Metaphilosophy* 31, nos. 1/2 (2000): 216.

7. For a compendious treatment of Margolis's view, see my "Interpretation, Relativism, and Culture: Four Questions for Margolis," in *Interpretation, Relativism, and the Metaphysics of Culture,* ed. Michael Krausz and Richard Shusterman (Amherst, N.Y.: Humanity Press, 1999), 105–24.

or judgments at all. Rather, they would be regarded as *commendations,* as in "I commend your listening to the musical passage this way" or "I commend your looking at the painting this way" or "I commend your reading the text this way" or, more directly, "Listen to the musical passage this way!" or "Look at the painting this way!" or "Read the text this way!" A commendation might draw attention to one or another feature of a work that would make it more or less conducive to hearing or seeing or reading it one way or another. Since commendations are not claims or judgments, they would not be truthlike, and so a pair of commendations could not be logically incompatible. According to a commendatory approach, the multiplist would unpack incongruence in terms of opposed but not exclusive commendations. Yet commendations are typically couched in contexts where certain results are expected or predicted. One typically commends with the expectation or prediction that the receiver will find the result satisfying, revealing, illuminating, interesting, engaging, or the like. And these expectations or predictions do involve claims or judgments that are truthlike. Indeed, "Listen to the passage this way!" is typically elliptical for "Listening to the passage this way will be revealing, illuminating, or satisfying." So let us bypass the commendatory approach and pursue a cognitivist understanding of opposition-without-exclusivity. I have no complete account of such an understanding, but we may make some headway toward one by considering the singularist's and the multiplist's treatments of two cases. At issue is the multiplist claim that in these cases incongruent interpretations may be admitted without logical contradiction, though they remain opposed in a soft sense.

(i) Consider the Indian practice (notably in the holy city of Benares) of burying its "morally pure" beings by weighing down and submerging their deceased bodies into the river Ganges. According to Hindu tradition (in which Buddhists also participate), the Ganges River is the embodiment of the life force itself. It is the source from which life begins, and it is the vehicle that transports the soul from one embodiment to another. The river is seen as a hallowed medium for transmigration. Since babies and such holy persons as Hindu Saddhus and Buddhist monks are taken to be morally uncontaminated, they are exempted from the more usual method of purification by cremation. As morally pure beings they are accorded the *honor* of being returned directly to the life source of the Ganges. Yet, from a secular or "scientific" perspective, where the Ganges River is merely taken to be badly polluted and germ infested, this practice amounts to a disrespectful method of *dumping* bodies. According to one interpretation, it would be appropriate to say that a given baby was *honored,* and according to the other interpretation, it would be appropriate to say that it was *dumped*. The case is made yet more complicated by the testimony that, in accord with the strong Indian prejudice against female births, most of the dead babies in the Ganges are female. The ostensible drowning and dumping of female babies is seen as offset by the honor of their return to the life-source Ganges.[8]

The singularist would hold that either the honored interpretation or the dumped interpretation or neither is admissible without *any* sort of opposition. Accordingly, one way to dissipate even the appearance of a soft opposition between candidate interpretations is to specify the interests that motivate an interpreter's assignment of salience to pertinent features. That is, in accord with the thought that one characteristic function of interpretive activity is to assign salience to, or to italicize, certain features of an interpretandum—a thought with which both singularist and multiplist can agree[9]—the singularist might say that, with respect to the interest of Hindu values, the "honoring" interpretation is admissible and that, with respect to "scientific" values, the "dumping" interpretation is admissible. Each interpretation in its own value context is fully self-consistent. One with Hindu interests will favor the "honored" interpretation, and one with "scientific" interests will favor the "dumped" interpretation. And there is no reason to confuse the matter by combining interests. Effectively, this way of dissipating an apparent opposition is to offer different objects-as-represented and to affirm that for each of these there is only one admissible interpretation. The features italicized in accord with one interpretation do not oppose the features italicized in accord with the other. And the singularist would hold that if one simultaneously has Hindu and scientific interests that generate different objects-as-represented, that should not bear on the logic of the situation.

Notice that in order to install the singularist condition of a one-one relation between interpretation and interpretandum (however many sets of such pairs may be so generated), the singularist must specify distinct objects-as-represented as distinct interpretanda. That is, that which a given interpretation interprets is different from that which another otherwise incongruent interpretation interprets. Put still otherwise, by performing this operation the singularist "pluralizes" interpretanda. He or she installs the singularist one-one relation between the "honored" interpretation and the baby-as-represented (italicizing certain sets of properties), and installs a one-one relation between the "dumped" interpretation and the baby-as-represented (italicizing other sets of properties).

In turn, the multiplist affirms that the pluralizing operation of separating clear and distinct interests (with attendant clear and distinct objects-as-represented) cannot always be successfully performed. Assigning salience to different features does not always result in different objects of interpretation. Accordingly, the multiplist says that sometimes there is a common thing that the objects-as-represented represent. And for such a thing, a multiplist condition would obtain between it and the multiple interpretations of it. The baby under a given description, for example, may exhibit features that answer to incongruent interpretations. If successful, this multiplist move would frustrate the singularist's pluralizing maneuver.

(ii) Now consider a different sort of case, but one that nevertheless reveals divergent treatments by singularists and multiplists. Composer, conductor, and musicologist Gunther Schuller comments on opposing interpretations by Arturo Toscanini and Wilhelm Furtwängler. Schuller says, "Toscanini and Furtwängler excelled in making their orchestras sing: Toscanini in a more simply lyric Italianate manner, where the song, the melody itself, was italicized and valued; Furtwängler in a more deeply expressive German way, with enormous stretch in his melodic lines, where the melody was always rooted in the underlying infrastructure and its harmonic tension."[10]

Toscanini's and Furtwängler's interpretations of Beethoven's *Eroica*, Symphony no. 3, for example, are not conjoinable in the innocuous sense that the faster and slower tempi respectively cannot be physically combined. On this the singularist and the multiplist agree. But what is at issue, as Schuller makes plain, is that each of these interpreters has a different conception of the work. They have different "critical interpretations" (as Novitz would say) of the work. That is, they stress which of its features should be italicized in order to bring out what each takes to be important about it. In accord with the singularist's handling of the previous case, the singularist would stress that the claim that one *should* italicize certain features is elliptical for the claim that *given certain interests* one should do so; Toscanini and Furtwängler are pursuing different sorts of interests issuing in different objects-as-represented, the first concerned with melodic lines and the second

10. Gunther Schuller, *The Compleat Conductor* (New York: Oxford University Press, 1997), 98. Note Schuller's fertile use of "italicized," amounting to the assignment of salience.

with harmonic tensions. And these interests and objects-as-represented do not compete in any significant way. They are not opposed, because they address different objects-as-represented. They address different interpretanda.

In contrast, the multiplist stresses that the interpretations are opposed in the significant sense that each interpreter—admittedly with different interests—assigns salience to different features of the same interpretandum. Toscanini's lyric-melodic interpretation and Furtwängler's harmonic-structural interpretation are opposed in that they affirm conflicting views about what *in the work should* be stressed, what interests *should* be fostered. Yet the interpretations are not exclusive. One does not rule out the other as inadmissible. The multiplist holds that the claim that one should italicize certain features opposes the claim that one should italicize others. And the opposition is soft in the sense that neither is thereby taken by the other to champion an interpretation that is inadmissible. The multiplist urges further that one cannot conjoin the italics of Toscanini and Furtwängler in a seamless unified interpretation—again, understood as respective conceptions of the work—for such a conjunction would no longer preserve the contributing italics. The italics of one would dislodge the italics of the other. It would not be Toscanini's and Furtwängler's italics combined, but something else again. As Peter Lamarque says in a literary context, "Too many saliences jostling for attention would blur, rather than enhance, literary interest."[11]

Novitz advances a distinct argument for singularism related to the pluralizing of objects-as-represented. It concerns the aims of interpretation. He seeks to avoid multiplism by introducing a sharp distinction between *elucidatory* and *elaborative* interpretation. He holds that elucidatory interpretation is the core sense of interpretation, and singularism obtains for elucidatory interpretation. This allows Novitz to concede that there may be numerous ways of elaborating a work. But for him elaborative interpretation is *"subjective, [and] largely gratuitous."*[12] More fully, Novitz says, "While it is true that . . . elaborations or imputations can affect the elucidatory interpretations that we offer, it does not follow from this that elucidatory interpretation imputes to the object it wishes to understand properties that then become a part of it."[13]

Novitz presses his point in the case of musical interpretation.

11. See Peter Lamarque, "Appreciation and Literary Interpretation," in this volume, page 306.
12. Novitz, "Against Critical Pluralism," in this volume, page 106, emphasis added.
13. Ibid., page 121.

A pianist, then, might seek the right way of rendering a score, and might find that some aspects of it are more easily grasped than others. Those that are puzzling or confusing stand in need of elucidation, and it is here that elucidatory interpretation is called for. . . . A pianist's performance of a musical work, or aspects of that performance, can be elaborative, and will be if the pianist subjectively and imaginatively elaborates on the score by "filling in" its indeterminacies without attempting to solve particular puzzles.[14]

I suggest that Novitz cannot sustain his distinction between elucidation and elaboration in terms of puzzle solving. Puzzle solving is involved when dealing with peculiarities of a score, but it is also involved when dealing with matters that Novitz would count as elaborative, such as musical personality and expression. In accordance with his view that "the performance of music . . . is the result of collaboration between composer and a particular performer on a particular occasion,"[15] composer Roger Sessions says,

[M]usical notation, despite all efforts on the composer's part to translate his wishes and intentions, can never be exact. In projecting the work, the performer *has to exercise individual judgment at many points;* a performance is a specific occasion and subject to specific conditions. If he is concerned at all with the impact the work is to make, he will be aware of these conditions and be affected by them. . . . the composer's text contains not only elements that must be considered as virtually invariable—pitch, relative note values, or the details of rhythmic articulation—but others that even under the strictest interpretation must be considered as variable according to the specific conditions under which the music is performed. To this category belong . . . dynamic indications, and such intangible but vital questions as the sharpness with which the larger rhythmic articulations are to be "brought out," or their timing and spacing—what we might call the "breathing" of music, the fraction of space which must occur between phrases or periods or sections if the listener is to gain the appropriate sense of movement.[16]

14. Ibid., page 105.
15. Roger Sessions, *The Musical Experience of Composer, Performer, Listener* (New York: Atheneum, 1962), 81.
16. Ibid., 78–79.

Sessions is surely right to say that in collaboration with the composer a musical interpreter must exercise judgments concerning such "variable elements" as those pertinent to the "breathing of music." That means that such judgments characteristically operate within a puzzle-solving mode. Further, Sessions is surely right to imply that such "variable elements" are not elaborative in a merely "subjective or gratuitous sense." So if the interpreter's elaborative contribution is not subjective and gratuitous but the result of mediated puzzle solving—where judgment is exercised—as Sessions's remarks suggest, then puzzle solving cannot successfully distinguish between elucidation and elaboration. Novitz's distinction between puzzle solving and non–puzzle solving is supposed to provide a way to distinguish elucidatory from elaborative interpretation. But puzzle solving is not coextensive with elucidation. It also applies to elaboration. Puzzle solving fails to distinguish elucidation from elaboration.

More generally, the distinction between elucidation and elaboration, if it can be drawn, seems to be illusive. And its illusiveness is reflected in the nature of that which is interpreted. In this connection Bruno Walter is driven to speak of *elasticity*. Walter says, "[A] work is capable of different interpretations and . . . , moreover, our own repeated performances of it need not, when allowance is made for spontaneity, entirely agree with each other. Faithfulness to the spirit knows no rigidity; the spirit of the work of art is flexible, *elastic,* hovering."[17]

Novitz seeks a firm distinction between elucidation and elaboration because he is generally concerned about the suggestion that "elaborative" interventions could alter the nature of the interpretandum. While he concedes the multiplicity of interpretive practices, Novitz is concerned to avoid the kind of "imputation" that one finds represented by such hermeneutic thinkers as Heidegger and Gadamer (from whom Margolis derives inspiration). Novitz is concerned about Gadamer's suggestion that interpreting (in Charles Guignon's and Gadamer's words) or "understanding is not so much reproductive as it is productive: it does not reproduce a meaning given in advance; instead, it cocreates the meaning and being of what it understands. . . . 'Understanding must be conceived as part of the event in which meaning happens, the event in which the meaning of all statements . . . is formed and actualized.' "[18]

17. Bruno Walter, quoted in Gunther Schuller, *The Compleat Conductor,* 93–94. The italics are Walter's. Note the affinity between Walter's "elasticity" and Torsten Pettersson's "pliability" in "The Literary Work as a Pliable Entity: Combining Realism and Pluralism," in this volume.

18. Charles Guignon, "Truth in Interpretation: A Hermeneutic Approach," in the present

Now, Novitz is concerned about imputation for fear that it would entail multiplism. But his fear is misplaced, for whatever misgivings one might have about imputationism in its own terms, it does not entail multiplism.[19] Imputationism holds that interpretive activity may impute properties to and thus alter the nature of a given object of interpretation. So, given different interpretive activities, the object could take on different properties. But such imputationism actually is compatible with either singularism *or* multiplism. Imputability is not sufficient to mandate multiplism. Indeed, in accord with the pluralizing procedure, a singularist could allow that interpretive activity alters an entity's nature, but yet affirm that in so doing different objects of interpretation would obtain. And for each newly constituted object of interpretation there is only one admissible interpretation. Under these conditions a singularist could accept the imputationist view.

The issue of commonness arises here again. Both singularism and multiplism require that competing interpretations address a common interpretandum. The judgment whether pertinent objects of interpretation are the same or sufficiently similar depends upon one's theory of identity. One might take (1) all, (2) some, or (3) an arrangement of properties of an object as fixing its identity. Accordingly, one might hold (1) that all properties of an object fix its identity, that a change in any of its properties entails a change in the identity of the object. This view of identity (let us call it the Leibnizian view) is too strong, for it rules out change of any selfsame thing over time. While the Leibnizian view arguably might hold for formalized languages, it does not apply to middle-sized objects or to the natural languages used to describe them in everyday discourse.

Alternatively, one might hold (2) that a subclass of properties of an object fixes its identity. That is, its "essential," or "core," properties serve as a criterion for its identity. Accordingly, not all of a thing's properties need to be invariant for it to remain the selfsame thing. While any change in the "essential," or "core," properties of an object would entail a change in the identity of the object, a change in nonessential properties would not. Yet doubts emerge about (2) when we consider that there may be circumstances under which the distinction between essential and nonessential (or "core" and "incidental") is not fixed and depends upon context of use. This leads

---

volume, page 276, quoting Hans-Georg Gadamer, *Truth and Method* (New York: Crossroad, 1988), 164–65.

19. Along with Hilary Putnam, Chhanda Gupta resists imputationism on other grounds. They endorse relationalism rather than imputationism. See Chhanda Gupta, "Constructive Realism and the Question of Imputation," in the present volume.

to the thought that perhaps no particular (set of) properties of a thing could inherently fix its identity. As Wittgenstein asks, "But where are the bounds of the incidental?"[20]

Accordingly, consider the thought (3) that a thing may be a selfsame thing on different occasions without holding would-be essential properties as fixed. According to (3) no given condition is taken to be invariantly essential. Wittgenstein champions this "family-resemblance" possibility when considering what might be "common" in two instances; he says, "Consider for example the proceedings that we call 'games.' I mean board-games, card-games, ball-games, Olympic games, and so on. What is common between them?—Don't say: 'There *must* be something common, or they would not be called "games'"—but *look and see* whether there is anything in common to all.—For if you look at them you will not see something that is common to *all,* but similarities, relationships, and a whole series of them at that."[21]

I stress that for either singularism or multiplism, in order for two or more interpretations to compete, they must address a common object of interpretation. And the claim of commonness of an object of interpretation must be grounded in a pertinent theory of identity. Further—and this is a point that will become central in Part II—insofar as one's theory of identity bears on the *nature* of the object of interpretation, it is an ontological theory in a wide sense. That is, in order to generate a contest between singularism and multiplism in the first place, some ontological theory of identity needs to be presupposed. It is in this wide sense that ontology is *relevant* to the ideals of interpretation. Yet it remains that both singularism and multiplism are logically detachable from realism, constructivism, and constructive realism—where these latter theories are understood to be ontological in a narrow sense. There are no entailment relationships between singularism and multiplism on the one hand and these narrowly construed ontological theories on the other hand.

In passing we should note that much of Novitz's article is given over to arguing against the thesis of cognitive intransparency, the view that objects as such—free of interpretive activity—are not accessible to apt interpreters. But he mistakenly thinks that the thesis of cognitive intransparency is crucial for multiplism. Even if the thesis of cognitive intransparency were false,

20. Ludwig Wittgenstein, *Philosophical Investigations* (Oxford: Basil Blackwell, 1958), para. 79, p. 37.
    21. Ibid., para. 66, pp. 31–32.

neither realism, constructivism, nor constructive realism would entail either singularism or multiplism. Specifically, realism (even of a transparent sort) does not entail singularism. Novitz's favored thesis of cognitive transparency is compatible with *either* singularism or multiplism. So his insistence on cognitive transparency does not secure the singularism he seeks to guarantee.

Yet Novitz is right to hold that indeterminacy, for example, may be handled in a singularist way. A singularist condition obtains where there is a one-one relation between interpretandum and interpretation. While indeterminacy does not entail a multiplist condition, it also does not entail a singularist condition. Novitz moves in the right direction when he says, "[I]f it is true that the score and the work are indeterminate in certain respects, this fact *must* be captured and relayed in the single right critical interpretation of the score and the work."[22] But Novitz overstates his point when he says that indeterminacy "must" be captured in a single right interpretation. It would have been enough had he said that it "might" be. The indeterminacy of an interpretandum does not entail its answering to a multiplist condition. A singularist condition might indeed obtain where the indeterminacy of an interpretation "matches" the indeterminacy of the interpretandum in question. Perhaps it might be best to say that for an indeterminate interpretandum it is *undecidable* whether it answers to either a singularist or a multiplist condition. The point is that, while multiplism is not entailed by the indeterminacy of pertinent interpretanda, neither is singularism.

(II)

I have said that the theories of realism, constructivism, and constructive realism—understood as ontological in a narrow sense—are detachable from the interpretive ideals of singularism and multiplism. To bring this claim into sharper focus I now rehearse the dialectic between realism and constructivism, followed by an explication of constructive realism.[23] To antici-

---

22. Novitz, "Against Critical Pluralism," in this volume, page 105, emphasis added.

23. Portions of the following section are taken and reworked from my paper "Ontology and the Aims of Interpretation: Toward a Constructive Realism," presented at the University of Delhi, January 16, 2001, a version of which will appear as "Interpretation and Ontology: A Synoptic View," in *Interpretation and Ontology: Studies in the Philosophy of Michael Krausz,* ed. Andreea Deciu Ritivoi and G. L. Pandit (Amsterdam: Rodopi Publishers, 2003).

pate: I shall urge that as a realist one may be a singularist or a multiplist. As a constructivist one may be a singularist or a multiplist. As an "internal" constructive realist one may be a singularist or a multiplist. And as an "external" constructive realist one may be *neither* a singularist *nor* a multiplist. *None of these ontologies uniquely entails singularism or multiplism and vice versa.* This does not mean that, if freighted with ancillary amendments, *particular* versions of these ontologies could not be *made* to entail either singularism or multiplism. It does mean that committing oneself *first* to either singularism or multiplism does not commit one to any one of these types of ontologies. Put otherwise, while *certain* freighted realisms, constructivisms, or constructive realisms may entail either singularism or multiplism, one's prior commitment to either singularism or multiplism commits one to neither realism nor constructivism nor constructive realism.[24] Yet, I suggest that wider ontological considerations that bear on the identity of objects of interpretation remain relevant to the theory of interpretation.[25]

How, then, are we to understand the general rubrics "realism," "constructivism," and "constructive realism"? In brief, realism is the view that an object of interpretation is fully constituted independently of interpretive practices. Constructivism is the view that at least some of an object's properties are constituted by interpretive practices. And constructive realism

24. For a fuller treatment, see my "Interpretation and Its 'Metaphysical' Entanglements," *Metaphilosophy* 31, nos. 1/2 (2000): 125–47. See also my *Limits of Rightness,* chap. 9. In the present volume Margolis continues to insist that I hold that there is *no* relation (in addition to no deductive relation) between interpretation and ontology. (See his footnote 27.) I have, in the article cited above, already corrected Margolis's mischaracterization of my view. But in his very latest book, *Selves and Other Texts* (University Park: Pennsylvania State University Press, 2001), 132, Margolis continues to mischaracterize my view when he says, by way of a would-be criticism of my detachability thesis, that "a ramified version of any of the metaphysical options offered *would* in all probability 'entail' some constraints on the theory of interpretation—and vice versa. In that sense, the denial of 'detachability' might mean no more than that *there cannot be a viable theory of interpretation that is not 'adequated' to one's metaphysics,* for without meeting that condition one's theory of interpretation would have no relevance or application at all." As the present chapter makes clear again, I agree that pertinent ontologies would provide some constraints on the (general) theory of interpretation. But none of the ontologies considered entails either singularism or multiplism. That latter narrower claim is what the thesis of detachability asserts. Margolis persists in equating the narrower with the more general claim. In so doing he manufactures a disagreement where there is none.

25. Note that relevance of ontological considerations that bear on the identity of objects of interpretation is a function of a given practice. While it is relevant in the present context of a theory of interpretation, it may be irrelevant in another practice. For example, when interpreting dreams, a therapist who is concerned to heal his or her patient may find the ontological issue of the identity of the interpretandum to be quite irrelevant to the interests and aims of the therapeutic practice.

holds that the very idea of *objects* of interpretation or the *existence* of such objects makes no sense independently of some constructing framework or symbol system. There are intramural differences between constructive realists. The *internal* constructive realist holds that it makes no sense to posit that there is *anything* beyond constructing interpretive frameworks. In contrast, the *external* constructive realist holds that one must posit that there is something beyond symbol systems or constructing frameworks—but for that "something" he or she withholds predicates of *objecthood* and *existence,* for these are taken by constructive realists generally to be internal to constructing frameworks. The external constructive realist holds that although it cannot be countenanced as real, some presystematic "material" needs to be appealed to in order to account for the construction of the real. The internal constructive realist holds that there can be no appeal to anything—real or otherwise—that precedes the symbol system. Both external and internal constructive realists agree that objecthood and existence are bestowed only within pertinent schemes.

Let us now rehearse the dialectic between realists and constructivists, to be followed by a fuller account of constructive realism. Realists stress the logical independence of the way things are from human representations of it. Usually this view is formulated in global terms, without specification of domains of inquiry. John Searle, for example, says: *"Realism is the view that there is a way that things are that is logically independent of all human representations. Realism does not say how things are but only that there is a way that they are."*[26]

Hilary Putnam characterizes metaphysical realism—or what I am simply calling realism—as holding that "the world consists of some fixed totality of mind-independent objects. There is exactly one true and complete description of 'the way the world is.' "[27]

On the other hand, constructivism rejects the thought that there is a world that consists of a totality of mind-independent objects. As Nelson Goodman says, "[W]e cannot find any world-feature independent of all versions. Whatever can be said truly of a world is dependent on the saying . . . informed by and relative to the language or other symbol system we use."[28]

26. John Searle, *The Construction of Social Reality* (New York: Free Press, 1995), 155, his emphasis.

27. Hilary Putnam, *Reason, Truth, and History* (Cambridge: Cambridge University Press, 1981), 49.

28. In Peter McCormick, ed., *Starmaking* (Cambridge, Mass.: MIT Press, 1996), 144. Further references to this anthology, which includes works of Nelson Goodman, Hilary Putnam, and Israel Scheffler, will be abbreviated in the text as McC followed by page number. Pertinent

Accordingly, any attempt to drive a conceptual wedge between unrepresented objects as such and objects as represented will fail, for any example of a would-be object as such would be represented somehow. And any represented object is nested in a symbol system or conceptual scheme of some kind or other. According to Goodman, this is inescapable. Nothing intelligible can be said about the world independent of world-versions. I have called this putative failure to drive a conceptual wedge between unrepresented objects as such and objects as represented the *constructivist's reductio* of realism. It tends toward the conclusion that constructivism must be global, that realism cannot be injected even in a piecemeal way. For the constructivist reductio applies to any candidate object offered by the realist, from no matter what domain of inquiry.

I take the claim that we make versions to be uncontroversial. Even the realist acknowledges this. More controversial, though, is the claim that in making versions we make the objects to which they refer, as when Goodman says, "We make a star as we make a constellation, by putting its parts together and marking off its boundaries" (McC, 145). A still more controversial claim is that some versions make worlds (McC, 145). Insofar as right versions make worlds and there are numerous right versions, there are numerous worlds. The multiplicity of right versions amounts to a multiplicity of worlds. Goodman says,

> [O]nce we recognize that . . . supposed features of the world derive from—are made and imposed by—versions, 'the world' rapidly evaporates. For there is no version-independent feature, no true version compatible with all true versions. Our so-called neutral version of motion is as prejudiced as any other; for if direction and speed and acceleration are relative to observer and frame of reference, so also is distance between objects. And . . . the objects themselves and the time and space they occupy are version-dependent. No organization into units is unique and mandatory, nor is there any featureless raw material underlying different organizations. Any raw stuff is as much the creature of a version as is what is made out of that stuff. (McC, 154)[29]

articles are as follows: Goodman, "On Starmaking," 143–47; idem, "Notes on the Well-Made World," 152–59; Putnam, "Irrealism and Deconstruction," 179–200; Scheffler, "Epistemology of Objectivity," 29–58; idem, "The Wonderful Worlds of Goodman," 133–41; idem, "Reply to Goodman," 61–64; and idem, "Worldmaking: Why Worry?" 171–77.

29. It is Goodman's use of the term "stuff" that prompts my formulation of external constructive realism in terms of it.

Now, even if particular objects are made by and nested in versions, how is it that *worlds* are thereby made? By a "world" Goodman means more than merely a collection of pertinent objects. Here I shall not pursue the difficulties involved in Goodman's notion of worlds or of many worlds. Israel Scheffler, for one, has done so with aplomb in articles reprinted in Peter McCormack's anthology *Starmaking*.

My aim here is to see to what extent the core claim of realism (namely, that the way things are is logically independent of human representations of it) can be reconciled with the core claim of constructivism (namely, that objects are intelligible only relative to the symbol systems or conceptual schemes in which they are nested).

One might be tempted to reconcile realism with constructivism by introducing a distinction between global and piecemeal strategies. A piecemeal reconciliationist might hold that in certain domains the distinction between discourse-dependence and discourse-independence holds and that in other circumstances the distinction does not. Accordingly, a star might be taken as the sort of thing that is discourse-independent, and a constellation might be taken as the sort of thing that is discourse-dependent. Yet this piecemeal approach falters as one recognizes the force of the constructivist reductio, namely, that even the boundaries of stars are designated in conventional ways. The constructivist's reductio tends toward the conclusion that constructivism must be global and that realism cannot be injected in a piecemeal way.

So consider another attempt, a global attempt, to reconcile realism with constructivism. Consider Putnam's heterodox view that *existence* and *objecthood* are internal to conceptual schemes. They do not precede such schemes. This suggestion accords with Goodman's constructivism (one might say "mere constructivism), but it goes beyond it in *specifying* that objecthood and existence are internal to conceptual schemes. Putnam says: "The idea that 'object' has some sense which is independent of how we are counting objects and what we are counting as an 'object' in a given situation is an illusion" (McC, 188). Putnam emphasizes the point when he says, " 'Objects' do not exist independently of conceptual schemes. We cut up the world into objects when we introduce one or another scheme of description. Since the objects *and* the signs are alike *internal* to the scheme of description, it is possible to say what matches what."[30]

As I said, according to Putnam, it is not only objects that are taken to be

---

30. Putnam, *Reason, Truth, and History*, 52.

scheme-relative. Existence is too. Putnam says that *"the logical primitives themselves, and in particular the notions of object and existence, have a multitude of different uses rather than one absolute 'meaning.'* "[31] In other words, "What objects does the world consist of? is a question that it only makes sense to ask *within* a theory or description."[32]

Notice that the claim that objecthood and existence are internal to conceptual schemes does not rule out the possibility that there is presystematic "input" (as Putnam says) or presystematic "stuff" (as I shall say) on the basis of which existing objects are to be constituted. That is, to concede that objects or existents are internal to conceptual schemes is not to affirm that there *is* nothing beyond conceptual schemes. One may concede that boundaries of stars, for example, are conventionally designated. But from this it does not follow that some undifferentiated stuff is not there before pertinent designations are made. It does not follow that there is nothing *there* yet to be made differentiated in a conceptual scheme. As Putnam himself says, "[W]hy should the fact that reality cannot be described independent of our descriptions lead us to suppose that there are only the descriptions?" (McC, 189).

It is in this vein that Putnam speaks of the construction of objects within systems of counting from "experiential inputs." Indeed, such "inputs" talk suggests that something is brought in from outside conceptual schemes. Putnam says,

> Internalism does not deny that there are experiential *inputs* to knowledge; knowledge is not a story with no constraints except *internal* coherence; but it does deny that there are any inputs *which are not themselves to some extent shaped by our concepts,* by the vocabulary we use to report and describe them, or any inputs *which admit of only one description, independent of all conceptual choices.* . . .The very inputs upon which our knowledge is based are conceptually contaminated inputs; but contaminated inputs are better than none.[33]

Now, I want to press Putnam about these "contaminated" inputs. Despite his emphasis on the internalism of world-features (along the lines sug-

31. Hilary Putnam, *The Many Faces of Realism* (La Salle, Ill.: Open Court, 1987), 19. Boldface and italic in the original text.
32. Putnam, *Reason, Truth, and History,* 49.
33. Ibid., 54.

gested by Goodman), Putnam leaves open the possibility that inputs might be external to conceptual schemes. Putnam is ambivalent about what these experiential inputs amount to. But Putnam's talk of inputs does suggest a strategy whereby a realist might affirm that there is precedent "stuff," or "materia" (as I called it in *Limits of Rightness*), that is not internal to some conceptual scheme.[34]

That strategy suggests an irenic constructive realism whereby, generally, *objects and their existence are conceptual scheme–relative. According to the constructive-realist proposal, "real objects" are subtended under a constructivist rubric, but they are not identified with that which may be posited as presystematically there.* So understood, Putnam can be seen as a constructive realist in the general sense that he holds that there is no nonpartisan way of identifying objects and their existence. And at least his language allows an "external" constructive realism in that prescheme inputs are invoked on the basis of which existent objects may be constituted.

While Putnam denies that "there are any inputs which are not themselves to some extent shaped by our concepts," and while he affirms that they are "conceptually contaminated," his view still allows the claim that there is presystematic stuff "upon which our knowledge is based." This would be enough to qualify him as an external constructive realist. (And were we to be swayed by Chhanda Gupta, in her following article, to revise this characterization of Putnam, to consider him an internal, rather that external, constructive realist, we should still benefit, dialectically, by considering the conceptual possibility of external constructive realism.)

One might observe that the "mere" constructivist (such as Goodman)

---

34. Chhanda Gupta insists that by "input" Putnam means something that is fully internal to conceptual schemes. While this may indeed be Putnam's intention, his choice of this central metaphor suggests an alternative view on which I capitalize to formulate external constructive realism. See Gupta's "Constructive Realism and the Question of Imputation," in the present volume.

But if by "input" Putnam does indeed mean something that is fully internal to conceptual schemes, then one might ask (as Bernard Harrison does) in what sense Putnam is a realist at all. Harrison formulates his challenge this way: "Putnam may indeed . . . speak of 'inputs' to conceptual schemes. But unless he has some way of saying why the MODE of 'input' is language-independent . . . , I don't see how this [sort of realism] can be more than a mere form of words, since if language penetrates as deeply as all that into our commerce with reality it must penetrate into anything describable as an 'input.' He is only a 'realist,' then, in the Pickwickian sense. . . . But that is such a minimal sense of 'realism' that I think those who have accused him of turning his back on realism altogether in his recent work have a point" (private communication, March 19, 2001; see also Bernard Harrison and Patricia Hanna, *Word and World: Reference and Linguistic Convention* [forthcoming]).

can allow the core claim of constructive realism, namely, that objecthood and existence are internal to conceptual schemes. But what distinguishes Putnam from Goodman is that Putnam allows experiential input, and this goes counter to Goodman's remark, "Any raw stuff is as much the creature of a version as is what is made out of that stuff" (McC, 154).

The core claim of constructive realism—again, that objecthood and existence are internal to conceptual schemes—allows but does not mandate that there is undifferentiated stuff (not yet ordained as existing or as real) beyond any conceptual scheme. Here, then, arises the intramural distinction between *external* and *internal* constructive realism. The external constructive realist allows the question, What presystematic "stuff" is there for the construction of "real" objects? The internal constructive realist does not. One who answers that there is undifferentiated stuff external to conceptual schemes (but not ordained as "existing") is an external constructive realist. One who answers that there is not is an internal constructive realist.

At this point one might ask, more fully, what distinguishes the "mere" constructivist position from that of the internal constructive realist. Both agree with the core claim of constructive realism. In response one might say that the difference is one of emphasis. Namely, while the internal constructive realist emphasizes that objecthood and existence along with all other world-features are internal to conceptual schemes, the "mere" constructivist does not. But perhaps it is more than a matter of emphasis. While "mere" constructivism talks of the scheme-relativity of world-features, internal constructive realism explicitly raises the question of the material from which world-features arise and explicitly answers that it too is scheme-relative.

What, then, is the difference between internal and external constructive realism? The internal constructive realist says that there can be no appeal to anything—real or otherwise—that precedes any conceptual schemes. The internal constructive realist holds that there is nothing *there,* outside conceptual schemes, or that one can make no sense of the claim that there is something *there.* In contrast, the external constructive realist says that, although it cannot be countenanced as embodying real objects, some pre-scheme undifferentiated "stuff" needs to be appealed to in order to account for the construction of real objects. The external constructive realist agrees with the internal constructive realist that real objects are not outside conceptual schemes or that one cannot make sense of the claim that real objects are outside conceptual schemes. But this agreement does not prohibit one's positing that there is something *there,* some undifferentiated stuff, outside conceptual schemes, from which real objects are constituted within conceptual schemes. The external constructive realist affirms that just to say that objects are made within conceptual schemes is not to say that there is *nothing* from which features emerge. In Kantian terms, if one were to posit that a noumenal realm were *there*—providing the undifferentiated "stuff" for the construction of real objects—one would be an external constructive realist. If, on the other hand, one were to forswear the noumenal realm, one would be an internal constructive realist.

Yet one might ask of the external constructive realist, In what sense of "is" can it be said that there *is* prescheme stuff? In response, the external constructive realist might say that the pertinent sense of "is" is a noumenal "is." It is a posit with no claim of existence. But what could that be? The external constructive realist could reply that "stuff" is an expression used to indicate the absence of any concept that is being applied to a subject. Its use is to show that one is not applying a significant concept to a subject. Kant's thing-in-itself (*Ding an sich*) or the noumenal world is such a subject. Accordingly, the notion of a noumenal world is a kind of limit of thought (*Grenzbegriff*) rather than a clear concept.

In response, the internal constructive realist might reply that this negative characterization of "stuff" still does not tell us in what sense one can affirm that the stuff is *there*, that it exists. On the contrary, the negative characterization only tells us why we cannot say that the stuff is there, or that it exists. So here is the dilemma: It would be contradictory for the constructive realist to say that the prescheme stuff is there, or that it exists, *in the constructive realist's internalist sense*. Alternatively, if the prescheme stuff is still said to be there, or to exist, the constructive realist must provide a positive characterization of the different sense in which it might be so. But that characterization remains to be provided. In short, at this stage we are left with either contradiction or incompleteness.

Yet, again, our central concern is with the relation of constructive realism to singularism and multiplism. In that regard, recall that in external constructive realism the prescheme stuff remains undifferentiated. No individuation of objects operates with respect to it. Consequently, one cannot ask of its nonexistent objects whether they are the same when addressed by otherwise contending interpretations. Thus, *external constructive realism does not admit of either singularism or multiplism, for both singularism and multiplism require that otherwise contending interpretations must address a common object of interpretation.* The undifferentiated stuff cannot satisfy a condition necessary for *it* to answer to either singularism or multiplism. On two occasions of interpretive activity, it cannot be said to be a *common* stuff. Thus, with respect to that stuff, neither singularism nor multiplism can arise. Notice, though, that with respect to the external constructivist's *once ordained objects* within pertinent schemes, either singularism or multiplism may obtain, just as they may obtain for the internal constructive realist's objects within such schemes.

Yet an internal constructive realist might still press the point that, even if one granted the stuff to the external constructive realist, that in itself would not explain the emergence of existent objects, for to do so would require the still further account of how an undifferentiated stuff might come to be differentiated in its resultant objects, how, that is, differentiation might arise from undifferentiation. For the external constructive realist there is the mystery of differentiation from undifferentiation. Correspondingly, for the internal constructive realist there is the mystery of the origin or material from which objects can come to be constituted. Mystery is to be found on both sides of this dialectic.

The dialectic between internal constructive realists and external constructive realists parallels the dialectic between constructivists and realists as first characterized. The internal constructive realist responds to the external constructive realist by saying that there is nothing external from which objects emerge. All input talk, all stuffness talk, is disallowed. There can be no stuff left outside the reach of conceptual schemes. And even talk of stuff, individuated or not, is intelligible only if nested in some discourse. The very posit of a prescheme stuff is itself scheme-dependent. The would-be noumenal "is" of external constructivism is an "is" without content. In reply, the external constructive realist insists that prior to discourse there must be a stage at which stuff resides. Otherwise the emergence of objects remains a mystery.

External constructive realism is neutral with respect to singularism or multiplism in that neither singularism nor multiplism are applicable to prescheme stuff. Such stuff cannot satisfy pertinent judgments of commonness. And internal constructive realism is compatible with singularism or multiplism because, within the realm of conceptual schemes, objects may be constituted so as to answer to either singularism or multiplism.

Notice that *I have endorsed neither internal nor external constructive realism*. Rather, my aim has been to show how internal constructive realism is compatible with either singularism or multiplism and how external constructive realism—in regard to its posited external stuff—is compatible with neither singularism nor multiplism. In either case, constructive realism entails neither singularism nor multiplism.

The argument that I have offered for the detachability of singularism and multiplism from the inventoried ontologies is an argument concerning detachability relative to entailment. That is, neither singularism nor multiplism entails realism, constructivism, or constructive realism, and vice versa. That does not mean that there is *no* pertinent relationship between these ideals of interpretation and these ontologies. As I have suggested, a particular kind of identity theory is necessary for the competition between singularism and multiplism to arise in the first place. And such a theory counts as ontological in a wide sense.

Accordingly, it is an ontological question whether, on a given occasion, it is appropriate to deploy the pluralizing strategy whereby a given object of interpretation should be pluralized into two or more, thus resulting in singularist conditions. In these nontrivial ways at least, ontology is relevant to the ideals of interpretation—despite the fact that neither singularism nor multiplism is uniquely entailed by realism, constructivism, or constructive realism.

To conclude, I note the following: (1) Neither realism nor constructivism nor constructive realism entails either singularism or multiplism. (2) The thesis of cognitive intransparency is not mandated by multiplism. So if the thesis is false, multiplism will not thereby be unseated. (3) Incongruent interpretations—which partly define multiplism—exhibit opposition-without-exclusivity. Incompatible interpretations do not exhaust the class of interpretations that are opposed. (4) The conjoining of two interpretations that italicize different features of a common interpretandum (as might be encouraged by singularists) alters the italics of each. The result is no mere conjunction into one interpretation but something else. (5) Whatever misgivings one might have about imputationism, it does not entail multiplism. It is also compatible with singularism. (6) The distinction between elucidation and elaboration cannot be drawn in terms of puzzle solving. And elaboration is not merely "subjective" or "gratuitous." (7) In order for two or more interpretations to compete, they must address a common object of interpretation. And a thing may be common on different occasions without having invariantly fixed "essentialist" properties. Finally, (8) insofar as pertinent theories of identity count as ontological in a wide sense, ontology is relevant to interpretation theory.

Constructive Realism and the Question of Imputation

Chhanda Gupta

Many in the realm of metaphysics limit their ontological options to certain dichotomies that polarize philosophical viewpoints. It is pointless, according to them, to make any reconciliatory effort to go beyond this polarization or to evolve a kind of fusion philosophy that would combine elements of both views. Realism and constructivism, usually seen as contrasting positions, can never therefore come to terms, these thinkers would urge. It is this contention that Michael Krausz questions in his excellent book *Limits of Rightness,* moving exactly in the opposite direction by collecting hybrid ontologies under the irenic heading of "constructive realism."[1]

In his inventory of irenic ontologies Krausz includes Putnam's "internal realism." My concern here is to show that even if "constructive realism" is imbued with internal-realist ideas in a very basic sense, it is debatable whether internal realism can be labelled "constructivist." All real things and their features are *relational,* an internal realist insists, but relativization need not imply *construction—imputation* or *projection.* The idea of a *relatively*

This chapter is a version of the postscript of the forthcoming reissue of Chhanda Gupta, *Realism versus Realism* (Lanham, Md.: Rowman & Littlefield), printed here with permission of the publishers.

1. Michael Krausz, *Limits of Rightness* (Lanham, Md.: Rowman & Littlefield, 2000), henceforth abbreviated as LR.

real world is different from that of a world *constructed*. If internal realism is to be brought under the banner of "constructive realism" at all, then the constructivism it incorporates must be *nonimputationist*. What, however, could be the prospect of this pacifist project of trying to combine realism and constructivism, be it imputationist or nonimputationist, one might ask, given the standard construal of the two opposed positions?

I

The difference between the two positions seems to be too sharp to make peaceful coexistence possible. The points of contrast usually noted are the following:

1a. "The basic idea of realism is that the kinds of thing which exist and what they are like, are *independent* of us and the way in which we find out about them; . . . how many planets there are in the solar system [for instance] does not depend on how many *we think* there are."[2]
1b. Constructivism, endorsing the antirealist denial of this, holds that things and their features do depend on us. Primarily regarded as a sociological view of scientific knowledge, it even goes so far as to hold that "scientists literally 'make the world.' "[3]
2a. Realism, in one of its epistemological versions, is characterized in terms of limits of knowledge, inasmuch as it postulates facts that are "recognition-transcendent." This seems to suggest a slant toward skepticism. Indeed, if the way something is, is *utterly independent* of the way we are and the way we think about it, then what could rule out the possibility of there being facts that are beyond the reach of our cognitive powers?
2b. Constructivism maintains that knowledge, and more specifically "scientific knowledge," "is 'produced' by scientists"[4] and is determined minimally (if at all) by the independent world. It maintains further that the object of such knowledge is a "construct" too. And so, contra the real-

2. Edward Craig, "Realism and Antirealism," in *Routledge Encyclopedia of Philosophy,* ed. Edward Craig (London: Routledge, 1998), 8:115.
3. Stephen M. Downes, "Constructivism," in *Routledge Encyclopedia of Philosophy,* 2:625.
4. Ibid.

ist's skeptical stance, it would argue: if the nature of what we know is due to the way we "construct" it through our experience and investigation, then how could there be anything about it that our cognitive faculties cannot recover?

3a. The object that knowledge aims to discover, according to realists, is a reality existing independently of knowledge. "Knowledge is of what is there *anyway*."[5] This conception of the object of knowledge has been called the "absolute conception of reality."[6] This conception, widely held by realists, may be interpreted in two ways. It may be empty, signifying only *whatever* it is that our representations of it represent. Or, it could suggest a fuller and more determinate notion of the world as it *really* is, understood in terms of its *own intrinsic* primary qualities, in contrast to what merely *seems to us*. It is this world, standing apart from the peculiarities of observers, that the scientists wish to explore, according to realists.

3b. Constructivists reject both these notions. The *object of knowledge* can never stand apart from *representations*. The only access to the world that we may have is via representations. The object of knowledge is what can be called "object-as-represented."

4a. Realists think of truth in terms of correspondence to facts that exist independently of how anyone thinks about them.

4b. Constructivists, who subscribe to the sociological view of knowledge, claim that the truth or falsehood of beliefs, particularly scientific beliefs, derives not from their relation to the world but from the social interests and practices of inquirers. "Truth and falsity of scientific beliefs can be established independently of any evidence from the real world."[7]

If so glaring is the difference on such major issues, then how can the debating parties show tolerance to each other and formulate the kind of mixed ontology that Krausz wants to develop? Krausz himself seems to have given an answer. He has discerned a common strategy that most of the "irenic ontologies" he considers appear to have adopted. The strategy seems to be that each party is allowed to retain its own party line even though it is entering into a coalition, so to say, with its philosophical "other." Thus

---

5. Bernard Williams, *Descartes: The Project of Pure Enquiry* (Harmondsworth, Middlesex: Harvester Press, 1978), 64.

6. Ibid., 64–66, 236–46.

7. Downes, "Constructivism," 625.

"constructive realism" has space for both "realism," as it is usually interpreted, and "constructivism."

II

The variety of "constructive realism" Krausz first discusses is the one advanced by Paul Thom. Thom remains committed to the typical realist-party
position when he posits a "representation-independent" object that precedes our interpretive activity. He reiterates the basic idea of realism noted
above, namely, that real things are independent of what we *take* them to be.
He calls such an independent object the "further object."

Yet Thom embraces constructivism also. Despite his conviction concerning the interpretation-independent "further object," he believes in imputational interpretations that *construct,* on *another level,* various "objects-as-
represented," or what Krausz calls "objects-of-interpretation."[8] Thom's ad-
vocacy of this kind of constructivism seems to stem from a loss of faith in
the foundationalist picture of a pure, uninterpreted factual reality, on the
one hand, and an attraction to perspectivism, on the other. These two traits
are distinctive marks of what Krausz has described elsewhere as the "interpretive turn" of our age.[9] The turn signals the replacement of the absolute
conception of realities having fixed and independent identities by dynamic
and competing interpretations of facts, interpretations that do not merely
describe these facts but also *shape* or *create* them. Thom's constructivism
celebrates this "interpretative turn" and subscribes to an "imputationist
view of interpretations."[10] In what way, however, can the strategy of keeping intact two radically opposed viewpoints within a composite ontology
succeed in maintaining peace? Does not the notion of an interpretation-
independent "further object" collide head-on with that of an "object-as-
interpreted"? Thom and Krausz think that there need be no such collision
as long as we recognize the distinction Thom draws between the level of the
"further object" and the level of the "object-of-interpretation." This can be
understood by considering the well-known example of the face-vase con-

8. LR, 26–27.
9. Michael Krausz and Richard Shusterman, eds., *Interpretation, Relativism, and the
Metaphysics of Culture: Themes in the Philosophy of Joseph Margolis* (Amherst, N.Y.: Humanity Press, 1999), 8.
10. See LR, 25.

figuration (reminiscent of Thomas Kuhn's "duck-rabbit"). A line drawing, which is a presented configuration, is the single "further object" that can be seen or interpreted differently—either as two facing heads or as a vase, by imputing "salience to certain features of the presented configuration." If "there are different saliences there are different intentional objects," or different *constructed* objects-as-represented.[11] So, like Thom, one can, on one level, be a realist with respect to the "further object" and, on another level, still be a constructivist with respect to the "object-as-represented." If anyone asks why a realist should posit the "further object," even after taking the "interpretative turn," the answer will be:

(i)   interpretation is "not spun out of nothing";
(ii)   there must be something—a "further object"—"that is interpreted"; and
(iii) an imputation of salience to certain features of the presented configuration or the "further object" would confirm the *propriety* of interpreting it in one way or the other.

Yet, no matter what rationale is offered for the admission of the "further object," the notion seems to be contentious. It is likely to create dissension between the partisan views that Krausz wants to harmonize. One might have problems with this notion because

(a)   the representation-independent "further object" seems to mirror Kant's noumenon if it is construed as an empty notion, that is, simply as something "that is interpreted" [as stated in (ii) above] or as "*whatever* the representations represent" [as in the first sense of the "absolute conception" of reality noted in point 3a of the previous section]. Given this empty notion, it would be hard to understand the passage from the *representation-independent* "further object" to the "*object-as-represented*," as in the case of noumenon and phenomenon, in view of the schism that divides them.

Of course, Thom would vehemently oppose this reading of his notion of the "further object." When he speaks of the "*features* of the presented configuration" or the "further object" to which saliences are imputed, he is surely not suggesting an empty notion of something that is featureless in

11. LR, 26.

relation to our cognition, like Kant's noumenon. In fact, when Krausz calls him an "external constructive realist," he resists this characterization on the ground that the "external object . . . does not have to be independent of all representation."[12] So, when he says that objects of interpretation are representations of *something prior*, the "something prior" in all likelihood is not intended to mean anything that is simply there. Rather, it should be taken to mean an individuated existent.[13] But then, substituting a fuller notion of an individuated "further object" for a bare "thereness" may generate a fresh problem.

(b)   One may agree that the object-as-represented is not "spun out of nothing." But if the "further object" out of which it is spun is an individuated object, a presented configuration with definite features, and if interpretation involves *selecting* some of these *presented* features, then where is the room for *construction*? Selection does not amount to *construction*. It only *represents* what is already *presented*, and so the object-as-represented might tend to collapse into the "further object," as Robert Stecker suggests. Krausz acknowledges the point. One could hold, he writes, that "there is no need to introduce a separate . . . object-as-represented—to account for the fact that people see the pertinent configuration differently. . . . There is only the [further] object seen one way or another."[14] Still, he takes sides with Thom and argues that when certain properties of the "further object" are singled out as salient, then such properties are not predicated of the "further object" *as such*. They are predicated of objects-as-represented. The imputed properties such as face or vase, for example, are part of the object-as-represented, but they are no part of the "further object."[15]

This, however is a point that raises further questions. Even if one agrees that certain *imputed* properties are brought into being by some favored interpretation, it would be wrong to suggest that they are *no part* of the "further object." For the newly imputed emergent properties are the selected features of the presented configuration as well, to which salience is assigned by various interpretive concerns. One may concede that the features of the

12. LR, 31. The line is quoted by Krausz from Paul Thom, "Rightness and Success in Interpretation," in the present volume, 55.
13. LR, 31.
14. LR, 26.
15. LR, 26.

"further object" by themselves are not the *sufficient condition* of the emergence of the imputed properties, but they are *necessary* nevertheless. One cannot rule out the rootedness of the emergent, or constructed, properties in properties that are part of the "further object." To say they are *no part* of the "further object" is to suggest that the emergent properties are *created* by the interpreter and the interpretation *alone*. And this account does not seem to coincide with Dewey's view of artworks, as Krausz claims. For even though Dewey's "art product" finds a parallel in Thom's "further object," and his "work of art" is an analogue of Thom's "object-as-represented," "Dewey defines a work of art as a complex, co-created by the experiencing viewer and the art product."[16] To insist, therefore, that "there is *nothing in the further object* as such that recommends that it should be seen this way or that"[17] is to go against Dewey's insight about the *cocreation* of the work of art by *both* the viewer and the art product. Moreover, it leaves unexplained how certain features of the "further object," selected as salient, would confirm the *propriety* of interpreting it in one way or the other.

A break between the parties that Krausz wished to join then seems imminent. If the "further object" is *interpretation-independent* and an interpretation is just a matter of *selection* of its *given* features, then Stecker's puzzle will be a threat to constructivism. If on the other hand there is *nothing* in the "further object" that recommends an interpretation and it is, on the contrary, the "object-as-represented" that transfers its interpretive elements to the "further object," then the latter will tend to collapse into the former. This obviously would be a blow to realism and would pave the path for *pan constructivism,* or a *"constructivist reductio,"* as Krausz says.

III

Thom's ideas find resonance in Krausz's account of realism and constructivism vis-à-vis an intriguing example. Krausz had seen a dead baby floating in the river Ganges at Benares and was told that the baby was *honored* by being returned to the river, which was a hallowed place according to Hindu tradition. Later on he encountered a parallel case, about a newborn being *dumped* in the shallow waters of Cobbs Creek in Philadelphia. Applying

16. LR, 30.
17. LR, 27.

Thom's distinction one could say that the *baby* in both cases is an *object as such*—a "further object" that is a *given* fact of the matter, autonomous and independent of interpretive practice. The "body honored" in the Ganges River case and the "baby dumped" in Cobbs Creek, on the other hand, are "objects-as-represented," objects *taken* in certain ways—as "honored" and "dumped"—within their respective cultural settings. The realists hold that however represented, there is a baby *as such,* and that whatever properties are imputed to objects-as-represented, namely, "honored" and "dumped," they are no part of the "baby as such." In contrast to this, the constructivists maintain that objects are never *given* but are always *taken.* There is no point in talking about the "baby as such." "Even minimally, as a baby, the object is always represented somehow. No object is presented independent of some representation of it."[18]

The problems noted in Thom's ontology seem to reappear.

1) If the "object as such" is an empty notion signifying a bare "thereness," then one may wonder whether it is fit to play any role at all in interpretation—even that of an interpretandum. Krausz is aware of the problem and observes poignantly that "objects as such" cannot be fixed independently of their representations, not even by *ostention,* as Wittgenstein showed. One needs a supplementing story, Krausz reminds us, for *identifying* the things pointed at.[19]

2) But if the realist replaces this problematic notion with that of an *individuated* object as such (or "further object") and makes interpretation a matter of *selection,* as previously noted, then this will jeopardize the *imputationist* thesis of constructivists. Will not this imperil the alliance between realists and constructivists?

3) The constructivists nevertheless would urge, as Krausz points out, that *just* the baby in both examples can never be made intelligible without being nested in some symbol system, though not the symbol system of Hindu tradition and that of the North Americans. We simply cannot make sense of an interpretation-independent "object as such."

4) A possible realist retort to this is anticipated by Nelson Goodman himself, a constructivist par excellence. "How can there be no fact, no content, but only alternative ways of describing nothing?"[20] Still, the

18. LR, 42; see also 37–38.
19. LR, 42.
20. LR, 44. The line is quoted by Krausz from Nelson Goodman, "Just the Facts Mam," in *Relativism, Interpretation, and Confrontation,* ed. Michael Krausz (Notre Dame, Ind.: Notre Dame University Press, 1990), 81.

constructivists believe that there is no reason to posit an interpretation-independent object as such that interpretations or "versions" are *about*. Krausz articulates the constructivist's answer succinctly: "[I]t is not the case that there was *nothing* that had been intentionalized. There was an intentional *something* that was further intentionalized."[21] The realists remain unconvinced. When intentionality is fully minimized, there must be an object as such at the limit.

Despite this growing dissension between the views, however, Krausz rightly continues his reconciliatory exercise. But to minimize discord and strengthen the reconciliatory tie, the strategy of leaving intact the standard construals of realism and constructivism needs to be altered. Krausz considers several versions of "constructive realism" other than Thom's and his own. In none of these versions, however, has there been a shift from the standard construal of realism and constructivism. The chart given below gives a brief sketch of these versions.

Each of these versions of constructive realism seems to be committed to the core contentions of realism and constructivism as they are standardly construed. Realism cleaves to the idea of things, properties, "materia," "power," and levels of discourse that are *interpretation-independent*. Constructivism considers nearly every thing to be *constructed* or *made* by interpretation. To avert tension stemming from such dichotomous contentions, a realist may give up the notion of a *transcendent interpretation-independent* reality, and a constructivist may cease to accept an imputationist view of interpretation. This precisely seems to be the line of thinking Putnam pursues.

IV

The notion of an interpretation-independent reality is a legacy of Kant's "thing-in-itself," or "noumenal objects," or "the noumenal world" as it is, collectively called. Putnam's "internal realism" is indeed an endeavor to "reassess and appropriate Kant's philosophical legacy,"[22] but this does not

---

21. LR, 45.
22. See the introduction by James Conant to Hilary Putnam's *Realism with a Human Face*, ed. James Conant (Cambridge, Mass.: Harvard University Press, 1990; paperback, 1992), xviii, xxiii.

Constructive Realism

Piecemeal constructive realism with respect to objects. There are representation-independent middle-sized objects with respect to which this version vindicates realism. But it subscribes to constructivism with respect to cultural objects. Yet this version may be vulnerable to the constructivist's reductio, for even sticks and stones seem to be nested in some symbol system.

Piecemeal constructive realism with respect to properties. Some properties, such as the mass of an electron, must be understood realistically, but some other properties, such as position and momentum, which electrons do not possess simultaneously, are to be given a constructivst treatment. Even this version can still be vulnerable to the constructivist's reductio.

Piecemeal constructive realism with respect to levels of discourse. Both realists and constructivists agree that there is at the first order a distinction between objects or properties that are representation-independent and those that are representation-dependent. But a second-order realist holds that this distinction is found, while a second-order constructivist thinks that the distinction is made. However, if this very distinction is constructed, then the first-order distinction should be between objects that are constructed in different ways. Here too there would be a slide toward global constructivism.

Constructive realism with respect to "real objects" internal to some representation system. "Real objects" may be regarded as intrasystemic and constructed. But this version has sub-types.

External constructive realism posits that there is something outside the symbol systems—the "materia" from which "real objects" are constituted. Rom Harré, a vigorous exponent of this version, contends that this external reality beyond symbol systems is power. What is there has the power to produce phenomena relative to what he calls "world-apparatus set-ups". Other exponents of a different type of this version are Bernard Harrison and Patricia Hanna. Besides Paul Thom and Hilary Putnam, who also are "external constructive realists" according to Krausz, there is Fritz Wallner. The "real," on Wallner's view, is constructed. But there is an order beyond this "real one," and this is the "environment." The reference to something beyond this "real one" qualifies Wallner's view as external constructive realist.

Internal constructive realism sponsored by Joseph Margolis, denies that what is out there can be spoken of even in terms of powers to afford phenomena, as Harré maintains, or to deliver true or false judgements about constructed objects and features, as Harrison and Hanna argue in their version of external constructive realism.

amount to an acceptance of Kant's notion of a *transcendent* noumenal reality. We "can form no real conception of . . . noumenal things," Putnam writes; "even the notion of a noumenal world is a kind of limit of thought rather than a clear concept." And even if he concedes that "we can't help thinking that there is *somehow* a mind-independent 'ground' for our experience," he adds that "attempts to talk about it lead . . . to nonsense."[23]

Still, one may contend that Putnam has not given up the notion of "noumenon" altogether. For when anyone makes a judgment about an external object—say a chair, he points out—a *power* is ascribed to *something* on Kant's view, a power that makes it look like a chair to the person making the judgment. So one could ask whether this something was a noumenal object. Of course, neither Putnam nor Kant, to whom this view is ascribed, maintains that this *something* is a *noumenal* chair to which the chair as it *appears* corresponds. There is no one-to-one correspondence between noumenal and phenomenal objects. But on Kant's view, any judgment about external or internal objects is to be interpreted nevertheless as saying that the noumenal world *as a whole* is such that this is the judgment that beings like ourselves would make. "Power is ascribed to *the whole noumenal world*."[24] However, does Putnam himself endorse this view? If he too posited a whole noumenal world that is supposed to provide the interpretation-independent "materia" for the construction of "real objects," then he might be called, in Krausz's words, "an external constructive realist," a realist who does not abandon the notion of a noumenon-like reality altogether. Given what Putnam says about the constructions of objects from "experiential inputs," Krausz describes him as an "external constructive realist."[25]

I wonder, however, whether this label can be applied, if the "external constructive realist" is one who holds that some *presystemic* materia must be admitted. Since the "very *inputs* upon which our knowledge is based are conceptually contaminated,"[26] according to Putnam, I do not know how it can be said that "his view allows the minimal claim that there is *presystemic* materia 'upon which our knowledge is based.' "[27]

It seems to me that Putnam's internal realism cannot be placed on a par with those versions of constructive realism in the chart, which remain com-

---

23. Hilary Putnam, *Reason, Truth, and History* (Cambridge: Cambridge University Press, 1981), 61, 62; henceforth RTH.

24. RTH, 63.

25. LR, 77.

26. RTH, 54.

27. LR, 77, italics mine.

mitted to the notion of a *presystemic interpretation-independent* reality—a notion that harks back to Kant's thing-in-itself.

Krausz himself has clearly expressed the central tenet of internal realism, namely, that "all things and their features should be understood in relational terms as expressed in [Putnam's] idea of *conceptual relativism.*"[28] This idea is not incompatible with realism. On the contrary, it is an integral part of his "internal realism," or "relative realism," as it might aptly be called. And this realism can be introduced "without helping itself to the notion of the thing in itself."[29]

At this point internal realism seems to coalesce with constructivism. Any notion of a presystemic transcendent reality is dropped. There even seems to be a slide toward global "property constructivism," for neither the properties of middle-sized objects nor the microstructural features of elements can escape the sweep of intentionality. But does this not amount to a "constructivist reduction" of realism, as Krausz says? How can internal realism syncretize constructivism with its professed realism?

A few points may be noted to understand how this syncretism could be possible.

1. Things and their features do exist independently notwithstanding their perspectival nature. Even if we cannot "view" them "from nowhere," they are *not of our own making,* the internal realists maintain just as realists do. They are not projections and reifications of our own conceptual and cognitive nature and are in this sense *nonepistemic.* This minimal sense of the *independence condition* can be adapted to the basic idea of realism noted at the outset of section 1. Indeed, the existence of planets does not depend on us. However, contrary to the standard construal of realism, internal realism maintains that "how many planets there are in the solar system" is a question that cannot be answered intelligibly without referring to us and our counting systems. And this brings it close to constructivism.

2. Krausz sums up the dual claim of internal realism very clearly. (a) Real things and their features are not anyone's making. (This is welcome to realism, though it is denied by constructivism.) But at the same time (b), the *condition of intelligibility* is built into the notion of an object (or reality) such that it can be intelligibly talked about only when construed

28. LR, 77.
29. Hilary Putnam, *The Many Faces of Realism* (La Salle, Ill.: Open Court, 1987), 17.

as thinkable, knowable, and describable.[30] (This is welcome to constructivism.) "No meaningful discourse is possible about anything, including its most fundamental features, unless it is an object, at least a putative object of some belief, conception, or knowledge. To stress *relativity* of things and their features to thought in this way, however, is not to deny that things exist whether or not we know or say anything about them. Relativity here means that things which we may or may not know, are *not transcendent,* that is, they are not trans-conceptual, trans-cognitive and trans-phenomenal."[31]

3. "External," or "transcendent," realists are opposed to this very idea of relativization. At most, they may grudgingly admit that an idea of secondary quality such as warmth can be *relativized.* Surely there is no sense in saying that an object itself is warm apart from the touching hand. But this, according to them, is only an *appearance,* something we *project* upon the thing that it really does not have. Internal realism, by contrast, holds that the object *really* has the warmth, though *relationally,* and that this feature is not a projection. The object may certainly have a subvisible structure and causal power, but this does not mean that it does not have warmth. *All* features, primary and secondary, are *relational,* but are *not unreal* for being relational. The way things *appear* is the way they *are.*

4. To appreciate how relativity is compatible with reality, one may follow Putnam by invoking a distinction between two kinds of nonepistemicity. In one sense, not acceptable to internal realism, things and their features are *radically nonepistemic.* This means things and their features are *entirely* independent of us. This is another way of saying that all our beliefs and conceptions may remain just as they are, while reality and truth about reality may be entirely different from *all* our beliefs and conceptions held true by us at several stages of our cognitive enterprise.[32] The "radically nonepistemic" is something *transcendent,* something that can transcend *all* states of knowledge. The kind of nonepistemicity that internal realism accepts, by contrast, is *nonepistemicity simpliciter.* In this sense the nonepistemic is *knowable,* though not a *projection* of the knowing mind. Things and their features are nonepistemic in the sense

30. LR, 83.

31. Chhanda Gupta, *Realism Versus Realism* (Calcutta: Allied Publishers in collaboration with Jadavpur University, 1995), x.

32. See Donald Davidson, "The Structure and Content of Truth," *Journal of Philosophy* LXXXVII (1990): 298.

that they are not of our own making. The features are *not projected* onto something that does not have them.

5. Projection means imposing something upon something else that does not have what we impose upon it. When a thing is believed to have some property, even a microstructural property, no realist, and also no internal realist, would say that this was a projection of the knowing mind or of a certain theory the knowing mind conceives at a certain stage of inquiry. The knowing mind or the theory it conceives does not *impart* the microstructural property to a stuff any more than the touching hand *imparts* warmth to a body that does not have it. Of course, the claim that the stuff really has the property that a theory conceives it to have is a defeasible claim. Some other theory may conceive it to have a different property. The fact remains that the stuff must be said to have the composition that *some* theory conceives it to have. We cannot meaningfully talk about anything that is *totally unrelated* to *all* our beliefs and conceptions.

If the term "construction" carries with it the idea of imputation—projection or ascription—it would be hard to find a place for it within realism, both "external" and "internal." A nonimputationist version of constructive realism, however, is resonant with internal-realist ideas. The kind of "constructive realism" that can properly be called irenic seems to be a realism minus absolutism and a constructivism minus projectivism.

Interpretation and the Ontology of Art

Robert Stecker

This paper first outlines a general account of interpretation in the arts that I have set out and defended in more detail elsewhere.[1] I then focus on an issue to which I have previously not given systematic attention, namely, the extent to which a theory of interpretation—in particular, my own theory—has implications for the ontology of artworks and vice versa. There are two issues. Assuming a distinction between works and texts (and more generally between works and structural types),[2] the first issue is whether, on the account proposed here, the object of interpretation is always the work, or whether it is sometimes instead the text. The second issue is whether the

I thank Stephen Davies, Jerrold Levinson, and Philip Percival for helpful comments.

1. This account is set out in "Art Interpretation," *Journal of Aesthetics and Art Criticism* 52 (1994): 193–206 (henceforth "Art Interpretation") and in *Artworks: Definition, Meaning, Value* (University Park: Pennsylvania State University Press, 1997), 133–85 (henceforth *Artworks*).

2. Not everyone accepts this distinction. Some identify work and structural type. For example, Nelson Goodman and Catherine Z. Elgin identify literary work and text in *Reconceptions in Philosophy and Other Arts and Sciences* (London: Routledge, 1988), 49–65. Peter Kivy identifies musical work and sound structure in a series of papers. See *The Fine Art of Repetition: Essays in the Philosophy of Music* (Cambridge: Cambridge University Press, 1993), 35–94. For a thorough survey of the debate over the relation of a musical work to its sound structure, see Stephen Davies, *Musical Works and Performances* (Oxford: Oxford University Press, 2001).

object of interpretation exists independently of what occurs or comes to exist after the work is created, or whether such things wholly or partly construct the work in some sense, and whether my account takes a stand on this issue.[3]

I. A Theory of Art Interpretation

I begin with a summary of a proposal, according to which (a) people interpret artworks with different aims; (b) such interpretation needs to be evaluated relative to aim; (c) the aims of some interpretations permit, indeed require, them to be evaluated for truth or falsity, while the aims of others do not; (d) among the former are those that aim to identify what an artist "does" in a work in a robust sense of "does" to be spelled out; (e) there is a single correct comprehensive interpretation with this aim for any given work; (f) one can also conjoin any true interpretations of a work (whatever their aims) to form ever more comprehensive true interpretations of it, though ones that may be too diffuse and unwieldy to be very useful; (g) everything that has been asserted so far is compatible with there being a plurality of good or acceptable interpretations of given a work.

To get at (a), let us begin with what looks like a fairly clear contrast between two situations where we are engaged in interpretation. The first situation is one in which we are interpreting someone's behavior. Suppose your friend Jim has begun waking up in the middle of the night, going out of the house and poking around his backyard, then going back to sleep. That is all you know about his behavior, based on a somewhat hasty telephone conversation. From this sparse information, you can think of many interpretations of your friend's behavior, which include:

i. He has insomnia, wants to get back to sleep, and believes that the best way to do this is to get a bit of fresh air.
ii. He is collecting night crawlers for an upcoming fishing trip.
iii. He has become psychotic and, believing traps are being laid, is attempting to find them and expose the perpetrators.

3. I have previously (in "The Constructivist's Dilemma," *Journal of Aesthetics and Art Criticism* 55 [1997]: 43–52) attempted to refute a more restricted version of constructivism according to which it is interpretations themselves that, in part or in whole, create the object of interpretation.

An interpretation, in this context, would be a hypothesis about the explanation of the behavior. It is safe to say that, while you can think of many interpretations, that is, many possible explanations of the behavior, some are correct, though they may be complex in, for example, including both i and ii. Although your initial aim is to consider possible explanations, this is in the service of finding the actual causes of Jim's behavior, and you would throw out those you can determine to be incorrect. You certainly wouldn't say something like "I accept i and ii because together they correctly explain Jim's behavior, but I also accept iii because it makes Jim's behavior a lot more interesting than i and ii do."

Turn now to interpretation in the arts, such as the interpretation of poetry. Here we do get the assertion of interpretations as different as i and iii, and we also seem to get two quite different attitudes toward the assertions of these. On one hand, just as in the case of the hypotheses put forward to explain Jim's behavior, different interpretations of a poem are regarded as rivals among which we need to choose, although, just as with i and ii above, it remains a possibility that some seemingly rival interpretations are part of a more comprehensive correct interpretation and hence not really rivals at all. The thought that interpretations of particular works are rivals is what creates interpretive controversies, of which there are many, including the famous controversies over James's *Turn of the Screw* and Wordsworth's poem "A slumber." On the other hand, there seems to be considerable tolerance of a plurality of interpretations of the same work, a critical culture that encourages such diversity and that often expresses skepticism about the idea of an objectively correct interpretation. There does not seem to be a concerted and cohesive effort to look at interpretations as hypotheses to be confirmed or disconfirmed, or to consider one critic's work as building on the work of another in order to discover a more comprehensive interpretive truth about a work.

Key here is that literary interpretation (and interpretation within other art forms) is more complex than interpretation of Jim's behavior in that in literary interpretation there is not one question that all interpreters are trying to answer, not one aim that they are all pursuing. Some seek to identify the artist's intention in creating the work. Some look for what the artist could have intended, where this allows for a number of different possibilities.[4] Others aim to discover what the artist does—for example, what atti-

---

4. Among the aims that fall under a search for what the artist could mean or intend are various versions of hypothetical intentionalism and conventionalism. On the former approach, we try to determine an intention that some audience (intended, original, ideal) would hypothe-

tudes get expressed—quite apart from, often in spite of, the artist's intention. (For example, Brenda Webster claims that "Blake's rhetoric often serves as a cloak or defense that distracts the reader, and Blake himself, from seeing the aggressive or selfish nature of the sexual fantasies he is portraying.")[5] Some may seek merely a way of making sense of a work, a way it can be taken, where this may or may not be something the artist could have intended. While this is quite rare among academic critics if only because more is professionally expected of them, it is, I suspect, much more common among lay interpreters, nonprofessional appreciators of the arts, and understandable given the constraints of time and a limited knowledge of many works encountered. What is not rare among professional critics is attempting to find a way of understanding a work against the background of a set of large, culturally significant ideas, myths or archetypes, or theories. (According to David Simpson, "Of all the major poets I know Blake is, along with Smart . . . and Joyce, . . . the most open to analysis in terms set out by Derrida.")[6] Some aims are instrumental. One such is to make a work relevant or significant to a certain sort of audience, to identify what is cognitively valuable in a work or to enhance the reader's aesthetic experience of a work. (In pursuing at least the first two of these instrumental aims, Laura Haigwood offers an interpretation of "Visions of the Daughters of Albion" and a criticism of earlier interpretations in part to show that "feminist criticism which reads feminine characters primarily as victims may unintentionally . . . reinforce assumptions which support the very oppression it opposes. My more general political motive for making such a point is to find new ways of empowering women readers by contributing to the refinement and

---

size as the artist's based on some weighting of epistemic and aesthetic considerations. Defenders of this view are Gregory Currie, "Interpretation and Objectivity," *Mind* 102 (1993): 413–28; Jerrold Levinson, "Intention and Interpretation in Literature," in *The Pleasures of Aesthetics* (Ithaca, N.Y.: Cornell University Press, 1996), 175–213; Alexander Nehamas, "The Postulated Author: Critical Monism as a Regulative Ideal," *Critical Inquiry* 8 (1981): 133–49; and William Tolhurst, "On What a Text Is and How It Means," *British Journal of Aesthetics* 19 (1979): 3–14. On a conventionalist approach, we try to determine what intentions are compatible with the artwork against a background on conventions in place when the work is created. A defender of this view is Stephen Davies, *Definitions of Art* (Ithaca, N.Y.: Cornell University Press, 1991). These two approaches do not exhaust the possible ways of approaching what an artist *could* have meant.

5. Brenda Webster, "Blake, Women, and Sexuality," in *William Blake,* ed. David Punter (New York: St. Martin's Press, 1996), 189. The references here and below to recent Blake criticism are motivated by an interest in finding out what aims are actually being pursued with respect to a poet and a body of earlier criticism with which I have some familiarity.

6. David Simpson, "Reading Blake and Derrida: Our Ceasars Neither Praised nor Buried," in *William Blake,* ed. Punter, 151.

clarification of our 'visions' of ourselves and of the internal and external sources of oppression.")[7]

(b) Interpretations should be evaluated according to their aim. It would be foolish to criticize Brenda Webster's interpretation of the attitudes expressed in Blake's poetry either because the attitudes she identifies are not ones that Blake intended to convey or because her interpretation does not maximize the aesthetic experience of the poetry. Her interpretation should be evaluated for its truth and for the light it sheds on Blake's work, and her claims might receive positive evaluation on both counts independently of Blake's intentions and the maximization of aesthetic experience, though not without having a bearing of some kind on the artistic appreciation of the poems.

(c) It follows from what has already been said that some interpretations require evaluation for their truth, consisting as they do of truth claims. Already cited is Webster's interpretation claiming that Blake expresses certain attitudes in his poems. Similarly, interpretations claiming that Blake intended to do or say certain things in his poems or (more interestingly, perhaps) that he intentionally did or said those things require this kind of evaluation. On the other hand, the situation is less clear with interpretations concerned with instrumental aims. They seem to claim at least that a work can be taken in a certain way (relative to some interpretive constraints, including perhaps a limited set of agreed-upon facts about the work) and that doing so will have certain benefits. But they can be construed as offering such a way of taking for our contemplation, without asserting that it holds, and then commending the benefits of so doing, in which case the only issue that is truth-evaluable is whether entertaining the interpretive proposal has the touted benefits. I'm inclined to think that most interpretations make at least weak claims (e.g., that a work could mean p, or can be taken as meaning p), but I want to leave open the possibility that some interpretations are neither asserted nor true or false.

(d) Among the interpretations that are truth evaluable are those that aim at a historically accurate statement of the things the artist does in creating a work that are artistically significant. When I speak of what the author does, I have in mind an open-ended list of acts that centrally include such things as saying, representing, expressing, presenting, alluding to, allegorizing, and so on. When I speak of a historically accurate statement of these

7. Laura Haigwood, "Blake's *Visions of the Daughters of Albion:* Revising an Interpretive Tradition," in *William Blake,* ed. Punter, 105.

things, I mean an identification of those doings that occur in virtue of the intention of the artist, conventions or traditions in place at the time of creation and that bear on the work, and any other relevant meaning-creating historical conditions. Much of what I have in mind here is covered by what the artist intentionally does in creating the work, but some of what the artist does, such as express certain attitudes, may be done unintentionally. What is not included here are things the artist does in virtue of circumstances that arise after the work is completed, even long after the artist is dead. Among these would be acts that make possible anachronistic interpretations, such as Blake's use of the phrase "dark satanic mills" in the poetic preface to the poem "Milton," which enabled later readers to understand this as a reference to the textile mills of the industrial revolution.

(e) Since the historically accurate statement mentioned above has many aspects, interpreters whose aims fall within the broad boundaries of this project may not see themselves as working toward a common goal. Nevertheless, just as there is one, possibly complex truth about what explains Jim's behavior, there is one, certainly complex truth about what the artist does in a work in virtue of his intentions and historical context. There may be disagreement about what this is, and this may or may not be settleable on the basis of available evidence, but these are epistemic matters that do not bear on the main contention. Hence ideally there should be a single correct comprehensive statement of what the artist does in a work (in the relevant sense).[8] I have argued elsewhere that we should distinguish this particular identification of the meaning of an artwork from identification of meanings it could have or can be taken as having and various significances that might be found in it by certain audiences.[9] For present purposes, however it is not necessary to insist on this claim.

(f) It is also true that we can conjoin (or disjoin) any truths, including any true interpretations, no matter how distinct their aims are. This would create some sort of fabric of interpretive truth, but one that does not represent a coherent project, and hence the point of attempting this is dubious. Further, there is no particular reason to suppose the number of true inter-

8. Unless such an interpretation cannot be expressed in a finite set of statements, in which case there would only be more and more comprehensive interpretations of what the artist does in the relevant sense.

9. In *Artworks,* 156–85. Jerrold Levinson, though he defends a somewhat different conception of work meaning, has come to a similar conclusion about the possibility of combining interpretations identifying the meaning of a work into a single comprehensive interpretation; see his "Two Notions of Interpretation," in *Interpretation and Its Boundaries,* ed. Arto Haapala and Ossi Naukarinnen (Helsinki: Helsinki University Press, 1999), 8–27.

pretations is finite (though, of course, the number that have been produced at any specific time is finite). Hence there is no reason to think that we would, by conjoining true interpretations, produce a single correct comprehensive interpretation of a work, if comprehensiveness consists in containing all the interpretive truth about the work.

(g) Ignoring the dubious project just mentioned in (f), there is no reason to think, even if all interpretations are truth evaluable, that they must all sensibly combine into a single correct comprehensive interpretation. The many ways of taking works for the sake of the many different interpretive aims that critics (amateur and professional) bring to the task of understanding and appreciation guarantee a plurality of acceptable interpretations for just about any work. This does not mean these interpretations are strictly logically incompatible, as is often claimed, but only that the aims of interpretation do not include one of combining all these disparate interpretations into a single many-headed monster.[10]

We can now see why it is inevitable that such a variety of interpretations are put forward in the case of artworks and why their variety invites such dispute. As long as we are individually and institutionally inclined to embody in our interpretive aims the many different interests we have in artworks, plurality is inevitable and acceptable. However, this does not prevent individual interpretations from being truth evaluable, which in turn quite sensibly renders them critically controversial. The theory proposed here still leaves unexplained some previously mentioned attitudes toward the interpretation of artworks. For example, it does not explain the widespread skepticism about the possibility of objectively correct interpretations. An explanation of this skepticism likely will not be found in a good theory of interpretation. One has to look elsewhere, in more cultural quarters, but this would be the subject of a different paper.

II. The Object of Interpretation: Work or "Text"

I shall take it for granted here that a defining feature of artworks is that they are objects (in a broad sense) that are produced in a particular historical context by some particular artist or artists. For at least some types of

---

10. This is a departure from views I have previously expressed. I was, in the past, more sympathetic to the monster just condemned. See *Artworks*, 149.

artworks, such as literary and musical works, this means that a defining feature of such works is a relation that holds between artist and historical context on the one hand and a structural type on the other. In the case of literary works, this type is the text. In the case of musical works, it is a "sound structure" as would be indicated by a score (in cases where the work is scored). (There are different ways of construing both text and sound structure. For example, a text can be conceived as a purely syntactic entity or one having semantic properties.) I know that this assumption is tendentious, but that does not really matter. It permits me to raise the issue whether the following three propositions are logically consistent: 1. Contextual variables, that is, authorship and historical context, are essential to a work's identity. 2. There is a single correct comprehensive interpretation of the work, which identifies what the artist does in the work, though this is usually set out in a number of less comprehensive interpretations (interpretation set A). 3. There are other acceptable interpretations *of the work* (interpretation set B) that are not combinable with interpretations in set A or with each other.

Here is an argument for the logical inconsistency of 1–3.

4. To the extent that contextual variables enter into the individuation of a work, only interpretations that respect all of these variables are acceptable interpretations of the work.
5. Only interpretations in set A respect all of these variables.
6. No interpretation in set B is in set A.
7. Therefore, interpretations in set B are not acceptable interpretations of the work.

It follows that interpretations in set B either are not acceptable interpretations at all or are acceptable interpretations of something other than the work, such as the text, in the case of literary works, or the sound structure, in the case of musical works.[11]

In evaluating this argument, we have to consider whether the premises are true. Premise 6 is true in virtue of the way we have defined the interpretation sets, but I doubt that both 4 and 5 are true. A lot depends on how we are to understand the vague idea of respecting "contextual variables," that is, essential facts about the origin of a work. Our evaluation of the

11. Propositions 4–7 represent an attempt to reconstruct an argument proposed by David Davies in "Interpretive Pluralism and the Ontology of Art," *Revue Internationale de Philosophie* 50 (1996): 577–92.

premises also depends on whether interpretations have to be true to be acceptable. If an interpretation can be acceptable but untrue, it is very unclear why it has to be consistent with some particular set of facts, even facts essential to identifying the works. Such inconsistency can only serve to make interpretations untrue, but not necessarily unacceptable. To put the argument in the best light, let's assume truth and acceptability go hand in hand.

Respect for contextual variables should entail consistency between them and one's interpretation. This is not a difficult condition to meet as long as care is taken about what one's interpretation asserts. If what it asserts is that a work *can be taken* in a certain way, or that it *could* mean so and so, then it can be consistent with contextual variables that imply the work *does* mean something quite different. So Blake's preface to the poem "Milton" can be taken as containing a reference to textile mills, even if facts about the origin of the poem imply that it doesn't contain one.

It may be objected that, if, as we have been assuming, the contextual variables determine the very identity of the work, then a work not only doesn't but couldn't mean something incompatible with these variables, since any work that did so mean wouldn't be the work in question. The legitimate point here is that there is *a sense* of "could" (which philosophers sometimes call the metaphysical sense) in which a work not only doesn't but couldn't mean things incompatible with the relevant originary facts about the work. Specifically, there is no possible world in which the work *does* mean those things. However, there are other senses of "could" that do not have this implication, and it is quite possible that what critics are asserting when making interpretive statements relies on one of these other senses. For example, it would make perfect sense to say, when one first hears of Jim's insomniac behavior, that it could be a symptom of psychosis. One thing we could mean is simply that, relative to our evidence or what we currently know, this is a possibility. Call this the epistemic sense of "could." Certainly it would be reasonable for critics (both amateur and professional) to use this sense, since critics quite commonly work with evidence that is incomplete. There is also what might be called a pragmatic sense of "could," where we assert that a work could mean one thing if we ignore or bracket off some other thing we do know about it for the purpose of pursuing a particular interpretive aim. Here, we intentionally bracket off certain facts about the work, even if we know they are essential to identifying the work, for certain interpretative purposes. So, for example, we may know a work has an essentially polemical aspect, but may want to bracket it off to see if we can find a more general significance in it.

So, if respect for contextual variables requires only that our interpretation be consistent with them, then premise 5 is false. Interpretations in set B also respect contextual variables if formulated with sufficient care or, alternatively, if taken in the right spirit.

Of course, something stronger can be intended by the requirement that we respect the contextual variables. One possibility would be to stipulate that only interpretations that make reference to *all* of them, or use all of them in their formulation, respect the variables. This stipulation would certainly exclude interpretations in set B from those that respect the contextual variables. But it would also exclude many, if not all, the individual members of set A, since it is unlikely that any would make reference to all contextual variables. So 5 would still be false, not for wrongly excluding interpretations in set B, but for wrongly including individual members of set A. This point could be circumvented by claiming that there is "really" only one interpretation in set A, the single true comprehensive statement of what the artist does in the work, and this interpretation does respect all the contextual variables in the current sense of "respect." Seemingly less comprehensive interpretations should be seen as really being part of the comprehensive interpretation.

However, there is another problem with the argument understood as requiring that an acceptable interpretation make reference to all the contextual variables essential to the work's identity. This is simply that this is not a reasonable requirement on *acceptable* interpretations. Nothing like such a requirement is recognized in any community of critics (amateur or professional). Nor is such a requirement reasonable, since it would imply that individual critics virtually never offer acceptable interpretations of a work. Hence, if we understand "respect" according to the current suggestion, premise 4 is almost certainly false. It would not quite be legitimate to conclude that the argument under consideration is unsound, since there might be a sense of "respect" that is both reasonable and according to which the premises are true. We can conclude, though, that it looks unlikely that there is such a sense, because we can see, emerging from the stated objections to the premises, a general dilemma that the argument faces. The dilemma is that, when the understanding of "respect" is reasonable (so that premise 4 is true), it fails to exclude interpretations in set B (so that premise 5 is false), and when it excludes those interpretations, it does so only at the cost of requiring an unreasonable understanding of "respect" (rendering premise 4 false). Hence, though we haven't demonstrated it, we have good reason to think the argument is unsound. Hence, also, we lack a good reason to think 1–3 is inconsistent.[12]

It should be added that I am not arguing that a structural type such as a text is never an object of interpretation. Structural types do exist, even if they should not be identified with works, and it might come about that one such turns out to be what a critic is interpreting. This could happen in more than one way. A sophisticated critic may prefer to consider how a structural type could be taken over what a work means. This may be so because such a critic may enjoy a sense of greater freedom in discerning what meanings could attach to a given structure. Alternatively, a critic might be operating under the false belief that the work is the text, in which case the most charitable way of understanding what such a critic is doing is that he or she is interpreting the text. Furthermore, it may be difficult to distinguish some interpretations of works that belong in interpretation set B from some interpretations of texts or other structural types, unless one can become clear about what the critic is aiming at.

III. Is the Meaning of a Work Constructed?

Let's stipulate that the meaning of a work is the significant artistic properties of a work that are at its core, that is, the properties we would have to take in to have a full appreciation of the work at a given time. In the somewhat technical sense of "constructed" intended here, an artwork is constructed if events that occur, or contexts, conventions, or traditions that arise, or objects that come into existence after the work is created, either directly contribute to *the meaning* of the work or contribute to a change in the work's meaning. Such a change can either be an accretion in meaning, that is, a simple addition to the current meaning of the work, or it can be a transformation in meaning, that is, a substitution of one meaning for another. Thus, if one were to claim that changes in the meaning of the word "mill" enable it in Blake's poem now to mean factories (of a certain type), though it meant something else when the poem was created, and hence that *the meaning* of the poem has undergone a change, one would be making a

12. In "Art Interpretation" and *Artworks,* 134–38, I have argued at length for the consistency of 2 and 3. The present discussion shows that adding 1 should not create problems.

constructivist claim. (Constructivists are people who think that a work's meaning is constructed). If someone were to claim that the pervasiveness of a Freudian conception of human psychology during a period within the twentieth century enabled one during that period to construe Hamlet's behavior (in *Hamlet*) as caused by an Oedipus complex, that would also be a constructivist claim. (On the other hand, suppose Freudian psychology is true and that Shakespeare recognized its truth regarding Oedipal matters, without, of course, connecting it to Freud, and incorporated this truth into *Hamlet*. Then we could also interpret the play in terms of the protagonist's Oedipal complex, but this would *not* be a constructivist claim.)

Among the things that might bring about a change in meaning would be, on some constructivist views, an interpretation, or perhaps the wide acceptance of an interpretation. On this view, interpretation would be seen as a vehicle for meaning creation, not merely meaning discovery. Note, however, that one can be a constructivist in the sense defined here and see all interpretation as discovery. It would be discovery not of the meaning fixed at the work's creation but of meanings that arise afterward according to historically shifting variables. On this alternative constructivist view, interpretations would have to be sensitive to, for example, new contexts or conventions that impinge on and change the meaning of the work, and thereby *discover* what are these changes in meaning. A work's meaning is not constructed if it is fixed when completed by the artist.

One thing that is clearly required for constructivism in the present sense to be coherent is that the numerically identical work persist through changes in meaning. This rules out as inconsistent or uncombinable with the present conception of constructivism an alternative conception according to which interpretations or some other things coming into existence after the creation of a work create a new *object* of interpretation (somehow on the basis of the work). If one conceives of construction as the creation of a new object, one not only cannot think of it as changing the meaning of the original work, but one cannot even think of such a construction as an interpretation of the original work. If a new object is created, it just couldn't, short of commitment to the truth of a contradiction, be the original work.[13]

---

13. Various versions of constructivism are sympathetically discussed, though not defended outright, in Michael Krausz, *Rightness and Reasons: Interpretation in Cultural Practices* (Ithaca, N.Y.: Cornell University Press, 1993). Constructivism of one sort or another is defended in Graham McFee, "The Historicity of Art," *Journal of Aesthetics and Art Criticism* 28 (1980): 302–24; idem, "The Historical Character of Art: A Reappraisal," *British Journal of Aesthetics* 35 (1995): 307–19; Joseph Margolis, "Reinterpreting Interpretation," *Journal of Aesthetics and Art Criticism* 47 (1989): 237–51; idem, *Interpretation Radical but Not Unruly: The New*

Given that, on the conception in force here, construction does not create a new object of interpretation, though it may create a change in meaning, what might be the identity conditions of an artwork if constructivism is correct? There is not one set of identity conditions required by constructivism, and the two proposals considered below are not intended to be exhaustive. Although it may seem paradoxical, it would be perfectly coherent for a constructivist to accept the historicist identity conditions very roughly stated in the previous section. That is, a work could be identified with an object (material object or structural type) "produced" by an individual or individuals in a certain context. Origin would fix the identity of the work, and changes in meaning would be contingent, though not unimportant, facts about it. Identity and meaning would be two different things not essentially related. An alternative constructivist view would be that meaning is essential to the identity of a work. This does not imply that one gets a new work with each change in meaning. Rather, it would require that only something that goes through *that* exact sequence of meanings could (in the metaphysical sense) be that work. If there were a work just like Van Gogh's *Potato Eaters* except that it had a slightly different meaning than the actual painting for a period of ten years (say from 1950–60), it would be a different work, on this view. Whereas, if origin fixes identity, we would have the same work.

Is constructivism as defined here consistent with the theory of interpretation outlined in the first part of this paper? The answer to this question is yes. The main reason this is so is that the constituent parts of the theory, (a)–(g), make no commitment concerning what constitutes the full meaning of a work. The theory mentions a number of different interpretive aims, and claims made by way of achieving those aims. It points out that many different such claims can be acceptable and even true if what is asserted is carefully formulated or taken in the right spirit (as if it were so formulated). Furthermore, it asserts that while some interpretations focus on what the artist does within the context of creation, other acceptable interpretations focus on the work in relation to other things, including later contexts into which it enters. Lest this be confused with the constructivism just outlined, remember this latter view claims that such interpretations discover, if not

Puzzle of the Arts and History (Berkeley and Los Angeles: University of California Press, 1995); Philip Percival, "Stecker's Dilemma: A Constructive Response," *Journal of Aesthetics and Art Criticism* (forthcoming); Richard Shusterman, *Pragmatist Aesthetics* (Oxford: Basil Blackwell, 1992); and Anita Silvers, "Politics and the Production of Narrative Identities," *Philosophy and Literature* 14 (1990): 99–107.

create, changes in the meaning of the work, whereas the theory I have endorsed here is officially neutral about that. Not every acceptable interpretation, on this theory, identifies part of the work's meaning, and no commitment has been made about which interpretations accomplish this.

Unlike some versions of constructivism I have discussed elsewhere,[14] the version in question here is perfectly coherent and consistent with our proposed account of interpretation. Furthermore, there do seem to be "objects" that change their meaning in the fashion predicted by this kind of view. The words of a language are objects of this type. They undergo changes in meaning—both accretions and transformations—of precisely the sort we have been discussing, and do so as a result of historical contingencies.

Are artworks, like words, objects whose meaning is constructed? As I indicated earlier, I have advanced an alternative view according to which the meaning of a work is identified with what the artist does that is artistically significant in virtue of his or her intentions and the context of creation. Call this traditional historicism, to give a name to this alternative to constructivism.[15] There are acceptable interpretations that do not do this, but, in my view, they aim not at identifying a work's meaning but at other things. There is no single overarching aim that all interpretations share.

I don't think there is an obvious right way to conceive the referent of "the meaning of a work," or anything like a general demonstration that a particular conception of this referent is the correct one. In favor, at least initially, of the traditional historicism is an attractive conception of work meaning as a species of utterance meaning.[16] The meaning of an utterance of a natural-language sentence is normally fixed by the semantics of the sentence and contextual and intentional features existing on the occasion the utterance is made. Thus, "I shall return" could be an expression of intention (and could be only if there is an intention to be expressed) and, if so, could more particularly be a threat or a promise. It could express a prediction. It could express a hope or fear, a premonition, a recurring anxi-

14. See Stecker, "The Constuctivist's Dilemma," and idem, "Pragmatism and Interpretation," *Poetics Today* 14 (1993): 193–206.

15. I borrow this term from Jerrold Levinson, who for the most part also endorses a traditional historicist view of work meaning. See his "Artworks and the Future," in *Music, Art, and Metaphysics* (Ithaca, N.Y.: Cornell University Press, 1990), 179–214. Stephen Davies has discussed the pros and cons of traditional versus constructivist historicism in "Interpreting Contextualities," *Philosophy and Literature* 20 (1996).

16. For more elaborate arguments defending the utterance model of work meaning, see Levinson, "Intention and Interpretation in Literature," 176–87; Tolhurst, "On What a Text Is"; and *Artworks*, 166–79.

ety. It could implicitly refer to a place or to something else. The meaning of the sentence tells us nothing about which specification is the right one for some particular utterance of that sentence. The right specification is in some way a function of speaker's intention and context of utterance on the occasion of utterance. Later events don't seem to change the meaning of an utterance, though they affect its truth and significance. McArthur's return to the Philippines did not change the meaning of his utterance of "I shall return" when he retreated from those islands, though it proved his words true (if they expressed a prediction) and gave them significance.[17]

A constructivist could counter this either by arguing that the meaning of an utterance can change or by arguing that utterance meaning is the wrong model for work meaning. In either case, an argument is most likely to begin with purported examples of meaning change.

IV. Percival's Examples

Let us begin with some examples from outside the arts.[18] Consider Bob's sign, a piece of board on which is inscribed the words "Back in five min-

17. In Chapter 15 of this volume, "Appreciation and Literary Interpretation," Peter Lamarque criticizes the utterance model. His criticism is blunted, however, by the fact that he takes utterance meaning to be something like sentence meaning, a view that all proponents of the utterance model would reject. Consider the following remark, directed against the utterance model: "These features [of *Moll Flanders*]—the 'pattern of theft,' the 'contradictions,' the 'double vision' of the heroine—are not properties of the linguistic *text* inherent in the language" (page 000, author's italics; see page 000 and note 20 for similar claims). It is precisely the point of those who endorse the utterance model that these properties of the novel are not properties of the linguistic text but properties that result from Defoe's *use* of the text to make the particular literary utterance that he does.

Contrary to what Lamarque claims, his excellent examples of critical writing about literature fit the utterance model very well, in fact better than his alternative idea that interpretations aim at an appreciative experience. Consider just one more example. J. Hillis Miller describes Dickens's *Our Mutual Friend* as a "drama of looks and faces" and a "conflict of masks" in which each character tries to hide his own secret and probe that of another character. In describing Dickens's novel in this way, Miller is aiming to point out an important theme about the nature of personal relations in the society that the work depicts, and one of the ways that theme is conveyed. It is no doubt true that Miller hopes that his interpretation will enable the reader to better appreciate the novel, but how is this appreciation brought about? Clearly it is by showing the reader something that Dickens does in the novel and that the reader may not otherwise notice. In other words, it is by enabling the reader to better understand Dickens's literary utterance.

18. The examples discussed below are all found in Percival, "Stecker's Dilemma," but the example of the vase painting was first presented in my "Constructivist's Dilemma."

utes." In Bob's language, these words mean "No trespassing," and Bob uses the sign to warn trespassers to keep out of his garden. Now suppose a thousand years later Sally digs up the sign in her garden. Sally's first thought is that this sign says, "Back in five minutes," and makes plans to use it in her shop window when she has to close to run a short errand. Everything works out fine. Sally puts the sign out, and people realize that she will be back in five minutes. Has the meaning of the sign changed?

If a sign should be understood on the model of an utterance, the meaning of the original sign did not change after Sally discovered the board in her garden or at any later time. Rather, Sally took the board and rendered it a sign that she would be back in five minutes by intending that it would be so used and placing it in a context where this intention was understood. Bob used the same board to make a different utterance. The fact that Sally's sign and Bob's sign made use of the same board with the same shapes inscribed on it should not mislead us into thinking that there is just one sign. There is one board, but two signs.

Notice that for Sally to transform the board into a sign that suits her purpose, she does not have to mistake it as having always indicated that someone would be back in five minutes. She could be an amateur archaeologist and know that the board was originally a no-trespassing sign. Perhaps hundreds of such signs have already been discovered in her area. So this sign has little archaeological value, but it could save Sally the cost of making a new sign.

Do we have to take a sign on the model of an utterance? I suppose not. We could take it as a semantic tool. A tool is an artifact made to fulfill one or more specific functions but that can acquire new functions in use. (There is more to a tool than this, but it won't affect what is said here.) I assume that the screwdriver was invented to turn screws, but people have discovered that it is also quite good for prying things open. It's fine to say that prying things open is a function of screwdrivers even if this was not intended when the tool was invented. Screwdrivers may cease to turn screws (because screws go out of use) but continue to exist to pry things open. If a sign is a semantic tool, it can acquire new semantic functions and still be the same sign. (Of course, a sign, like virtually anything that has a material embodiment, can acquire nonsemantic functions as well.)

Next consider an idol, a piece of carved wood intended to stand in for the god Nur. It fulfills this function for several hundred years. Eventually, though, it becomes lost in a region where the god Artifa is worshiped. Rediscovered, it comes to stand in for the god Artifa for several hundred years.

Perhaps it is intentionally put forward as an idol of Artifa by a particular individual. Alternatively, perhaps it is generally misconstrued as having been made to serve this function, and its treatment as such eventually establishes a social convention to use it so. Finally, it might be known that it was intended to be an idol of Nur, but the pragmatic tribal members decide it would be a handy stand-in for Artifa. It's a fact that one carved figure stands in for the god Nur for several hundred years and later stands in for the god Artifa for several hundred years. There is one carved figure. But is there one idol or two? I would be inclined to say two, just as I was inclined to say there were two signs. But I'm fully cognizant that there is no obvious right answer, and perhaps no fact of the matter.

Now consider an imaginary painting, a pictorial work of art. The painting resembles the faces/vase ambiguous figure but in fact, since it was painted in a land that forbids the representation of the human face, was intended simply as a representation of a vase. So it was understood when it was initially exhibited in the land. However, the painting is moved to a conquered region whose people relish the representation of the human body. They see faces as well as a vase, and a rumor begins that this is a subversive painting cleverly representing human faces under the guise of being a vase picture. This becomes established in the local art history, and generations in the conquered land take the painting this way, long after independence is regained.

I believe the proper way to understand the situation with the painting is clearer than in the previous two cases. A work of art does not change its meaning either on the basis of "innocent" miscontrual or the fact that a new way of taking it is "handy." Sometimes the artist who created a painting is misidentified. For example, some paintings attributed to Rembrandt were actually done by lesser members of his school. When these attributions are corrected, it is not uncommon for our understanding and evaluation of the painting to change, even if an earlier understanding is well established in art history. The discovery that the vase painting was neither intended nor received (by its original audience) as an ambiguous and subversive figure, and that the contrary view was based on a false rumor, would require a similar art-historical and critical reevaluation.[19] It's plausible to conclude that un-

19. An interestingly different example is provided by A. E. Housman's poem "1887 written on the occasion of Queen Victoria's Golden Jubilee." Here the poet's *expressed* intention was that the poem be simply patriotic with no irony, but from the moment of publication it was often read as ironic. Such a case is intrinsically less clear, even from an intentionalist point of view, because the total evidence about the poet's intention does not point in a single direction.

derstandings of a work based on misconstrual are given up no matter how well established, once the misconstrual is uncovered and even if the misconstrual is based on something other than mistaken authorship, unless other grounds are found for them. Further, if misconstruals are not uncovered, they will not be genuine agents of meaning change. In a similar vein, we don't believe poems change their meaning when a word used in the poem acquires a new meaning and it is handy to interpret the poem according to this new meaning. The relevant meaning of the word is the one that it had (assuming it had only one) when the poem was written.

If the above is correct, then, when we are dealing with artworks, we don't face the uncertain choice we needed to make in the examples concerning signs and idols. With artworks, when there are socially enshrined misconstruals or reconstruals (based on pragmatic considerations of "handiness"), we need say *neither* that a work has changed its meaning *nor* that a second work has come into existence. Rather, we should say that the work means one thing but is being taken in another way, for reasons that may or may not be legitimate.

This is not to say that we have established that neither of the choices we faced in the earlier nonart examples would ever confront us when considering artworks. Had Robert Rauschenberg put forward a sequel to his *Erased de Kooning Drawing*, 1953, called *Unerased de Kooning,* it is plausible that he would have transformed artwork by de Kooning with one content into a distinct artwork by Rauschenberg with a different content. Perhaps there can also be examples of meaning change within the history of a single artwork. A more plausible avenue to explore might be cases where later events amplify original meaning rather than obliterate it in virtue of misconstrual or pragmatically motivated reconstrual.

V. Levinson's Examples

Jerrold Levinson is, in general, more of an opponent than a friend of constructivism.[20] He is also one who endorses an utterance model of work meaning. However, for a limited class of cases, he defends the existence of meaning change in artworks or at least meaning amplification. These are

20. The examples that follow are taken from "Work and Oeuvre," in *The Pleasures of Aesthetics*, 242–73.

cases where, purportedly, what we discover in later works within the oeuvre of an artist changes the meaning of an earlier work of that artist. That someone of Levinson's temperament reaches this conclusion might seem to lend extra support to a limited constructivism, since it is tempting to suppose that the weight of evidence must have broken through a tendency to believe the contrary. But, of course, the evidence has to be evaluated on its merits.

Levinson's view is that two conditions have to be met for meaning change to occur. Condition 1 is that the earlier and later works be properly seen as products (or parts) of a single extended artistic act. Condition 2 is that the later part of this act (the later work or its creation) change what is most reasonably construed as the intention with which the earlier work was made. These two conditions, to be properly appreciated, need to be seen against the background of Levinson's theory of work meaning. His view (hypothetical intentionalism) is that the core meaning of a work, its utterance meaning, is the intention most reasonably ascribed to it by an ideal audience. Notice that the conditions on meaning change are tied to his hypothetical intentionalism. Otherwise, the fact that it is most reasonable to attribute one intention at one time, and a different intention at a later time, does not indicate a change of meaning. It could merely indicate that a meaning already fixed at the earlier time is better *understood* at the later time.

Notice also that if hypothetical intentionalism were keyed to actual audiences, it would invite quite radical changes in meaning, unless we chose a single privileged actual audience. This is because actual audience members would be in varying epistemic situations regarding which intention each of them would most reasonably attribute to the creator of a work. This would vary not only between individual and individual but between one generation and another, given the different facts that would be available to each as well as the differing conceptual and theoretical orientations of each. However, one could assume that much of this variation would be smoothed out in the case of the ideal audience.[21] Nevertheless, even an ideal audience would necessarily have to come to different conclusions at different stages of the artistic act, unless we could implausibly attribute to it knowledge of the future. Alternatively, we might say the meaning of the work is not fixed (an ideal audience is not in a position to judge) until the artist's most extended artistic act is complete. If we go this route, we could not say that the meaning of a work changes over time, but we would still say that the meaning of

21. Not that there is a simple or obvious way of choosing a single ideal audience. For a discussion of the problems, see *Artworks*, 197–202.

a work is determined by things that occur well after the work is completed. I take it this would be in the spirit, if not the letter, of constructivism.

Could there be other events, *not* part of the creative act, that occur after the work is completed and alter which intention can most reasonably be ascribed (in effect contradicting the first condition for meaning change)? This question I postpone until after we have examined examples of oeuvre-related meaning change.

The first example concerns Mahler's Third and Fourth Symphonies. Here it seems quite plausible that the first condition is met, that is, that the creation of these musical works can be considered part of a single extended artistic act. This has to do with the special circumstances of composition of the symphonies, which were closely intertwined. It is much more doubtful that the crucial second condition is met, that is, that knowledge of the second work changes the meaning of the first. Exactly how this happens turns out to be "very difficult to say. . . . Perhaps, when we have them both, then knowing that redemption comes in the succeeding symphony retrospectively frames the despair of the preceding one, tempering its sting."[22] Perhaps, but this conclusion is so subjective that we should question whether it qualifies as a filling-out of meaning rather than one possible way of taking the Third Symphony. We can equally well take this work as just different in emotional tone than the Fourth and note with interest that this is so despite similarities in other musical respects.

I take this problem with the Mahler example to carry over to Levinson's other examples as well, though I will confine the discussion to just one of these. Levinson suggests that after looking at Mondrian's pure abstractions of 1917, "perhaps" we can see in the already highly abstract landscapes of 1914 and 1915 a teleological content of striving to isolate the structural essence of the visible world. One might see that, but one might also claim that one sees a more inchoate or ambivalent intention in the earlier paintings, or, yet again, one might claim that those earlier works are sufficiently abstract that, when combined with some knowledge of Mondrian's sensibility, one can discover the striving without the help of the later paintings. The matter is too indeterminate, the choices too subjective, to make a strong case for the claim that the later works alter or complete the meaning of the earlier ones.

However, another point about the Mondrian example that needs to be made is that, in this case, we don't have the same convincing evidence that

22. Levinson, *The Pleasures of Aesthetics,* 254–55.

the first condition is met. The Mahler case is based on an appeal to biographical information about the circumstances of composition. Nothing like this is offered for the Mondrian case. Rather, we have similarities of form or structure in the paintings being compared. Since inclusion in the same oeuvre is not sufficient to establish a single artistic act, it is not clear that such similarities are sufficient either. The idea that there is such an extended act is unclear in these, if not in all, cases. This is because of the speculative or subjective character of various ways of taking the connection between the two works.

None of this shows that the sort of meaning change contemplated in these examples could never occur. Perhaps the best place to look for such an occurrence would be in works that are explicitly connected, such as a trilogy of novels. But the failure of the examples examined raises the question why clear cases are not easier to come by.

Light can be shed on this by returning to the question, postponed above, whether condition 2 can hold without condition 1 and whether the fact that it can would provide a hypothetical intentionalist sufficient ground on which to claim that work meaning has been altered or completed. One example that has been proposed in support of this possibility is the case in which critics are only able to discern a core artistic property of a work in the light of the preeminence of that property in the work of later writers. Thus it has been claimed that the Kafkaesque aspect of earlier writers could only be properly understood in the light of the work of Kafka, or that the artistic purpose of the dense and abstruse aspects of Melville's later prose could only be understood in the light of early-twentieth-century writing.[23] Of course, no one is claiming that we should see the earlier and the later writers as participating in a single artistic act, but it is being claimed that the intention most reasonably attributed to the earlier writer changes with the advent of the later one(s). Doesn't that suffice, from a hypothetical-intentionalist viewpoint, to indicate a change in meaning?

The right thing to say about these cases is that, insofar as we are talking about core aspects of the meaning of the earlier works and not merely ways of taking them or the significance they come to have for later generations or the greater appreciation of their artistic properties in virtue of this signifi-

23. Mcfee, "The Historicity of Art," uses the Kafkaesque example. Silvers, "Politics and the Production of Narrative Identities," uses the Melville example. Levinson attempts to reply to the latter by claiming that what has changed is the evaluation of Melville's later prose, not the understanding of its meaning. But this seems wrong because what came to be appreciated was the point of the convolutions, which is a matter of literary meaning.

cance, their meaning was and is always there, and the later works only help us to see it. But how can a hypothetical intentionalist say this? Only by giving ideal audiences the ability to discover such meaning without knowledge of the later works. Such a claim might not be implausible, because it seems to be contingencies that make actual audiences blind to meaning.

These considerations create a very narrow hoop through which a defender of intra-oeuvral meaning change would have to jump. One would have to identify a core aspect of a work's meaning, not merely an optional way of taking it, a significance it has, or a greater appreciation of the work based on one or the other of these, and further, it would have to be an aspect of meaning necessarily unavailable to an ideal critic (audience) absent knowledge of the artist's later work. We haven't shown that this condition could not be met, but we haven't seen it met. We haven't seen, by the way, that it could not be met in the inter-oeuvral case either. What we do know is that it won't be easy to meet it.

VI. Conclusion

In this paper I have sketched a theory of interpretation. I have argued that it is compatible with many theories about the object of interpretation and the meaning of a work. It is compatible with the work's always being the object of interpretation, but also with the text's (structural type's) sometimes being the object. It is compatible with many views about a work's meaning, including both constructivism and traditional historicism. This does not mean that all these views are equally plausible. Even very modest versions of constructivism, in particular, are hard to defend, but I have not argued that they are false.

Can Novel Critical Interpretations Create Art Objects Distinct from Themselves?

Philip Percival

The "interpretations" at issue in the title above are (token) states of mind or (token) utterances attributing some meaning to some object: they do not include performances of artworks. An interpretation is "critical" when it is made by someone other than the agent who produced the object interpreted and attributes what I will call a "critical" meaning of the kind commonly attributed by art critics;[1] it is "novel" when the meaning it attributes has never before been attributed to that object. An interpretation literally "creates" an art object if and only if it brings into existence an object that did not exist prior to the interpretation being made, and that object is (identical to) an art object. The qualification "distinct from themselves" is included in the title to sidestep the possibility that some interpretations of art objects are themselves art objects. I use the term "object" generically for any kind of entity, not for a specific kind of entity distinct from, for example, events or properties.

A natural answer to my title's question is that (mere) critical interpretations cannot create art objects distinct from themselves. In contrast, the

I would like to thank Jim Edwards for helpful comments on an earlier draft, and the Arts and Humanities Research Board for funding research leave during which the paper was completed.

1. For the moment, I leave which kinds of meaning are "critical" unspecified. I explain and discuss my reasons for so doing shortly (section 1.i).

somewhat iconoclastic answer given by "radical constructivism" is that novel critical interpretations of art objects, at least when they are "apt," *always* create art objects distinct from themselves.[2] Though I argue that radical constructivism is false, I find in it no incoherence of a kind that would force the "natural" answer to my title's question upon us. Indeed, I hold that answer false too.

I. The Structure of Radical Constructivism

I.i The best way to appreciate the motivation for, and nature of, radical constructivism is to approach it via Bob Stecker's (1997) critique. Though he "quickly reject[s]" the doctrine, his grounds for so doing are not perspicuous. Stecker (1997, 43) characterizes radical constructivism as the view that "every new interpretation creates a new work, even if each starts out from the same 'text.' " His next sentence elaborates this view: "On this view, the only difference between an artist and a critic or an interpreter is that the artist creates a 'text' that gets made into a work by being given an interpretation, while the critic or interpreter borrows a text." Surprisingly, however, his main argument against radical constructivism, which he states immediately, seems to attack a somewhat different doctrine: "[The doctrine that] what we receive from an artist [is] essentially blank until given an interpretation [is] doubly wrong [since] no one takes what they receive from artists in this way (quite rightly), and, if they did, they would do no better with what they received from critics. . . . The buck has to stop somewhere; something has to *have* meaning rather than be given it, or the giving of meaning will not be possible." This argument is ineffective for two reasons. As characterized, "radical constructivism" need not embrace the doctrine objected to, while both objections to that doctrine are in any case unsatisfactory. To maintain that each novel interpretation of an object creates a new object is not to deny that the object interpreted has a meaning. Hence, radical constructivism can deflect the argument by repudiating the doctrine

2. Following Wolterstorff (1975), performances of artworks are "works of art," but not themselves artworks. Moreover, performances of artworks are also "interpretations" of them (in a sense different from the one I employ in this paper). Though the questions arise as to whether radical constructivism should extend its doctrine concerning artworks to works of art, and its doctrine concerning interpretations to performative interpretations, I do not consider them further.

that "what we receive from an artist [is] essentially blank until given an interpretation" and holding instead that though what we receive from an artist (typically) has meaning, each novel interpretation creates a new work (with a different meaning). Moreover, while the observation that "no one takes what they receive from artists [as blank]" is certainly inaccurate with respect to some mediums (like abstract sculpture and painting), and probably inaccurate with respect to all of them (if only because of the existence of certain constructivists), when charitably read the observation that if anything is to be given meaning, something must have it is not inconsistent with the view that "what we receive from an artist [is] essentially blank." This view is respected by the supposition that token sentences or token mental attitudes constituting (critical) interpretations possess meanings independently of interpretations (of *them*), but that artworks do not possess meanings independently of critical interpretations. And while this supposition alone is strong enough to launch the claim that novel critical interpretations create new artworks, it is not ad hoc. As Stecker himself suggests,[3] there can be no unreflective presumption that the cases of art and nonart run parallel: perhaps it is in the nature of art that in its case conditions otherwise sufficient for the meaningfulness of nonart objects are inoperative or subverted. Moreover, to adopt a different tack, a critical interpretation that attributes a meaning need not itself have the kind of meaning attributed. For example, an utterance that attributes a certain symbolic significance to a certain grouping of fruits need not itself "symbolize" anything in the same sense: that it should have a specifically linguistic meaning suffices. It cannot be simply presumed that the class of critical meanings (i.e., the meanings attributed by critical interpretations) includes specifically linguistic meanings. Understanding a language seems like a very different matter from understanding even a literary work.[4] The radical constructivist might plausibly maintain that even in the literary arts, critical interpretation *proper* only begins once the relevant linguistic meanings have been identified, its purpose being to attribute meanings of another kind—namely (where relevant), symbolizations, ironies, wider significances, morals and points, character motives, plot structures, pictorial representations, and so forth. On this conception, linguistic meanings are external to critical interpretation: they are involved in literary criticism only because in the literary arts the basis for attributions of critical meanings is mostly constituted by linguistic mean-

3. In this volume, page 161.
4. Cf. Peter Lamarque's contribution to this volume, Chapter 15.

ings. So even to admit that something must have (linguistic) meaning if any-thing is to be given (critical) meaning need not be to deny that "what we receive from an artist [is] essentially blank" *with respect to the meanings that matter.*

An even quicker, albeit implicit, objection to radical constructivism that occurs later in Stecker's (1997) paper is no more compelling. Once again, one of its presuppositions is at odds with radical constructivism as Stecker has defined it. In writing that "Krausz recognises the unacceptability of radi-cal constructivism, and so is eager to avoid the view that every interpreta-tion has its own unique object," Stecker (1997, 49) implies that radical constructivism is committed to the view that "every interpretation has its own unique object" and that this view is incorrect. Yet this commitment is very far from any commitment entered into by radical constructivism on his initial characterization. Indeed, that characterization's commitment is to the opposite view. If an artist interprets a text he has fashioned, while a critic interprets a text he has borrowed, interpretations by artist and critic alike focus, at least on occasion, on the same object (a given text). But in that case a second critic can interpret an object—the text—that is identical to the object interpreted by the first critic. Stecker's primary characterization of radical constructivism as the view that "every new interpretation creates a new work, *even if each starts out from the same text*" (my italics), appears expressly designed to admit just this possibility: it surely includes the words "even if" as much to reflect radical constructivism's view that diverse criti-cal interpretations may have a common object—the "text"—as to express the view that supposing novel critical interpretations can create new works is consistent with supposing they can have a common object. Presumably that is why Stecker immediately elaborates this characterization by saying that the radical constructivist has the critic interpreting a text (and creating a work) that the artist himself fashioned and interpreted (creating a different work). Nothing in radical constructivism on Stecker's characterization pre-vents it from holding that different work-creating critical interpretations can have the same object, and much within it commits it to maintaining that they can.

I.ii Since Stecker offers no further arguments against the doctrine, his "quick rejection" of radical constructivism is therefore premature. Nevertheless, if his treatment is to be relied upon, radical constructivism is indeed confused: for on that treatment it makes contradictory claims about the objectivity or reality of critical meaning. On the one hand, when he is attacking the doctrine, Stecker says radical constructivism holds that "what we receive from the artist is blank." This implies that it holds that nothing we receive from the artist has critical meaning. On the other hand, when he is characterizing the doctrine, he says it holds that an artist creates a work by interpreting a text he has fashioned. This surely implies that radical constructivists allow that something—the work—has critical meaning, for the supposed (critical) meaningfulness of works is one of the main motivations for the text/work distinction. Accordingly, unless Stecker's radical constructivist is trying to make more than is warranted of the notion of "what we receive"—holding that while an artist creates a (critically meaningful) work by interpreting his text, what critics receive is the (critically meaningless) text and not the work—it appears that he both says and denies that some art objects have critical meaning.

There may be nothing but confusion to this tension. But rather than attribute to radical constructivism contradictory theses, we do better to distinguish two opposing lines of thought. They have two premises in common. First, an artist creates a work via his own interpretations of something else he has fashioned, a "text." Second, there is nothing an artist does or achieves via interpretative attitudes toward his text that a subsequent critic does not do too. Call these premises "Text/Work Distinctness" and "Artist/Critic Parity" respectively. They play different roles. While Artist/Critic Parity is distinctive of constructivism per se, Text/Work Distinctness is characteristic of the radical version: without it, Artist/Critic Parity could only engender the "moderate" constructivist's view that novel critical interpretations *modify* (the properties of) existing artworks, but do not create new ones.

The argument to radical constructivism from these premises bifurcates into two lines of thought because of an uncertainty over the import of Text/Work Distinctness. The claim that an artist creates a work by interpreting his text might be glossed over: it is not *literally* the case that something comes into existence bearing critical meaning via the artist's interpretative attitudes. Alternatively, this claim might be taken literally. Being incompatible, these alternatives yield two horns of a dilemma with which radical constructivism challenges its opponents:

> *First horn:* Suppose no art objects have critical meaning. Then works—critically meaningful objects—do not *really* exist. In that case critics' interpretations are not constrained by critical meanings, and critics too can certainly be supposed to "create" works via their

interpretations in whatever nonliteral sense artists themselves "create" them.

Second horn: Suppose some art object—a work created by the artist's interpretation of a "text" he has fashioned—has critical meaning. Then, even so, since there is nothing that an artist does when interpreting his text that a critic does not do too when interpreting it, (novel) critical interpretation of something *other* than this bearer of meaning—namely, the text of the work—will create some further meaningful object (a new work).

Though the horns of this dilemma are skeletal, even so flimsy a structure is profitably imposed upon radical constructivist argumentation. In resisting it, I argue that the first horn is inapplicable—literally, that there are objects that possess critical meanings (artworks among them)—and that at best there is none but a grain of truth in the contention of the second.

II. Inapplicability of the First Horn: Realism About Critical Meanings

Intentionalism about artworks holds that a typical artwork has critical meanings determined by the artist's interpretative intentions: because the artist intends that his work should have certain critical meanings while meeting certain (other) necessary conditions—a matter that can be glossed as "successfully realizing his intentions"—he creates a work having those meanings.[5] The first horn of the dilemma just sketched holds this account to be misguided: the artist's intentions don't determine critical meaning in this way, because nothing *really* has critical meaning. It is some such error-theory or subjectivism about the critical meaning of art objects that Stecker seems to have had in mind both when he supposed that radical constructivism holds that "what we receive from an artist [is] essentially blank until given an interpretation" and when he objected that "[t]he buck has to stop somewhere; something has to *have* meaning rather than be given it, or the giving of meaning will not be possible."

---

5. "Creates" does not mean "literally creates." Intentionalism is neutral as to whether artists create their works in the literal sense.

Though I have expressed disagreement with some of Stecker's critical remarks concerning the repudiation of "realism" about meaning,[6] I agree with him to this extent: whether or not it is *incoherent* to suppose meanings are *always* conferred on their bearers by interpreters, that some physical particulars have certain meanings is a fact no less objective than is the fact that there are objects having certain masses.

The distinction I made earlier between "linguistic" meaning proper and "critical" meaning is important here. What one makes of it will depend on the details of one's philosophy of language, but the fact remains that natural languages exhibit phonetic, syntactic, and semantic rules that are altogether more constraining than are even Gricean "conversational" rules, let alone "rules" of, for example, symbolization. Accordingly, one who denies the objectivity of specifically linguistic meanings will be led to deny it of (all) critical meanings, but not necessarily vice versa. Since agents' intentional attitudes (states of mind) are commonly held to underpin such meanings, the radical constructivist can attack intentionalism at three junctures: intentional attitudes, linguistic meanings, and critical meanings.

Only three sorts of consideration might lead one to reject realism specifically about intentional attitudes and linguistic meaning. The one most prominent in literature about art interpretation turns on the attractiveness of some kind of holism about interpretation. However, even if interpretation is holistic in a way that sustains the thesis of indeterminacy of interpretation, this thesis does not ground the view under consideration. Indeterminacy of linguistic meanings (of utterances) or intentional properties (of mental states) is not absence of them: the distinction between true and false attributions of linguistic meaning or intentional properties remains. To say that an utterance or mental state is subject to indeterminacy of interpretation is merely to say that there are some apparently distinct attributions of linguistic meanings or intentional properties to it that are equally correct (relative to some scheme of interpretation). It is not to say that no interpretation of it is incorrect. Indeterminacy of interpretation is not the doctrine that anything goes (relative to some scheme of interpretation): it is the doctrine that attributions of linguistic meaning to utterances and intentional properties to mental states are not determined to uniqueness (independently of schemes of interpretation).[7]

6. Here and throughout I use the phrase "realism about Xs" to characterize the doctrine that Xs exist or that objects exist having Xs.

7. The classical sources for indeterminacy of interpretation are Quine 1960, 1970, and Davidson 1973. See Wheeler 1986 for parallels between Davidson and Derrida. See Lewis 1974 for constraints on interpretation additional to those Davidson initially proposed, and for

The two remaining considerations serve the radical constructivist no better. The first repudiates intentional attitudes en masse as fictions of an old unsuccessful theory—folk psychology—which, it is held, we can now see good reason to reject.[8] However, this contention should not persuade: until we have a theory better than folk psychology, it is a promissory note—a product of bad methodology (if not of scientism too). The second consideration mixes a kind of physicalism with a kind of conventionalism. The linguistic meaning of a physical object does not supervene on its intrinsic physical properties: for example, two physically duplicate token sentences might differ in all their semantic properties (because produced by speakers belonging to different linguistic communities). It follows that the intrinsic physical properties of an object are not, in general, individually or jointly identical to any linguistic meaning it possesses. But a physicalist might think that there are no intrinsic properties other than physical properties. Hence, on the further assumption that an object's properties are exhausted by its intrinsic properties, it would follow that no physical object has linguistic meaning. However, whether or not physicalism is correct, this consideration is also misguided. It is wrong to suppose that if some property is not among the intrinsic properties of an object, that object does not have that property. Though being the husband of Hilary is not one of Bill Clinton's intrinsic properties, it is (as I write) one of his properties nevertheless. Denying that the linguistic meanings of written signs, or the intentional attitudes of human beings, are intrinsic to them does not stop the meanings or the attitudes from being real (extrinsic) properties of them.[9] On the correct model,

the hope that those constraints are strong enough to ensure determinacy. Since the supposition that they are not strong enough to ensure it is consistent with linguistic meanings' and intentional attitudes' being determinate relative to a scheme of interpretation, indeterminacy of interpretation does not introduce a disanalogy with masses and velocities: these too are only determinate relative to a frame of reference.

8. See Churchland 1981.

9. Still less does it prevent meanings from being real properties of those nonphysical objects—for example, types of some kind—that some have thought artworks to be (see section IV below). However, it is difficult to see how an artist could identify a meaningful nonphysical object if no physical object has meaning. Note that while it is uncontroversial that a particular object's meaning does not supervene upon its intrinsic physical properties, it is less clear that none of a human being's intentional attitudes does so. To be sure, it is now generally held that many intentional attitudes do not supervene on an agent's intrinsic physical properties: a physical duplicate of myself on Twin-Earth thinks that glass A contains water while I think that glass B contains water. But this much "externalism" about intentional attitudes does not rule out a level of "content" at which a physical duplicate of myself must have *some* intentional attitudes (directed at contents of that level) in common with me. I am persuaded, for example, that a physical duplicate of myself (now, as I write) would have to be consciously having experiences as if there were *an object in front of him.*

the linguistic meanings of certain physical particulars are (or at rate supervene upon) highly complex relational properties that, like Clinton's being
married to Hilary, involve multifarious psychological and social facts (and
no doubt much else besides).

Once intentional attitudes and linguistic meanings are admitted outside
the arts, there is no reason not to admit critical meanings outside them too.
If, with respect to any indeterminacy-induced relativity to a scheme of interpretation, it is an objective fact that this morning I asked for a coffee, it is
an equally objective fact that while drinking my coffee I sketched a caricature of Bill Clinton. In the light of certain complex facts, the sounds I vocal-
ized amounted to asking for coffee. In the light of certain other complex
facts, the lines I produced on a napkin amounted to a drawing that represents Bill Clinton leering.

Upon reflection, meanings outside the arts do not rely on any convention-
ality or purpose that art objects necessarily lack or subvert. This much is
evident in the case of linguistic meanings. Whatever the complexity or the
scope of the facts in virtue of which Joyce spoke English conversationally
on occasion, facts of that ilk ensure that English is the language to which
the opening sentence of *Ulysses* belongs. It is slightly less evident in the
case of nonlinguistic critical meanings that the relevant mechanisms remain
operative in the arts. Because such meanings arise by a mechanism that is
less rule-bound than is the mechanism by which linguistic meanings arise, it
is harder to say anything so clearly correct about, for example, the point,
significance, moral, character motives, or symbolizations of *Ulysses*. But
this is immaterial: not all truths are evident. Nevertheless, clear-cut cases of
nonlinguistic critical meanings possessed by artworks are easily given (as in
section III.ii, below). Admittedly, it has been held characteristic of an artwork that it should be subject to multiple critical interpretations.[10] However, supposing this claim to be correct would not preclude the extension of
critical meanings from nonart physical particulars such as conversational
utterances to physical particulars such as the manuscript of *Ulysses* and,
hence, to artworks (such as *Ulysses* itself). There being artworks and critical
meanings such that those artworks possess those meanings (with respect to
any indeterminacy-induced relativity to scheme of interpretation) is consistent with the claim that for each artwork there are (and ought to be) critical
meanings that are incompatible but equally apt.

10. Goodman and Elgin 1988, 55.

III. Failure of the Second Horn: Against Artist/Critic Parity

III.i With respect to any slack induced by indeterminacy of interpretation, people have intentional attitudes, inscriptions and utterances have linguistic meanings, and certain entities, artworks among them, have critical meanings. When an artist successfully realizes his intentions, his activities ordinarily result in a work bearing certain critical meanings. According to the second horn of the dilemma with which radical constructivism's opponents are challenged (section I.ii), this much is grist to its mill: artist and critic are on a par, so if the artist literally creates a work via (novel) interpretative attitudes directed at his text, the critic does too.

If Artist/Critic Parity is to support radical constructivism via Text/Work Distinctness, text and work must be different objects. This fact is obscured by Stecker's claim that according to the radical constructivist "the artist creates a 'text' that gets made into a work by being given an interpretation." Indeed, on its most natural reading this claim militates against radical constructivism by holding that the artist first fashions a text and then completes the work by giving the text an interpretation so as thereby to confer certain artistic properties upon it (i.e., the text). For in that case the artist's completing interpretation merely changes the properties of the text: just as a student eventually becomes an academic upon being suitably trained, the text becomes an artwork upon being suitably interpreted by the artist who fashioned it. Artist/Critic Parity could then have no more than the consequence that subsequent novel critical interpretations confer new properties on an object that is both a text and work. It could only lead to moderate constructivism's doctrine that every novel critical interpretation modifies an artwork.

Text/Work Distinctness can only combine with Artist/Critic Parity to yield radical constructivism if it is construed literally. It must be read as holding that despite being directed at the text, an artist's completing interpretation creates a new object distinct from the text. The resulting artwork must be, not the text suitably modified (in the way in which the resulting blacksmith is an apprentice suitably modified by training), but a different object.

III.ii The suggestion that an artist's interpretative attitudes determine a work that is not identical to his "text" is controversial quite independently of the status of radical constructivism. Whether it can be sustained is a matter to which I will return (section IV), but for the moment it suffices to observe that the radical constructivist critic's need to sustain it places him in a dilemma of his own. If, to be on a par with the artist, he mirrors the artist's interpretative activity and interprets the text and not the work, he is vulnerable to the charge of missing the point. But if he interprets the work and not the text, he, unlike the artist, is confronted by an object that already possesses critical meaning: he appears to relinquish the claim of Artist/Critic Parity on which radical constructivism relies.

This simple dilemma shows that radical constructivism is incorrect. It is the second horn that is crucial, since even if some critical interpretations are directed at texts (and texts lack critical meaning), others are (explicitly!) directed at works. Some critical interpretations directed at works explicitly aspire to attribute meanings that the work actually possesses. (*Some* critical interpretations are *assertions* after all!) Call such interpretations "deferential." Since a critical interpretation is only "novel" when it attributes a meaning that has never before been attributed to the work, a novel deferential interpretation attributes a meaning that the artist did not intend it to have. For some kinds of critical meaning, this ensures that the meaning attributed is not one the work possesses and, hence, that corresponding deferential critical interpretations are simply false. Consider a fictional work in which repeated reference is made to black cats. Irrespective of how neatly the supposition that these cats symbolize evil fits the story, or of the extent to which black cats symbolize evil in the cultural milieu or literary tradition in which the author wrote or in which the critic interprets, if the author didn't intend these cats to symbolize evil, then they don't. However, while intentionalism is correct with respect to the occurrence of symbols in artworks, this is not to say that it is correct for critical meanings of all kinds. The "weak" intentionalist doctrine that there are kinds of critical meaning such that a work possesses a meaning of that kind if and only if the artist successfully realizes an intention that it should possess that meaning must be distinguished from "strong" intentionalism's view that all critical meanings have this property. Although strong intentionalism is incorrect,[11] the

11. Section VI below briefly justifies this claim with respect to such "higher-level" critical meanings as "significances" and "morals." The status of intentionalism with respect to lower-level "linguistic" meanings is rather subtle and turns on the well-known "linguistic division of labor." Most of the time at least, literary artists are no different from anyone else: they speak with both direct intentions to express a certain meaning and indirect intentions to defer to "correct" usage. Consequently, a work can have (or embody) linguistic meanings the artist did not directly intend: as in humdrum speech, a novelist might use the word "molybdenum," having little idea what this word means while at the same time intending, as speakers of English ordinarily do, that it mean whatever experts take it to mean. Moreover, as in the everyday context, a novelist's words can mean something quite different from what he or she directly

truth of weak intentionalism refutes radical constructivism. Those deferential critical interpretations which attribute meanings a work does not possess and that are therefore false do not automatically create another work. Once a critic falsely takes work W's black cats to symbolize evil, it is not automatically the case that a new work W* is created that is parallel to W save for the fact that its black cats symbolize evil. Merely false interpretations of an object do not create a sign or create a meaning. A dog scratches out a shape in the sand on Brighton beach, "Labour will win the next election." This (token) shape means nothing, and falsely supposing otherwise by deferentially interpreting it as meaning that Labour will win the next election does not alter that fact. To "interpret" a token shape (or sign) by attributing a linguistic meaning to it is to do one of two things: it is to make a claim about the intentional attitudes of the agent(s) who produced the shape (or sign), or it is to express one's own resolve or intention to use the shape in a certain way (as a sign). In the case of critical meanings like symbolizations, an artist does the latter: he creates a work by "interpreting" his text in view of certain interpretative intentions he has with respect to the object—a text say—that he fashions. A critic who "deferentially" interprets a work as symbolizing something does the former: lacking the requisite intentions, he fails to create a work when his interpretation attributes a novel symbolic meaning (and is therefore false). *Some* novel critical interpretations therefore fail to create artworks.

The same consideration also undermines the moderate constructivist's claim that novel critical interpretations, at least when they are apt, always modify artworks. One deferentially interpretative mistakenly false attribution of a meaning to a work no more alters that work (by conferring that meaning upon it) than does falsely attributing to Jones a desire to steal his neighbor's lawnmower alter him or falsely attributing arsenic to a sample of pure water poison it. Mistakenly supposing that a work W symbolizes evil by black cats no more results in W's coming to symbolize evil in that

---

intends them to mean. If I were transported while asleep to a place that is just like London save for the fact that the language spoken there shares only the phonetic and syntactic features of English, I might inadvertently say something offensive (and unrepeatable) when uttering "It is a lovely morning" to the first person I met. The innocence of my intentions cannot alter the fact that what I said was offensive. The literary arts are no different in this respect. Symbolization, however, is another matter. Even if "morning" in this language has the same meaning as "stick" in English, and even if the person I greet takes my reference to a stick to symbolize something crude, I have not thereby employed crude symbolization, and nothing crude has in fact been symbolized. In this case the innocence of my intentions is crucial.

way than it results in a new work W* that is just like W save for the fact that its black cats symbolize evil.

IV. Text/Work Distinctness

IV.i Radical constructivism is incorrect: novel critical interpretations do not *always* create new artworks. But is it even possible for them to do so? Typically, an artist creates in an obvious sense: he combines words or notes (or sounds) that were never before so combined; he daubs paint on a canvas in a novel way; he fashions clay or stone to produce something the like of which has never been seen. But a mere critic does not dirty his hands in this way: he simply muses about the upshots of such activity. How then could he possibly create new artworks akin to those created by artists themselves? The question can seem merely rhetorical in the case of the plastic arts, where artworks are widely thought to be physical particulars. Here, especially, the activities of artist and critic can seem so different that the idea that they could sometimes issue in a common product appears utterly implausible.[12]

However, while this skeptical line of thought has some credibility, it fails to come to grips with the doctrine of Text/Work Distinctness. If an artist's combining notes or words, daubing paint, or molding clay is in itself a matter of mere text creation, while work creation relies on interpretative attitudes additional to those essential to text creation, the fact that a critic does not dirty his hands is beside the point. Were novel critical interpretations sometimes on a par with the work-creating interpretative attitudes of artists, critics would sometimes create works.

---

12. There is no analogous objection to the claim that critical interpretation sometimes modifies artworks. The intentional properties of a statue do not supervene on its intrinsic physical properties: they are conferred by beings who themselves enjoy such intentional states as perceiving as, intending, and believing. Some artworks therefore possess some properties the natures of which are such that changes in them do not require intrinsic changes of the kind artists themselves effect by adding bars, words, paint, clay, or the like when creating their artworks. It follows that a dependence of the intentional properties of some artworks on critical interpretation is not precluded by the most basic categories to which intentional properties and critical interpretations belong. It was because of this apparent ontological asymmetry that I was led earlier (in Percival 2000) both to follow Stecker (1997) in dismissing the radical version of constructivism and to part company with him in defending a (weakened) moderate version of it. However, Stecker's discussion (in this volume) of my examples persuades me that my earlier conception and appraisal of the apparent ontological obstacles to the idea that critical interpretations can create artworks was superficial.

IV.ii As its name suggests, Text/Work Distinctness generalizes a distinction made initially in the literary arts. Clarifying the notion of a literary text involves at least a clarification of the conditions under which two particulars token the same text. The condition Currie (1991, 325) proposes as sufficient for this is that the two particulars should "have the same semantic and syntactic properties." Whatever one makes of this as a contribution to an "analysis," it is sufficiently close to ordinary usage as to be unexceptional as a stipulation. The question then becomes whether two particulars that token the same text in this sense are bound to token the same work. And Currie is right to maintain, contra Goodman and Elgin, that they are not. Smith feels down, and it is apparent to his colleagues. His friend encourages him with an e-mail saying "you look great today"; his enemy harasses him with an e-mail saying the same. Though the two e-mails token the same text, their (broader) intentional properties are not the same: one is sincere, the other sarcastic. The same phenomenon can arise in literature. If a manuscript entitled "Northanger Abbey" by Anne Radcliffe is discovered and is word for word identical to Jane Austen's manuscript of her novel of that name, we would have two manuscripts that token the same text, but different works: Austen's novel is ironic, Radcliffe's isn't.[13]

The distinction just drawn turns on the fact that two physical particulars having the same syntactic and semantic properties can nevertheless differ in "meaning" broadly construed, and hence critical meaning. Similar considerations point to an analogous distinction in the case of musical compositions. A notion of "text" can be introduced whereby two scores, or two particular sequences of sounds, token the same "text" if they are, in an obvious sense, sound duplicates. But sound duplicates can differ in critical meaning. A motif scored in the manuscript of Tchaikovsky's Fourth Symphony symbolizes (portentous) fate. But the same motif scored in a physically duplicate manuscript produced simultaneously and independently by Schmaikovsky does not symbolize fate. Mozart's *Musical Joke* is a joke; Bozart's similarly scored, albeit differently titled, work is not. In such cases, two scores token the same "text" but not the same work.

IV.iii However, while this distinction is relatively straightforward, it is not a distinction of the kind involved in the supposition that the work created

---

13. Goodman and Elgin would try to accommodate such a case by insisting that both manuscripts instantiate a single work that *can* be read as either ironic or not. But there is no more substance to this move than there is to denying that there is any sense of "remark" in which the two e-mails I described token different remarks.

via the interpretative intentions that an artist directs at his text is an object distinct from that text. It has been drawn as if "text" and "work" were determinables such that two particulars might fall under the same determination of "text" while falling under different determinations of "work," in the manner in which two particular animals might fall under the same determination of "species" but different determinations of "subspecies." If there is no more than this to the text/work distinction, then, for example, a writer's interpretative intentions toward his text—as thus far conceived, the physical particular he has created by putting words on a page or speaking—don't create a new object. They merely ensure that his text falls under a certain determination of the determinable "work."

In the light of this failure, there are two strategies by which to pursue the doctrine of Text/Work Distinctness being sought. The first grafts on to the distinction already drawn the supposition that works (and texts) are (primarily) identical to certain types, not to certain tokens. On this view, terms like "Ulysses" or "Beethoven's C-sharp Minor String Quartet" and phrases like "the text of Ulysses" refer, respectively, to types that are restrictions of the (different) types referred to by the terms "artwork" and "text." A second quite different strategy seeks to generalize a distinction many have found attractive in the plastic arts. Unreflectively, we identify a sculpture or a painting with a physical particular: Vigeland's monument to Abel is identical to a physical particular located in Oslo; Gris's *Portrait of Picasso* is located in Chicago. Yet even when circumstances are most propitious for identifying a painting or statue with a canvas or hunk of stone, the fact that paintings and statues appear to have modal properties different from those possessed by canvases and hunks of stone seems to prevent the identification. Suppose the statue *Goliath* consists of a lump of clay, Lumpl, and that *Goliath* and Lumpl not only came into being at the same time but ceased to exist at the same time too. It remains the case that Lumpl could have survived in the interim a squashing that *Goliath* could not have survived. Since identical objects cannot have different properties (modal or not), *Goliath* appears not to be identical to Lumpl.[14] Both strategies gel with the thought that an artist determines a work by directing interpretative intentions at something else—the relevant text in the case of the first strategy, and the relevant (eventually work-constituting) physical object in the case of the second. A physical duplicate of Lumpl might not compose a statue, and Lumpl itself might not have composed a statue either if, for example, the

14. See Johnston 1992 and Rudder Baker 1997.

artist who fashioned it had done so unthinkingly in an effort to produce an object massive enough to weigh down his roof in a gale.

IV.iv The distinction proposed in the Lumpl/*Goliath* case is not confined to the plastic arts. Mrs. Scrabble leaves a message for Mr. Scrabble by arranging a string of letters on the kitchen table so as to form a token of the sentence "Julie is coming to dinner, and I will be home at six." The object comprising the mereological sum of these letters might have survived scrambling before Mr. Scrabble saw it; the token sentence couldn't have. Prima facie, then, the sentence is not identical to that object. That is, just as it seems obligatory to distinguish statue from composing object, so too does it seem obligatory to distinguish (token) linguistic sign from the object that composes it. Applied generally in the literary or musical arts, this distinction between sign and composing object operates differently from the distinction between text and work already deemed inadequate for the radical constructivist's purposes. That distinction had identified a sense in which two manuscripts might token the same text while tokening different works, so that, on that way of speaking, one particular—a manuscript—bears both linguistic and critical meaning. In contrast, the analogue to the Lumpl/*Goliath* distinction just drawn for the literary or musical arts distinguishes the bearer of critical meaning from the object that composes it.

IV.v The two versions of Text/Work Distinctness still in play have different prospects of grounding the claim that artists literally create their works by interpreting their texts. That physical particulars of the kind involved in the Lumpl/*Goliath* distinction should have a temporal existence is more credible than is the thought that types should do so. Levinson (1980), by identifying literary and musical works with types he calls "indicated" structures, tries to reconcile the view that they are types with the idea that they are literally created by artists. For example, he identifies a musical work with a certain kind of "S/PM structure-as-indicated-by-X-at-t," where "S/PM" is a sound structure generated in a certain way (typically, on certain instruments), X is the composer, and t the time of composition. But whatever the merits of this proposal, Levinson's further claim that types of this kind only come into existence when X indicates S/PM at t threatens untenable consequences. If, for example, "[t]he Ford Thunderbird . . . is a metal/glass/plastic structure-as-indicated (or determined) by the Ford Motor Company on such and such a date [that] begins to exist as a result of an act of human indication or determination," then either it was not the case two weeks beforehand that the Ford Thunderbird would come to exist in (what was then) two weeks time, or facts involving entities can exist at times at which those entities do not exist. Neither alternative is palatable. Admittedly, the same consideration suggests that the sense in which the existence of, for example, *Goliath* is temporal is not literal either: unless it was not true the day before the statue *Goliath* came to exist that it would come to exist the day after, or that facts about *Goliath* can predate its existence, *Goliath* must always have existed. Nevertheless, even if existence is literally timeless, a good sense remains in which a physical particular like *Goliath* might be said to be created by the sculptor, a sense that does not extend to literary and musical works if they are identified with types. Even if the existence of *Goliath* is timeless, it might well be counterfactually dependent on the actions of the sculptor: if the sculptor hadn't done such and such, *Goliath* would not have enjoyed (timeless) existence. But if the literal existence of a type having the form "S/PM structure-as-indicated-by-X-at-t" is timeless, there is no reason to think that it is similarly counterfactually dependent: this type is abstract, and a fortiori X's actions do not bear causal relations to it.[15]

IV.vi So, basing Text/Work Distinctness on either the identification of literary and musical works with types or on the distinction between artworks that are physical particulars and the physical particulars that compose them, involves problems so to speak "internal" to the project of establishing that artists (sometimes) create their artworks. There are also problems with both bases that are independent of, and therefore "external" to, that project.

---

15. Actually, this distinction in terms of counterfactual dependence is itself problematic, since modal reasoning parallel to the temporal argument for the conclusion that existence is timeless gives the conclusion that existence is necessary. If Bill Clinton's parents had never met, he would not have been born. But in this counterfactual situation, there would surely have been facts about Bill Clinton: it remains true in this situation that he might have been born, that he would have been born if his parents had met in such and such circumstances, and so forth. So if there can only be facts about him in situations in which he exists, it must be the case that he would have existed even if he had never been born. I doubt there is an asymmetry between the temporal and modal cases that makes this style of argument cogent in the former but not in the latter. Still, even if there isn't, another good sense remains in which artworks that are physical particulars are dependent on the actions of artists. Even if *Goliath*'s existence is timeless and necessary, its intrinsic properties are not. Prior to being constructed *Goliath* did not occupy space and was not composed of clay, and if it hadn't been sculpted, it wouldn't have occupied space or been composed of clay. It is the sculptor's actions that result in *Goliath*'s coming to have these properties. By contrast, for example, the intrinsic properties of the Ford Thunderbird, as conceived by Levinson, are neither temporal nor contingent. Being a type, its intrinsic properties are not affected by the temporal, contingent activities of motor manufacturers.

Those confronting the distinction drawn at the level of particulars are most acute. The supposition that there are types that are identical to (some) artworks involves an extravagant ontology it would be best to do without if possible. But this is an issue as deep as they come, and repeated attempts across the ages to do without such an ontology have not been entirely successful. By contrast, the Lumpl/*Goliath* distinction generates anomalies that are local: we are asked to accept both the existence of two physical objects entirely coincident in their spatiotemporal locations, and the creation of one of the two—*Goliath*—by mere acts of mind. It is reasonable to try to avoid these consequences by rejecting one of the premises on which the Lumpl/*Goliath* distinction is based. Perhaps the supposition that Lumpl might have survived squashing but *Goliath* could not have is incorrect. Alternatively, perhaps this supposition is consistent with the supposition that *Goliath* is identical to Lumpl. On Lewis's counterpart theory of *de re* possibility, to say Lumpl might have survived squashing is to say that there is a counterpart relation with respect to which a counterpart of Lumpl survives squashing; to say that *Goliath* might not have survived squashing is to say that there is no counterpart relation with respect to which a counterpart of *Goliath* survives squashing. But in that case an explanation is available of why Lumpl might have survived squashing when *Goliath* couldn't have even though Lumpl is identical to *Goliath*: the names "Lumpl" and "Goliath" invoke different counterpart relations.[16]

IV.vii It is a metaphysical issue, as yet unresolved, whether there are such entities as "texts" or such entities as "works," and whether the latter are distinct from the former. If there are such entities, it is likewise unresolved whether "works" are created by artists and, if so, in what sense. But suppose there are works, that they are distinct from texts, and that artists typically create them via interpretative attitudes directed at their texts. Can a critic's interpretative attitudes toward a text create a work too?

V. Artist/Critic Parity

V.i The interpretative attitudes of critics—those who adopt interpretative attitudes toward texts others have fashioned—can at least aspire to be on a

16. See Lewis 1971. Lewis's way out is criticized and rejected in Johnston 1992 and Rudder Baker 1997.

par with those of artists. Not every critical interpretation aspires to attribute to an object a critical meaning that object already possesses: there are critical interpretations that are not "deferential." And among critical interpretations that are not deferential, some are "appropriative": these interpretations aspire to *confer* a critical meaning upon an art object.

An appropriative critical interpretation might be "cynical," in that the critic who pursues it does so caring not one jot whether the object he interprets possesses the meaning he attributes, or whether the artist's own interpretative intentions were to create a work that does not have that meaning. In particular, a critic might seek to confer some critical meaning upon an object he takes to constitute some works of conceptual art, knowing full well that the meaning he seeks to confer is quite different from the meaning the work actually has. Indeed, in so doing he might hope to destroy the work, in the sense of hoping that its meaning will come to be forgotten and "lost."

One might think that an appropriative critical interpretation of some physical object constituting an artwork needn't be cynical, on the grounds that an artist might have had commonly known interpretative intentions that in effect "sanction" subsequent conferrals of meaning. However, that an artist might consciously defer to subsequent critics does not warrant the view that appropriative critical interpretations can be "innocent." Certainly, I might take junk, stick it together in a way that I find fascinating, and say, "I reckon that must mean something profound," meaning: "I intend that the meaning of this particular I have fashioned out of junk is that profound meaning which will eventually be (successfully!) articulated by an imaginative and wise critic." But even if there is only one profound critical meaning that is apt for the junk-object I have fashioned, and that meaning is eventually identified after much controversy during which alternative profound critical meanings are advanced and eventually rejected as inapt, the moment at which the one apt critical meaning is identified cannot be the moment at which my junk-object acquires that meaning. For in this scenario it possesses that meaning all along. The case differs from the ordinary one only in that the interpretative intentions I direct at my junk-object involve identifying a meaning under an unusual description. In the ordinary case a meaning is identified explicitly under some such description as "the meaning of life is the number 45": in the extraordinary scenario such a meaning is identified implicitly under the description "the profound meaning that will eventually be identified by a . . . critic." As such, this scenario is analogous to a commonplace linguistic division of labor. Though I don't know the difference in meaning between "aluminium" and "molybdenum," when I answer "aluminium" to the question "Is that piece of metal aluminium or molybdenum?" I assert that it is aluminium. Here I confer this much meaning on my token utterance indirectly by deferring to the intentions of expert speakers; in the extraordinary scenario I likewise confer a profound meaning on my junk-object indirectly by deferring to the intentions of expert critics. Consequently, the extraordinary scenario is not one that invites "innocent" appropriative critical interpretations.

However, although appropriative critical interpretations cannot be innocent, nonappropriative critical interpretations can be innocently work creating. Outside of the arts, the phenomenon is straightforward. Jones writes "back in five minutes" on a board and buries it. Smith digs it up many years later and displays it in his shop window. Smith's employment of the board is innocent: he thinks it means "back in five minutes," though in fact it means "trespassers keep out," since that is what those words mean in the language monolingual Jones wrote. Yet, despite the fact that at no time did Smith or any of his contemporaries have conscious intentions to disregard the meaning of the board, it eventually comes to mean "back in five minutes." Once the distinction is drawn between sign and composing object (the board), this eventuality is the (innocent) creation of a new sign. The case of art is no different. A faces/vase ambiguous canvas that is embraced by a conquered people who innocently take it to constitute a (subversive) representation of faces eventually comes to constitute that much even if it was in fact painted by an artist belonging to a conquering culture in which the representation of the human form was so taboo that faces were never before seen in a painting. Again, Text/Work Distinctness would guarantee that this is tantamount to the innocent creation of a new work.[17]

V.ii In replying to the claim in Percival 2000 that certain examples suggest that critical interpretations can sometimes modify artworks, Stecker (this volume, Chapter 9) appears to concede that in some nonart circumstances innocent critical interpretations can indeed create a new object—a sign. But he insists that in the case of art, critical interpretations cannot create new artworks. His attitude, then, appears to be that while there is no *metaphysical* incoherence to the idea that mere critical interpretation can create new artworks, this idea is nevertheless incorrect because nonart examples in

17. These cases are discussed in Stecker 1997, Percival 2000, and Stecker's contribution to this volume (Chapter 9). Stecker does not admit meaning change or work creation in the case of the faces/vase ambiguous canvas.

which mere interpretation creates a new object are disanalogous to the case of art.

Sometimes his reason for taking the two cases to be disanalogous seems to appeal to the practice of art interpretation:

> Understandings of a work based on misconstrual are given up no matter how well established, once the misconstrual is uncovered and even if the misconstrual is based on something other than mistaken authorship, unless other grounds are found for them. Further, if misconstruals are not uncovered, they will not be genuine agents of meaning change. In a similar vein, we don't believe poems change their meaning when a word used in the poem acquires a new meaning and it is handy to interpret the poem according to this new meaning.[18]

However, for Stecker to appeal to critical practice at this point is surprising, since he has previously observed that critics have many aims, some of which do not involve a deferential respect for authorial intentions or interpretation-independent meanings. From his own perspective, then, he does not challenge the thought that artworks might be created by interpretations that are cynically appropriative. In any case, that he appeals to our practice is at least partly explained, I suspect, by his pluralist response to its heterogeneity. Yet the various critical aims Stecker identifies sit less comfortably with one another than he would have us believe. The controversies over constructivism and intentionalism are not philosophical appendages external to an easygoing pluralism that exists among critics themselves. Art critics don't just differ in their critical aims. They disagree over what the aims of criticism should be. This shows that the controversy over whether mere interpretation can create works is in part a normative one. For this reason, even if the practice to which Stecker appeals were more homogeneous than it is, it couldn't settle the matter of whether critical interpretation can create artworks. Stecker himself implicitly indicates the normative status of the issue when he writes: "With artworks, when there are socially enshrined misconstruals or reconstruals (based on pragmatic considerations of 'handiness'), we need say *neither* that a work has changed its meaning *nor* that a second work has come into existence. Rather we *should* say that the work

---

18. In this volume, pages 175–76. Note that in my terminology Stecker's "misconstruals" are deferential interpretations that are incorrect.

means one thing but is being taken in another way, for reasons that may or may not be legitimate" (my italics in the second sentence).[19] What we should or should not say is a normative issue. Normative issues are not settled by any description of practice. Even if everyone agreed that some socially enshrined misconstrual/reconstrual is simply a case of an artwork that means "one thing . . . being taken in another way" (rather than the creation of another artwork), the question whether we ought to agree as much would still arise. The crucial issue is this: irrespective of what our practice actually is, should we always deny that an artwork comes into existence when, for example, critical interpretations exhibit a way of looking at an existing art object that is artistically exciting and unprecedented but that is quite divorced from the artist's own interpretative intentions?

V.iii Artworks can have a value divorced from their status as artworks: a painting might serve as a table; a literary work might help improve one's memory. Call the value that an artwork has as a work of art "art-value." It is the business of critics to help us appreciate the art-value of artworks. Since this value is not independent of the meanings artworks have, it might be held to follow that critics ought to help others identify those meanings. Yet it does not follow. Suppose that X puts paint on canvas C with the intention of representing R, by which to symbolize S, so as to suggest P, and that his intentions are thereby successfully realized in a work W. I claim that if C can be seen as representing R^*, by which to symbolize S^*, so as to suggest P^*, and if a critic attributes this meaning to C in a cynically appropriative manner or the members of some culture innocently assume C to constitute a work that does so represent, a new artwork W^* will come to exist that does so represent. But doesn't this claim neglect the question of art-value? Won't there be a bar on W^*'s coming to be if it cannot have more art-value than W or if, from the point of view, so to speak, of art, neither critic nor culture ought to view C this way?

V.iv To suppose that one ought never to ignore or discard an artist's artwork in favor of another artwork generated by a critical interpretation that clashes with the artist's intentions is to suppose that the value of an artist's artwork trumps all other values. In effect, that it does so is claimed by Noël Carroll, on the grounds that art is about communication and communion

19. In this volume, page 176.

between souls: the art-value of an artwork lies in what its creator *says* to his audience by means of it: "[T]o the extent that communication or communion is among the leading purposes of art, authorial intention must always figure in interpretation, at least as a constraint on whatever other purposes we seek" (Carroll 1992, 124). But Carroll is muddled here. The quoted passage comes at the end of an article in which he has been concerned to argue against what he calls the "anti-intentionalist" view that art criticism is entirely independent of authorial intention in that an actual artist's intention is never relevant to critical interpretation. But even if Carroll is right to maintain that we have a "conversational" interest in art, in that there is something of value to be gained from understanding what, through his artwork, the artist has to say, and that the value a critic might gain by exploring his own interpretation of, for example, a canvas does not "trump" the value of understanding the artist, it does not follow that the conversational value of art trumps other values. But the sentiments of the quoted passage can only be sustained if conversational value is trumping in this way. Only if conversational value is trumping does authorial intention constrain critical interpretation; only if conversational value is trumping is it never right for critical interpretation to cut itself free from an artist's intentions and create novel artworks.

That's one non sequitur in Carroll's argument. Here is another. Suppose the conversational value of an artwork is trumping. This does not mean that there is no value to the artist in artistic activity: it means that the critic should be concerned to uncover the artist's intentions. But this conclusion gets Carroll what he wants only if artists are distinguished from critics by the criterion of "fabricator of the text." Yet there is nothing in Carroll's "conversational hypothesis" itself that justifies this criterion. Indeed, such a criterion begs the question. A conversation involves a speaker and an audience. Van Gogh paints a canvas and speaks through his painting *The Potato Eaters*. Knowing the value of communing ("conversationally") with the soul of van Gogh, the critic Jones listens. But Jones might well tire both of listening and of explaining what van Gogh has to say to others. He might be so bold as to suppose he has something to say through the canvas of *The Potato Eaters* more interesting than what van Gogh had to say through it. In that case, Carroll's "conversational" view of art itself encourages the critic Jones to cut himself free from the constraints of van Gogh's intentions and interpret van Gogh's canvas so as to initiate a conversation. If Jones were to do this with any facility, critical interpreters would do well to listen not to van Gogh but to Jones. The artwork their conversational interest in art should have them look out for is Jones's *Potato Eaters*, not van Gogh's.[20]

V.v There is nothing in the nature of art or art-value or "criticism" (broadly construed) that precludes the severing of critical interpretations from an artist's own interpretative intentions. But even were what critics have to say through texts invariably more interesting than what artists have to say through them, artists would not be dethroned or some myth of the artist as genius exposed and buried. The production of a mere text is no mean feat, even if some critic's interpretation of it is superior to that of the artist's. Indeed, the art-value that arises from the interpretation of a text is often minimal in comparison to the value of the text itself. This is particularly evident in many instances of sculpture and music (and is a way of articulating a truth in formalism).[21]

Nevertheless, the liberties sometimes profitably taken by critics (and especially performers) with works notwithstanding, in practice the limitations of critics differ starkly from those of the artists who produce texts. Generally, artists are either relevantly more knowledgeable or more intelligent or more sensitive or more imaginative or more passionate about their works than the rest of us. Many constructivists seem to have some kind of political objection to the suggestion that critics ought to exhibit deference to artists' intentions and, hence, to their artworks and their meanings. But they forget that humility is a virtue among those whose talents are more humble.

On the other hand, the best artists successfully realize their intentions. This is not just to say that they successfully create objects that possess the properties they intended their artworks to possess. It means that those properties are accessible to their audience via the text itself.[22] It follows that a

20. These criticisms do not contest the core of Carroll's idea that art is conversational. Moreover, I find Lamarque's critique of that idea (this volume) unpersuasive. In particular, the obscurity and depth of art is beside the point: conversations can have the same features (and the ones we most care about do). So too can the conversational theory of art accommodate the fact that the contributions of literary critics are "radically different from those common among participants of conversations." It can explain this difference as reflecting the difference between contributing to and commenting upon a conversation.

21. See Zangwill 1999.

22. I don't mean to deny that even the best artworks have properties relevant to their art-value that are inaccessible through the text itself. My point is that making all the properties relevant to art-value manifest in the text is a regulative ideal that the best artists come close to achieving. For example, some facts pertaining to the political life of Elizabethan England that are not manifest in *Julius Caesar* enhance the art-value of Shakespeare's play. But it is only because critical meanings sufficient to establish that play as having considerable art-value are

concern to ascertain artists' intentions via the artists themselves instead of the text reveals as much the inadequacy of the artist as the conscientiousness of the critic. Remarks attributed to Shostakovich illustrate both morals. To be sure, he writes:[23]

> I discovered to my astonishment that the man who considers himself its greatest interpreter does not understand my music. He says that I wanted to write exultant finales for my Fifth and Seventh Symphonies but I couldn't manage it. It never occurred to this man that I never thought about any exultant finales, for what exultation could there be? I think it is clear to everyone what happens in the Fifth. The rejoicing is forced, created under threat, as in *Boris Godunov*. It's as if someone were beating you with a stick and saying, "Our business is rejoicing, Our business is rejoicing."
>
> What kind of apotheosis is that? You have to be a complete oaf not to hear that. . . . People who came to the premiere of the Fifth in the best of moods wept.

But this is not to say that in his view critics should be concerned to establish an artist's intentions independently of the artist's text. Immediately beforehand, Shostakovich writes: "Awaiting execution is a theme that has tormented me all my life. Many pages of my music are devoted to it. Sometimes I wanted to explain that fact to the performers, I thought that they would have a greater understanding of the work's meaning. But then I thought better of it. You can't explain anything to a bad performer and a talented person should sense it himself." Critics do well to respect artists' interpretative intentions and hence their works. But artists do well to provide for critics from another age in their texts.

---

manifest in its text that one would go to the trouble of investigating such facts. Nor does the realization of the artist's intentions in a text require that these intentions be manifest *to everyone* (including, for example, people whose cognitive faculties are impaired or have yet to reach maturity). On the contrary, the deepest works are manifest only to the deepest interpreters, and an artist will often exploit knowledge that is common only to his or her contemporaries. Nevertheless, a text successfully treating deep issues will itself often have something to say to everyone, since depth tends to be universal. Everyone knows, for example, what a political murder or a triangular relationship is.

23. *Testimony: The Memoirs of Dmitri Shostakovich* (London: Faber & Faber, 1979), 183–84. This book is said to reproduce (in translation) memoirs related to, and then edited by, Solomon Volkov. In part because of its political import, whether Shostakovich did in fact relate any such memoir is hotly disputed.

VI. Concluding Remarks: The Variety of Critical Meanings

This paper has been written in the spirit of compromise. I have argued against radical constructivism while at the same time resisting the suggestion that critical interpretations can never create artworks. I have done so by arguing both that there are critical meanings that some artworks literally possess (so that, normally, deferential interpretations that attribute conflicting meanings to those artworks are simply false without further ado) and that there are nevertheless other circumstances in which, given the doctrine of Text/Work Distinctness, critical interpretations can lead to the creation of a new artwork (in whatever sense the original artist's interpretative attitudes created a work). The argument has paid little attention to the nature of those "critical" meanings attributed by critical interpretations. Although my discussion of Stecker's treatment of radical constructivism (section I, above) has invoked the thought that critical interpretations may not attribute linguistic meanings, all that my argument strictly requires of critical meanings is that they include symbolizations.

Nevertheless, as Peter Lamarque has observed (this volume, Chapter 15), the class of critical interpretations is exceedingly heterogeneous, so much so that even my supposition that all interpretations attribute (critical) "meanings" is rather strained. At the very least, then, there can be no presumption that what holds good for one sort of critical meaning regarding the philosophy of interpretation holds good for another. Upon reflection, although the identification of semantic (linguistic) meanings (of words, etc.) plays a minor role in even literary criticism, it plays a role even so, and however unrepresentative they may be, such semantic meanings should therefore be admitted to the class of critical meanings. In that case I have identified two sorts of critical meanings that artworks actually possess such that meanings of one sort—symbolizations—are possessed in virtue of the artist's explicit intentions, whereas meanings of the other sort—semantic meanings—are possessed in virtue of something else (namely, the practice of the community in which the artist writes, together with his or her resolve to defer to that practice).[24]

The case is different again if we ascend further up the hierarchy of critical interpretations to levels (of literary criticism) at which talk of attributed

24. See footnote 11 above. Lamarque himself denies that symbolization in an artwork is determined by the artist's actual intentions (this volume). In so doing he seems to succumb to the sort of error he is concerned to warn against, unjustifiably running together "symbolic" with "thematic" content.

"meanings" is most strained. At this level we encounter the "significance," in the broadest sense, of a work, its "themes" or "points" or "morals." Here critical interpretation might seem least constrained by prior objective properties of the work, since the work—in the literary case, in the guise of the fictional world constituted by the comings and goings of fictional characters—comes closest to breaking free both from the intentions of its author and from its social and historical context. To be sure, authorial intention or social or historical context can determine the significance, point, or moral of the (sufficiently rich) fate of fictional characters in some respects. That much is shown, for example, by the fact that some texts could be successfully written either sincerely or ironically. However, in other respects fictional lives can have significance, points, and morals that can no more be determined or constrained by authorial intention than could those of actual characters whose lives run exactly parallel to them. Consider a fictional work in which female characters are given social and sexual roles at variance with those given to male characters. Some respects in which this asymmetry is potentially significant are entirely insensitive to authorial intention. For example, the question whether the submissiveness of the female characters' sexual postures constitutes their sexual oppression by males can amount to a question, simply, about one aspect of the nature of sexual relationships. Clearly, irrespective of what prompts it, such a question is to be answered not by any "criticism" that is specifically "literary" but by a philosophical inquiry making full use of data from various social (and even biological) sciences. That intentionalism fails, therefore, with respect to "higher-level" critical meanings of this kind is no cause for constructivist celebration. Intentionalism is incorrect for such meanings only because they are "possessed" by artworks in a sense that is more "objective," not less, than is the sense in which artworks "involve" symbolizations determined by artists' interpretative intentions.

References

Carroll, N. 1992. "Art, Intention, and Conversation." In *Intention and Interpretation,* edited by G. Iseminger, 97–131. Philadelphia: Temple University Press.

Churchland, P. 1981. "Eliminative Materialism and Propositional Attitudes." *Journal of Philosophy* 78:67–89.

Currie, G. 1991. "Work and Text." *Mind* 100:325–40.

Davidson, D. 1973. "Radical Interpretation." *Dialectica* 27:313–28. (Reprinted in his *Inquiries into truth and Interpretation.*)

Goodman, N., and C. Elgin. 1988. *Reconceptions in Philosophy.* London: Routledge.

Johnston, M. 1992. "Constitution Is Not Identity." *Mind* 101:89–105.

Levinson, J. 1980. "What a Musical Work Is." *Journal of Philosophy* 77:5–28.

Lewis, D. 1971. "Counterparts of Persons and Their Bodies." *Journal of Philosophy* 68:203–11. (Reprinted in his *Philosophical Papers Volume 1*, 47–54. Oxford: Oxford University Press.)

———. 1974. "Radical Interpretation." *Synthese* 23:331–44. (Reprinted in his *Philosophical Papers Volume 1*, 108–18. Oxford: Oxford University Press.)

Percival, P. 2000. "Stecker's Dilemma: A Constructive Response." *Journal of Aesthetics and Art Criticism* 58:51–60.

Quine, W. V. O. 1960. *Word and Object*. Cambridge, Mass.: MIT Press.

———. 1970. "On the Reasons for Indeterminacy of Translation." *Journal of Philosophy* 67:178–83.

Rudder Baker, L. 1997. "Why Constitution Is Not Identity." *Journal of Philosophy* 94:599–621.

Stecker, R. 1997. "The Constructivist's Dilemma." *Journal of Aesthetics and Art Criticism* 55:43–52.

Testimony: The Memoirs of Dmitri Shostakovich. London: Faber & Faber, 1979.

Wheeler, S. C., III. 1986. "Indeterminacy of French Interpretation: Derrida and Davidson." In *Truth and Interpretation*, edited by E. LePore, 477–95. Oxford: Blackwell.

Wiggins, D. 1980. *Sameness and Substance*. Oxford: Blackwell.

Wolterstorff, N. 1975. "Towards an Ontology of Art Works." *Nous* 9:115–42.

Zangwill, N. 1999. "Feasible Aesthetic Formalism." *Nous* 33:610–29.

PART III

The Literary Work as a Pliable Entity: Combining Realism and Pluralism

Torsten Pettersson

I

The literary work exhibits an intriguing combination of variability and stability. On the one hand, an obvious consequence of the interpretive process
is diversity: fully qualified readers continually produce different and often
nonconverging interpretations of a given work. This seems to suggest that
the interpreter constructs the meaning of the text wholly or in part. The
resultant diversity, on this view, follows naturally from the diversity of the
interpretive methods, background assumptions, interests, and values that
are brought to bear in the course of this construction. But on the other
hand, it is also clear that interpreters regularly use the text as a standard
against which they test the adequacy of interpretations put forward by
themselves or by others. This seems to support the opposite inference that,
instead of being constructed on the basis of the interpreters' values and interests, interpretations correspond or seek to correspond to the work conceived as an entity independent of the interpretation.

Literary works are thus both chameleons and touchstones. This is the
central epistemic paradox of interpretation. In what follows, I first attempt
to demonstrate that the paradox cannot be resolved by denying the validity
of one of its components: I show, in the face of assertions to the contrary,

that multiplicity and correspondence are both genuine, and not merely apparent, characteristics of interpretation. After this critique of monism and constructivism, respectively, I present an account of the nature of the interpretive process and the literary work, an account that accommodates both the chameleon and the touchstone qualities of the work. In conclusion, I comment on the kind of epistemological realism that this account represents.

II

A conception of interpretation that is well attuned to the work's touchstone qualities is monism: the idea that there is a single correct interpretation of a literary work and that therefore the work's chameleon qualities are illusory or must be relegated to some realm of reflection and speculation separate from interpretation proper.

Monism can in principle be established on four different foundations. At least in theory it can be reader-based, since, regardless of the degree of determinacy in literary works, a sufficiently homogeneous community of readers with the same worldview and the same values may formulate a reading that for them represents the single correct interpretation. Thus each member of a closely knit community of devout Christians might spontaneously arrive at the conclusion that *King Lear* is essentially a demonstration of the horrors of a paganism that has no recourse to the God of Christianity. In totalitarian states and authoritarian classrooms orthodoxy has on occasion been enforced by canonical readings and mandatory reading techniques. But in modern Western societies these cases are so obviously exceptions to the rule of heterogeneous reader response that purely reader-based monism does not seem to have any advocates in present-day aesthetic theory.

Second, it may be argued that literary works are so highly and tightly structured that, with the exception of a small number of idiosyncratically ambiguous works (such as *The Turn of the Screw*), they will, after sufficient scrutiny but without recourse to external evidence, be seen to admit of only one interpretation. Other readings are mistaken or can be included in the single correct interpretation. This was Monroe C. Beardsley's view. He only supported it with a brief defense of one reading of Wordsworth's Lucy poem (and a rejection of a competing reading),[1] without coming to terms with the enormous diversity of interpretations that was in evidence even then.[2] In the three decades that have passed, the continuing spate of competent nonconverging interpretations has made the idea that mere scrutiny of the work will yield a single correct interpretation even less plausible; at the beginning of the twenty-first century, purely work-based monism has few, if any, champions.

The third type of monism is context-related. It takes account of the work but also relates it to some supposedly stable context that is privileged over other possible contexts as a vantage point from which the work takes on one particular appearance. An interesting example was orthodox Marxism of the reductive kind. Its logic was this: (1) It is a fact discovered by scientific Marxism(-Leninism) that the base determines the superstructure and a historical fact that in a given society at a given time that determination takes a certain form. (2) A literary work has one true meaning determined by the position that the work and its author occupy in this historical context. (3) Armed with historical knowledge and a Marxist methodology, the critic can relate the work to this context and arrive at the single correct interpretation of its meaning. In all its staggering confidence, this is an intriguing line of argument. But in this explicit and overtly assertive form context-related monism is now defunct.

The fourth form of monism, and the only one that is alive and kicking today as a serious option in aesthetic theory, is intentionalism.[3] That term, as has become increasingly clear in the last decade, does not so much refer to a single position as cover a group of related but different stances. Consequently, any manifestation of anti-intentionalism must specify its focus. In

1. Monroe C. Beardsley, *The Possibility of Criticism* (Detroit: Wayne State University Press, 1970), 29; cf. 45–47.

2. Only a few years later it was, for instance, possible for Stanley Corngold to review no less than 128 interpretations of a well-known story in *The Commentator's Despair: The Interpretation of Kafka's "Metamorphosis,"* National University Publications—Series on Literary Criticism (Port Washington, N.Y.: Kennikat Press, 1973). Beardsley would perhaps have taken the unsatisfactory line that most of them are not interpretations at all; he felt that, for instance, Freudian or Marxist or Christian readings are better designated as *"superimpositions"* (*The Possibility of Criticism,* 43–44, Beardsley's italics).

3. Intentionalism may appear to be a variety of context-related criticism, but strictly speaking it is not. *Qua* intentionalists, critics may refer to the various personal and social contexts surrounding an author, but only if the contexts can be construed as evidence of his or her intention to determine the meaning of a given work. If they cannot, they are not, from an intentionalist point of view, pertinent to the interpretation of that meaning, however alluring the parallels between them and the work may be.

the present context, my aim is not to deny that authors' attitudes may determine some features of works or to demonstrate that their intentions are always irrelevant to our interpretations of their works. The critique of intentionalism presented below is directed at the radical monistic variety that purports to determine the single correct interpretation (conceived as the one that renders the meaning intended by the author of the work).

Intentionalism, then, need not be oriented toward the single correct interpretation.[4] Nevertheless, that orientation has loomed large in intentionalism ever since E. D. Hirsch Jr. advocated its adoption in academic criticism and P. D. Juhl insisted that "there is in principle one and only one correct interpretation of a work,"[5] so that intentionalists continue to refer to authorial intention as a useful means of disambiguating literary works.[6] Indeed, for many theorists the attraction of intentionalism resides in the tidy solution it seems to offer to the logical dilemma of interpretations that are logically incompatible but, in terms of purely textual criticism, equally admissible.

However, whatever other advantages and drawbacks it may exhibit, intentionalism cannot substantiate monism. First, the single correct interpretation cannot in practice be established. If, following Steven Knapp and Walter Benn Michaels, we consider textual meaning inherently intentional,[7] there can be no question of complete disambiguation. The work regarded as an embodiment of the author's intention will mean whatever it can mean in purely textual interpretation, with the possible exception that patently anachronistic readings can be ruled out. If, on the other hand, we espouse

---

4. Thus the "moderate intentionalism" advocated by Paisley Livingston, "Intentionalism in Aesthetics," *New Literary History* 29 (1998): 831–46, limits intentionalism to a subset of interpretations, thereby allowing for interpretive variety in other subsets.

5. See E. D. Hirsch Jr., *Validity in Interpretation* (New Haven: Yale University Press, 1967), and P. D. Juhl, *Interpretation: An Essay in the Philosophy of Literary Criticism* (Princeton, N.J.: Princeton University Press, 1980) (the quotation from Juhl's book is from p. 199).

6. Thus there is a focus on disambiguating the beginning of a poem by Gerard Manley Hopkins in Gary Iseminger, "An Intentional Demonstration?," in *Intention and Interpretation,* ed. Gary Iseminger (Philadelphia: Temple University Press, 1992), 76–96; and Livingston, "Intentionalism in Aesthetics," 842–43, argues that the actual intentionalism he favors will disambiguate *The Turn of the Screw,* whereas hypothetical intentionalism will not. Nevertheless, the aim of securing determinacy also appears in the hypothetical intentionalism of Jerrold Levinson, "Intention and Interpretation: A Last Look," in *Intention and Interpretation,* ed. Iseminger, 221–56 (esp. 236), as well as in the fictionalist intentionalism of Alexander Nehamas, "The Postulated Author: Critical Monism as a Regulative Ideal," *Critical Inquiry* 8 (1981): 133–49 (esp. 144–47).

7. See Steven Knapp and Walter Benn Michaels, "The Impossibility of Intentionless Meaning," in *Intention and Interpretation,* ed. Iseminger, 51–64.

the Hirschian project of securing the author's intention in evidence external to the text, disambiguation fails on other counts. Every author's life is enmeshed in a wide variety of personal, social, economic, career-related, and existential contexts. It may be difficult enough to determine what the author's reaction was to the circumstances prevailing in one of them at a certain time. If, for instance, our aim is to disambiguate a poem that hovers between affirmation and despondency, shall we decide on the former on the grounds that the author was happy because of his recent marriage, or on the latter on the grounds that he was unhappy because of his father's death (and he was likely to write a poem that reflected one of these frames of mind)? Even if there is reliable evidence that determines the author's reaction in one context, there remains the often insuperably difficult task of weighing different contexts against each other. For example, Thomas Gray's *Elegy Written in a Country Churchyard* can be interpreted as a satire aimed at the social order, an attempt to alleviate the author's loneliness, or an enactment of his low spirits, pushed as far as an imagined death.[8] All these divergent readings have a reasonable claim to representing Gray's intention, as they can, respectively, be linked to well-attested social, personal, or medical facts that can be assumed to have preoccupied him at the time of writing: his relatively low social standing (in relation to aristocratic friends), his lack of close relatives, and his neurasthenia. There is no nontendentious way of privileging one of these contexts over the others, and consequently no possibility, even with reference to authorial intention, of securing a single correct interpretation of the *Elegy*.[9] Once this incommensurability of contexts has been grasped as a general point, it is not hard to understand why it is rare for critics to agree on a single correct interpretation of any work, even when the purview of textual interpretation is extended to include the author's intention.

The second reason why intentionalism cannot substantiate monism is that the assumption of a univocal authorial intention geared toward one coherent meaning is misguided. Instead, the author's overriding intention is surely in many cases the resolve to produce a work that will be as highly

8. These are, respectively, the interpretations presented by F. W. Bateson, "Gray's *Elegy* Reconsidered," in his *English Poetry: A Critical Introduction* (London: Longmans, Green & Co., 1950), 181–93; Thomas R. Carper, "Gray's Personal Elegy," *SEL: Studies in English Literature, 1500–1900* 17 (1977): 451–62; and Brian Cosgrove, " 'Ev'n in our ashes live their wonted fires': Privation and Affirmation in Gray's 'Elegy,' " *English* 29 (1980): 117–30.

9. *Mutatis mutandis,* this is also an argument against the claims of context-related monism.

appreciated as possible. And at least since Romanticism, this includes the requirement of a rich meaning potential, that is, multiple interpretability. The work with one clearly establishable meaning would seem square and uninteresting; if anything, it will therefore be the writer's intention to avoid producing such a work![10]

Third, even if writers regularly had a clear and univocal semantic intention and we could decide what contextual facts reliably indicate what it was, we would still not be able to arrive at a single correct interpretation. This is because discoverable authorial intentions do not cover more than some portions or aspects of the work. Typically, such intentions are of two kinds. One has to do with such "local" matters as idiosyncratically private word meaning or symbolism and the identification of intended reference in *romans à clef*. In this case some building blocks for an interpretation are provided, but by no means an interpretation of the work as a whole. In the other typical case, the intended meaning is overarching but general in nature, for instance, if we decide that Henry James intended the ghosts in *The Turn of the Screw* to be taken as real. At an important bifurcation, this disposes of one class of readings (the no-ghosts readings). But it still leaves open a host of interpretive questions, such as the nature of the evil represented by the ghosts, the extent of the children's possible complicity and depravity, as well as the appropriateness of the governess's reactions to the events. These questions clearly admit of a wide variety of interpretive answers: the disambiguation by reference to authorial intention is much more limited than many intentionalist discussions suggest. With the possible exception of some very short works, it clearly falls short of establishing a single correct interpretation displaying a reasonable coverage of main issues in a given work.

For all these reasons, then, not even monism of the most viable, intentionalist kind holds water. The ability of the work to support a variety of nonconverging interpretations[11] must be accepted as a fact with which all theories of literary interpretation have to come to terms. In other words, in this domain it is impossible to sustain the kind of realism (espoused implicitly by Beardsley, Hirsch, and other monists) that regards the work as a

---

10. Except when nonartistic intentions such as the exposure of social abuses predominate, as in Harriet Beecher Stowe's *Uncle Tom's Cabin* and Upton Sinclair's *The Jungle*.

11. The ultimate reasons for this ability are, first, that the interpretation of a literary work consists in selecting and combining what I have called "implications" and, second, that the number of implications a word sequence may have is indefinable. See my "Incompatible Interpretations of Literature," *Journal of Aesthetics and Art Criticism* 45 (1986): 147–61.

stable univocal entity that can ultimately be grasped in a single coherent interpretation. Let us now look at constructivism, the most readily available alternative.

III

Constructivism holds that interpretations of literary works are not accounts of their objects but projections from critical stances and sets of values. It obviously deals well with interpretive multiplicity—which it can ascribe to the multifarious methodologies and values available to readers in a pluralistic society—but it is scuttled by other characteristics of interpretation. This can be demonstrated with reference to Stanley Fish's 1980 study, which remains the paradigmatic statement of constructivism in literary theory.

Fish, as is well known, claims that "[i]nterpreters do not decode poems; they make them"[12] in accordance with the conventions of the interpretive community to which they belong. There may be substantial agreement among them, but this, "rather than being a proof of the stability of objects, is a testimony to the power of an interpretive community to constitute the objects" (338). There is, Fish argues, "no core of agreement *in* the text," only some agreement concerning "the ways of *producing* the text" (342, Fish's italics). But if this was true and publicly accepted possible meanings of words in the text (independent of any interpretation) counted for nothing, any established strategy should be applicable to any literary work (or any work of the same type, if we allow some differentiation of strategies according to genres and periods). One should be able to argue that the protagonist of *Othello* is prevented from enacting his desire for revenge by an incestuously motivated identification with his uncle. This is certainly an accepted strategy, applicable to *Hamlet*. So, if the source of the "mechanisms for ruling out readings [. . .] is not the text but the presently recognized interpretive strategies for producing the text," as Fish puts it (347), why cannot this strategy be applied to *Othello* as well?

Fish does not confront the objection in precisely this form, but he does discuss a similar example suggested by Norman Holland: why is it unacceptable, within the framework of the present literary community, to inter-

12. Stanley Fish, *Is There a Text in This Class? The Authority of Interpretive Communities* (Cambridge, Mass.: Harvard University Press, 1980), 327. Further references will be given parenthetically in the text.

pret Faulkner's "A Rose for Emily" as a story about Eskimos? The reason, Fish maintains, is that "there is at present no interpretive strategy for producing" the story "that would result in the emergence of obviously Eskimo meanings" (346). He then goes on to explain that such an interpretation might become possible if it was revealed that Faulkner always believed himself to be an Eskimo changeling and if critics elaborated a symbolic or allusive system showing the presence of this newly discovered "fact." Here Fish curiously shifts his ground. The concept of an interpretive strategy no longer designates the assumptions that govern our interpretations by allowing certain types (such as "nature versus culture") and disallowing others (such as spiritistic messages). Instead, the concept has turned into the equivalent of an acceptable interpretation of an individual work (an Eskimo reading of Faulkner's story) and the conditions of its acceptability (Faulkner's supposed belief that he was an Eskimo). When confronted with awkward evidence, Fish has thus been forced to abandon his meaningful, though misguided, claim that our reading is wholly governed by institutional conventions fashioning the literary work in their image: he cannot maintain, as he should be able to in order to support his theory, that even now the Eskimo reading is acceptable, since elaborate allusive systems constitute well-established interpretive strategies (for instance, in interpretations of Blake and Yeats) and since the text, in Fish's view, can offer no resistance. Fish's claim has in fact become circular: an interpretation is admissible if it can be produced by a recognized interpretive strategy, but that strategy includes all the considerations that in each individual case make the interpretation admissible. Thus Fish is unable to prove that correspondence with the work (as an entity independent of the interpretation) is not one of these considerations.

A further counterargument arises from the fact that it is possible to persuade readers to abandon their interpretation by pointing to parts or aspects of the work that the interpretation cannot accommodate. This fact is in itself awkward for constructivists because they deny that argumentative reference "past" an interpretation to the work is possible: there is, on their view, no such independent entity. They will of course reply that in such cases the interpretation is not challenged by reference to the work, but by another set of principles for producing the work (Fish, 353), that the disagreement is a "metacritical" one about the validity and elaboration of the approaches themselves.[13] But this defense breaks down on two counts. First,

13. Susan L. Feagin, "Incompatible Interpretations of Art," *Philosophy and Literature* 6 (1982): 133–46 (the quotation is from p. 139).

as we have seen, the reason why a certain interpretive strategy is admissible with regard to one tragedy by Shakespeare but not to another is not meta-critical. It concerns, not the strategy as such, but the relevance of its application. Because of qualities that must be independent of the interpretation (since it remains constant), one text responds satisfactorily to a given strategy, and another one does not. Second, it would seem that we can invalidate an interpretation with reference to the text even without providing an alternative interpretation in any reasonably strong sense of the word. We can simply point out that none of the meanings that certain words in the text may conceivably have, according to native speakers of the language, "fits" the interpretation and admit that these words pose a problem we are also unable to solve. Thereby we have referred to the text without substituting an alternative interpretation "presiding over its production" (Fish, 354): we have been unable to "produce" the text (i.e., understand it in a certain way) at all.

These, to my mind, are strong arguments against constructivism and for the necessity of some kind of realism in our understanding of literary interpretation. Furthermore, like the earlier arguments for the inescapable pluralism of our interpretive practice, they reinforce the initial paradox: the literary work genuinely confronts us both as a touchstone and as a chameleon.

IV

What we need to resolve the paradox is a conception of the literary work that posits neither the solidity of monistic realism nor the fluidity of constructivism. The apposite conception, I believe, should be based on a recognition of a quality of the literary work that I propose to call "pliability." It consists in the ability of the work to offer for our perception different patterns that may be disparate and even incompatible but that are nevertheless constrained by the work's particular application of linguistic means of expression, literary conventions, and culturally available assumptions about the world. Pliability thus differs both from the ultimate immovability assumed by monistic realism and from the indiscriminate malleability suggested by constructivism. While a cultural artifact is by no means analogous to a physical object, it may be useful, as a purely heuristic visual aid, to remind oneself of the qualities of pliable physical objects. They can assume an indefinable number of different shapes, but only within the bounds set by the extent and durability of their structure. Furthermore, the parts of that structure are interdependent in the sense that the shaping of some of them in one particular way limits the possibilities of shaping other parts. In the same way the literary work, on my account, consists of elements whose interpretability, though indefinably wide, is constrained both by their own constitution and by (the interpretation permitted by) other elements.

I proceed to illustrate the workings of pliability by means of three examples drawn from Shakespeare. The first has to do with the occurrence of a specific event: In *Othello,* has Emilia slept with the protagonist? The second tests an interpretation of a short passage in *Hamlet.* The third, to diversify the illustrations as much as possible, is by contrast situated on a high level of thematic abstraction: is the world presented to us in *King Lear* invested with or devoid of a metaphysical dimension? A characteristic of the questions emerging from *Othello* and *King Lear* is that they admit of diametrically opposed answers. They may therefore serve the further purpose of showing that the possibility of logically incompatible interpretations is not the monstrosity (to be combated, for instance, by recourse to monistic intentionalism) that it is taken to be in some quarters. Once the mechanisms of pliability have been grasped, incompatibles need cause neither scandal nor concern.

In *Othello,* the question of Emilia's fidelity first surfaces in a comment in her husband's, Iago's, soliloquy:

> I hate the Moor
> And it is thought abroad that 'twixt my sheets
> He's done my office. I know not if't be true,
> But I for mere suspicion in that kind
> Will do as if for surety.[14]

This is in itself a good example of pliability in an individual passage. On the one hand, one may say in defense of Emilia's fidelity that rumors are notoriously unreliable and that even Iago does not seem to take this one very seriously. He throws in a reference to it as a casual afterthought prefaced by "And," not by "Because," which would establish the possible liaison as a reason for his hatred of Othello. On the other hand, the odd use of

---

14. William Shakespeare, *Othello,* ed. E. A. J. Honigmann, Arden Shakespeare (Walton-on-Thames: Thomas Nelson & Sons, 1997), 1.3.385–89. Further references to act, scene, and lines in this edition will be given parenthetically in the text.

"And" does not dislodge the fact that Iago's shrewd mind dwells on the rumor, in which, furthermore, there may conceivably be some substance, since after all no rule states that all rumors are unreliable. Thus the same passage may be taken to suggest either Emilia's innocence or her culpability.

One can imagine the possibility that the play would later provide conclusive proof for one of these alternatives. In that case the pliability of the passage would be specious; in the larger structure its import would be fixed either as a manifestation of paranoia on Iago's part or as a palpable fillip to his crusade against Othello. But in fact the pliability is genuine and extends throughout the following relevant passages.

The interpretation that Emilia has slept with Othello can bring out that pattern in the following fashion: Emilia reveals her flirtatiousness by allowing herself, without objections, to be kissed by Cassio (2.1.97–103); Othello thinks of her as "a subtle whore, / A closet, lock and key, of villainous secrets" (4.2.21–22), which suggests that he knows her to be adulterous (as well as a keeper of Desdemona's secrets); in conversation with Desdemona, Emilia explicitly describes adultery as "a small vice" (4.3.68) that a woman may well cultivate for the proper rewards; and in her final confrontation with Othello, a commander whom she owes respect as a woman of the people, she is so astonishingly abusive—"thou art a devil" (5.2.131), "O gull, O dolt, / As ignorant as dirt!" (5.2.159–60)—as to suggest a secret ground of familiarity between them.

The interpretation that Emilia is innocent of adultery "bends" these passages in the opposite direction: Emilia is merely courteous to Cassio; Othello's reference to her as "a whore" is only occasioned by the link in his mind between her and her supposedly unfaithful mistress, Desdemona; Emilia's designation of adultery as "a small vice" is mere banter calculated to buoy the despondent Desdemona; and her uninhibited abuse of Othello is explained by her extreme horror and disgust at his murder of Desdemona. This interpretation may in addition emphasize the fact that Emilia spontaneously speaks to Desdemona of the frequent groundlessness of jealousy (3.4.159–62) and that she and Othello display no signs of undue familiarity when left alone together (4.2.1–19). The opposite interpretation will, on the other hand, explain the former as a clever piece of indirect self-exculpation and the latter as a passing encounter that in this respect proves nothing.[15]

---

15. Interpretive arguments of this kind may seem to deal with fictional characters as if, paradoxically, they were real people. However, interpretive statements such as "Emilia has been unfaithful" are in fact shorthand for "The play represents Emilia as having been unfaithful" (the assumption being that in so doing it relies on our understanding of human behavior

Taken together, these suggestions of fidelity or infidelity support each other, so that in each case there emerges a pattern that squares satisfactorily with the possibilities of interpretation offered by individual passages. In other words, the play in this respect displays a dual structure that can be "bent" into one of two shapes, each of which blocks perception of the other. We are thus faced with an object unamenable to accounts that partake of the monistic realist's assumption of a univocal object that can ultimately be perceived in a certain fixed way.

One might choose to look at the matter in another way. Instead of describing two conflicting patterns, one would hold the question of Emilia's (in)fidelity in abeyance on the grounds that there is no compelling evidence for either alternative. Rather than two distinct alternatives, one would attempt to bring out, in this respect, a fuzziness of the play akin to Ingarden's notion of *Unbestimmtheitsstellen*. The work could then be described as univocal but partially indeterminate or "incomplete." This, I would argue, may be a perfectly viable conception of such instances of undecidability in which the work offers very little information, particularly if the matter at hand is relatively unimportant for an interpretation of the work as a whole. But in the case of Emilia, the availability of considerable evidence for either alternative tends to press upon us a choice between two possible patterns instead of encouraging us to leave the question open. Furthermore, the latter strategy would also be unsatisfactory because so much of our interpretation of the play hinges on making a decision about Emilia's behavior: as the case may be, Iago emerges as either maniacal and deluded in his suspicion of her or as perceptive and even justified, up to a point, in his campaign of retribution against Othello; Othello, correspondingly, appears as an innocent victim of Iago's machinations or as a philanderer taken to task for his reckless promiscuity.

Because of such ramifications, literary interpretations in general tend to bring out one of the clearly etched patterns allowed by the work rather than leave matters hanging in the balance. One could even argue that this is what interpretation is all about: confronted with objects of cognition that strike us as unclear or puzzling, we do not, in interpreting them, rest content with that impression but make a series of informed and coordinated decisions and determinations in order to attain clarity and understanding. This general goal can usually be reached by different routes, resulting in different and possibly nonconverging interpretations.

---

and motivation). This kind of interpretation is therefore no more paradoxical than other attempts to determine the meaning of a literary work.

For a number of reasons, then, my emphasis on a conjunction of different patterns in *Othello* and in literary works in general cannot successfully be replaced by an analysis in terms of univocal indeterminacy. Similarly, the constructivist argument that interpretations fill in gaps in a partly or completely blank work also fails to provide a viable alternative. The duality we have observed results from a given construction of one set of elements in *Othello,* not from the lack of such a construction. Hence, as I have already suggested, if the construction was different, we might not find any pliability at all in this particular matter. This would be the case if, for instance, Othello's reflection (4.2.21) quoted above read "This is a subtle whore / *As I have known her be when she seduc'd me*" (where the italicized line is my addition to the text). This would conclusively establish Emilia's infidelity and controvert the interpretation that Iago's suspicion of her is entirely unfounded.[16] To return to the actual form of the play, one interpretation that it effectively rejects is the claim that Iago *is convinced* (as opposed to *suspects*) that Emilia has been unfaithful. The words already quoted from his soliloquy, "I know not if't be true" (1.3.387), are sufficiently fixed in English usage to prevent such a reading, even though, as an explanation of Iago's hatred of Othello, it would seem plausible in the context.

This combination of flexibility and resistance—an important characteristic of pliability—also appears in detailed textual criticism. Take the following passage from *Hamlet,* where Polonius speaks of his response to Hamlet's courtship of his daughter Ophelia, which he considers unseemly:

> And then I prescripts gave her,
> That she should lock herself from his resort,
> Admit no messengers, receive no tokens;
> Which done, she took the fruits of my advice,
> And he, repelled—a short tale to make—
> Fell into a sadness, then into a fast,
> Thence to a watch, thence into a weakness,
> Thence to a lightness, and, by this declension,
> Into the madness wherein now he raves
> And all we mourn for.[17]

16. Up to this point, that interpretation could nevertheless temporarily play a part in our reception of the play, as an element of suspense and insecurity that is here resolved conclusively.

17. William Shakespeare, *Hamlet,* ed. Harold Jenkins, Arden Shakespeare (London: Methuen, 1982), 2.2.142–51. Further references to act, scene, and lines in this edition will be given parenthetically in the text.

Consider the interpretation that Polonius's point is that he does not blame Hamlet for anything, provided only that Ophelia reveals that she had a part in the courtship equal to that of her suitor. Such an attitude is certainly in evidence elsewhere in Shakespeare when a widowed middle-aged father comments on an undesirable suitor; it is expressed in Brabantio's words about his daughter Desdemona and the protagonist in *Othello:* "If she confess that she was half the wooer, / Destruction on my head if my bad blame / Light on the man" (1.3.176–78). Up to a point, the interpretation suggested could also be applied to Polonius. One could argue that he is mistaken in his conviction that Ophelia "took the fruits of [his] advice" and rejected Hamlet's advances. As a later indication of this, Hamlet's denunciation of women—"You jig and amble, and you lisp" (3.1.146)—can be taken to apply in particular to his interlocutor, Ophelia, revealing her flirtatiousness. Thus Ophelia could indeed have played a part comparable to Hamlet's in the courtship, and Polonius, who might well suspect as much, could be considering a more favorable attitude toward their liaison, provided that he finds both parties committed to it. In context, then, the interpretation applicable to Brabantio could also fit Polonius.

For all that, it is obvious that Polonius's speech simply cannot be read in the same way as Brabantio's utterance. For one thing, the concatenation of sentences separated by the words "Which done [. . .] And [. . .] And" cannot be read as a conditional "If . . . then." For another, Polonius's references to himself—"I prescripts gave her" and "all we mourn for"—cannot by any means be construed as some kind of pledge or promise on his part. The interpretation cannot mold the text in the way that constructivism considers possible.

On the other hand, this is not to say—as the monistic realist would—that there is only one mark, of which the suggested reading falls short. On the contrary, this part of Polonius's speech, though far from dense or difficult, clearly raises some interpretive questions. To what extent is his judgment of Hamlet sincere, and to what extent influenced by his need to justify his own actions to the king and queen (whom he takes to frown on Hamlet's advances to Ophelia)? To what extent is he mistaken about the prince? We know that he is wrong to believe that Hamlet, who has decided to "put an antic disposition on" (1.5.180), is really mad. But is Polonius entirely wrong, or is Hamlet's melancholy in part due to Ophelia's behavior toward him? Different answers, and combinations of answers, to these questions are perfectly admissible, as are, consequently, different and nonconverging views of Polonius as a stupid windbag, a devious manipulator, or a judicious, if somewhat verbose, student of human nature.

Like a literary work as a whole, Polonius's speech thus exhibits considerable flexibility, but only within the limits of its construction. When those limits are transgressed, it resists a would-be interpretation even when it is plausible in the context as well as established in another similar case in Shakespeare. A literary work, to repeat, is indefinably *pliable,* that is, neither fixed nor indiscriminately malleable. That is the solution to the epistemic paradox of literary interpretation.

To turn to *King Lear,* there is no doubt that the play presents an exceptionally harrowing sequence of atrocities and calamities: the harsh disowning of Cordelia, the humiliation of Kent in the stocks, the exposure and derangement of Lear in the storm, the blinding of Gloucester, the murder of Cordelia in prison, and the death of Lear while poring over her dead body. One group of critics sees in the play as a whole (as distinct from statements made by individual characters) a bleak exposition of meaningless suffering and a denial of providence and an afterlife. They may seek support in three elements in the play. First, they habitually refer to the surprising and shocking deaths of Cordelia and Lear after their tender meeting and reconciliation, relatively late in the play, have suggested a final respite from suffering: "the deaths to no purpose of Lear and Cordelia controvert any providential redemption in the play's decisive, closing movement."[18] Second, time and again expressions of hope or belief in the ministry of the gods are dashed immediately and pointedly by the advent of further calamities, as when Edgar persuades himself to accept his lot, only to be devastated by the sight of his blinded father (in the first scene of Act 4), or when Lear's appeal to the heavens is followed by the outbreak of the storm (in the fourth scene of Act 2), which will lash his defenseless body: "Sequential ironies, which reflect a tendency of the play, are exposed like a series of trapdoors in *Lear.*"[19] Third, a telling conclusion can also be drawn from the mock suicide that Edgar arranges to restore his blind father's will to live and his faith in the gods. After Gloucester has supposedly jumped off a cliff, Edgar persuades him that he has been saved by the gods: "Therefore, thou happy father, / Think that the clearest Gods, who make them honours / Of men's impossi-

18. J. Stampfer, "The Catharsis of *King Lear,*" *Shakespeare Survey* 13 (1960): 1–10 (the quotation is from p. 9).

19. William R. Elton, *"King Lear" and the Gods* (San Marino, Calif.: Huntington Library, 1966), 330.

bilities, have preserved thee."[20] However, as Frank Whitehead has pointed out, there is a distinct irony in the fact that belief in such gods "can only be preserved by means of a cheap imposition upon a blind and helpless old man."[21]

Critics in the opposite camp maintain that the suffering detailed by the play, though real and terrible, is not meaningless: it is allowed, or even ordained, by providence and prepares the good characters for the afterlife by subjecting them to a process of redemptive growth. Such interpretations may point to the fact that the frequent invocations of various deities are given an increasingly Christian slant as the play proceeds;[22] and they may discover substantial parallels linking many characters with biblical figures and suggesting a symbolic pattern of salvation through suffering (particularly the suffering of Cordelia viewed as a Christ figure).[23] They may also emphasize the analogy between the main plot and the subplot: "So when we consider that both Gloucester and Lear have erred, have misjudged their children, have suffered terribly as a consequence, but have come (independently) to kindred wisdom, this clearly creates the impression that their suffering is an *ordained* suffering. We gain the impression that divine powers have acted to punish but also to enlighten these erring noblemen. A repeated pattern implies a pattern-maker."[24]

Though aware of each other, these two groups of critics rarely engage in a point-by-point debate with their polar opposites. However, one can see how each of them could reasonably deal with the counterevidence. The "nihilists" could say that the features the "redemptivists" call attention to are indeed elements in the play but that they only serve to inflate our expectations of a happy ending; when those expectations are defeated, the effect is all the more shattering, and so is the blow to any conception of a metaphysically based world order. The redemptivists, conversely, may grant the valid-

20. William Shakespeare, *King Lear,* ed. Kenneth Muir, Arden Shakespeare (Walton-on-Thames: Thomas Nelson & Sons, 1997 [1972]), 4.6.72–74.

21. Frank Whitehead, "The Gods in *King Lear,*" *Essays in Criticism* 42 (1992): 196–220 (the quotation is from p. 207).

22. J. C. Maxwell, "The Technique of Invocation in 'King Lear,' " *Modern Language Review* 45 (1950): 142–47.

23. Cherrell Guilfoyle, *Shakespeare's Play Within Play: Medieval Imagery and Scenic Form in "Hamlet," "Othello," and "King Lear,"* Early Drama, Art, and Music Monograph Series, 12 (Kalamazoo: Western Michigan University, Medieval Institute Publications, 1990), 111–27.

24. Cedric Watts, "Main Plot, Sub-Plot, and Paradox in *King Lear,*" in *King Lear: William Shakespeare,* ed. Linda Cookson and Bryan Loughrey (London: Longman, 1988), 11–18 (the quotation, with Watts's italics, is from p. 16).

ity of the observations made by the nihilists: the play recognizes the fact that there is, in this world, real suffering that may seem to dash all hopes and expectations and make a mockery of the whole idea of providence. But this, the redemptivists may argue, is part of the suffering necessary for purification and, furthermore, an example of the Christian conviction that God moves in mysterious ways: He may allow everything to look irremediably bleak but nevertheless presides over the events and holds out the possibility of salvation.

Both parties, then, are able to accommodate the relevant evidence, so that the worldview of *King Lear,* like the question of Emilia's fidelity, allows of two opposite and incompatible interpretations. It should be noted, however, that apart from differences in scale and complication, these two cases illustrate two different mechanisms in the workings of pliability. In the case of Emilia's fidelity, the two sets of arguments are able to *supersede* each other. To perceive Emilia as being merely courteous to Cassio is to extirpate the perception of her as flirtatious; to construe her lighthearted comments on adultery as a sign of adulterous proclivities is to erase their appearance of mere banter. When one set of observations prevails, the other is suppressed. In the case of *Lear,* on the other hand, the two sets of arguments exemplified *subsume* one another. Rather than banish the redemptivist's observations, the nihilist integrates them into a larger structure; and vice versa. When one set of observations prevails, the other is subordinated.[25]

Despite this difference in their mechanisms, both examples display an important feature of pliability: its lack of logical reciprocity. In our dealings with other kinds of entities—physical objects in particular—we are used to a state of affairs where an argument for p is, by logical necessity, an argument against not-p. But this, as we have seen, is not true of a pliable entity such as a literary work. The valid arguments for Emilia's fidelity and for the nihilism of *King Lear* do not rule their opposites out of court. For the latter to be established as equally valid, they need only show that they are capable of dealing with the relevant counterevidence in their particular way, by supersession or subsumption,[26] and of presenting a pattern of observations that are mutually supportive and consistent with relevant passages in the text.

25. This, however, is not to deny that when the highly complicated question of the worldview of *King Lear* is pursued in all its ramifications, there may be areas where opposing arguments are able to supersede each other.

26. Or by some other means, such as questioning the reliability of a speaker or narrator. This procedure is exemplified in my "Internalization and Death: A Reinterpretation of Rilke's *Duineser Elegien,*" *Modern Language Review* 94 (1999): 731–43.

Pliability, then, allows both p and not-p to be correct. By the same token, it sustains the coexistence of interpretations—such as those advocated by different schools of criticism—that are nonconverging in the sense that they cannot coherently be combined into a more comprehensive interpretation (even though they may be logically compatible). Hence, although there is no single correct interpretation, there may be many different correct interpretations. Each of them actualizes one of the patterns that are determined by the work as potentialities created by its particular application of linguistic and literary conventions as well as culturally available assumptions about the world. Because of this interaction between the work and conventions of reading and understanding, I prefer not to use the common locution that the meaning established in a successful interpretation is *in* the work. However, since that meaning is determined by the work's particular actualization of such conventions, it is on my account found, not made, by the interpreter. That account, in other words, constitutes a form of realism: one that is best termed "pluralistic realism."

V

The existence of incompatibles need not pose a threat to realism if that stance is broadly understood to be the conviction that objects of cognition and their properties exist independently of our conception of them and are in principle amenable to human inspection and comprehension. As Michael Krausz has been concerned to demonstrate, realism can in principle be combined with multiplism (pluralism) as well as with singularism (monism).[27] Nevertheless, as Krausz also points out, "the combination of the singularist and the ontological realist is rather orthodox; such a realism characteristically assumes that a real entity answers to a unique interpretation" (162). Similarly, in his analysis of contemporary varieties of realism, John Wright concludes that "the idea that Realism can be explicated as the doctrine that there is just One True Theory does seem to have a fair amount of truth in it."[28] No doubt this is so because incompatibles appear to call into question

27. Michael Krausz, *Rightness and Reasons: Interpretation in Cultural Practices* (Ithaca, N.Y.: Cornell University Press, 1993), chap. 6 and passim. A further reference to this work will be given parenthetically in the text.
28. John Wright, *Realism and Explanatory Priority,* Philosophical Studies Series, 71 (Dordrecht: Kluwer Academic Publishers, 1997), 33–34.

the most basic rationale of realism: if p and not-p are both accepted as correct statements about an entity E, it would seem that they do not so much refer to independently existing properties of E as project properties onto E, since E surely cannot *be* one thing as well as its opposite. The flaw in this kind of reasoning, we now realize, is the assumption that all objects of cognition are necessarily univocal. On the contrary, by virtue of their pliability, some are protean and multiform enough to support both logically incompatible and otherwise nonconverging statements. They *can* be one thing as well as its opposite.

This realization makes it easier to uphold realism in the cultural domain. To do so, one need not apply the monistic realists' elaborate strategies[29] designed to deny what is in the last resort undeniable: that many cultural phenomena support equally admissible incompatibles. This is true at the very least of artworks, many different kinds of texts (nonliterary as well as literary), and the character traits of human beings.

The pluralistic realism that accommodates the chameleon qualities as well as the touchstone qualities of such entities differs in many ways from the dominant monistic form of realism. It is not, as we have seen, wedded to bivalent logic. It allows a multiplicity of legitimate conceptions and perspectives—while its acknowledgment of the independently existing touchstone qualities of objects of cognition effectively counteracts all suggestions that anything goes. It does not see the accumulation of knowledge, in many cultural fields, as a road toward some ultimate goal; instead, it celebrates the never-ending actualization and deployment of the potentialities of the objects of cognition. Finally, compared to its monistic cousin, pluralistic realism has to devote more attention to understanding the identity of such objects to obviate the danger—present in theoretical discourse, though only marginally in such practices as literary criticism—that their multiformity is mistaken for disintegration.

In most of this, pluralistic realism, it is interesting to note, bears a marked resemblance to the "robust relativism" advocated by Joseph Margolis. There is a real dividing line: my inspection of the literary work's touchstone qualities has led me to insist, in a way that I take to be unacceptable to

---

29. A useful typology of such strategies is provided by Stephen Davies, "Relativism in Interpretation," *Journal of Aesthetics and Art Criticism* 53 (1995): 8–10, under the heading "Explaining the Problem Away." I have attempted to defuse some of those strategies by means of a detailed analysis of four incompatible interpretations of Gray's *Elegy* in my *Literary Interpretation: Current Models and a New Departure* (Åbo [Turku]: Åbo Academy Press, 1988), 53–74.

Margolis,[30] that a successful interpretation elicits a possible pattern determined by the construction of the work itself (though one that may be dormant and in need of keen-sighted detection). But in all other respects enumerated in the previous paragraph, pluralistic realism and robust relativism are remarkably similar. As I see it, they both position themselves on a middle ground where, despite the borderline that separates them, they are closer to each other than they are, respectively, to the monistic realism and the radical relativism that occupy the extreme opposite ends of the epistemological spectrum.

This suggests that the time-hallowed distinction in Western philosophy between realism and idealism/constructivism is in the process of being radically modified,[31] perhaps to be abandoned at some point in the future. The increased attention devoted in the last few decades to the epistemic nature of cultural artifacts has paved the way for a realization that in the cultural domain various traits of these two seemingly contradictory stances must somehow be combined. Pluralistic realism is one attempt at such a combination.

30. Cf. two often-quoted passages in Joseph Margolis, *Art and Philosophy* (Atlantic Highlands, N.J.: Humanities Press, 1980), where interpretation is said to comprise "the added contribution of the interpreter" (111) and "aesthetic designs" are described as something that can be "rigorously *imputed* to particular works when they cannot be determinately *found* in them" (160, Margolis's italics). In his recent "Replies in Search of Self-Discovery," in *Interpretation, Relativism, and the Metaphysics of Culture: Themes in the Philosophy of Joseph Margolis,* ed. Michael Krausz and Richard Shusterman (Amherst, N.Y.: Humanity Books, 1999), 337–408, Professor Margolis summarizes and amplifies his earlier views without clearly distancing himself from them in this respect (372). However, since he also emphasizes the inevitable "symbiosis" of "the disjoint 'contributions' of the 'brute world' and the 'sense-bestowing' functions of human subjects" (374), he may now find the whole distinction between imputing and finding less useful.

31. Cf. Richard J. Bernstein, *Beyond Objectivism and Relativism: Science, Hermeneutics, and Praxis* (Oxford: Basil Blackwell, 1983), and Joseph Margolis, *The Persistence of Reality,* vol. 1, *Pragmatism Without Foundations: Reconciling Realism and Relativism* (Oxford: Basil Blackwell, 1986). Note, however, that there are also considerable differences between these two stances, as can be seen from the critique of Bernstein in Joseph Margolis, *The Truth About Relativism* (Oxford: Basil Blackwell, 1991), 32–37 and 166–69.

The Multiple Interpretability of Musical Works

Stephen Davies

In this chapter I discuss the role of interpretation in the performance and reception of musical works specified by scores.[1] Five types of interpretation (notational, editorial, performative, work-descriptive, and performance-descriptive) are likely to be involved, and in none of these is it customary to assume there is one correct interpretation.

Notational Interpretation

Performers can use others' musical works or ideas as the starting point for their own improvisations and variations, as in much jazz. Often, though, their goal is to present a performance of the composer's piece, rather than something inspired by, or after, it. For example, they intend to perform Haydn's Symphony no. 100. If this is their aim, they must undertake to

For their help I thank Robert Stecker, Jerrold Levinson, and John Fisher.

1. Not all musical works are for performance. For instance, electronic pieces issued as discs are not. They are for playback, which may have a ritual character but does not involve the creative and interpretative contributions made by performers. Also, not all musical works are specified by scores. They can be perpetuated within purely oral traditions.

follow the instructions Haydn directed to his work's potential performers, since it is by issuing such instructions that composers authorize and specify their works. For Western classical music, these instructions are communicated in a score, a musical notation historically connected to and reflective of the composer's acts of work creation. In undertaking to perform the given work, the performers commit themselves to obeying its score. Here, then, is the first kind of interpretation: the interpretation or reading of the score.

Like all symbol systems, musical notations are not self-explanatory; they are not transparent in their significance. Moreover, they cannot be interpreted according to any simple algorithm. Of the instructions expressed in the score, not all are of equal force. Some, such as written out cadenzas in the eighteenth century, are recommendatory without being work-specifying; at that time the performer was free to improvise her own cadenza, even if one was recorded by the composer. Furthermore, even where they connect to work-determinative instructions, not all notations are to be taken at face value. Rhythmic values marked as dotted sometimes should be played as double-dotted; melodies that are written as "plain" sometimes require decoration. And finally, much that is required for the successful presentation of a work is not indicated in its score. For instance, the composer will assume that the violin's strings are tuned to the standard intervals and that its player will use an orthodox bow, playing the strings with the hair and not the wood. With respect to such matters, only departures from the norm, such as "col legno," are indicated in the score.[2]

To read a score, the player needs knowledge of what might be called purely notational conventions. For example, an accidental applies to all other notes at the given pitch in the same measure unless and until it is explicitly countermanded. In addition, she needs to understand and appreciate the performance practice that is assumed by the composer as a heritage shared with the musicians he addresses. To be blunt, she needs to know what a violin is and how to play it, what counts as "fast," and so on.

Performance practices are mutable; they vary from place to place and

2. The composer may include in the score annotations or written comments that are not instructions about what is to be done or sounded by the performer. If the conventions of music making do not allow such features to be work-indicative, they are not part of the work's specification. These annotations may be irrelevant to the music (e.g., the shopping reminder "buy more beans"), or they may be revealing of it (such as Beethoven's "Must it be? It must be!" in his String Quartet in F, op. 135). In the latter case, they indicate the composer's thoughts, intentions, or feelings and are thereby suggestive of rewarding interpretative approaches, though they go beyond the work-determining function that is central for scores.

time to time. I mentioned above that the composer assumes the string players will employ standard bows in the orthodox fashion, but the design and
shape of the bow, as well as the manner of holding and using it, have
changed considerably over the centuries. What counts as "standard" or
"orthodox" is relative to historical periods. When it comes to interpreting
the work's score, the performance practices to be considered are those of the
composer's day. In order to understand and follow the composer's work-
determinative instructions, the score must be interpreted in light of the notational conventions and performance practices the composer shared with the
musicians he was addressing. The score can seem to be transparent to the
work it encodes for the contemporary musicians to whom it is directed.
When the performers are distanced from the composer's musico-historical
situation, as is inevitable when they aim to play pieces from prior times or
other cultures, the proper interpretation of the score might depend not only
on considerable scholarship but also on the mastery of instruments and
playing techniques that are unfamiliar. A great deal of study, along with
sensitivity in using techniques and instruments that are not of the contemporary variety, might go into recognizing and executing the work-determinative instructions recorded by the composer.

Consider the example below. A number of questions will occur to the
player. How much should the opening chord be arpeggiated? Should the
first sixteenth note be given its full rhythmic value or shortened? In measure
two, how long should the grace note be? How quickly should the trill be
played, and should it end with a turn? How should the passage be bowed?
Should vibrato be used, and, if so, are there rates of oscillation that would
be unacceptably wide or narrow or fast or slow? Should the accents on the
first and third beats of the measure be strongly marked? Are the indicated
phrasings and decorations required, or only recommended? Most of these
questions will have straightforward replies if the player can identify the
work's vintage. If the music dates from 1720, the answers may not be the
same as they would be if it was composed in 1920.

The instructions issued within scores often are indefinite. "Allegro"
means "fast" (literally, it means "cheerful"), but what is a fast tempo?

Usually it is one falling between, say, eighty to a hundred beats per minute. So long as a performance of a work with a tempo marked as "allegro" falls within that range and holds consistently to its choice throughout the relevant section, it complies with the work's tempo specification. Tempo is among the work's identifying features, but the relevant tempo covers a range (only a narrow band of which should be employed in any particular performance). To put the point differently: the work-determinative instructions may be indefinite just so long as the work itself is indefinite in the relevant respects. Any particular performance must resolve the indefiniteness one way or the other, but many resolutions are consistent with the faithful presentation of the work.

Can an interpretation of the composer's score be *correct?* A performer who intends to discover in the score the composer's work-determining instructions reads the score incorrectly if she appeals to conventions and practices differing from those used by the composer. She might play a C-sharp, failing to realize that the note should be read as a natural, or she might decorate in the wrong place or in an entirely inappropriate style. If readings can be incorrect, they can be correct also. A correct reading would be one that captured the composer's directives and appreciated their relative weight.

Is there *only one* correct interpretation of the composer's score? Well, it might be that the score indicates allegro as the only correct tempo for a movement, or forte as the volume. Since only one tempo and one volume is indicated, there is a sense in which there is only one correct interpretation for each notational aspect. These indications are indefinite, however. At the level of actual performance, a range of finely graded options is consistent with what is instructed. The performer deals with concrete notes, rhythms, timbres, volumes, and tempos. She must work with particulars, not abstract types, even if it is the latter the composer specifies. More than one sounded realization can be consistent with the notation's proper interpretation, and, in that sense, there is not only one correct interpretation of the composer's score.

Editorial Interpretation

We tend to think of works as ordered sets of pitched tones because it is at that level of detail that we hear performances. Many pieces are not so fine-grained as this, however. For instance, their scores specify notes, rhythms, or chords at the level of general types rather than that of particular tokens. This is the case with figured bass notations in the eighteenth century, which indicate a bass line and the chordal skeleton that overlays this, but leave it to the performer to flesh out the bare framework. And the same applies to a contemporary score directing the performer to role dice to settle which notes are to be given or the order in which the sections are to be played.

Indefiniteness must be distinguished from ambiguity. The vagueness implicit in "Andante" or figured bass notation indicates an *indefiniteness* in the work and does not represent an inadequacy or problem with the notation itself. (It is not as if the work is more definite, with the notation inadequate to convey this.) By contrast, *ambiguities* in the score equivocate over or fail to specify details that should be definite because they are work-constitutive. In a typical case of ambiguity, two scores purporting to be of the same work differ in details that are work-identifying in pieces of that kind and era. This could arise because of a copying error or because of a notational slip made by the composer. Such ambiguities are indicative of notational errors and misrepresent the work's identity. In yet other cases, ambiguity can be introduced deliberately. Bruckner revised many of his symphonies after their initial publication. If a composer does this, without indicating any particular rendering as authoritative, then there is an ambiguity that is best defused by talk of the work's multiple versions. For instance, Stravinsky gave *Petrushka* two incarnations, and it is appropriate, therefore, that a particular performance specifies which version it follows.

To complicate matters, notations can be overdefinite. This occurs where they record details of a performative interpretation that go beyond the work's indefiniteness. If we have two scores of a late-eighteenth-century concerto, and one contains a written cadenza while the other indicates merely where the cadenza should be, there is no ambiguity. The performance practice of the day allowed cadenzas to be improvised. The written-out cadenza is not work-constitutive. It is either a record of a performance option that once was taken or a recommendation that the performer is free to ignore. The scores differ because the one indicates details of interpretation that go beyond the work, whereas the other merely indicates the respect in which the work is indefinite. For contrast, imagine that two versions of the score of a late Beethoven quartet differ in that a flat is canceled by a natural in the second violin at measure 100 of the first movement in the one but not in the other. In this case, we are likely to be facing an ambiguity, because Beethoven's late quartets, like others of the time, are not indefinite in the (relative) pitches of the notes that compose them.

Ambiguity invites editorial interpretation. If it arises from a copying error, the composer's original takes precedence. If the error is the composer's, the editor corrects the slip. If there is uncertainty about which alternative should be favored (though we know both cannot be right), the editor must exercise her judgment if she is providing a performing edition. In some cases, it will be appropriate to tag the work with "version of 1837." In others, the editor will have to commit herself to one path or the other. Such decisions should be footnoted in the score.

From the way they are discussed by musicians and musicologists, indefiniteness, overdefiniteness, and ambiguity are often conflated. That is understandable, given that we are not always well situated to draw the distinction in considering old music, because our knowledge of the background of practice assumed by such music is inadequate. Such epistemic limitations do not undercut the usefulness of the distinction, however, and it can be applied clearly enough in many cases. A second basis for confusion resides in the fact that indefiniteness and ambiguity present the performer with similar difficulties and uncertainties. If she is to play the work, she cannot avoid committing herself to producing a specific sonic outcome. From her point of view, it makes no difference whether she faces a range of options because the score accurately represents the work's indefiniteness or because the score contains an ambiguity. In both cases she must go beyond the score in settling the concrete details of her performance.

Nevertheless, the distinction is crucial to the proper description of the choices the performer makes. In the first instance, that in which the performer resolves an indefiniteness in the work by choosing to play one way or another, her selection determines how she will realize and interpret the work. That decision focuses on how to deliver the work once its specification has been recognized. By contrast, the resolution of ambiguities in the work's notation is directed at a pragmatic identification of the work and, as such, is logically prior to matters of interpretation. Performative interpretation can begin only when the work that is to be the object of interpretation has been located and identified.

Is there one correct resolution for each ambiguity in a score? Where the ambiguity is deliberate, the editor should record rather than resolve it. It would be ontologically tidier if each work was specified unambiguously, but there is no reason to think the identity of a musical work is seriously undermined by its existing in several closely related versions. Musical works are robust enough to survive minor multiplicities. The craving for neatness is ideological, not ontological. Where the ambiguity is accidental, however, it should be removed if possible. In effect, the composer's creative intention is decisive, and we can sometimes know what that was, because our knowledge of the composer's works and other music of the time allows us to identify a notational solecism as such. In many cases, though, we cannot be sure if an ambiguity is deliberate and, if not, how it should be treated. In some others, we cannot even be confident in distinguishing score ambiguity from indefiniteness.

Performative Interpretation

A performance is replete with sound. Some of this sonic filigree is distinctive to the particular performance; other detail belongs (predicatively) to the work and will be common to accurate performances of it. I call musical works "thick" or "thin," depending on how much of the performance's detail is constitutive of the piece. The less the minutiae of an accurate rendition are work identifying, the thinner is the work and the more indefinite it is. The more the detail of the performance belongs essentially to the piece, the thicker and more definite it is.

In the nineteenth century, it became the norm for Western classical works indicated by scores to specify notes and rhythms in sequences of particular individuals, tempo as beats per unit time, and instrumentation according to rather specific instrument types (for example, "violin"). Basically, every note to be sounded was indicated in the notation, along with many other details of the performance, and all these features were work-determinative. If one takes such works as paradigms of musical pieces, one might be tempted to decide that composers of prior times could not conceive of their creations as musical works and that we apply the notion anachronistically when we impose it on the music of those earlier periods. An alternative, the one I prefer, simply regards the works of the nineteenth century as thicker than those of earlier times, which were more indefinite and sometimes specified note types rather than particular tokens. There was not a radical upheaval in the practice of the nineteenth century, one separating it entirely from prior approaches to music; rather, there were changes that can be fully appreciated only as developing out of (and reacting against) earlier musical activities with which they were continuous in many vital respects.

Generalizing incautiously, one could say that the trend after the invention of musical notations was toward the specification of works that are thicker in their constitutive properties. The notation became more exhaustive. Sometimes this meant only that work-determinative details resident in the performance practice (such as required decorations) were taken into the notation, but in other cases (as in the move from verbal to metronomic tempo specifications), this change probably corresponded to a thickening of the work itself. In any event, the notation became increasingly complex, instruments and ensembles became more standardized, the competence of musicians improved, printing became more widespread, and composers were less frequently involved in the presentation of their works. In consequence, more details of the work came to be notated and accepted as work-determinative.

There is a gap between a performance and the features that constitute the work the performance is of. Where works are specified by scores, the performance always is more detailed than the piece. In other words, musical works specified by notations always are indefinite with regard to some features of their sonic embodiment, while performances always are replete. Provided the performer is in control of the sounds she produces, it is she who decides how to bridge this gap. Where the composer's instructions are indefinite, she must choose what is to be sounded or how it is to be done. The performer's interpretation is generated through these choices. In order to have the work sound out, the performer must go beyond it, since the work's specification underdetermines many of the performance's sonic features. As a result, many different sounding performances can be equally and ideally compliant with the composer's work-identifying directives. In other words, faithfulness to the work is consistent with significant differences between performances, and these differences will be attributable to the performer's interpretation.

The thinner the work, the more interpretative opportunities it affords the performer. Indeed, if the work is very thin (as is the case with many Tin Pan Alley songs), almost all the value and attraction will lie in the interpretive aspect of performance. The thicker the work, the more the performer will take as her task the work's delivery to the audience for their contemplation. But even if the work is very thick, there remains considerable scope for the performer's interpretation, and the differences between performances are apt to be as interesting as what they share. Earlier I observed that nineteenth-century classical works were usually thicker than their predecessors. Yet it is plain that the symphonies of Brahms, say, are subject to a variety of interpretations. This is because their work specifications remain indefinite in many crucial respects, even if their scores specify each and every note to be played. If a note is marked as forte, still the performer must decide just how loud it is to be; if the melody is phrased, still the performer must decide how to articulate that phrasing. The musician controls an extraordinary range of options and shades regarding attack, decay, dynamics, articulation, color, pitch, and timing—far more than is specified in regular notations (and far more than could be indicated in any functionally useful notation, as is apparent when one considers the quantity of 1s and 0s needed to specify musical files digitally). Moreover, she controls the way in which elements succeed each other to build themes, sections, and movements. In playing the phrase of the moment, there are very many ways she can shape it in order to bring out or suppress its connections to what has preceded and will come later. In exercising these options, she creates the performative interpretation.

I have said the musician's interpretation of the work is expressed in the choices she makes in performing it. It might be objected: only those choices that are guided by an overall vision of the work could contribute to an interpretation; moment-by-moment decisions disregarding the whole do not qualify as interpretative.

There is a crucial unclarity in this objection. If the claim is that the performer must be able to describe an overarching interpretive vision and to say how local decisions contribute to achieving this, it is mistaken. I suspect that many highly skilled performers do not concern themselves with large-scale form and the like, being more involved with the minutiae of the moment. They might quite reasonably expect the form to take care of itself, so to speak, so long as they give due attention to the appropriate microstructures. Moreover, the kind of practical skill displayed by the performer is not always verbally expressible. Certainly, we would expect the performer to be able to tell us where the melody begins and ends and to show the usual verbal signs of musical literacy, but someone can satisfy this expectation without being able to recount a plausible and coherent narrative that makes sense of the work's totality and relates it to far-sighted performance decisions. Instead, we expect the musician to rely on her intuitions about what seems right, or seems to work, in taking her choices. Which gets us to the other side of the ambiguity: if "being guided by an overall vision of the work" means relying on musical intuitions honed through careful practice and repeated playings of the piece, then it is not clear that an objection is being raised to what I wrote earlier. As I said, the interpretation that is the performer's overall vision of the work arises from her choices, assuming she relies on her musical judgment and experience in making them. (If her play-ing seems to be spontaneous and to focus more on the moment than the totality, she should be understood to be offering an interpretation under which these reactions are plausible responses to the work's qualities and mood.)

A different way of emphasizing that the player's interpretation presup-poses her executive competence and a musical judgment informed by famil-iarity with the piece, or with stylistically similar ones, is to insist that she be able to own the interpretation that is given. For the interpretation to be hers, she must be able to take responsibility for producing it. This explains why we attribute the interpretation to the conductor, not the orchestral members, in the case in which the conductor decides for the group. And it acknowledges that one individual might play an interpretation that is another's, not her own, by slavishly copying everything done (decided by) the other. This last observation brings to light another point: just as works can have different performances, so too can interpretations. A particular interpretation can be instanced in distinct performances manifesting the same set of choices.

The function of a performative interpretation is to reveal the work in a certain perspective. If successful, the interpretation shows off the work clearly and (if possible) to advantage, allowing it to be understood and ap-preciated. Performative interpretations should be internally consistent so long as the work can be heard that way, because an account of the work that makes it seem incoherent is unlikely to do it justice. Moreover, the connection or proximity of parts usually should be stressed. Dramatic changes in mood, style, or technique are appropriate in interpretations only where they are called for in the work's specification (or in the established performance practice for such pieces). Despite what I have just written, lus-terless or episodic performances can offer good interpretations if they are of works designed to exhibit such qualities; some works aim to represent repetitive, inhuman mechanisms or mindless disorganization and are best revealed through interpretations exemplifying these properties.

If it is the prime function of interpretations to present an interesting, revealing, and enjoyable perspective on the piece that is performed, then the value of a given interpretation will depend in part on the audience's knowl-edge and experience. What will be experienced as interesting or revealing in a performance of Beethoven's Symphony no. 5 relies on the listener's history of involvement with the work and playings of it. In standard cases, the pro-fessional musician can reasonably assume that she is dealing with a musically experienced audience. Under special conditions, it can be obvious that this is not the case, however, and this recognition should affect the interpretation offered. The interpretation that is apt for an audience of tyros is not so when offered to a convention of spent music critics.

Is there only one correct performative interpretation? No. Many are consistent with the faithful delivery of the work. Some of these will be poor, despite being true to the work. For instance, they might be uncompelling, implausible, and tasteless. Even among good interpretations, there is no reason to expect similarity. Indeed, we value works for the fecundity of interpretations to which they give rise, and we positively value variety and contrast among interpretations. One rendition might stress drama and tension, where the other gives more weight to the lyric and expressive; one might invest the whole with an energetic undertow, while the other is more relaxed; one might treat the piece's moods as merely successive, while another tries to connect them within some wider narrative; one might give each climax full power, while the other accumulates their impact by building each a little more than its predecessors. The multiplicity of legitimate performative interpretations must be plain to anyone who has experienced many different performances of, say, Tchaikovsky's Symphony no. 6.

Descriptive Interpretation of the Work

A performance embodies or instances the work it is of. Because the performance provides the primary route of access to the work, and because the performance would not exist as such independently of the piece it is of, there is a relation of mutual dependence between the two. Moreover, a performative interpretation shows the work in a certain light, but without describing it. By contrast, what I call descriptive interpretations of the work are verbal accounts that exist independently of the work and its performance.

A musically self-aware performer might develop her own descriptive interpretation of the work. Or she might learn of and agree with a descriptive work interpretation developed by another person. In these cases, the descriptive work interpretation is likely to inform and affect the musician's performative interpretation. Similarly, a listener, critic, or analyst might come to a particular descriptive interpretation under the influence of a given performance. Nevertheless, the connection between these two modes of interpretation is not as strict as that of logical entailment. Different performative interpretations might be equally consistent with and illustrative of a given descriptive interpretation of the work, and different descriptive interpretations might be compatible with and exemplify a single performative interpretation.[3]

The function of a descriptive interpretation is like that of a performative interpretation, in that it tries to find a manner of charactering the work as a coherent whole, but whereas the latter does this sensuously, by presenting the work in a certain way, the former is discursive. It provides a description or narrative that, if successful, tracks the course of the music and explains why it progresses as it does. The descriptive interpretation can be thought of as an adjunct to the listening process; it recommends an appropriate (rewarding, revealing) way of listening to the work.

Descriptive interpretations can be very diverse. Consider the following accounts of Beethoven's *Grosse Fuge* (op. 133), which was the original finale of op. 130:

Roger Fiske writes in these terms:

> Here is a brief analysis of the tremendous fugue:
> *Introduction.* The theme in unison octaves . . . I shall call it A for brevity; next, three transformations of A, as they will occur in the three main sections of the fugue (fast, fairly slow, *scherzo*), but in the reverse order. All this takes less time to play than to describe.
> *First Fugue.* A double fugue. A being the counter subject; the main subject has wide leaps and a dotted rhythm. The energy generated in this section is overwhelming; the music is cruelly difficult to play and usually sounds a bit of a scrape. Very loud all through.
> *Second Fugue.* Fairly slow. A is again the countersubject and does not appear for some bars. Very soft all through.
> *Third Fugue. Scherzo.* A, here the principal subject, sounds very jaunty in 6/8 rhythm. This is a long section with reminiscences of what has gone before.
> *Coda.* Based largely on the dotted-rhythm subject in the First Fugue.[4]

---

3. For discussion of these and other relevant issues, see Jerrold Levinson, "Performative vs. Critical Interpretation in Music," in *The Interpretation of Music: Philosophical Essays,* ed. Michael Krausz (Oxford: Clarendon Press, 1993), 33–60.

4. Roger Fiske, "Ludwig van Beethoven (1770–1827)," in *Chamber Music,* ed. Alec Robertson (London: Penguin Books, 1957), 94–140. The quote is from p. 134.

William Kinderman says:

> The parade of fugal themes in the "Overture" anticipates the main sections of the great finale in reverse order. As Kramer points out, this sequence proceeds from the clearest thematic statement to the most obscure—the gapped form of the subject that serves as counter-subject in the huge opening section in B♭. Conversely, the main sections of the fugue unfold with a sense of progress from the obscure to the coherent; the most basic form of the subject is withheld until the final passages. The most emphatic assertion of this principal fugue subject in the tonic B♭ occurs only in the closing section marked *Allegro molto e con brio*, where it is prefaced by brief reminiscences of two of the other main sections (now recalled in the proper order). In the *Grosse Fuge* Beethoven combines smaller movements into a composite form using variation technique, while employing unusually elaborate rhetorical devices of premonition and reminiscence. In these respects the quartet finale bears comparison to the choral finale of the Ninth Symphony.[5]

Charles Rosen has this to say:

> Beethoven's development of the fugue is best comprehended within the context of the transformation of the variation. The two fugal finales—the *Great Fugue* op. 133 (the last movement of the String Quartet op. 130) and the fugue of the *Hammerklavier*—are both conceived as a series of variations, each new treatment of the theme being given a new character. Like the last movement of the Ninth Symphony, they both have the harmonic tensions characteristic of sonata-allegro form, along with its sense of a return and extensive resolution. They both, too, impose upon this another structural idea of several movements: this is particularly evident in the *Great Fugue,* which has an introduction, Allegro, slow movement (in a new key), and Scherzo finale as almost completely separate divisions; but the D major section of the *Hammerklavier* Fugue also provides a perceptible sense of slow movement before the stretto-finale. No one model, however, can exhaust the variety of ways in which Beethoven was able to integrate the fugue into a classical structure. . . . The aspect

5. William Kinderman, *Beethoven* (Oxford: Oxford University Press, 1995). The quote is from pp. 305–6. Reprinted with the permission of Oxford University Press.

of many of these late works is not ingratiating; to many, the *Great Fugue* is disagreeably harsh. But when it is played, as it should be, as the finale of the B flat Quartet op. 130, there is nothing eccentric in this harshness. . . . What makes some of these works appear wilful is that they are uncompromising.[6]

Melvin Berger describes the piece as follows:

The intense and often frenzied *Grosse Fuge* baffles many listeners with its giant leaps, clashing dissonances, and overwhelming rhythmic drive. Harold Bauer . . . believed that the work was misinterpreted. "The *Grosse Fuge* is more like a glorified polka-scherzo," he said. "People play it as if it were profoundly mystical which it is not. They put philosophy into it instead of music." Most other interpreters and analysts disagree. They are stirred by its rage and vehemence and are awestruck by its grand proportions and symphonic elements. It is a brilliant paradigm of various fugal techniques, some harking back to the polyphony of Bach, others looking ahead to the advanced musical thinking of Liszt and Wagner. The brief opening section, marked *Overtura* by Beethoven, resembles the introduction to an opera, but instead of presenting tunes from the opera it sets out four different statements of the main fugal subject. It is first presented in broad, loud, accented tones: the next statement is much faster and rhythmically altered. The tempo then slows for a quiet, smooth, legato statement of the same theme. A final presentation, first violin alone, reveals the melody in note-by-note fragmentation. The *Overtura* is followed by the *Fuga*, the fugue proper, which starts with the violin flinging out a subsidiary subject, an angular, leaping melody against which the viola pounds out the fragmented main subject. For over 124 measures of the fugue Beethoven does not drop below a relentless *fortissimo* ("very loud") dynamic level, with accents to add even more power to the wild music. Then suddenly the music quiets, the key changes, and another fugal episode, based on the subsidiary theme and the main subject ensues, all *pianissimo* ("very soft"). The third episode, faster in tempo, is based on a rhythmic transformation of the main theme. Varied sections follow, all growing from the same

---

6. Charles Rosen, *The Classical Style: Haydn, Mozart, Beethoven* (London: Faber & Faber, 1971). The quote is from pp. 440–45.

material though reworked and refashioned into an amazing variety of shapes and forms. The coda offers fleeting glimpses of the different subjects in a similar manner to the *Overtura* and then builds to still another climax and abrupt ending.[7]

Sidney Finkelstein observes:

> There are four main themes, which are musically connected but have each its distinct individuality. The introduction presents two of them, one which will be heard throughout the work, of great upward leaps of a seventh and a sixth, and another more relaxed and tender, flowing in sixteenth notes. After a repetition of the first theme, and the hesitant contrasting statement of the second theme, the fugue proper begins on a third theme, which has a strong rhythmic impact with its double "hammer blows." This theme is heard in succession from first violin, second violin, viola and cello, and in the rich fugal texture the introductory theme is heard as a counter-melody. Triplets give rhythmic variety as it runs its fierce course. Then comes the long, tender and plaintive interlude of rippling sixteenth-note figures, *Meno mosso e moderato,* using the second theme announced in the introduction. It is busily contrapuntal but not fugal. The tempo then changes to *Allegro molto e con brio,* and the fourth theme is heard, bright and dancing. The higher instruments devote themselves to it. A sudden modulation, without break, inaugurates a new development. The cello forcefully announces the opening theme of the work, under drooping figures by the second violin. It is taken up in turn by the viola, second violin, and first violin, and a new double fugue is on the way. It moves through complications to a succession of searing climaxes, of high notes antiphonally answered by low notes, or low by high. Finally the dancing theme is heard again, and the work moves to a meditative conclusion based on the first fugue theme.[8]

J. W. N. Sullivan offers this account:

> In the great Fugue of the B flat Quartet the experiences of life are seen as the conditions of creation and are accepted as such. The Fugue

7. Melvin Berger, *Guide to Chamber Music* (New York: Doubleday, 1985). The quote is from pp. 71–72. Reprinted with the author's permission.

8. Sidney Finkelstein, notes to a Vanguard (Recording Society) 1971 four-LP set by the Yale Quartet. Reprinted with permission of Vanguard Classics USA. Copyright 1971 by the Omega Record Group, Inc., New York.

has been called an expression of the reconciliation of freedom and necessity, or of assertion and submission, and the terms may pass since they suggest the state of consciousness that informs the Fugue, a state in which the apparently opposing elements of life are seen as necessary and no longer in opposition. Beethoven had come to realize that his creative energy, which he at one time opposed to his destiny, in reality owed its very life to that destiny. It is not merely that he believed that the price was worth paying; he came to see it as necessary that a price should be paid. To be willing to suffer in order to create is one thing; to realize that one's creation necessitates one's suffering, that suffering is one of the greatest of God's gifts, is almost to reach a mystical solution of the problem of evil, a solution that it is probably for the good of the world that very few people will ever entertain. Yet, except in terms of this kind, we cannot represent to ourselves the spiritual content of the Grösse Fugue. The fugue opens with such an expression of unbridled energy and dominant will that it seems about to break the bounds of the string quartet. This vigorous, striving life is very different from the almost subhuman furious activity of the Fugue of the Hammerklavier Sonata, although it seems to promise an equally headlong course. But, with the entry of the opposing G flat major episode it changes its character. We become aware that a truly indescribable synthesis has been effected. There is no effect conveyed to us of anything being yielded up or sacrificed. Nevertheless, there is a change, a change that makes us conscious that opposites have been reconciled, although the Fugue marches to its close in indestructible might. This Fugue is certainly, as Bekker has rightly insisted, the crown and *raison d'être* of the whole B flat major Quartet.[9]

How should we characterize these descriptions of the *Grosse Fuge?* A first point draws attention to the fact that many make comparisons with related works. Plainly, performative interpretations cannot draw such comparisons to the audience's attention; at best, the performer can hope the listener will make relevant connections for himself. Here, then, is an advantage discursive reflection has over musical production: it can help explain what hap-

---

9. J. W. N. Sullivan, *Beethoven* (Harmondsworth, Middlesex: Penguin Books, 1949), 142–43 (first published by Jonathan Cape, 1929).

pens in a given work by reference to how other pieces in the same genre or oeuvre are both similar and different.

Two other features are shared by all these accounts: each uses low-level technical terms (like pitch names), and each describes properties of the music by reference to the way it is experienced (energy, tension, harshness).

The interpretations differ considerably in the proportions with which they mix the technical and the nontechnical. Fiske does no more than sketch the piece's geography. Kinderman goes further in that he discusses devices of premonition and reminiscence. Rosen outlines how a multimovement pattern here is superimposed on a fugal structure relying more on variation than on traditional techniques of fugal development. He makes salient for unreflective listeners features they would easily miss, features that enrich the experience and the appreciation of the music when apprehended. As explanations of the music's progress, these three stories restrict themselves largely to musical technicalities. By contrast, Berger and Finkelstein pay no less attention to the mood conveyed by the piece than to its structure.

Sullivan's is the least technical and the most ambitious story. He sets out to discover the source of the piece's profundity: it reconciles apparently irreconcilable tensions, thereby intimating a solution to the problem of explaining why a benevolent, omniscient, and omnipotent God would tolerate the existence of undeserved suffering and evil. In my view, Sullivan is too quick to infer the composer's emotional and psychological commitments from the nature of the music. That inference cannot be guaranteed to go through, even if it is more plausible for Beethoven than for many others because he was so obviously trying to convey his personal response to the world through his music. Furthermore, I regard Sullivan's conclusions as pure whimsy, as going far beyond anything that can be substantiated solely by reference to the music and the context of its creation. But I quote Sullivan not to ridicule his excesses. I do so, instead, because he makes clear that the fullest explanation of the music's progress must take account of what he calls its "spiritual content." I think his exposition of this content owes a great deal to fancy, but I allow that he has taken on a more demanding and yet crucial task than the other critics in trying to address what is so humanly compelling and impressive about Beethoven's piece.

It might be argued that the point of a person's descriptive interpretation is to lead her interlocutor to an experience of the music's coherence. Any story—no matter how metonymic and fantastic—must be judged a success so long as it generates the desired experience. Sullivan's account will be as good as any other if it does the trick. I disagree, however. Though I am helped in following and understanding Prokofiev's *Peter and the Wolf* by the narrative that it illustrates, an equivalent story concerning Fred and the Serval is not an interpretation of Prokofiev's Symphony no. 5, even if it succeeds as a prop by leading me to hear the work in some appropriate fashion. Neither is a story about the relation between creativity and suffering an interpretation of a work if that story bears no connection to the parts of the work and the manner in which they succeed and relate to each other. A descriptive interpretation must be about the work it characterizes. As such, it must deal with the work's elements (including expressive and not merely formal features) as contributing or not to the fashion in which the music unfolds, develops, and ends. A descriptive interpretation must be answerable to the work it is of. If we expect it to produce an appropriate experience of the work, we do so because we take it to be consonant with and responsive to the articulation of the work it outlines.

Should technical analyses be distinguished from descriptive interpretations? I think not. They have a specialist audience, but they are best regarded as a subset within the wider realm of descriptive interpretations.[10] Accounts that confine themselves to technical niceties usually are incomplete as interpretations because there is more to most pieces than is uncovered by a reckoning of formal or musical elements narrowly construed. Most music has an expressive character, and the treatment of this usually is no less significant within the work than is attention to structure. Moreover, the expressive and the formal are not intrinsically opposed and in many cases cooperate in propelling and shaping the course of the work.

This is not to say that accounts of mood, color, and expressiveness can be reduced easily to technical descriptions, or vice versa. The two kinds of description are not perfectly intertranslatable. They are complementary, though, not opposed. The listener who is not technically minded might gain as much (and much the same) from metaphorical descriptions as the musicologist gets from an analysis.

Is there one true descriptive interpretation of the work? One might think so if one believed that a giant disjunction of each interpretative possibility could be achieved or would make sense. But that amalgamation would be an open-ended hodgepodge, rather than a singular, definitive interpretation.

10. For discussion of the relation between analyses and performative interpretations, see Edward T. Cone, *Musical Form and Musical Performance* (New York: Norton, 1968); Wallace Berry, *Musical Structure and Performance* (New Haven: Yale University Press, 1989); John Rink, ed., *The Practice of Performance: Studies in Musical Interpretation* (Cambridge: Cambridge University Press, 1995), pt. 3.

Alternatively, one might think so if one believed the work means only what its composer intended. But there is no reason to assume composers always have clear intentions about the significance or proper description of their work, or any reason to think there could not be more in the work than passes through the consciousness of its composer. Moreover, the fact that descriptive interpretations apply one medium of meaning and communication (the discursive) to a quite different one (the musical) provides a reason for expecting multiple mappings and relationships, rather than a neat one-to-one correspondence.

Notice, though, that this conclusion does not endorse theories insisting that interpretation is radically subjective or massively underdetermined. Descriptive interpretations can be false: it is not true that Beethoven's Symphony no. 5 is about the invention of the coffee percolator. And descriptive interpretations can be inapt and unrevealing. Also, the assessment of a descriptive interpretation is grounded publicly through a process that measures it against the work and against competing interpretations. There may be no one best descriptive interpretation, but this does not entail that all conceivable descriptions of the music are on a par.

Descriptive Interpretation of the Performance

If works exist as abstract particulars, distinct from the set of their possible performances, and if performances possess features that do not belong to the works they embody, we will need to be careful in distinguishing between the performance and the work as the object of a descriptive interpretation. Not everything that is true of the latter will apply also to the former.

In the previous section, I gave examples of descriptive interpretations of Beethoven's *Grosse Fuge*. These interpretations are of the work, not of any performance of it. The descriptive interpretations provided by music analysts and the authors of program notes are bound to be of this kind. Where a particular performance is discussed, the primary focus still can fall on the work embodied in it. Plainly though, there are descriptive interpretations that target the performance rather than the work. The newspaper notices written by professional music critics usually devote attention to creative features of the given performance. These accounts could have the function I have earlier stressed for interpretations—that of making sense of the object of interpretation, which, in this case, is the original contribution made by the performers. They would do so where they are presented to other audience members or the performers. More often, though, such notices function as reports addressed to people who were not present at the concert and, hence, who cannot test how much sense the accounts make of the events they retell.

Is there one true descriptive interpretation of the performance? This is unlikely for reasons like those in terms of which I denied that there is one true descriptive interpretation of the work.

Conclusion

Where the musician's goal is to play the composer's work, ambiguities in the notation by which that work is conveyed present problems, though these sometimes can be resolved easily enough by allowing that the given work exists in more than one version. Scores, even where they are not ambiguous, always are indefinite about much the performer will do and achieve in sounding out the work. They are so because the works they identify are similarly indefinite. This is not to say that such works are deficient. To the contrary, they are indefinite because they are created for performance. That they can be multiply interpreted is inevitable.

Something similar could be said of singular works, such as oil paintings, and of multiple works whose instances are more or less identical, such as printed novels. They, too, lend themselves to multiple descriptive interpretations. But they do not celebrate their interpretability as works created for performance do. The very mode by which the latter works are promulgated, in instructions that underdetermine the concrete details of their realizations, acknowledges and promotes the creative skill required for their rendition. In being designed for multiple and different performances, they are also created for multiple and different interpretations. They cannot be instanced independently of their being interpreted. The possibility of their various interpretations is integral to their nature and value as art.

Right Answers: Dworkin's Jurisprudence

Rex Martin

Critics sometimes charge that contemporary liberalism is committed to a monolithic and universalist scheme of values and that liberal accounts of political justice and proposals for public policy are deeply and inevitably skewed, even flawed, by these very commitments. Sometimes the charge is focused on liberalism's alleged privileging of certain values, for example, the values of personal autonomy or atomistic individualism. And sometimes it focuses on the claim, purportedly made by leading liberal theorists, that there is a single best interpretation of political justice, for example, or of the law and what it requires in given cases. John Rawls (especially in his book *A Theory of Justice*) and Ronald Dworkin, two leading contemporary liberal theorists, are typically cited among the "usual suspects" on both these charges, but especially the second one.

Dworkin's work has primarily been in the area of philosophical jurisprudence, and he has an international reputation and a standing there comparable to (but not quite as high as) that of Rawls in political philosophy. I want in the present paper to concentrate on Dworkin, in particular.

I want to thank David Reidy, Stephen Mathis, Karen Bell, and Peri Roberts for many valuable discussions, over the last several years, on Dworkin, and also to thank my colleagues Ann Cudd, Richard DeGeorge, and Russ Shafer Landau for their helpful comments on an earlier draft of the present paper.

Critical opinion, predominantly, leans to the view that Dworkin has quite consistently, throughout his career, espoused the idea of a single right interpretation. His theory of jurisprudence is taken to be almost a paradigm of the deployment of that idea.

Indeed, Rawls—in a brief contrast of his current views, in *Political Liberalism* (PL), with those of Dworkin—adds, as an aside, after a lengthy footnote on Dworkin, that "the idea of public reason [in Rawls's own PL theory] does not mean that judges agree with one another, any more than citizens do, in the details of their understanding of the constitution" (Rawls 1996, 237; for the long footnote, see 236–37 n. 23). H. L. A. Hart (Dworkin's predecessor in the chair of jurisprudence at Oxford) says, in one of his last published pieces, that Dworkin "has argued that apart from some trivial exceptions there are no such cases [of what Hart calls judicial "discretion"], since as he has famously said, there is always a single 'right answer' to any meaningful question as to what the law is on any point arising in any case."[1] And Paul Kelly, a knowledgeable interpreter, in an introductory essay on Dworkin in one of the leading British political-theory textbooks, says that Dworkin holds that "there is in principle a right answer to each controversial 'hard case' "; Kelly goes on to gloss this claim further: "The 'right-answer thesis' excludes the possibility of any middle ground between two controversial claims in law or morality. If one is true, then the other cannot also be true at the same time and must therefore be false" (1996, 284; see also 285).

Again, then, we come back to the idea that Dworkin's "right-answer thesis" means or implies that there is always a *single* right interpretation "as to what the law is on any point arising in any case" (as Hart puts it), even in the most controversial of cases. This seems to be the agreed-upon, indeed the canonical, reading of Dworkin's theory of adjudication. In this brief paper on Dworkin I'd like to challenge this prevailing reading and to suggest an alternative account.

In his seminal paper "Hard Cases" Dworkin lays out three main theses for defense: that for any case there is always a correct decision in law for a judge to make (always a "right answer"), that all cases in law involve rights (in some essential way), and finally that rights are "trumps" (as Dworkin

---

1. See Hart 1994, 306 n. 272. The editors describe the text of this note as "an alternative beginning" to section 6 of the postscript; they add that they have included this alternative version in the published text "here, as it was not discarded."

liked to put it).[2] The first two theses are closely connected, and I concentrate on them in the present article. In Dworkin's subsequent paper "No Right Answer?" these two key theses are elaborated at length.[3]

The issue Dworkin principally wants to address in this paper is whether there are "gaps" in the law, whether judges have discretion in hard cases. Lawyers seem, quite naturally, to assume bivalence in the law; for example, either a contract is valid or it is not; a person charged with a criminal offense either is or is not guilty; in a civil case someone before the court either is liable for costs or is not liable (MOP, 120). Furthermore, these bivalent results are fully "dispositive": if a contract is valid, then a judge has a duty to enforce it (duty to do A); if it is not valid then a judge has a contrary duty (that is, has a duty to do not-A). Thus, assuming bivalence and the pervasive importance of "dispositive concepts" (such as valid or guilty or liable) in law, there should be right answers (that is, definite duties to decide/ act) for judges. Indeed, in principle there are *always* right answers.

What Dworkin does, then, is to test this thesis by considering two main objections to it, which he then tries to rebut. The first of the two objections simply denies bivalence; it does so by suggesting that there is often a "third possibility" (MOP, 121). The objection here draws on an interesting ambiguity. For example, we might say that serving on a jury, when one is called, is just. Now, suppose one doesn't take on such a task; is that *un*just? It may not be. Thus, there may be a zone, often an ill-defined one, between positively just and positively *un*just. Thus, if A is positively just, then not-A would include *both* the *un*just and that which is neither positively just nor positively unjust.

The second objection differs from the first in that it does not say that the law itself officially incorporates "third possibilities" within its main categories (that, for instance, contracts can be valid/invalid/inchoate); rather, it simply says there are good reasons why we can't always decide exactly what the law says or requires. Thus, for example, it could be argued that the law is vague; it has "open texture" (it says "no vehicles in the park," without

---

2. "Hard Cases" was originally published in the *Harvard Law Review* (1975); it was reprinted unchanged as chapter 4 in a collection of Dworkin's papers published under the title *Taking Rights Seriously* (1978, hereafter TRS).

3. This paper was originally published as "Is There Really No Right Answer in Hard Cases?" in the *N.Y.U. Law Review* (1978); it was reprinted virtually unchanged as chapter 5 in another collection of Dworkin's papers published under the title *A Matter of Principle* (1985, hereafter MOP).

saying exactly what is meant by a vehicle, or "no sleeping in railway stations," without specifying exactly what counts as proscribed sleeping). Or it could be said that judicial arguments and judicial decisions are inherently controversial and that what is inherently controversial, what is not demonstrably the case, cannot be decided simply yea or nay.

The first objection is the more challenging of the two; indeed, it is pivotal. So I will focus on it. The objection continues by suggesting that duty may be similar to justice in being, in effect, trivalent. Thus, if there can be an intermediate zone of "neither . . . nor" in the case of duties, there is, in such a zone, no definite duty one way or the other. A judge has no duty to enforce something (as the judge would have were the contract positively valid) and no duty to not enforce it (as the judge would have if the thing were positively *in*valid). Rather, conduct here (including judicial conduct) is not fully mandated by norms; there is no duty either way; one has a degree of discretion. Even judges do.

In short, we find (as in the two objections we are considering) a variety of possible sources of "gappiness" in law, and, hence, of judicial discretion, by looking to such concepts as justice and duty and to legal language more generally.[4] Now, curiously, Dworkin does seem to think that duty is like justice. It can be mapped out in a similarly trivalent fashion. For Dworkin, then, the alleged gap in law cannot be closed by reference simply to the *concept* of duty. If the gap is to be closed, it must be closed in another way.

In simplest terms Dworkin closes the gap by turning to the character of legal reasoning itself. Of course, the story Dworkin tells about judicial reasoning is by no means simple. He constructs an elaborate theory, centering on the labors of an ideal judge named Hercules, to make his argument. And I will turn to that theory shortly.

For now, though, I want to complete the line of reasoning Dworkin followed in his "No Right Answer?" paper. Judges try to determine what decision should be made, given the law, in an individual case. It is the judge's job, the judge's duty, to reach the best decision, all relevant legal factors considered. And people before the bar are entitled to such a decision (MOP, 122). This is not necessarily because there is some preexisting right there.

---

4. Dworkin revisits these objections in a more recent paper, Dworkin 1996, at 129–39, esp. 136–39.

Dworkin's views on judicial discretion have been much criticized, from the very beginning. For his earliest views here, see Dworkin 1963; for an interesting early criticism, see MacCallum 1963.

It's simply that the judge has this very definite duty, and corresponding to it is a definite right of someone.

Dworkin is not saying that there's always a concrete right in law (analogous, say, to the right to liberty of conscience) and that the judge's job is to make out (to find or discern or appropriately construe) that right, then to decide who has it, and to give the entitled thing (the thing legitimately claimed) to that person. Rather, Dworkin is saying simply that judges have definite duties to make the best decision, one way or the other, and that people have rights relative to those duties.

In sum, Dworkin's central claim here is that a system of law, construed broadly to include certain substantive principles embedded in law, has resources such that judges, taking the law as it is, can be said to have a duty to make the best decision. And we have seen how Dworkin used that idea to underwrite one of his main theses, the thesis that for any given case in law there is always a right involved.

But we have not yet determined whether the central claim also implies that there is in a given case one and only one right judicial decision. To explore this question further, we now turn (albeit briefly) to Dworkin's ideal agenda for judges, Herculean jurisprudence.

Let us begin with a bit of background. In "Hard Cases," Dworkin moves away from the Rawlsian contract apparatus, as a justificatory mechanism, and adopts instead a method familiar from jurisprudence: the "constructive" model for developing background principles, in which the judge or legal scholar examines the relevant body of law and precedent in order to construct "a scheme of abstract and concrete principles that provides a coherent justification for all common law precedents and, so far as these are to be justified on principle, constitutional and statutory provisions as well" (TRS, 116–17). In a more recent book, *Law's Empire* (1986, hereafter LE), a treatise rather than a collection of essays, Dworkin develops the notion of constructive interpretation, under the name "law as integrity," in a systematic way.

Law as integrity requires that judges try to take on board and stay true to existing law and its inbuilt resources so much as possible. Such judges are guided, of course, by a vision of what the legal and political history of the country has been and what its political institutions can be said to add up to (see LE, 398). Hercules (as the ideal judge in this model of law as integrity) uses the same method throughout. Hercules gives priority to localized legal principles (tailored to the case and anchored by "fit" to existing judicial precedents, public convictions about statutes, concrete rights).

For example, Hercules might be hearing a case that concerns compensation for emotional injury in an automobile-accident case. And he might find two candidate principles to be the most compelling of those he considers eligible: (1) that the law allows full compensation for all (emotional) injury caused by careless driving, or (2) that the law allows compensation but limits it if it'll be very costly to the liable party.[5] These are instances, just two instances, of a vast array of localized principles that judges might consider in deciding cases. In the end Hercules decides for (1) here; the deciding consideration is, apparently, the ready availability of automobile insurance to cover injuries to third parties—again, a quite localized consideration. (See LE, 258, 267–71, esp. 269–71.)

Of course, other more general controlling principles will also be in play. If the judge is considering a statute (as was not the case here), then judicial deference to the legislature and its well-founded convictions about public policy will be a controlling principle. And if the judge is considering previous judicial decisions (as was the case here), then the judge has to have a good sense of the various norms at work in a given department of law, as the judge tries to bring together the relevant strands in a decision. Thus, in the instant case, that would include judicial consideration of such strands as liability for accidental injury, for severe emotional distress as itself an injury, even for such distress when it is suffered well away from the scene of the accident (the nub on which this particular case turned). Thus, the principle of local priority (of giving great weight to extant norms within a well-developed department of law) is another general controlling principle.[6]

Finally, Hercules must also juggle a variety of considerations of principle—involving such high-order values as (a) justice and rights, (b) democratic procedures (or fairness, as Dworkin calls it in LE), and (c) procedural due process—as part of the background to the decisions he makes. Even so, he uses localized legal principles and relevant general controlling principles and the facts pertinent to the case as the main focus of his decision. The background principles and values that Hercules does call on are not abstract (not perfect platonic justice, for example) but, rather, are in an embodied and mediated form, as determined from within the particular system of law in which they are viewed as ingredient, for example, from within British law

5. See LE, 246–50, esp. 249–50. The case under consideration here is *McLoughlin v. O'Brian* (1983), a British case (1 A.C. 410, reversing [1981] Q.B. 599), which Dworkin takes as one of the sample "real-world" legal disputes that law as integrity is called upon to resolve in a principled way (see LE, 23–29).

6. For further discussion of the principle of local priority, see LE, 252–54, 402–3.

or American law. (For the discussion of such principles as embedded, see TRS, chap. 4; also pp. 40, 66–67, 79; and LE, chap. 11.)

Dworkin attempts to bring all the judge's work into one and the same frame: there's a distinctive procedure (just described) that Hercules uses throughout, and uses at all levels, in all his prodigious interpretive labors. Thus, constitutional analysis (as set out in LE, chap. 10) should be similar, in deep ways, to precedent-based common-law adjudication (LE, chaps. 7 and 8) and to statutory construction (LE, chap. 9). This notion of using the same approach at all the main levels, and not just at the level of common law, is an additional element of integrity in Dworkin's current theory, where the judiciary is instructed to speak with one voice.

We are now ready to turn to the issue that first attracted our interest in Dworkin's jurisprudence, the issue of one right answer. Dworkin's view here can be put as follows: "It's not the case that there's no right answer." Or, alternatively, there's (always) a right answer. Now, this claim can be read in two distinct ways: (*a*) that there is always *a* right answer, though there could be more than one, and (*b*) that there's one and *only one* right answer.

Suppose we took the first answer (answer *a*). This answer would not work for Dworkin's theory when applied to a *single* judge. Why not? Because it still leaves room for discretion as to which "right answer" is chosen by that particular judge. (And if there are no gaps in the law, as Dworkin hypothesizes, then there is no room at all for such legally unguided discretion.) So the thesis that there's one or more right answers could be applied only *systemically,* to judges (in a given legal system) overall.

This, then, becomes the focal point of disagreement between the two answers: if we look at the issue systemically (systemwide), can we say, for Dworkin's theory, that there is always (*a*) at least one right answer, but possibly more than one, or (*b*) one and only one right answer? Dworkin's answer, curiously enough, seems to favor (*a*). Thus, we find him saying, at the very end of his book:

> Our main concern has been to identify the branching points of legal argument, the points where opinion divides in the way law as integrity promises. For every route Hercules took from that general conception [law as integrity] to a particular verdict, another lawyer or judge who began in the same conception would find a different route and end in a different place, as several of the judges in our sample cases did. He would end differently, because he would take leave of

Hercules, following his own lights, at some branching point sooner or later in the argument.

[The reader] must ask how far he would follow me along the tree of argument, given the various interpretive and political and moral convictions he finds he has after the reflection I have tried to provoke. If [the reader] leaves my argument early, at some crucial abstract stage, then I have largely failed him. If he leaves it late, in some matter of relative detail, then I have largely succeeded. I have failed entirely, however, if he never leaves my argument at all (LE, 412–13).

It is clear to me that Dworkin does not regard law as integrity, the general conception of jurisprudence he advocates, as one and the same thing as Hercules' reasonings. And he does not think that a judge, operating within the lines of that general conception, is in error to "take leave of Hercules" at some point. Just as Hercules, paradigmatically, gives a right answer, other judges, even when departing from Hercules' answer, could also be taken as giving right answers. (See also LE, 239–40, 256.)

In my judgment, the best way to gloss Dworkin's theory here is to distinguish between what is true of a single judge and what is true of a panel of judges (or, in the most general case, of a single judicial system). Let us take these up in turn.

For any given conscientious judge who applies Hercules' method, in a relatively mature and complex legal system, there is one and *only one* determinate right answer in a given case, as I've already said. Here's how one could show this: if two different Herculean judges agreed literally on everything—agreed "preinterpretively" on what counts as law in a given system (an agreement we can expect from *all* lawyers, judges, and jurisprudents), agreed on the relevant facts of the case, agreed on the law (the propositions of law) and on the history of politics/law and on an interpretation of the political institutions in their country, agreed about the relevance of the same localized principles and general controlling principles in the case at hand, and agreed about the main background principles (especially justice and fairness) and the interpretation and the preferred ordering of these—they'd reach the *same* decision.

We can call this the argument from Hercules' clone. What works for Hercules and Hercules' clone works for Hercules alone: there's one (and only one) determinate decision a given Herculean judge would reach. Thus, one (and only one) determinate right answer is the regulative ideal for Herculean jurisprudence, as applied to a single judge (see TRS, 279; LE, 261,

266). The judge's job then, taking account of all the resources of the law, is to try to reach that right answer for a given case.

One could notch things up a bit and say that in Herculean jurisprudence there is *always* one and only one right answer that will be reachable by a given judge in any given case. But Dworkin would, I think, deny this (see LE, 273). In short, even where we said that in principle there's always one and only one right answer, it doesn't follow that a given judge, even one who reasons in the best Herculean fashion, will always reach it—or that the judge in this case will be able to *prove* the answer reached (see LE, viii–ix).

The theory that there's always one and only one right answer (though it may not always be reached) runs into real problems, however, when we imagine a *panel* of such judges who must reach a single decision through discussion and voting.

Dworkin avoided this problem, initially (and for several years), by making Hercules the sole judge. But once Hercules is elevated to the Supreme Court (LE, 379), the problem cannot be avoided.

Note how Dworkin handles it there; he says Hercules doesn't have to "compromise" to "gain the votes of other judges" (LE, 380–81). This could mean that the other judges, not being Herculean, simply follow his lead. Well and good. But if it's possible that Herculean jurisprudence can be done by judges who aren't Hercules' *clone,* or by judges who don't simply defer to Hercules, then what?

Here we need to distinguish the Herculean project, or Herculean jurisprudence—the way Hercules typically proceeds, taking account of all the resources of the law, to render judgment—from the convictions of the judge named Hercules. Hercules is an example of a judge who follows the ideal method of adjudication, granted, but he is a judge with particular beliefs and convictions as well; Hercules isn't the LAW PERSONIFIED (see LE, 239).

Suppose, then, that there is a judge Athena who follows the same *method* as Hercules; but she and Hercules (unlike Hercules and his clone) do not necessarily agree on everything else. Specifically, though they agree "preinterpretively" on the sources of law, on what counts as law in their common jurisdiction, they might well disagree on the relevant facts, disagree on the law (the propositions of law) and on the history of politics/law and on an interpretation of the political institutions in their country, disagree about the relevance of the same localized principles or about the general controlling principles in the case at hand, and disagree about the main background principles (especially justice and fairness), at least with regard to the interpretation and the preferred ordering of these values. Or they might merely disagree at *some* of these points. In either case, they'd not reach the *same* decision.

Thus, just as the argument from Hercules' clone showed that for any two judges identically the same, jurisprudentially speaking, there would be one and only one right answer, so the same argument from Hercules and Athena shows that for any two judges equally Herculean in method but differing jurisprudentially there would be more than one right answer reachable by the same method: one answer for Hercules, a different one for Athena.

And if we supposed yet a third judge, Nestor, who, though Herculean in method, might differ markedly from the other two in substantive matters of jurisprudence, then we'd still have right answers—but three different ones this time. If these judges all sat on the same bench, there might be an impasse. We don't know how things would go (but one or more would probably compromise, or one would be outvoted).

This is not, however, a disaster for Dworkin's theory (as many might suppose). Dworkin's theory is intent on denying that there is no right answer. But one or more than one right answer is compatible with this denial. I have suggested that for a single judge, following the Herculean method with due diligence, there is in a given case one and only one determinate right answer. But for a panel of judges or for a whole judiciary of judges, all equally Herculean in method and all equally diligent, there could in principle be more than one right answer. And, given the way the world is and given Dworkin's own statement in the matter (at LE, 412–13), there probably would in fact be more than one right answer. Conscientious judges, Herculean judges, can and will differ (see LE, 256).

Let me briefly elaborate my central claim here. The basis for a Herculean decision can always be found within the resources of the law. And these resources (as I've described them) are capacious enough that a determinate judicial decision, with a suitable legal rationale, can always be reached in principle. There is no need for Hercules ever to go outside the law's resources to reach a judicial decision, and there's no need for him to use discretion, to fill in gaps in the law. Thus, Herculean jurisprudence provides no space for judges to use personal predilections or to import favored political goals as a proper basis, or as an essential feature, of adjudication.[7]

But one cannot just read off "correct law" from an examination of the

---

7. The last sentence here is intended to distinguish Dworkin's views sharply from those of what he called legal pragmatism (a version of legal realism). For discussion, see LE, chap. 5 (esp. p. 152); also LE, 378.

resources of the law. Rather, in using these resources, the judge, through careful and reflective consideration, has to come to certain convictions about what the law actually requires in a given case. Constructing a correct decision, a sound one, is always an interpretive project. Interpretation here must range over a great number of dimensions (and I have tried to make clear what these dimensions are in my account of the Herculean method), and interpretive choices have to be made within each dimension. Thus, an individual judge (Hercules, say), in conscientiously working through these dimensions and choices, will be able to come to a single determinate best answer. All this is part of being a Herculean judge within the confines of law as integrity.

But different judges, starting with the same resources but having made somewhat different interpretive choices and developing different convictions than has Judge Hercules, may come up with sound answers that are significantly different from his. Thus, in a single legal system there may be *several* sound decisions for a given case, reachable by judges equally Herculean in method. And each of these is a right answer, given the differing acceptable interpretive strategies deployed.

This reading of Dworkin is markedly different from the canonical one with which we started, and one is entitled to ask how the canonical view has gained such a foothold. I think the answer is twofold. (1) When Dworkin first posed the question of determinate best answers in given cases, he did so by drawing on the example of a *single* judge (Judge Hercules) who, using the resources of the law (but staying strictly within those resources), was able to come to a single determinate right answer for a given case. (2) And the interpretive character of Hercules' project was not stressed in this initial account. So long as Dworkin stayed with these original motifs, as he did for about a dozen years, the one-right-answer thesis made perfect sense, and the canonical reading took hold. But once we depart from these two key starting points, as Dworkin did in his later writings, the one-right-answer thesis is no longer the only available reading.

In *Law's Empire* interpretation is brought center stage.[8] This does not affect Dworkin's central claim—respecting a single judge following the Herculean method with due diligence. Here that judge, through careful and reflective consideration, ranging over all the resources of the law, has come to certain convictions about what the law actually requires in a given case;

---

8. For Dworkin's main discussion of the interpretive approach he favors, see LE, chaps. 1–3, esp. pp. 47–55, 65–68, 90–95.

for that one judge (be it Hercules or Athena) there is in a given case one and only one determinate right answer. But once Dworkin brings in the idea of a whole system of judges or a panel of judicial equals, all of them deploying differing interpretive strategies, the reading I've suggested becomes not only appropriate but inevitable: that for a *panel* of judges or for a whole judiciary of judges, all equally Herculean in method and all equally diligent, there could in principle be more than one right answer (one for Hercules, another for Athena, and so on).

This reading does not supplant the canonical reading *for a single judge;* it continues to be the case here that there is, for that judge, one and only one determinate best answer in a given case. But it does force an amendment on the one-right-answer thesis for a panel of judges or for a whole judicial system. Here more than one right answer is possible—indeed, to be expected. How many such answers there are will depend on how many Herculean judges there are, other than Hercules and Hercules' clone. And this amended reading is, I think, closer to Dworkin's texts and to his overall line of reasoning.

In the end, I have argued (as the best way to read him) that Dworkin is not committed to there being, across the board, a single right interpretation. A similar argument could, I think, be advanced for Rawls.[9] If this is so, interesting new opportunities for dialogue within liberalism and between it and its critics may be opened with this realization.

Bibliography of Relevant Writings

Dworkin, Ronald. 1963. "Judicial Discretion." *Journal of Philosophy* 60:624–38.
———. 1978. *Taking Rights Seriously.* 2d impression (corrected). Cambridge, Mass.: Harvard University Press. (A collection of articles by Dworkin, originally published in 1977; the 1978 printing includes "Appendix: A Reply to Critics," 291–368.) (Cited as TRS)
———. 1985. *A Matter of Principle.* Cambridge, Mass.: Harvard University Press. (A collection of articles by Dworkin.) (Cited as MOP)
———. 1986. *Law's Empire.* Cambridge, Mass.: Harvard University Press. (Cited as LE)
———. 1996. "Objectivity and Truth: You'd Better Believe It." *Philosophy and Public Affairs* 25:87–139.
Hart, H. L. A. 1994. *The Concept of Law.* 2d ed. With a postscript edited by Penelope Bulloch and Joseph Raz. Oxford: Oxford University Press.

9. I have attempted to make such an argument in my chapter on Rawls in *Political Thinkers: A History of Western Political Thought*, ed. David Boucher and Paul Kelly (Oxford: Oxford University Press, 2002).

Kelly, Paul J. 1996. "Ronald Dworkin: *Taking Rights Seriously.*" In *The Political Classics: Green to Dworkin,* edited by Murray Forsyth and Maurice Keens-Soper, 263–87. Oxford: Oxford University Press.

MacCallum, Gerald C. 1963. "Dworkin on Judicial Discretion" (with "Addendum: Afterthoughts"). In *Legislative Intent and Other Essays on Law, Politics, and Morality,* edited by Marcus G. Singer and Rex Martin, 168–77. Madison: University of Wisconsin Press, 1993. (MacCallum's essay and the addendum were published for the first time in this edited collection of 1993.)

Rawls, John. 1971. *A Theory of Justice.* Cambridge, Mass.: Harvard University Press. (A revised edition was published in 1999.)

———. 1996. *Political Liberalism.* New York: Columbia University Press. (This is the paperback version of the book originally published in 1993. This paperback version is unchanged in content from Rawls 1993, except that it has a second [paperback] introduction, xxxvii–lxii, and adds Rawls, "Reply to Habermas," from the *Journal of Philosophy* 92 [1995]:132–80, as Lecture IX.)

14

Truth in Interpretation: A Hermeneutic Approach

Charles Guignon

The concern with determining what counts as a correct interpretation has been central to hermeneutics since its inception. Hermeneutics, understood as the art or theory of interpretation, first arose as a discipline during the Reformation, as the Reformers sought to provide guidelines for grasping the truth of Scripture.[1] It continued to be seen as an auxiliary discipline in theology until the nineteenth century, when Friedrich Schleiermacher and Wilhelm Dilthey formulated the idea of a *general hermeneutics* whose goal is to provide a method for understanding any form of human expression whatsoever. In its expanded form, methodological hermeneutics focused on understanding authors' intentions rather than the truth of texts, but the issue of correct interpretation remained a primary concern.

By the twentieth century, the methodological conception of hermeneutics was itself called into question. In the minds of Martin Heidegger and his student Hans-Georg Gadamer, the whole project of formulating rules for interpretation—and, indeed, the whole preoccupation with method—was seen as a by-product of an overblown conception of the importance of scien-

---

1. For a concise account of hermeneutics, see "What Is Hermeneutics?" in Frank C. Richardson, Blaine J. Fowers, and Charles B. Guignon, *Re-envisioning Psychology: Moral Dimensions of Theory and Practice* (San Francisco: Jossey-Bass, 1999).

tific method and questions about knowledge. In their view, epistemology and "methodologism" are themselves loaded down with questionable ontological assumptions that can distort our view of what actually goes on in trying to understand human expressions. The centrality given to method leads us to suppose that we are, at the most basic level, knowing subjects, or minds, who are set over against objects we want to interpret and understand. The gap between subject and object, which creates the traditional epistemological puzzle concerning our knowledge of objects in the "external world," poses even more pressing problems in the human sciences, where the object itself is seen as merely an outward expression of the inner intentions of another subject. Given the presumed distanciation between knower and known, it is hard to see how we can ever gain a correct understanding of the mental acts that animate texts and other human creations. From the standpoint of methodological hermeneutics, then, there seems to be an unbridgeable gap between interpreter and textual meaning, with the result that the entire project of interpretation becomes deeply problematic.

To deal with this problem, Heidegger and Gadamer shift the focus of hermeneutics from epistemological concerns, which center on the proper method for interpreting humans and their creations, to *ontological hermeneutics*, which attempts to get clear about the *being* of the entities that interpret and understand, namely, ourselves. On this view, the problem with methodologism is that it starts out from an uncritical and distorted conception of our initial predicament as humans: the conception of the disengaged knowing subject. In order to bypass the assumptions of traditional epistemology-centered philosophy, ontological hermeneutics begins by working out a careful, detailed description of our everyday experience of things, prior to reflection and theorizing. This phenomenology of *being-in-the-world* provides an alternative to the subject/object picture of mainstream epistemology, a way of seeing ourselves as "always already" having some understanding of the surrounding lifeworld by virtue of the fact that we are agents with a grasp of how things count in our culture. The transformed picture of our basic condition that arises from phenomenological hermeneutics aims at undercutting standard puzzles about the possibility of correct interpretation and opening the way to richer, more illuminating ways of grasping what actually goes on in interpretation. The plausibility of this new way of thinking of our situation as interpreters results not from arguments but from the way this alternative description is able to make sense of phenomena that remain baffling in mainstream approaches.

Given the shift to ontological hermeneutics, it might seem that the whole question of truth would simply drop out of sight. But truth remains a central concern in the writings of Heidegger and Gadamer, in part because both these thinkers are intent on avoiding what Gadamer calls "interpretive anarchism." In what follows, I want to sketch out and defend the account of interpretation that appears in contemporary hermeneutics. As should become clear, ontological hermeneutics leads to a position that is pluralist or multiplist about interpretation—it holds that there may be a number of true interpretations of the same phenomenon—but it is also realist in holding that interpretation must be faithful to the object being interpreted.

Truth as Disclosedness

Heidegger's description of human existence (or *Dasein,* the German word for human existence, usually left untranslated) makes understanding central to human beings. What is distinctive about Dasein, Heidegger says, is "that there is some way in which Dasein understands itself in its being, and that to some degree it does so explicitly."[2] What this means is that humans are beings who have some sense of who they are and what they are up to as they go about the daily business of living. They have what Heidegger calls a "vague, average understanding of being," a background of understanding that is found not so much in explicit mental activity as in the tacit know-how we embody as we handle our affairs in familiar situations. In activities such as preparing a meal or taking care of chores, our understanding is made manifest in our skillful dealings with things. Understanding is a matter of " 'being able to manage something,' 'being a match for it,' 'being competent to do something' " (BT, 183) in everyday contexts.

It should be clear, then, that Heidegger does not use the term *understanding* in the limited sense of a cognitive capacity for grasping others and their creations. On the contrary, understanding is what is definitive of humans as such: *"Understanding of being is itself a definite characteristic of Dasein's being"* (BT, 32). We can get a grip on this conception of understanding if we see that the root of this term contains the idea of a "stand" (more obvi-

2. Martin Heidegger, *Being and Time* [1927], trans. J. Macquarrie and E. Robinson (New York: Harper & Row, 1962), 32, henceforth cited parenthetically as BT. The translators' use of the uppercase in translating the German word for being, *Sein,* is potentially misleading. I use the lowercase to emphasize the fact that the word "being" is just the ordinary word for the way things are.

ously so in German than in English). To say that humans are the beings that understand is to say that we are always *taking a stand* on our being in what we do. We care about our lives and, whether we do so consciously or not, are all making something of our lives in our activities. Life is a project in which past, present, and future are bound together in our undertakings. Heidegger tries to capture this dynamic unified conception of human existence by saying that Dasein is a "happening" or "movement." To be human is to exist as an ongoing *event,* as a life-story extending "from birth to death."

A consequence of this conception of human existence as an event is that humans (and, as we shall see, many human creations) have a distinctive temporal nature. Where brute natural objects can be seen as merely persisting though time, as "enduring presence," humans are constantly taking over what has come before in the light of fundamental concerns about where it is all going and what is yet to come. Humans do not exist in time, then; they exist as *temporalizing,* as making their lifetimes in the way they carry forward the past in trying to achieve something for the future. This dynamic conception of human existence as an unfolding life-course, or life-story, points to two aspects of Dasein's underlying temporal structure. The first fundamental dimension of Dasein's being, a dimension that defines the existential experience of the "past," is our *thrownness,* or *situatedness,* in the world. We always find ourselves already caught up in the midst of concrete situations, involved in prior commitments, and engaged in the undertakings laid out in the social world we find around us. The fact that we are always contextualized in a meaningful public lifeworld is referred to as our *facticity.* As we grow up into our historical culture, we are initiated into the forms of life and practices of our community, with the result that, from an early age, we come to act as "one" acts in everyday contexts. We are initially and for the most part participants in what Heidegger calls the "they" or "anyone." In learning the public language, for example, we come to experience the world according to schematizations and principles of ordering deposited in that language. Because our understanding is socially constructed in this way, Heidegger can say that what "articulates the referential context of significance" of the familiar lifeworld is nothing other than the "they itself" (BT, 167). On this view, then, our facticity, or embeddedness in the public world, is seen not as an impediment to understanding but rather as the window that first makes possible any understanding at all. All understanding and interpretation are guided and shaped by the shared background attunement that is opened by our historical culture.

The second structural dimension of Dasein's being, corresponding to the "future," is called *projection*. In our active lives, we are not just objects located in the present. Instead, we are always "ahead of ourselves" in pressing forward into possibilities of being and acting made accessible in our public world. Our being is essentially *futural* in the sense that we stand out into an open array of possibilities offered us by our cultural context, and we are always under way in realizing our lives in the stands we take on those possibilities. If you are permissive and unconcerned in dealing with your children, for example, you are contributing toward defining your identity as a "negligent parent," as this possibility is interpreted in our world. As long as you continue to act in this way, your *being* (that is, your *identity* as a person) is something that is coming to take a distinctive shape and content. In Heidegger's vocabulary, the specific way you project yourself into the future in your actions defines your being. In this sense, you just *are* what you make of yourself in the stands you take in taking up the public possibilities made accessible in your community.

As an unfolding event, human existence is always enmeshed in a concrete world, where the term *world* is understood in the existential sense it has in expressions such as "the world of theater" or "the academic world." We are, in a phrase made familiar by Heidegger and Merleau-Ponty, "being-in-the-world." Heidegger's description of agency in a familiar workshop shows how there is a mutual interdependence between agent and lifeworld in familiar practical situations. It is only because we actually go out and vote that voting booths and ballots have the meaning they have. But it is only because voting places and the institution of voting have the meaning they have that we are able to *be* voters in the first place. As this example shows, a world is always a culturally and historically shaped context of significance, and it is prior to and definitive of the things and people that show up in the world. The human lifeworld, seen as a "unified phenomenon" interweaving agents' purposes, cultural interpretations, and historically shaped settings, is a meaning- and value-laden totality.

As Heidegger employs it, then, the term *understanding* is designed to capture the sort of skilled mastery of practical situations embodied in our ways of projecting ourselves into possibilities of action. Understanding therefore embodies a certain "fore-structure," or prior sense of things, that gives our dealings with the world a direction and focus. We find ourselves involved in a matrix of functional relationships defining the context of action (our fore-having); we see things in their relations to other things as determined by our motivations and interests (fore-sight); and we operate within the system of articulation provided by our language (fore-conception). This "preunderstanding" determines in advance our concrete ways of taking things.

The term *interpretation* (*Auslegung*, literally, "laying out") refers to our ways of explicitly working out our preunderstanding by taking things *as* such and such in our practical dealings with the surrounding lifeworld. Interpretation is "the working out of possibilities projected in understanding" (BT, 189). For example, a churchgoer entering a church has a prior understanding of this context as a place of worship—in Heidegger's vocabulary, the churchgoer's preunderstanding *discloses* this context as having a particular meaning. As the person goes about appropriating the context by using what appears in the church—kneeling in the pew, saying the rosary, entering the confessional, lighting a candle—the context becomes articulated into a particular "as-structure." In taking something *as* something, Heidegger says, one *discovers* or *uncovers* entities in a particular way. Interpretation, as a discovering of what is there, "lets things be" in the sense of letting them have a specific significance in this context. This picture of interpretation once again reveals the reciprocal interplay between context and agency. The worshiper can *be* a worshiper only because of the meaning of this setting, while the setting can *be* a sanctified ground only because of the practices of this and other worshipers. On Heidegger's account, human agency in concrete contexts lets the holistic context of being-in-the-world emerge as a *clearing,* or *disclosedness,* in which both agent and worldly entities can come to *be* the specific sorts of entities they are.

Heidegger's characterization of everyday existence as an unfolding event embedded in a lifeworld offers us a transformed way of thinking about our situation as humans. On this account, human existence is seen as having both a passive and an active component. As thrown into a world, we always find ourselves "already" bound up with a context of culturally and historically constituted possibilities of understanding that determine our possible choices and ways of understanding things. At the same time, as a projection into those possibilities, we are always articulating the background of intelligibility into a configuration of meaning that is our own.

When life is understood in this way, it is found to have the kind of circular structure that is characteristic of textual interpretation. According to traditional hermeneutics, textual interpretation is always caught in a circle. Any interpretation must start out from some *preunderstanding*—some set of anticipations and expectations about what the text as a whole is trying to say—and it will interpret particular passages in the light of the prior grasp of the whole. It will then use the interpretations of specific passages to revise and reconfigure its initial understanding of the whole. This circular structure has the consequence that, in textual interpretation, there can be no access to "raw facts" or "brute data" to ground a reading of a text. As Heidegger's says, "If, when one is engaged in a particular concrete kind of interpretation, in the sense of exact textual interpretation, one likes to appeal to what 'stands there,' then one finds that what 'stands there' in the first instance is nothing other than the obvious undiscussed assumption of the person who does the interpreting" (BT, 192). Since everything one encounters is already encountered through the lens of one's preunderstanding, there is no exit from this framework of anticipations to an uninterpreted given that can legitimate one's interpretations.

On Heidegger's view, the *hermeneutic circle* is built into life itself. Given our facticity, we must always start out from where we are—from our holistic "vague, average understanding" of what things are all about. This means that our ways of taking things in our dealings with the world are inevitably colored in advance by that prior understanding. But it would be wrong to think that this circularity is a limitation or constraint on our ability to grasp things, for it is only because life has this circular structure that things can show up as counting in determinate ways. There can be better and worse interpretations—Heidegger says we should avoid letting our preunderstanding be influenced "by fancies and popular conceptions," so that we can "make the scientific theme secure by working out these fore-structures in terms of the things themselves" (BT, 195). But, as we shall see, this reference to "things themselves" (*Sache selbst*) does not imply that there can be a direct, unmediated access to uninterpreted facts.

The conception of Dasein as a clearing, or disclosedness, paves the way to Heidegger's radically new way of thinking of truth. Section 44 of *Being and Time* sets out to show that the traditional concept of truth as correctness, as correspondence between a proposition and a fact, is grounded in a more "primordial" form of truth, a conception of truth Heidegger finds implicit in the Greek word for truth, *alētheia,* which literally means "unforgetfulness" or "un-concealing." The claim is that truth as correspondence, through which entities are "un-covered" or "dis-covered" in specific ways, is made possible by a prior "dis-closing" that opens a space in which anything at all can show up *as* such and such. Since this disclosing occurs through the thrown projection of Dasein, Heidegger can say that what is true in the most primordial sense is Dasein, where Dasein, as being-in-the-world, is understood as the coming-into-presence of a meaningful world in which things can show up as counting in determinate ways.

The conception of truth as a dis-closing or opening of world remained central to Heidegger's writings throughout his life. In the writings following the appearance of *Being and Time,* however, he came to think of the idea of an "event of truth" less as something that humans *do* than as something that *happens to* humans. The shift in emphasis is evident in a set of lectures delivered in the thirties, "The Origin of the Work of Art,"[3] which contain a powerful description of how the appearance of a temple in ancient Greece opened up the world of the Greek people. According to this description, it is the work of art that provides the clearing in terms of which entities can appear on the scene. Heidegger says, for example: "Standing there, the building holds its ground against the storm raging above it and so first makes the storm manifest in its violence" (OWA, 42). The temple is a world-defining work of art: it lets a *world* emerge as a field of meanings in terms of which entities can *be* the entities they are: "Tree and grass, eagle and bull, snake and cricket first enter into their distinctive shapes and thus come to appear *as* what they are" (OWA, 42, my emphasis).

The description of the temple makes it clear that, in Heidegger's view, *humans themselves,* as beings with specific sorts of concerns and commitments, first gain their concrete identity through the world that is opened by the work. "The temple, in its standing there, first gives to things their look and to men their outlook on themselves" (OWA, 43). The temple defines what is at stake for a people: "It is the temple-work that first fits together and gathers around itself the unity of those paths and relations in which birth and death, disaster and blessing, victory and disgrace, endurance and decline acquire the shape of destiny for human being" (OWA, 42). Turning to a different sort of artwork, Heidegger says that in a great tragedy "the battle of the new gods against the old is being fought. . . . [The tragedy] transforms the people's saying so that now every living word fights the battle and puts up for decision what is holy and what unholy, what great and what small, what brave and what cowardly, what lofty and what flighty, what master and what slave" (OWA, 43).

The lectures on art bring to prominence the idea of an "event of being" in which a truth, understood as a disclosure or opening up of a world, first

---

3. Martin Heidegger, "The Origin of the Work of Art," in *Poetry, Language, Thought,* trans. A. Hofstadter (New York: Harper & Row, 1971), hereafter cited as OWA.

occurs. The world lays out the context of possibilities of understanding in terms of which a community can come to see what is at issue for them. "The world is the self-disclosing openness of the broad paths of the simple and essential decisions in the destiny of a historical people" (OWA, 48). What that world *is,* is defined by the decisions the community makes in taking up the challenge posed by a work. Heidegger says that the meaning of the work is determined by future generations of *preservers,* who carry it forward in their ways of making it relevant to their own context. Seen from this standpoint, the very *being* of the work—that which defines its identity and meaning—is something that is open-ended and futural. The being of the work, like the being of a life-story, is an event in which what has come before, what is currently happening, and what is yet to be are knitted together into a unified unfolding.

The lectures on art illuminate another theme that is central to Heidegger's later thought. Heidegger claims that any event of truth, by opening up a world in which things can count in specific ways, at the same time closes off other possible ways things can show up. In other words, any event of truth, as a dis-closing or un-concealing, is at the same time a concealing: the act of tearing things out of the darkness and illuminating them simultaneously lets other aspects of things recede into darkness. So, for example, Greek tragedy, in illuminating the heroic dimension of life, closed off possibilities of meek acceptance highlighted by the Christian tradition, and the new images of Christ suffering on the cross that appeared at the end of the first millennium displaced earlier visions of the soon-to-return Christ the King.

It follows that any form of disclosedness that comes to define a world for a community must be seen as concealing alternative possibilities of interpretation and understanding. If texts and text analogues are always open to new interpretations given new perspectives, then no single interpretation of an artwork or human creation can ever be regarded as absolute in the sense of being the sole admissible interpretation. Glossing Nietzsche's well-known claim that truth is an "error," Heidegger writes: "Truth . . . i.e., what is constant and fixed, because it is the petrifying of any single perspective, is always only an apparentness that has come to prevail, which is to say, it is always an error."[4] The outcome of this train of thought is a perspectivism according to which things can show up only relative to a perspective or

---

4. Martin Heidegger, *Nietzsche,* vol. 1, *The Will to Power as Art,* trans. D. F. Krell (San Francisco: Harper & Row, 1979), 214.

frame of reference. What is misleading, on this view, is to suppose that one appearance or perspective is the ultimate or final truth about what things are. Heidegger expressly defines "dissembling" as treating an appearance or perspective as if it were *being* in some absolute sense: dissembling occurs, he suggests, when appearance "covers itself over as appearing, inasmuch as it shows itself as Being."[5]

These passages suggest the following picture of Heidegger's later conception of truth. At various times in history there have been events of truth that determine how entities will show up as mattering and how things are to be assessed relative to that clearing. As long as a world endures and continues to define the parameters for interpreting what appears in that world, successive generations of interpreters will tend to interpret things along the guidelines laid out by that world. Interpreters go wrong, on this view, when they assume that the framework of understanding that guides their interpretations is the ultimate and absolute way things are. When people let a particular framework of understanding become petrified (as is happening with our current technological understanding, according to Heidegger), then interpreting activity falls into a rut. Interpretations, as it were, go dead. When this happens, truth—understood as a dynamic interplay of revealing and concealing—is covered over. Yet, insofar as any emergence of truth is possible only against the backdrop of what is currently concealed, there is still the possibility, even when a world goes dead in this way, that a new world will come into existence. The appearance of a new world is described by the later Heidegger as a "gift" of being, something humans receive rather than make. But even though humans cannot create a new world by fiat, there can be extraordinary humans (thinkers and poets) who, by recovering forgotten ways of understanding and taking a "leap" into a new way of relating to things, play a crucial role in bringing about a new "event of truth."[6]

Understanding Human Creations

In his immensely influential work, *Truth and Method,* Gadamer takes over the core ideas of Heidegger's hermeneutic ontology and applies them to

5. Martin Heidegger, *Introduction to Metaphysics,* trans. G. Fried and R. Polt (New Haven: Yale University Press, 2000), 114, translation slightly modified.

6. For an excellent account of how this works, see Hubert Dreyfus, "Heidegger on the Connection Between Nihilism, Art, Technology, and Politics," in *The Cambridge Companion to Heidegger,* ed. C. B. Guignon (Cambridge: Cambridge University Press, 1993).

reflections on what is involved in understanding works of art, history, and language. It has been noted that the title of this work might have been "truth *or* method," since Gadamer's underlying claim is that the sort of method that has been so successful in the natural sciences tends to obscure the truth in the human sciences. For Gadamer, in our actual encounters with humans and their creations there is "an experience of truth that transcends the control of scientific method."[7] Scientific method calls for a stance of detached, disengaged objectivity in which one sets aside all prejudices and prior assumptions in order impartially to record data and formulate hypotheses. In the human sciences, in contrast, one can understand only if one is fully engaged, employing one's prior assumptions in order to grasp the object of investigation in its relevance for one's current motivations and aims.

The difference between the natural and human sciences can be clarified in terms of the fundamental difference in the nature of the objects studied by each. Where the natural sciences can assume that there is an antecedently existing object "out there," with features that are what they are independent of us and our practices, the human sciences should recognize that what counts as an "object" in its investigations is constituted in part by the interpreting activity of the person who is trying to understand. We can see why this is the case if we consider what historians do in trying to understand the First World War.[8] Until the 1940s, this war was understood as "The Great War" or "The War to End All Wars," an understanding that reflected the experience of the time. After the Second World War, however, the earlier war came to be called World War I, and it was seen as a precursor to "the Big One" in the forties. In a related way, the events in the second half of the twentieth century have led people to call World War II "the last good war." Presumably each generation of historians will rethink those wars in the light of new developments and interests. In view of these considerations, Gadamer concludes, "This is precisely what distinguishes the human sciences from the natural sciences. Whereas the object of the natural sciences can be described *idealiter* as what would be known in the perfect knowledge of nature, it is senseless to speak of a perfect knowledge of history, and for this reason it is not possible to speak of an 'object in itself' toward which its research is directed" (TM, 285). *Truth and Method* continues the ontological trend in hermeneutics to the extent that its primary concern is to clarify

7. Hans-Georg Gadamer, *Truth and Method* [1960], trans. J. Weinsheimer and D. G. Marshall (New York: Crossroad, 1989), xxii, henceforth cited as TM.
8. This example comes from Georgia Warnke, *Gadamer: Hermeneutics, Tradition, and Reason* (Stanford: Stanford University Press, 1987).

what understanding and human creations must *be* for the human sciences to have this distinctive character.

Gadamer begins his reflections on art by opposing our actual experience of works of art to the view dominant in modern aesthetic theory. In contrast to the aestheticist tradition, which sees an artwork as a thing with sensuous qualities that produce special sorts of experiences in an audience, Gadamer wants to recover an older appreciation of the work as something that expresses a *truth* about how things are. The conception of art as an event of truth is worked out by looking at the difference between tragedy in life and tragedy on the stage. People who have had some experience in life have an insight into the tragedy in life and can discern life's tragic dimension. But the tragedy in life seldom takes a final coherent form, because life always stands out into an open-ended future where new developments may transform the significance of what is now happening. We see the tragic only intermittently and through a glass darkly.

Gadamer points out that it is only when a tragic event in life comes to have the kind of coherence and unity of meaning characteristic of a drama that it really manifests the tragic dimension of life. "Now if, in a particular case, a context of meaning closes itself and completes itself in reality, such that no lines of meaning scatter in the void, then this reality is itself like a drama" (TM, 112–13). And it is only when life achieves the level of coherence and clarity of the dramatic work that the *truth* of the tragic comes to be realized in life. But this implies that tragedy on the stage, insofar it has the kind of closure and unity of meaning that clearly manifests its tragic aspect, achieves a "superior truth" in comparison to what runs through life: the play "produces and brings to light what is otherwise constantly hidden and withdrawn" and so lets this course of events *be* the tragedy that it always already is (TM, 112). The world that is revealed in the artwork realizes and defines what is only inchoate and tacit in actual life. "The world that appears in the play of presentation does not stand like a copy next to the real world, but is that world in the *heightened truth of its being*" (TM, 137, emphasis added). Through the work, what is generally concealed is now brought to light, with the result that "everyone recognizes that this is how things are" (TM, 113). The joy we derive from art is not grounded in an aesthetic experience, but is instead the joy of a particular type of knowledge: "the joy of knowing *more* than is already familiar," of grasping dimensions of life that are normally concealed. In the artwork, "what invites our attention is how true it is—i.e., to what extent one knows and recognizes oneself" (TM, 114).

The conception of art as an event of truth provides a basis for understanding Gadamer's general claims about human phenomena such as texts and history. First, following suggestions in Heidegger, Gadamer proposes that we see such phenomena not as objects simply on hand but rather as ongoing events whose meaning is realized and defined by our ways of engaging ourselves with them. A literary work, for example, is not a thing with a meaning fixed from the outset; it is an event in which the textual meaning (and so the very *being* of the text *as* a text) comes alive and is formed by different readings over time. It follows that understanding is not so much reproductive as it is productive: it does not reproduce a meaning given in advance; instead, it cocreates the meaning and being of what it understands. As Gadamer says, "Understanding must be conceived as part of the event in which meaning happens, the event in which the meaning of all statements . . . is formed and actualized" (TM, 164–65).

Second, the description of art makes it clear that Gadamer is presupposing the conception of truth formulated by Heidegger. Like Heidegger, Gadamer thinks that truth in ordinary circumstances should be regarded as correctness, that is, as the correspondence between judgment and fact. Truth is a matter of "telling it like it is." But he also thinks that, when it comes to understanding human phenomena, truth is not just a static mirroring of some fixed state of affairs in the world. Instead, truth is a way of letting something emerge and come into the light in a determinate way, of letting something present itself *as* such and such. Since the ways things come to presence are determined by our "horizon" of interests and motivations at any given time, what counts as *true* will always be relativized to a particular context or perspective. On this view, then, truth is not so much a matter of having a correct picture of something as it is a matter of capturing in an illuminating way some of the aspects of a thing that are germane given the motivations and preunderstandings we have at a particular time. Like Heidegger, Gadamer holds that cases of true assertion are made possible by a background of un-concealment, which provides the horizon in terms of which anything can show up as a topic for our asserting and knowing.

For Gadamer, the meaning of a text is inseparable from the actual ways the text is read and understood throughout history. Just as a play comes alive and fully *is* the play it is only in its productions, so the text's *being*—its identity as a text—is realized only in its readings. Thus, interpreters bring to realization the being of the text through their interpretations. Gadamer also claims that new readings of the text will always produce new interpretations. This is the case because every reading of a text is always guided by what Heidegger calls the "fore-structure of understanding" that members of a community bring to a text. Gadamer uses the word *prejudice* to refer to the pre-judgments that give interpreters their shared prior viewpoint and orientation toward the text. Because each new generation of interpreters will bring a somewhat different horizon of prejudices to the text, it follows that new readings will produce new meanings, and those new meanings will then become components of the history of interpretations defining the text. This history of readings should not be seen as leading to progressively better and better interpretations. "Understanding is not, in fact, understanding better," he writes. "It is enough to say that we understand in a *different way, if we understand at all*" (TM, 296–97). It is a consequence of our finitude as historical beings that there can never be a "final" "correct" meaning for a text. There is only the unfolding history of interpretations generated by different horizons of understanding.

Textual interpretation is therefore open-ended. But this open-endedness does not lead to an interpretive anarchism according to which any interpretation is acceptable. Much of *Truth and Method* is devoted to showing the constraints and criteria that actually structure our interpretive practices. All interpretations grow out of and help to constitute the world of a historical community. Our sense of what things are all about is always determined by the traditions—"the variety of voices in which the echo of the past is heard"—that determine "what seems to us worth enquiring about and what will appear as an object of investigation" (TM, 284, 300). The *principle of effective history* points out how our current interpretations and the historical horizon of the text are always intertwined as part of a common tradition. It should be clear from this account of textual interpretation why understanding a text is not a matter of recovering or reconstructing the original intentions of an author. What actually occurs in interpretation is a movement toward what Gadamer calls a *fusing of horizons*. Every text embodies a horizon of understanding about some subject matter (*Sache*), and the aim of the interpreter is to grasp the horizon of the text in order to gain an insight into the subject matter. Of course, interpreters must always start out from the horizon of the historical culture in which they find themselves. But the goal of interpretation is neither to get into the mind of the other nor to assimilate the text to one's current frame of reference. The goal of interpretation is to *reach an understanding* about the subject matter, where the word "understanding" is used in the sense of "coming to an agreement" about some topic.

Interpretation therefore aims at discovering the *truth* about the subject

matter by means of a dialogical exchange between the questions the interpreter brings to the text and the answers the text provides in addressing the
matter at hand. This interplay of question and answer usually transforms
not just the text but the interpreter as well: it makes the horizon of the
text accessible to the interpreter's frame of reference while simultaneously
transforming the interpreter's initial horizon of understanding and so transforming the interpreter. Such a fusing of horizons is always possible, Gadamer says, because both text and interpreter already stand in "the one
great horizon" (TM, 304) that defines a shared historical reality and attunes
both interpreter and text to common interests and understandings.

Gadamer also suggests that there are certain "formal" criteria that govern our ways of interpreting a text. There is, first of all, the "anticipation of
completeness," the expectation that, because "only what constitutes a unity
of meaning is intelligible," the text one is trying to understand will have a
complete meaning (TM, 294). Needless to say, this does not imply that
every text actually *has* a complete meaning; it only tells us that any activity
of interpreting is guided by an expectation that things will come together
or add up in some way in the end. In addition, Gadamer holds that our
interpretations should be guided by an "anticipation of truth," the advance
assumption that the text has something to say to us and that we can learn
something from it if we are open to what it says. This regulative idea governing interpretation arises once we get rid of the assumptions of aestheti-
cism and recover the older idea that texts make a claim to truth—that they
have something to say about "how things really are."

These general features of interpretation help Gadamer deal with the question, What basis do we have for claiming that interpretations are not arbitrary? This question is addressed in the course of reflecting on the discussion
of the hermeneutic circle in *Being and Time*. Recalling Heidegger's description of preunderstanding, Gadamer observes that a person "who is trying
to understand a text is always projecting. He projects a meaning for the text
as a whole as soon as some initial meaning emerges in the text." Every
reading involves a projection because all readings operate under the "anticipation of completion" and because interpretation is always guided by a
horizon of interests and motivations that dictates in advance the questions
the text is supposed to answer and the answers that can make sense. "Working out this fore-projection, which is constantly revised in terms of what
emerges as [the interpreter] penetrates into the meaning, is understanding
what is there" (TM, 267). What keeps this circular relation between preunderstanding and readings of passages from being a vicious circle, according

to Gadamer, is the ideal reader's openness to changing his or her presuppositions in the light of what emerges in reading the text. This is what Heidegger meant when he spoke of not letting our interpretations be guided by "fancies and popular conceptions," but "working out [our] fore-structures in terms of the things themselves" (BT, 195). As Gadamer puts it, "Working out appropriate projections, anticipatory in nature, to be confirmed by 'the things' themselves, is the constant task of understanding" (TM, 267).

It should be noted that Gadamer gives no account of how misinterpretations are *in principle* to be ruled out. All he offers is a phenomenology of reading that shows how we normally move toward interpretations we regard as sound. We all know "the experience of being pulled up short by the text," Gadamer points out (TM, 268). Such an experience gives us good reason to think we can move toward a correct interpretation so long as we see the text as having something important to say to us and are willing to give up or revise our assumptions if the text undercuts them. In Gadamer's words, "a person trying to understand a text is prepared for it to tell him something. That is why a hermeneutically trained consciousness must be, from the start, sensitive to the text's alterity" (TM, 269). What is crucial to reaching a nonarbitrary interpretation, then, is remaining sensitive to the otherness of the text and recognizing that one's own prejudices are just that: prejudices that give one a point of entry into the text but may need to be revised or abandoned in the light of what the text says. Textual interpretation therefore requires a stance of self-criticism: "The important thing is to be aware of one's own bias, so that the text can present itself in all its otherness and thus assert its own truth against one's own fore-meaning" (TM, 269).

Hermeneutics and Multiplist Realism

The final conception of interpretation we find in ontological hermeneutics might be called a plural realism or multiplist realism.[9] Hermeneutics is committed to ontological realism insofar as it holds that interpretation is concerned with understanding human creations with determinate features that exist in the real world. On this view, an interpretation is *true* only if it

---

9. Hubert Dreyfus uses the term "plural realism" in his *Being-in-the-World: A Commentary on Heidegger's "Being and Time," Division* I (Cambridge, Mass.: MIT Press, 1991), 262.

captures what is really there in the object of interpretation. Yet hermeneutic thinkers are also multiplists insofar as they hold that there can be a number of different true interpretations of the entities studied by the human sciences. In other words, they agree with Gadamer that, given the fact of our finitude, there is "something absurd about the whole idea of a unique, correct interpretation" (TM, 120). Georgia Warnke has summed up this view as follows. Hermeneutics holds that "different interpretations of a work can reveal dimensions of meaning of the work that were previously obscured or hidden," and it can do this because "different interpreters approach [a text or text analogue] with different experiences and concerns, view it from within different contexts, and come at it from the vantage point of different interpretive traditions."[10]

The distinctive sort of realism found in ontological hermeneutics must be understood in the light of the conception of *being* this view presupposes. Hermeneutics holds that the mainstream tradition of Western thought has been mistaken in supposing that the being of entities should be thought of in terms of *substance,* where substance is seen as that which underlies and remains constant through change. Ontological hermeneutics sets out to replace this substance ontology with what might be called an *expressivist ontology,* a view that sees the *being* of entities as consisting in their ways of emerging-into-presence or coming-into-being through time.[11] For an expressivist ontology, the being of an entity is not something static and simply given. It is instead the ongoing event through which the determinate characteristics of the entity are brought to realization in the light of a specific opening or clearing. In Heidegger's words, entities appear on the scene and, in so doing, "give themselves an aspect"—that is, they appear in a certain light.[12] We then encounter the aspect those things present in the clearing that defines our world. As an example, Heidegger refers to the way a city can present different aspects to us in relation to different situations and frames of reference. We encounter a city as dangerous and crime-ridden, or as warm and neighborly, or as a cultural Mecca, or as a frightening labyrinth, and so forth. But to say we encounter things only under aspects is

10. Georgia Warnke, *Legitimate Differences: Interpretation in the Abortion Controversy and Other Public Debates* (Berkeley and Los Angeles: University of California Press, 1999), 9.

11. I discuss this ontology in "Truth as Disclosure: Art, Language, History," in *Heidegger and Praxis,* ed. T. J. Nenon, vol. 28, supplement to the *Southern Journal of Philosophy* (1989): 105–20, and in "Being as Appearing: Retrieving the Greek Experience of *Phusis,*" in *A Companion to Heidegger's "Introduction to Metaphysics,"* ed. R. Polt and G. Fried (New Haven: Yale University Press, 2001).

12. See *Introduction to Metaphysics,* 108.

not to say that we cannot encounter the things themselves, as if a veil of representations blocked our access to the entities. For when we see different aspects of the city, *we are seeing the city itself.* What we encounter and deal with in our lives are the things that are actually there, not sensory data or mental representations of those entities.

Our ability to encounter entities is made possible by a clearing opened by our shared, cultural ways of being-in-the-world. This clearing is called *truth* in the sense of *a-lētheia,* un-concealment. Since there are different clearings at different times and under different circumstances, Heidegger says that things "stand in different truths."[13] In a similar way, Gadamer concludes that we must understand differently if we are to understand at all. The hermeneutic conception of interpretation therefore maintains that there can be more than one admissible interpretation of the same entity. But it is important to see that this pluralism does not depend on, say, claims about propositional contents being relative to conceptual schemes. Rather, the point is that a multifaceted reality presents different aspects depending on the kind of clearing that is opened at any time. In Heidegger's language, reality contains an "essential fullness" that can never be fully captured by any one interpretation.[14] Things show up in different ways given different clearings, not because interpretations are *underdetermined* by the data (as happens in the natural sciences), but because human phenomena are *overdetermined* in the possible meanings they can have. Things embody multiple possible meanings, and different interpretations reap different possibilities.

For hermeneutic theorists, interpretation is a creative act—it is a "re-creation," Gadamer says, though not of the author's creative act, but of the work itself insofar as it presents the meaning the interpreter finds in it (TM, 119). With respect to the metaphors of *making* and *finding,* we might say that interpretation is a matter of both making and finding: we find what makes sense and we make something of what we find. A good interpretation must be creative, lighting up and configuring possibilities inherent in things in illuminating ways, yet faithful to what it sets out to grasp.

A pressing question for a theory of interpretation of this sort is how to account for incompatible, conflicting, or incommensurable interpretations. It should be obvious, given what we have seen so far, that in many cases

13. Martin Heidegger, *What Is a Thing?* trans. W. B. Barton Jr. and V. Deutsche (Chicago: Henry Regnery, 1969), 26.
14. For this notion of the *Wesensfülle* of nature, see Martin Heidegger, "Science and Reflection," in *The Question Concerning Technology and Other Essays,* trans. W. Lovitt (New York: Harper & Row, 1977), 174.

conflict will be only apparent. Since truth is always relativized to a context of interests and aims, most cases of apparent conflict can be resolved once one grasps the contexts to which claims of correctness are relativized. In cases where two interpretations are indexed to one and the same context, it will presumably turn out that one interpretation *can* be said, relative to the standards internal to that context, to be better or truer than the other. Judgments about what is "truer" and "better" pose no problems here, for multiplism does not lead to an "anything-goes" anarchism with respect to interpretations.

If judgments of this sort are possible, however, it seems that the hermeneutic picture of interpretation should be able to give some account of how evaluative judgments are to be grounded. Yet ontological hermeneutics, as we have seen, understands itself as describing what actually happens when we understand and interpret, not as making prescriptions. The description of understanding reveals that all interpretation is caught in a hermeneutic circle, and this shows us that our interpretation of a particular passage in a text is guided by the "fore-meanings," or "prejudices," that make up our culturally and historically conditioned preunderstanding. Insofar as these prior projections determine what can count for us as data or facts, we have no access to an uninterpreted given that could ground our interpretations. But neither can we turn to an overarching standard of reason that could adjudicate among conflicting interpretations, for, as Gadamer says, "the idea of an absolute reason is not a possibility for historical humanity. Reason exists for us only in concrete, historical terms" (TM, 276). Though there is always room for discussion about the relative merits of different interpretations, this discussion will rely on standards that are relative to the frameworks of interpretation in play, and therefore cannot give us a higher court of appeal.

But if all interpretations are caught in a hermeneutic circle, how can arbitrariness and misunderstanding be avoided? Gadamer answers this question by offering some remarks on how interpretations actually work. He points out that, even though "every interpretation must begin somewhere," it must seek "to supersede the one-sidedness which that inevitably produces" (TM, 471). One-sidedness is avoided when interpreters are reflective about their own prejudices: instead of "approach[ing] the text directly," the interpreter explicitly examines "the legitimacy—i.e., the origin and validity—of the fore-meanings dwelling within him" (TM, 267). Distortions and misinterpretations result not from prejudices, which are inescapable prerequisites to any understanding, but from "the tyranny of hidden prejudices" that make us deaf to what is said (TM, 270). Moreover, Gadamer holds that the ideal interpreter is always guided by the things themselves, where the "things" are the truths concerning the subject matter addressed by the work. Where interpretation is thought of as an open-ended conversation aimed at reaching the truth about a subject matter, "correctness" has to be conceived in terms of hearing what the text has to say, and this means being open-minded and not imposing one's prejudices onto the text.

The fact that interpretations grow out of and feed back into an unfolding cultural heritage provides another basis for talking about "better" interpretations. Heidegger emphasizes the *historicity* of our understanding, the fact that our interpretations spring from and help to transmit a background of understanding that is deposited in our inherited language and practices. To be authentic, on Heidegger's view, is to understand one's life as repeating the possibilities of one's heritage and as *preserving* what is important from the past in the project of realizing the destiny of one's community.[15] Gadamer also emphasizes the fact that our interpretations, as part of an unfolding tradition, draw on the past and contribute to what is to come in a community's life. For example, Gadamer talks about the role of "the Classical" in laying out guide rails for new creative activity, and he emphasizes the role played by the *application* of a work from the past to new contexts in determining the validity of an interpretation. The "criterion of correct understanding," Gadamer says, is "harmony of the details with the whole," but we must expand our understanding of the "whole" to embrace the entire stream of history if we are fully to grasp this principle (TM, 291).

Hermeneutic theorists point to a cluster of considerations that may prove relevant to assessing interpretations in particular cases. For example, they would claim that, all other things being equal, good interpretations are maximally *comprehensive,* making sense of the text in its context as this is part of the wider flow of history. "Comprehensive" here does not mean all-inclusive, as if all the different aspects of text and context could be melded and synthesized into one homogeneous and fully intelligible soup. On the contrary, since we start out from a "variety of voices" that do not allow for a synthesis (*Aufhebung*), faithfulness to tradition involves preserving this dissension as much as it seeks to fuse horizons (TM, 284). One might also claim that good interpretations are open-ended in the sense that they make

15. Heidegger's conception of the historicity of interpretation is made more complex by his claim that interpretation must do "violence" to the text and that the most primordial interpretations achieve a "new beginning" in history. These complexities cannot be dealt with here.

manifest the fact that every revealing of possibilities depends on concealing other possibilities. The best interpretations therefore reveal that the possibilities they disclose are just that, *possibilities,* and that other possibilities of interpretation are therefore possible.

Ontological hermeneutics holds that we neither need nor can formulate rules or procedures applicable to every instance of interpretation. Nothing general can be said about interpretation aside from descriptions of what usually goes on. But our actual practices show that we have no real need for anything more than clear-sightedness about what we in fact do. Our ability to identify good interpretations and come up with them ourselves shows how deeply engrained interpreting is in us, the beings whose own being is interpretation.

Appreciation and Literary Interpretation

Peter Lamarque

It seems unlikely that there is a single right interpretation of the term "interpretation," not only because the concept crops up in a multiplicity of domains but because in certain particular domains the concept is essentially contested. Nowhere is the very idea of interpretation more problematic or more contested than in its application to literature. It is not that there is widespread disagreement about what kinds of critical commentary might *count as* literary interpretation or even, within fairly broad bounds, what counts as perceptive or worthwhile interpretation. The problem comes principally at the level of metacriticism, in identifying the principles of interpretive reasoning, the aims of interpretation, the criteria for judging between competing interpretations, or the very nature of the objects interpreted.

Perhaps, though, we are wrong to expect some definitive answer to these metacritical conundrums. Why should there be an essence of literary interpretation, waiting to be discovered, that has so far eluded generations of theorists? Perhaps the metacritic, in exploring the limits of interpretation, is more like the critic, constrained certainly in recognizable ways, seeking clarity, plausibility, conformity to shared intuitions and widespread practice, but in the end addressing a subject matter that is intrinsically indeterminate. Such at least is the meta-metacritical line I take in this essay. I do not deny that there are truths about literary interpretation—I shall outline some—nor do I hold that on matters of controversy any opinion is as good as any other. My method is this: I shall commend a certain picture of the interpretive enterprise in literary criticism, contrasting it with other levels at which interpretation supposedly occurs; I shall engage the singularism/multiplism debate at each stage;[1] but I will pull back from the claim that the picture I offer is the one and only right way that interpretation must be applied to literature.

The Distinctiveness of the Literary

In developing this picture, I assume one fundamental truth, namely, the distinctiveness of literary works as objects of interpretation. Exactly what is distinctive about literary works among other kinds of linguistic expressions remains contested, and more detailed truths on this score must be elicited with care.[2] I will not offer a definition of literature, since I am not convinced that any substantive, noncircular, set of necessary and sufficient conditions is available. But I am sure that if there were such conditions, they would not, and could not, rest at a purely linguistic level—in terms of textual, semantic, or rhetorical features that all and only literary works share. The essential properties, such as they are, must include relational properties, making reference to participants in a practice, their attitudes, expectations, and judgments.[3] More on that later. In my characterization of the literary realm an added complexity arises because the picture I seek to promote links the nature of literary works essentially with the species of interpretation that I favor.

But we cannot take any step for granted, and the distinctiveness of the

1. I adopt the terminology from Michael Krausz, for whom "singularists hold that . . . the range of ideally competing interpretations should be conclusively narrowed to a limit of one" and the "multiplist allows that the range of ideally admissible interpretations in some practices should be multiple": *Rightness and Reasons: Interpretation in Cultural Practices* (Ithaca, N.Y.: Cornell University Press, 1993), 42, 44.

2. I should emphasize that I am taking for granted a restrictive (modern) notion of "literature" as "imaginative literature." There are broader senses. I discuss the delimitation of the term "literature" in my article "Literature" for the Routledge *Companion to Aesthetics,* ed. Berys Gaut and Dominic Lopes (London: Routledge, 2000).

3. For detailed development of this idea, see Peter Lamarque and Stein Haugom Olsen, *Truth, Fiction, and Literature: A Philosophical Perspective* (Oxford: Clarendon Press, 1994), pt. iii, and my *Fictional Points of View* (Ithaca, N.Y.: Cornell University Press, 1996), chap. 12.

literary needs further defense and elaboration. Although there has been widespread agreement among metacritics that, whatever else might be said, literary works are distinct *in ways that affect how they are interpreted,* even this view has been challenged in recent years. The challenge is most notable among those who aim to revive support for versions of intentionalism in literary criticism.[4] A common move in such arguments is to insist on the application to literature of paradigms of meaning drawn from extraliterary contexts, for example, ordinary conversation or "utterance meaning."

Nowhere is this assimilationist strategy more evident than in Noël Carroll's defense of "modest actual intentionalism." A central plank of Carroll's argument against "hypothetical intentionalism" is the claim that there is no difference in kind between the interpretive practice appropriate for literature and what he calls "ordinary interpretation," as applied to conversation or, more generally, to human action. For Carroll the fact that we normally seek to uncover actual intentions in these other areas is a prima facie reason for supposing that the search for actual intentions should govern literary (and artistic) criticism: "Outside the literary and artistic contexts, we generally interpret utterances, gestures, and other forms of symbolic behavior with an eye to retrieving authorial intentions. Modest actual intentionalism takes literary and artistic interpretation to be on a par with ordinary interpretation."[5]

Let us pursue Carroll's argument a bit further, even though I am not inclined to get drawn into the debate between "actual intentionalism" and "hypothetical intentionalism," because the notion of interpretation I propose rejects the very framework in which that debate is set up. Carroll addresses some remarks by Jerrold Levinson that present the more standard view that there is something distinctive about, in Levinson's words, "the practice of literary communication." Here is Levinson, drawing on the point, in defense of hypothetical intentionalism: "Although in informative discourse we rightly look for intended meaning first . . . , in literary art we are licensed, if I am right, to consider what meanings the verbal text before

4. For example, Noël Carroll, "Art, Intention, and Conversation," in *Intention and Interpretation,* ed. Gary Iseminger (Philadelphia: Temple University Press, 1991); idem, "The Intentional Fallacy: Defending Myself," *Journal of Aesthetics and Art Criticism* 55 (1997): 305–9; idem, "Interpretation and Intention," *Metaphilosophy* 31 (2000): 75–95; Gary Iseminger, "An Intentional Demonstration?" in *Intention and Interpretation,* ed. Iseminger; idem, "Actual Intentionalism vs. Hypothetical Intentionalism," *Journal of Aesthetics and Art Criticism* 54 (1996): 319–26; Paisley Livingston, "Intentionalism in Aesthetics," *New Literary History* 29 (1998): 831–46.

5. Carroll, "Interpretation and Intention," 81.

us, viewed in context, *could* be being used to convey, and then to form, if we can, in accord with the practice of literary communication to which both author and reader have implicitly subscribed, our best hypothesis of what it is being used to convey."[6] Levinson is appealing to a practice associated with the reading of literature that he believes differs, with regard to the role of intentions, from the practice of ordinary conversations. Carroll's objection is that in characterizing this practice Levinson is "making some extremely substantial empirical claims about the nature of our literary practices," and he, Carroll, is "not convinced that the evidence will bear out these claims."[7]

My response is that perhaps the evidence from critical practice is indecisive as between the two kinds of intentionalism, but the evidence is surely overwhelming in another respect, namely, that literary works, apart from the question of intention, are *not* treated as though they were contributions to a conversation. The kinds of comments that are standard in literary interpretation, the kinds of interest taken, the focus of attention, are radically different from those common among participants of conversations. The analogy between literary works and conversation, which is at the heart of Carroll's theory of interpretation,[8] seems hopelessly weak *when pursued beyond the intentionalist debate.* The quite proper appeal to practices— even to empirical evidence about those practices—shows up the disanalogies glaringly.

First of all, we should note how odd it is even to speak of *interpretation* in a conversational context. Only exceptionally would interpretation be necessary or appropriate for a remark in a conversation and would usually arise on occasions when conversations break down (with the suspicion, for example, that things are being hinted at, hidden, not honestly or straightforwardly spoken). Normally, conversational remarks are grasped (their meaning grasped) and responses elicited without any deep reflection and without any need for *interpreting.*

But, second, to pursue a more substantial point, consider the typical focus of interest in literary interpretation, as exhibited in the following unexceptional passage of critical comment:

6. Jerrold Levinson, "Intention and Interpretation in Literature," in *The Pleasures of Aesthetics* (Ithaca, N.Y.: Cornell University Press, 1996), 196. The passage is quoted in Carroll, "Interpretation and Intention," 86.

7. Carroll, "Interpretation and Intention," 86–87.

8. He develops a theory of what he calls "our conversational interest in artworks" as offering a new perspective on the relation between artists and audiences: Carroll, "Art, Intention, and Conversation," 118f.

A society in which personal relations reduce themselves to a struggle for dominance develops that drama of *looks* and *faces* which is so important in *Our Mutual Friend*. Scenes in the novel are frequently presented as a conflict of masks. Each person tries to hide his own secret and to probe behind a misleading surface and find the secrets of others. The prize of a successful uncovering is the power that goes with knowing and not being known. Bella Wilfer finds that the Boffin household has become a confrontation of stealthy faces: "What with taking heed of these two faces, and what with feeling conscious that the stealthy occupation must set some mark on her own, Bella soon began to think that there was not a candid or a natural face among them all but Mrs. Boffin's." In the same way the Lammles exchange hidden looks over the heads of their unconscious victim, Georgina Podsnap, and Silas Wegg reads stories about misers to Mr. Boffin. In this case, as in the others, the master of the situation is the man whose face is an opaque nonreflector and remains unread.[9]

The focus of this snippet of literary analysis is on the development and illustration of one aspect of a general theme ("personal relations reduce themselves to a struggle for dominance") in Dickens's *Our Mutual Friend*, through examining the symbolic role of *looks* and *faces*. Instances of the symbols are cited and connected and a general conclusion drawn. This is a small part of a wider effort at exploring the literary interest of the novel. Themes, symbols, the citing and linking of textual evidence, the redescription of local incident, the drawing of conclusions, as illustrated in the passage, are the very stuff of literary interpretation. *But they are quite alien to ordinary conversations.* Nor is this just a contingent consequence of the pedestrian nature of most conversations, that is, that they don't *as a matter of fact* contain symbols or themes or elicit this kind of interest. Attention of the kind directed toward a text by the quoted passage is singular and, on the face of it, peculiar. If a contribution to a conversation did elicit this kind of response, then the flow of conversation would be entirely disrupted; the contribution would be treated as something other than an exchange of views, indeed *as if* it commanded attention in its own right, in other words, *as if* it were a literary work (or a part of one) in itself. If we are looking

9. J. Hillis Miller, afterword to *Our Mutual Friend*, by Charles Dickens (New York: Signet Classics, 1964), 906.

for the distinctiveness of literary works, then we must concentrate on the distinctiveness of ways of talking about them.

The important underlying point is this: different objects of interpretation command different modes of interpretation, which in turn have different aims.[10] We are called upon to interpret all manner of actions, texts, and phenomena—a cryptic remark, a political speech, legal rulings, a passage from the Bible, philosophical theses, dreams, flashes in the sky, Rorschach blots, Wallace Stevens poems, delinquent behavior, someone's absence from a meeting. Although we might find some generic formula that binds all these interpretive enterprises together—seeking to "make sense" of something or "understand" it better—the differences are more striking than the commonalities.

The idea I seek to promote is that a central component of *literary* interpretation properly so called—that part which makes it distinctive of literature—has less to do with *meaning* as such, or with *understanding,* than with *appreciation* of a special kind.[11] This appears to go against an almost universally held tenet in discussions of interpretation, that to interpret is necessarily to seek meaning. I am not denying, which would be perverse, that literary critics are concerned with meaning. My skepticism about meaning arises principally at the level where metacritics speak of "the meaning of the work," and yet, I argue, it is at that level (differently described) that the enterprise of literary interpretation exhibits its essential character.

The consequences of this refocusing are soon apparent in the singularism/multiplism debate. The idea of a "single right interpretation" is commonly taken to imply a "single determinate meaning," but if literary interpretation does not aim for meaning, then it does not aim for a single determinate meaning. Also, if interpretation is associated with appreciation, then singularity and rightness needs to apply to appreciation. Yet, given the multiple facets of a literary work, there is little theoretical pressure to postulate a single correct appreciation for each work.

To aid the discussion I will avail myself of a distinction—or a version of a distinction—drawn by Monroe C. Beardsley that has largely been lost

10. These points are elaborated in more detail in my essays "Marks and Noises and Interpretations," *Semiotica* 108 (1996): 163–75, and "Objects of Interpretation," *Metaphilosophy* 31, nos. 1/2 (2000): 96–124.

11. I acknowledge at the outset my debt here to Stein Haugom Olsen, who has been developing just this line in the past twenty years, notably in his book *The End of Literary Theory* (Cambridge: Cambridge University Press, 1987). I hope I can do a little more than merely repeat his arguments—through expanding and consolidating the position—but the groundwork is all his.

from view: between, in his own terms, "explication," "elucidation," and "interpretation." For Beardsley, to *explicate* is "to determine the contextual meanings of a group of words"; to *elucidate* is "to determine parts of the world of the work, such as character and motives, that are not explicitly reported in it"; and to *interpret* is "to determine the themes and theses of a literary work, given the contextual meanings of the words and a complete description of the world of the work."[12]

Explication, or the Recovery of Verbal Meaning

Explication, with its concern for "relatively localized parts" of works,[13] is, of the three, the most obviously and unproblematically concerned with *meaning*. But it does not inevitably involve *interpretation* (in a standard sense, as well as in Beardsley's more restricted sense). That "dun" means "dimmed" in Shelley's line "With whose dun beams inwoven darkness seemed" is not a product of interpretation; and it seems straightforwardly a case of a "single determinate meaning." Often what is sought in explication is the recovery of information that was once common knowledge.

I do not want to brush aside the importance of explication or deny that there are difficult theoretical issues about it, including what Beardsley calls its "logic," but I will restrict my discussion to one or two observations with implications for literary interpretation of the kind I favor.

First, explication in criticism most readily lends itself to the appropriation of models of meaning from outside literary practice. Beardsley himself famously proposed that "a model of all explication" is "the explication of a metaphor."[14] When metacritics appeal to extraliterary paradigms—metaphor (Beardsley), conversation (Carroll), utterance meaning (Levinson, Stecker), utterer's meaning (Iseminger)—the appropriation, if convincing at all, is likely to be at its most convincing at the level of explication. After all, if the meaning of sentences (or sentence parts) is being investigated, then more general theories of sentence (or word) meaning will be candidates for application. However, models of meaning appropriate at the level of explication (for localized meanings) should not be *assumed* applicable at the level

---

12. Monroe C. Beardsley, *Aesthetics: Problems in the Philosophy of Criticism,* 2d ed. (Indianapolis: Hackett, 1981), 401, 403.
13. Ibid., 130.
14. Ibid., 144.

of whole works. The assumption that an entire novel, like *Our Mutual Friend,* possesses a meaning in a manner even analogous to that of an individual sentence, utterance, or metaphor is not justified, at least not merely from premises about what is relevant for explication (of parts of works).

Second, explication, however carried out, is not, in the literary case, an end in itself but a stage toward a fuller appreciation of a work as a whole. Admittedly, the relation between explication and work interpretation is far from straightforward. It is complicated, for example, by worries about the hermeneutic circle. Segments of a work might not be explicable independently of an overall view of the work, yet the overall view might depend on meanings assigned to segments. The point is familiar enough. It is illustrated in the well-known crux about "buckle" at the start of the sestet of Gerard Manley Hopkins's sonnet "The Windhover":

> Brute beauty and valour and act, oh, air, pride, plume, here
>   Buckle! AND the fire that breaks from thee then, a billion
>   Times told lovelier, more dangerous, O my chevalier!

There is debate as to whether the first sentence is in the imperative or indicative mood. Also, the word "buckle" can mean "join together" or "break under the strain," and the alternative, and contradictory, meanings could be associated with a hopeful, joyous vision in the poem as a whole or something darker and more ominous.[15] There is no clear-cut solution to this critical conundrum, no independent authority for a preferred reading, and it seems that both senses, at a textual level, must be acknowledged. The explicator's task can go no further, in this instance, than pointing out the double meaning, for the verbal context alone cannot eliminate one meaning definitively. It is only at the level of interpretation (applied to the complete sonnet) that decisions about how to respond to the alternative readings must be taken: perhaps to highlight one meaning over the other, perhaps to keep the tension alive and to emphasize the role of other tensions throughout the poem, as between Christ's humility and his soaring power. The thematic vision is left finely poised, in many ways troubling like the poem itself.

But the theoretical point stands, that explication is subordinate to interpretation at the level of the literary work. The ambiguity in "buckle" only matters because of its effect on an appreciation of the work as a whole, and

15. For a useful survey of different meanings attributed to the line, see *The Poetical Works of Gerard Manley Hopkins,* ed. Norman H. Mackenzie (Oxford: Clarendon Press, 1990), 382–83.

interpretive decisions will rest on evaluative factors, weighing up what best supports the literary interest of the poem, in concordance with the explicator's findings elsewhere. However, although interpretation, in a sense, selects meanings, the notion that a text, in Beardsley's phrase, "means all it *can* mean" is at best only a half truth.[16] Explication should certainly explore *possible* meanings at a textual level, but the task of delimiting meaning is more important to the interpretive exercise than that of multiplying meaning (a point, it should be noted, that still remains neutral on the singularist/multiplist issue). Too much meaning at the level of explication is more likely to hinder than aid appreciation. Readings in the style of William Empson or Roland Barthes, which merely catalogue what sentences or words could mean without showing the interpretive benefits, are at best incomplete and unsatisfactory.[17]

Third, the search for meaning at this level is not in itself sufficient to mark off the literary from the nonliterary. Every kind of text invites explication, and the procedures for recovering meaning at a *sentential* level will not differ markedly from case to case. Perhaps that is the intuition behind Carroll's position. The attempt to identify something distinctive about literary meaning in explication—as, for example, Beardsley's notion of "semantical thickness"[18]—usually founders because it rests on a single paradigm of literature, in this case, poetry. We would not expect sentences in a novel, for example, to be charged with meaning in the way that characterizes meta-

16. Beardsley, *Aesthetics,* 144.
17. Consider a not untypical passage from William Empson discussing some lines from *Macbeth:*

> If th'Assassination
> Could trammel up the Consequence, and catch
> With his surcease, Success; that but . . .

words hissed in the passage where servants were passing, which must be swaddled with darkness, loaded as it were in themselves with fearful powers, and not made too naked even to his own mind. *Consequence* means causal result, and the things to follow, though not causally connected and, as in "a person of consequence," the divinity that doth hedge a king. *Trammel* was a technical term used about netting birds, hobbling horses in some particular way, hooking up pots, levering, and running trolleys on rails. *Surcease* means completion, stopping proceedings in the middle of a lawsuit, or the overruling of a judgment; the word reminds you of "surfeit" and "decease." (*Seven Types of Ambiguity,* 2d ed. [London: Chatto & Windus, 1947], 49–50)

Admittedly Empson's purpose is to illustrate a type of ambiguity, but on its own the explication fulfills no interpretive function.
18. Beardsley, *Aesthetics,* 129.

phoric poetic imagery. This reinforces the claim that literature is not definable in linguistic terms alone.

A fourth point is that explication *per se* is value-neutral: a matter of understanding, not of appreciating. Understanding is common to different kinds of texts, while appreciation will differ according to assumptions about the practices in which the texts are located. Expectations about what is valuable in, say, philosophical works differ from expectations associated with works of imaginative literature. These value-laden expectations will inform both the aims and procedures of interpretation. Interpretation seeks out those qualities which the practice defines as valuable.

Finally, the dispute over a "single right interpretation" is often at its most intense in connection with explication, for it is at this level that questions about intention first intrude. However, because this is not the level at which distinctively literary qualities reside, we should not let the intentionalist issue overwhelm the discussion. There does seem to be a reasonable aspiration for explication, like all inquiries into meaning, to seek determinacy as far as possible. Even where no single meaning emerges unequivocally—as in the "buckle" case—at least the explicator seeks a determinate *range* of possibilities. Nor does it seem anything but arbitrary to delimit, at this stage, acceptable sources for the determination of meaning, including reliable indications of authorial intention. The test for relevance will come at the level of interpretation, where the selected meanings are put to work.

Elucidation, or the Recovery of the World of the Work

Elucidation, in Beardsley's sense, is the quest for details about a narrative—what occurs in the world of the work—that are not made explicit in the narrative itself. Beardsley gives these examples: "What did Hamlet study at Wittenberg? What is the minister's secret sin in Hawthorne's short story, 'The Minister's Black Veil'? . . . Who was Mrs. Dalloway's great-grandfather? How many years does Tom Jones live after the story ends?"[19] There are countless questions of this kind, arising in all narrative fiction, and they come in different degrees of seriousness.

It can seem strained to talk of "meaning" for many of these questions. Are speculations about the future life of Tom Jones concerned with the

19. Ibid., 244.

meaning of the novel (or parts of the novel)? Theories of meaning—utterance meaning, conversational meaning, metaphorical meaning—seem to have no natural application in this context.[20] But many such questions undoubtedly do concern interpretation, if not always of the distinctive literary kind.[21] There is no settled consensus about the principles for reasoning to what is "true in fiction." Kendall Walton has described what he calls the "mechanics of generation" (i.e., elucidation, in Beardsley's terminology) as "very disorderly."[22]

For our purposes, again just a few observations in relation to the "single right interpretation" should suffice before moving to the third kind of interpretation. First, it is clear, as with explication, that there are many cases where a determinate right answer is accessible under "elucidation." Many physical facts not made explicit in narratives—about the internal organs of fictional characters or modes of transport or distances between places—are readily inferable against common assumptions. Likewise, there are many cases where a radical indeterminacy arises from gaps in narratives (the weather on a particular day, a character's private thoughts at all times). No principle of interpretation will yield a determinate answer in such cases. But more to the point, no answer is *needed,* since, for most such cases, the missing "facts" are irrelevant to an appreciation of a work's literary qualities.

Of more interest are the cases between the clearly determinate and the clearly indeterminate. But what we find here is a shift from "elucidation," as in the paradigm of "truth in fiction" discussed by Beardsley or Walton or Gregory Currie or David Lewis, to more specifically literary concerns. A striking case might be the nature of Ophelia's madness. Nothing in the nar-

20. Robert Stecker believes that "the broad notion of utterance meaning . . . is adequate for determining this kind of content," but he should have taken more heed of his own example, whether Juliet's blood, in *Romeo and Juliet,* is made of molecules or humors, which seems to show that questions about "fictional truth" do not reduce, in any straightforward way, to questions about textual *meaning:* Stecker, *Artworks: Definition, Meaning, Value* (University Park: Pennsylvania State University Press), 178–79.

21. Gregory Currie characterizes this kind of inquiry as "narrative interpretation": "Interpretation and Objectivity," *Mind* 102 (1993): 413–28.

22. "Implications seem not to be governed by any simple or systematic principle or set of principles, but by a complicated and shifting and often competing array of understandings, precedents, local conventions, saliences": Kendall Walton, *Mimesis as Make-Believe: On the Foundations of the Representational Arts* (Cambridge, Mass.: Harvard University Press, 1990), 169. Walton considers two broad principles—the Reality Principle, according to which what is true in the fictional world is partly determined by how things are in the actual world, and the Mutual Belief Principle, according to which the determining factor is not how things are but how they were believed to be in the author's community—but argues that both face strong counterexamples.

rative of *Hamlet* tells us precisely what the physical or psychological causes of her madness are. Elaine Showalter, in an illuminating essay, has tracked the different conceptions of Ophelia's madness from the Elizabethan period to our own times.[23] For the Elizabethans, Ophelia suffered from "female love-melancholy or erotomania" (Showalter's terms);[24] Ellen Terry, in the late Victorian era, "led the way in acting Ophelia in feminist terms as a consistent psychological study in sexual intimidation, a girl terrified of her father, of her lover, and of life itself";[25] for the early-twentieth-century Freudians Ophelia has "an unresolved oedipal attachment to her father . . . [and] has fantasies of a lover who will abduct her from and even kill her father, and when this actually happens, her reason is destroyed by guilt as well as by lingering incestuous feelings";[26] finally, feminists in the 1970s viewed her madness as "protest and rebellion . . . [her as] the hysteric who refuses to speak the language of the patriarchal order."[27] Perhaps some of these conceptions might be dismissed as fanciful, but unlike more limited inquiries into "truth in fiction," any final assessment of them must be informed by an overall view of the play and the contribution that Ophelia is seen to make. There is no "single right" Ophelia. Her properties, like those of all characters, are radically indeterminate. Genuine interpretation is involved, but where it matters, it looks less like a quasi-factual inquiry into "truths about a fictional world" than like developing a *conception* of a work of art.[28] In the case of drama, different conceptions will be manifested in different productions.

Both explication and elucidation, in Beardsley's senses, can (but need not) involve interpretation, although the former is more closely linked with meaning as such. Neither is exclusive to literature or indicative of what is distinctive or valuable about literature. All texts require explication to some degree, and elucidation is required for all, not just literary, narratives. These inquiries are value-neutral. Both also allow, uncontroversially, for instances of "single right interpretations," or determinate meanings. Both also admit of unresolvable indeterminacies. But among the latter we can identify cases

---

23. Elaine Showalter, "Representing Ophelia: Women, Madness, and the Responsibilities of Feminist Criticism," in *Shakespeare and the Question of Theory,* ed. Patricia Parker and Geoffrey Hartman (London: Methuen, 1985).

24. Ibid., 81.

25. Ibid., 89.

26. Ibid., 90.

27. Ibid., 91.

28. For a further discussion of the tension between talk of "worlds" and of interpreting works, see my *Fictional Points of View,* chap. 4.

that matter and cases that seem merely peripheral. I have argued that the indeterminacies that matter—the contradictory meanings, the significant narrative gaps—will always defer, in any attempted resolution, to a higher level of interpretation involving the work at large and, what is more important, to questions about the *interest* of the work and its *value*.

Literary Interpretation, or the Characterizing of Literary Qualities

It is to that further inquiry that we must, at last, turn, for it is only at this level, I maintain, that we reach the realm of literary interpretation properly so called. It is perhaps for this reason that Beardsley was inclined to restrict the term "interpretation" to what he called "themes" and "theses."[29] In fact I will not be adopting Beardsley's theme/thesis distinction, for I am inclined to think that this is a distinction not between themes and something else but between ways of characterizing themes. Literary themes, which serve to exhibit a work's unity, are identifiable with more or less specificity: as abstract concepts (pride, despair, jealousy, ambition), as noun phrases (the futility of war, the conflict between desire and duty), as propositions (fate disrupts the best-laid plans), or in other forms besides. The question of "literary truth," as implied in the idea of "thesis," is best kept separate from the question of interpretation.[30]

Themes characteristic of the most valued literary works involve conceptions and "issues" that are central and perennial preoccupations for a culture, usually arising in philosophical or theological contexts as well. Yet in their summary formulation, especially in propositional modes, the themes can seem banal and vacuous (which only compounds the "truth" problem). Standardly, the focus of interest at the thematic level rests not in the bare statement of a theme but in the manner in which the theme is elicited and

29. Here are some of Beardsley's examples: "We say that the theme of *Wuthering Heights* is the quest for spiritual contentment through harmony with both good and evil forces of nature; of *War and Peace,* the endless rhythmic alternation of youth and age, life and death, ambition and resignation." Theses, on the other hand, unlike themes, are bearers of truth: "Critics say, for example, that Shakespeare's *Tempest* embodies a mystical view of life; that Upton Sinclair's *The Jungle* is a protest against the injustices suffered by the poor under a free-wheeling economic system; that there is implicit Platonism in Spenser's 'Epithalamion' and Shelley's 'Epipsychidion.' " Beardsley, *Aesthetics,* 403–4.

30. The nature and role of "literary truth" is discussed at length in Lamarque and Olsen, *Truth, Fiction, and Literature.*

supported through interpretation. The unifying "vision" of a literary work resides not in thematic summary but in the complex manner in which elements of the work—character, incident, symbol, verbal structure—are subsumable under themes of general interest. Although the terms in which a theme is formulated will often be derived from the work itself, the theme's elicitation as an organizing principle of the work demands, and is a product of, a kind of imaginative reconstruction on the part of a reader.[31] Appreciation of a literary work, qua literary work, is constituted by just such a reconstruction of the work's underlying themes; the exercises of explication and elucidation are subordinate to this ulterior aim. But we must move slowly to consolidate this picture because ideas like "imaginative reconstruction" and "organizing principle" raise difficult questions regarding the "single right interpretation."

First, the matter of meaning. It is at least not *obvious* that complete works, unlike parts of works, can intelligibly be said to possess "a meaning" or, if they do, that it is anything like the meaning ascribed to sentences, utterances, or words. As Stein Haugom Olsen has pointed out, it is hard to know how to fill in the blank in "the meaning of *Macbeth* is . . ." or even "the meaning of Hume's *Treatise* is. . . ."[32] Metacritics are so used to speaking of "the meaning of a work" that they have failed to reflect on its oddity. Often—not always—the phrase is taken to mean "the themes of the work" or what it is "about." So to say, as Wilson Knight does, that "*Macbeth* is a profound and mature vision of evil" would be to give the play's meaning (or part of it). Yet it is hard to put this statement into the meaning idiom, for example, as a filler for the blank above. And thematic content, at least literary thematic content, is quite unlike semantic content.

What matters, though, is not a quibble about words. What matter are misleading assumptions that can creep in when a certain vocabulary is taken for granted. Consider, for example, Robert Stecker's claim that "work meaning," as he calls it, is broadly equivalent to "utterance meaning."[33] I focus on Stecker's contribution partly because of the explicitness of his formulation but also because he is rare in actually addressing—albeit dis-

31. The terms "organizing principle" and "imaginative reconstruction" come from Olsen, *The End of Literary Theory*, 15, 16.

32. See the essays "Text and Meaning" and "The 'Meaning' of a Literary Work" in Olsen, *The End of Literary Theory*.

33. Other supporters of utterance meaning in literary interpretation include William Tolhurst, "On What a Text Is and How It Means," *British Journal of Aesthetics* 19 (1979): 3–14, and Levinson, "Intention and Interpretation in Literature."

missing—the question of the oddity of the phrase "the meaning of a work."[34]

Here is how Stecker defines utterance meaning: "Utterance meaning specifies what someone says or conveys by using certain words on a particular occasion in a particular context."[35] Yet immediately the difficulty arises regarding how to apply this definition to a whole work, say, a lengthy novel. What could *on a particular occasion* mean for a novel that took several years to write, was edited and reworked before publication, or was perhaps published in monthly sequels? And what is the *particular context* in which the work was "uttered"? It cannot be anything comparable to the context in which, say, a remark in a conversation is uttered. The relevant context in the literary case is not the moment when the author put down his or her pen (or picked it up) but a broadly conceived *literary* context, a historical period, a location in a tradition, a juxtaposition with other works.

The simple paradigm that gives point to the notion of "utterance meaning," as it does to "utterer's meaning," namely, a sentence spoken or written on an occasion, does not and cannot apply to something as extensive as a complete literary work. Sentential meaning, at the core of utterance meaning, is a function, partially, of semantic and componential rules, incorporating singular reference, predication, and syntactic structure. A sentence is a semantic unit to which truth-conditions are applicable. Nothing comparable occurs at the level of whole works, and nothing comparable will explain the elicitation of literary features. It is not merely the complexity of a work that makes the difference. For the sentences that constitute a text only come to constitute a literary work when embedded in a practice, which marks them as suitable objects for "literary" attention.

There are two principal reasons, I suggest, why metacritics have favored notions like "utterance" or "utterer's" meaning: first, they run together explication and other forms of literary interpretation (a look at their examples shows this); second, they assign the highest theoretical priority to the debate about authorial intention. Both positions distort the more interesting features of the literary institution. Explication at sentential level, we have seen, is not peculiar to literature and is subordinate to interpretation, which aims to exhibit distinctive literary qualities. There would be no point in explicating a text if there were not broader aesthetic ends in view. And the intention

34. Stecker (in *Artworks*, 157–62) discusses the problems posed by Stein Haugom Olsen about "the meaning of a work."
35. Stecker, *Artworks*, 167–68.

debate should not be all-encompassing. Suppose we were to follow what I take to be fairly widespread practice among critics and adopt a relaxed view about intention: *where intentions are available and known, make use of them; where they are not, make do.* I suggest that even in the light of that attitude the most interesting questions about literature still remain: why literary works are valued, what makes them distinct from other kinds of works, what rewards are to be had from reading them, how the literary development of themes differs from their development in other modes of discourse, what basis there is for the selection of canonical works, and so forth.

It is often said that literary interpretation has the aim of increasing "understanding," and that notion might seem innocuous enough. But again "understanding" fits much more naturally at the explication level than at the thematic level. Here is an example. On the face of it Daniel Defoe's novel *Moll Flanders* (1722) is not difficult to understand. It is a rollicking story full of incident and colorful characters. Even the title page tells us what to expect: it is about a woman "Who was born in Newgate, and during a Life of continu'd Variety for Threescore Years, besides her Childhood, was Twelve Year a *Whore,* five times a *Wife* (whereof once to her own Brother) Twelve Year a *Thief,* Eight Year a Transported *Felon* in *Virginia,* at last grew *Rich,* Liv'd *Honest,* and died a *Penitent.*" For a modern readership a certain amount of explication might be necessary—eighteenth-century terminology, customs, places, laws, the sorts of things a good critical edition would explain in footnotes—as a condition for a full understanding. But once the story is grasped and local explication completed, what more is there to *understand?*

Yet nothing up to this point has touched on the *literary* properties of the work, why it should be deemed a literary classic, why it rewards attention. Only interpretation, focusing a particular kind of attention, will reveal the *interest* or *value* of the work from a literary point of view. Many novels of the period (at least through the eighteenth century), of a superficially similar nature, neither invite nor reward interpretation; the effort would not be worthwhile. But a substantial critical literature has built up round *Moll Flanders,* and in spite of the famous denunciation of Defoe by F. R. Leavis in *The Great Tradition* and the equivocal judgment of this novel by Ian Watt in *The Rise of the Novel,* positive statements of the novel's achievement, encouraged by plaudits from James Joyce, Virginia Woolf, and E. M. Forster, are now numerous. What has happened is that new perspectives on the novel have been opened up that deepen, not so much *understanding*, as *appreciation*.

Terence Martin, for example, invites us to see unity in the novel through "the significance of the pattern of theft": "if we examine the details of theft, we find . . . that the second large part of the novel operates as an attempt to win back the relative security of the first part: Moll's desire for economic security manifests itself in a series of adventures which testify to the quality of this desire by falling into a significant episodic pattern."[36] Arnold Kettle, in a defense of *Moll Flanders* against the criticisms of Ian Watt, suggests: "The whole nature of Defoe's book—its construction, its texture, its detail, its vitality, its power to move us—is determined by his awareness of the contradiction between Moll's human aspiration and the facts of the human world she lives in." He describes in detail how much of the attempted resolution of this "insoluble" contradiction "takes the form of ambiguous or ironical statement."[37] Robert Alan Donovan sees different modes of irony unifying the novel:

> There is, for example, the irony implicit in Moll's assumption that the guilt of her life is her own rather than that of the heartless and venal society that has produced her. There is also an irony of a particularly devastating kind in Moll's innocent acknowledgment . . . that an immoral act is nullified if the perpetrator is ignorant of its moral bearings. The agent's ignorance, in other words, not only excuses him, it changes the nature of his act. . . . But the fundamental, shaping irony of *Moll Flanders* is the double vision of the heroine.[38]

Like the earlier interpretive comments on *Our Mutual Friend*, such remarks are typical of the literary treatment of a text. We *could* say, following metacritics like Stecker, that the comments involve "work meaning" and help increase "understanding." But we are not *forced* to use this idiom, and as I

36. Terence Martin, "The Unity of *Moll Flanders*," in *Moll Flanders*, Norton Critical Edition, ed. Edward Kelly (New York: W. W. Norton, 1973), 363. Originally published in *Modern Language Quarterly* XXII (1961): 115–24.

37. Arnold Kettle, "In Defence of *Moll Flanders*," in *Moll Flanders*, Norton Critical Edition, 395. Originally published in *Of Books and Humankind*, ed. John Butt (London: Routledge, 1964), 55–67.

38. Robert Alan Donovan, "The Two Heroines of *Moll Flanders*," in *Moll Flanders*, Norton Critical Edition, 403. Originally published in *The Shaping Vision: Imagination in the English Novel from Defoe to Dickens* (Ithaca, N.Y.: Cornell University Press, 1966).

have suggested, to emphasize meaning, especially "utterance meaning," in the context of works, is only misleading. What we are brought to understand is not the work's meaning but its interest. With the help of the critics we come to understand *why it is worth reflecting further on the novel*. The interpretive comments enhance appreciation of the novel's literary, or aesthetic, features. These features might be entirely missed by someone who follows the story in all its details and is fully apprised of all the sentence meanings in the work. Yet they are the features—and others besides—which give the work its literary interest and in virtue of which the work can be called "literary," rather than merely "fictional." These features—the "pattern of theft," the "contradictions," the "double vision" of the heroine—are not properties of the linguistic *text* inherent in the language. They "emerge" only under imaginative reconstruction. This is precisely why the age-old question whether thematic features are "in" a text or "imputed to" it is wrongly conceived. They are not *in the text* in the way that semantic meanings might be, yet they can come to be seen as *in the work* once the work has been identified as an appropriate object of (literary) interpretation.[39]

Now some clear and striking consequences for the "single-right-interpretation" debate come to light. Interpretation at a literary or thematic level does not aspire to a single determinate meaning, because it does not strictly aspire to meaning at all. Its aim is to reveal the value of a work, why it merits attention, and to draw out the perspectives under which that value is manifested. But there is no obligation to suppose that there must be a single right perspective on the novel or any single reason why it is worth reflecting on. The question about determinacy of meaning seems strangely out of place in this context. An analogy might be with perspectives on works in dramatic or musical performance. Few would hold that for each play or musical work there must be a single right performance, even though performances are judged for their effectiveness and fidelity to the work.

Literary interpretation with the aims I have attributed to it is essentially an imaginative exploration of a work's thematic content on the assumption of an aesthetic payoff. It seeks to identify and characterize features that show the work to be of literary interest. These features—patterns, thematic unity, interconnectedness of parts—are "emergent," features a work possesses *under a conception*. Hillis Miller characterizes a mirror motif in *Our Mutual Friend*: "To see a Veneering dinner party reflected in 'the great look-

---

39. For more on the distinctions between "text" and "work" and between "in" and "imputed to," see my "Objects of Interpretation."

ing-glass above the sideboard,' to see the vain Bella admiring herself in her mirror, or to see Fledgeby secretly watching Riah's reflection in the chimney-glass is to witness a concrete revelation of the way the lives of such people are self-mirroring. The reflection in the mirror is emptied of its solidity and presented as a thin surface of appearance hiding fathomless depths of nullity."[40] It would be wrong to suppose that the image of the mirror, fulfilling this symbolic function, is an intrinsic part of the *text* (i.e., sentences) of the novel, even though the occurrences described are objectively present. Again, someone could grasp all the meanings at the sentential level—and follow the narrative events—yet fail to apprehend the *gestalt* of this recurring image.[41] The position is comparable to that described by Frank Sibley, who claimed that knowledge of nonaesthetic properties is not sufficient for the appreciation of aesthetic properties, which requires further modes of discrimination.[42] The mirror becomes an item of literary interest only relative to a certain perspective on the novel and scenes within it, as the critic describes. What is happening here is related to what Krausz calls the assigning of "salience,"[43] on the further assumption that the saliences in this case are not value-neutral. Yet there is little theoretical pressure to postulate a single right assignment of saliences.

There is, though, immense theoretical pressure, quite properly, to delimit the range of acceptable or admissible interpretations, even if short of convergence on a single interpretation. The question of what constraints apply remains contested among metacritics. Yet, setting the intention issue aside, enough is broadly agreed to produce a robust barrier against "nihilism," at the thematic level: consistency with the text, plausibility against reasonable background assumptions, comprehensiveness, and an imaginatively reconstructed connectedness of elements.[44] A further factor, which underpins the

40. Miller, afterword to *Our Mutual Friend*, 905–6.

41. Stecker tries to show that Olsen cannot keep appreciation, in a value-laden sense, distinct from understanding, in a value-free sense, by supposing that a computer could be programmed to recognize literary aesthetic features. But it is highly improbable that a computer could do more than pick out recurrences of elements; the task of characterizing the *interest* of these recurrences, the roles they might play, seems to need a human mind. In a further argument Stecker simply seems to be begging the question against Olsen by insisting that an *understanding* of aesthetic features (like the mirror symbol) is a precondition of *appreciating* them (Stecker, *Artworks*, 162–63).

42. F. N. Sibley, "Aesthetic Concepts," *Philosophical Review* 68 (1959).

43. Michael Krausz, *Rightness and Reasons: Interpretation in Cultural Practices* (Ithaca, N.Y.: Cornell University Press, 1993), 68, 77.

44. For a useful account of these constraints, see Stein Haugom Olsen, *The Structure of Literary Understanding* (Cambridge: Cambridge University Press, 1978).

other constraints, should also be prominent: how *illuminating* an interpretation is,[45] in particular the extent to which it exhibits some value to be had in attending to the work as literature.

Interpretations are open to challenge under the criteria listed.[46] Does this mean that interpretations have truth-values? The matter is not easily settled. First of all, the question is misleading because good interpretive readings are made up of multiple propositions fulfilling different functions: redescribing, summarizing, explicating, connecting (consider some of the examples above). Constituent propositions are likely to range from undisputed truths to speculative hypotheses to imaginative redescriptions. Again, it is a mistake to take as paradigmatic of interpretation the straightforward assertions of meaning typical of explication, just as it is a mistake to think that every interpretation can be encapsulated into, and stands and falls on the strength of, a single summary proposition.

But, second, the significant truths in interpretation (i.e., those that serve to identify one interpretation among others) are truths about emergent properties. The claim that there is a mirror symbol in *Our Mutual Friend* and that it stands for the "concrete revelation of the way the lives of such people are self-mirroring" is a claim not about a semantic property but about a feature that "emerges" under the perspective of an interpretation. The question then arises whether the interpretation satisfies the criteria listed. It might be argued, for example, that this purported symbol doesn't add up to much, doesn't afford fruitful connections in thinking about the rest of the novel.

Those tempted to distance interpretation from truth might offer an antirealist construal of interpretive descriptions. Roger Scruton has proposed such a view for aesthetic descriptions in general:

> [T]he acceptance condition of an aesthetic description may not be a belief but may rather be some other mental state which more effec-

45. Another term adopted from Stein Haugom Olsen: see his "On Unilluminating Criticism," in *The End of Literary Theory*. Olsen criticizes the use of "esoteric knowledge" in interpretation where this knowledge is not widely accessible to the very community of readers who help constitute the literary "institution."

46. A vigorous debate is going on in Renaissance studies about the merits or otherwise of "cultural materialist" readings of Shakespeare, in the light of influential works like Jonathan Dollimore's *Radical Tragedy* (Brighton: Harvester Press, 1984). It is becoming increasing clear, though, that the textual evidence cited by critics like Dollimore in their appropriation of Shakespeare to a radical antihumanism involves much distortion and misreading: see, e.g., Tom McAlindon, "Cultural Materialism and the Ethics of Reading; or, the Radicalizing of Jacobean Tragedy," *Modern Language Review* 90 (1995): 830–46.

tively explains the point of aesthetic description. To agree to an aesthetic description is to "see its point," and this "seeing the point" is to be elucidated in terms of some response or experience. . . . Hence aesthetic descriptions need not have truth conditions in the strong sense, and to justify them may be to justify an experience and not a belief.[47]

A similar line, in the literary context, is suggested in Olsen's claim that an interpretive description "defines an experience."[48] If "right" in "single right interpretation" implies "true," then such antirealism would further weaken the hold of singularism. But it would be a mistake to give up the truth-seeking aspiration of interpretation altogether. Room must be left for reasoned support and *groundedness* in texts. The emphasis, though, drawing on antirealist intuitions, must be on the fact that the interpretive truths that matter are truths of a peculiar kind, characterizations of objects (i.e., literary works) whose very identity is tied to the kinds of interpretive comments they elicit.

Can there be incompatible interpretations? Perhaps the "Windover" case is one such, or the well-worn example of *The Turn of the Screw*, where the ghosts are interpreted as real or as mere figments of the governess's mind.[49] It seems highly unlikely that two formally incompatible interpretations will have exactly equal merit and satisfy standard criteria (including statements of authorial intention, if need be) without inclining one way or the other. But suppose they do. We would then have to say that here are two ways—entirely at odds with one another but equally rewarding and equally faithful to the text—in which attention can be focused on a work. The oddity is not in the need to relativize—for salient properties are always relative to interpretive perspectives—but in the fine balance achieved by such opposing visions.

I am not persuaded that Stecker's distinction between true and "acceptable" interpretations is a useful way of reconciling singularism and multiplism (what he calls "critical monism" and "critical pluralism"). He suggests (qua "pluralist") that "acceptable" interpretations are typically neither true nor false (they can be false, but never true), and he elaborates this by instancing those that "may aim at enhancing the aesthetic value of a work."[50] He

47. Roger Scruton, *Art and Imagination* (London: Methuen, 1974), 55.
48. Olsen, *The End of Literary Theory*, 123.
49. Stecker discusses the example: *Artworks*, 119.
50. Ibid., 136.

also holds (qua "monist") that all true interpretations can be conjoined into a single, comprehensive, true interpretation. Neither move is satisfactory. The conjoining (in Krausz's terms, "aggregating")[51] of all "true" interpretations for the sake of a "single right interpretation" has neither practical benefit nor theoretical legitimacy under the view of interpretation as appreciation. There could be no coherent *experience* that conjoined all perspectives deemed admissible (or "true"), even if these were not directly contradictory. Too many saliences jostling for attention would blur, rather than enhance, literary interest. Stecker's account has divorced interpretation from experience (appreciation)—a consequence of the emphasis on meaning. But the defense of pluralism looks no better, because it implies that the merely "acceptable" is a second-best standard of interpretation and it fails to acknowledge the role of interpretive truth even where the aim is "enhancing . . . aesthetic value."

We should be content, I conclude, with the benign multiplism implied by the picture of interpretation I have offered. There is plenty of room in critical practice for the intuitions of the singularist. The aspiration and the achievement of the "single right interpretation" are unequivocally in evidence in explication and elucidation. By drawing attention away from the emphasis on meaning at the level of the work and toward appreciation of literary works as distinct objects of interpretation, I hope to have shown how to sidestep some of the more intractable metacritical debates (e.g., about intention) while still characterizing a recognizable practice. But I do not believe, as I announced at the start, that the "aesthetic" approach to interpretation is the only acceptable approach, because I am resigned to acknowledge that there are legitimate alternative interpretive aims and that the concept is, and will remain, contested.

51. Krausz, *Rightness and Reasons*, 58.

PART IV

Hypothetical Intentionalism: Statement, Objections, and Replies

Jerrold Levinson

1. In an earlier essay I defended at some length a view on literary interpretation that I call *hypothetical intentionalism*.[1] The view centers on the idea that a literary work should be seen as an *utterance,* one produced in a public context by a historically and culturally situated author, and that the central meaning of such a work is thus a form of *utterance meaning,* as opposed to either *textual meaning* or *utterer meaning.*[2] Utterance meaning, in turn, is understood on a pragmatic model according to which what an utterance means is a matter, roughly, of what an appropriate hearer would most reasonably take a speaker to be trying to convey in employing a given verbal vehicle in the given communicative context. As applied to literature, and fleshed out in certain ways, what this amounts to is this: the core meaning of a literary work is given by the best hypothesis, from the position of an appropriately informed, sympathetic, and discriminating reader, of authorial intent to convey such and such to an audience through the text in question.

---

1. See "Intention and Interpretation in Literature," in my *Pleasures of Aesthetics* (Ithaca, N.Y.: Cornell University Press, 1996). (An earlier version appeared in *Intention and Interpretation,* ed. Gary Iseminger [Philadelphia: Temple University Press, 1992].) In a related vein, see my "Messages in Art," also in *The Pleasures of Aesthetics.*

2. For an initial statement of the view, see William Tolhurst, "On What a Text Is and How It Means," *British Journal of Aesthetics* 19 (1979): 3–14.

Thus hypothetical intentionalism is a perspective on literary interpretation that takes *optimal hypotheses about authorial intention,* rather than the *author's actual intention,* to provide the key to the central meaning of literary works.

Since the key notion here is that of a best hypothesis on the part of readers, which would seem to entail the consideration by them of a variety of hypotheses, it might seem that hypothetical intentionalism was committed to a picture of literary interpretation as a species of what I have elsewhere characterized as CM, or "could mean," interpretive activity, as opposed to DM, or "does mean," interpretive activity, the latter aimed at identifying what, if anything, something does mean, with the former concerned rather with what, in a manner of speaking, something might mean.[3] But this is where a distinction between heuristic (instrumental) and final (intrinsic) engagement in CM interpretive activity is important. For hypothetical intentionalism, CM engagement with a work is purely instrumental, and not undertaken for its own sake. The consideration of various possibilities of construal serves only to identify what is in fact the best hypothesis—that is, the most explanatorily plausible and, to a lesser extent, aesthetically charitable construction we can arrive at—regarding a work's intended import. What a work in fact means, however multifaceted that may be, remains the focus of inquiry.

2. Does a view like hypothetical intentionalism allow for a multiplicity of distinct, at least nominally incompatible interpretations, when interpretation is being conducted ultimately in a DM, or determinative, spirit? The answer is yes, in virtue of the existence of ties, roughly speaking, among distinct and competing hypotheses as to a work's import. That is to say, nothing precludes there being, in a given case, two or more informed hypotheses, framable as to authorial intent, that are explanatorily and aesthetically optimal. Even so, there are ways to view such multiplicity so that it becomes, from a certain angle, unitary. I suggest that it is always possible, in principle, to combine competing reasonable first-order interpretations of a work so as to embrace them as a totality from a more encompassing perspective.

The fact that we have no logical notion handy for representing the ensemble of acceptable interpretations taken together does not show that the most

3. See "Two Notions of Interpretation," in *Interpretation and Its Boundaries,* ed. A. Haapala and O. Naukkarinen (Helsinki: Helsinki University Press, 1999). (The present essay is a modification and expansion of the last part of that 1999 essay.)

correct and comprehensive interpretation of a work of art is anything other than that ensemble. The logical notions that naturally suggest themselves, conjunction and disjunction, are both, in different ways, misleading or unsuitable. We don't wish to say that the overall correct interpretation of W, where R1, R2, R3, are individually acceptable interpretations of W, is just R1 *or* R2 *or* R3, nor do we wish to say that it is just R1 *and* R2 *and* R3. Rather, it is each and all of R1, R2, and R3, and yet not their simple conjunction or disjunction. The best, most correct and comprehensive, interpretation of a work of art subject to multiple individually justifiable or revealing readings must be an interpretation that enfolds all such readings: a kind of *global* or *subsumptive* reading, so to speak, one that acknowledges all the individually acceptable readings and puts them in relation to one another. That, at any rate, is the sort of perspective I am inclined to adopt toward those examples of multiple acceptable yet incompatible readings that have figured so prominently in discussions of artistic interpretation, prompted by works such as Kafka's *Castle,* James's *Turn of the Screw,* Beckett's *Waiting for Godot,* and De Kooning's *Woman* paintings.[4]

To make this a bit more concrete, my global, or subsumptive, interpretation of, say, Kafka's *Castle* might run roughly as follows. "*The Castle* reasonably admits of theological, bureaucratic, psychoanalytical, existential, and epistemological readings, and in ways that can be related to one another, mostly reinforcingly; on the other hand it does not reasonably admit, say, of entomological (castle as teeming beehive), chivalric (castle as prison of beautiful damsel), or oneiric (castle narrative as dream report) ones, nor do such readings relate reinforcingly to any of those already acknowledged as admissible." There can be little doubt that if the individual interpretations of *The Castle* invoked above, for example, the theological or bureaucratic ones, have merit, then the best interpretation, *tout court,* of Kafka's novel will be an *inclusive* one having more or less the form indicated. If that is borne in mind, the narrowly logical problem of reconciling multiple distinct and individually meritorious readings of such a work, with which philosophical discussion has been excessively preoccupied, will seem of reduced importance or even to have disappeared.

4. A similar perspective is advanced by Robert Stecker, "Art Interpretation," *Journal of Aesthetics and Art Criticism* 52 (1994): 193–206. "Though all true statements are conjoinable, that may not be the best way to hook up a pair of true interpretations into a more comprehensive true interpretation. . . . If *The Turn of the Screw* is intentionally ambiguous, it doesn't represent the governess as battling with hosts *and* having hallucinations. . . . Better, the novella is such that it can be correctly read either as representing the governess as battling ghosts or as representing the governess as having hallucinations" (201).

3. But what, more precisely, is the form of global, or subsumptive, interpretations of the sort I have invoked above? The form of such an interpretation, I*, would seem to be something like this: "W's meaning is such that it is partly given by/aptly viewed under interpretation 1, partly given by/aptly viewed under interpretation 2, . . . and partly given by/aptly viewed under interpretation n," where those embedded interpretations, I1, I2, and so on, are understood as first-order subinterpretations subject to the higher-order interpretation, I*, that subsumes them, though not simply disjunctively or conjunctively.

Among such global, or subsumptive, interpretations, we might further want to distinguish ones that, like the above, are simply *collective* (or enumerative) from ones that are *integrative* (or hierarchical), and thus include an account of the relations of importance or centrality obtaining among the subinterpretations brought together in the global interpretation.

Admitting global/subsumptive interpretations of an integrative/hierarchical, rather than simply collective/enumerative, sort does open the door to possible ties among competing interpretations, ones that put different weights on or differently position the subinterpretations they acknowledge in common. For from a hypothetical-intentionalist perspective, two different ways of organizing the individually attractive subinterpretations of a work in relation to one another might be equally plausibly hypothesized, in light of all the appreciatively relevant data, to be what the contextually understood author would ultimately have wanted readers to grasp. Still, given how subtle the differences are likely to be between two such integrative/hierarchical readings acknowledging all the same individually acceptable subinterpretations, multiplicity at this level, even if not ultimately eliminable, must surely strike one as not much of a qualification on the idea of there being such a thing as *the* meaning of a literary work, *grosso modo*.

4. It will be no surprise that the doctrine of hypothetical intentionalism has failed to win universal acceptance among theorists of interpretation. Textualists, deconstructionists, and actual intentionalists still abound. What is more, the unconverted, and particularly actual intentionalists, have not been shy to voice their criticisms of the doctrine. Thus I outline here some brief responses to objections that have been raised to a hypothetical-intentionalist account of literary meaning such as I have proposed, whose bare bones were sketched above. The basic idea, recall, is that on such an account literary meaning, the object of literary interpretation in a determinative mode, is constitutively bound not to what a historically untethered text

might be saying or to an author's actual, psychologically real semantic intentions in composing the text—even ones that might be said to have been "successfully realized" in the text—but to our best *hypothesis*, as ideally comprehending readers, as to what the concretely situated and publicly available author's semantic intentions were in composing and presenting the text he or she did.

Objection 1: Drawing a veil of ignorance across some aspects of a work's actual creative history and not others, as a hypothetical-intentionalist approach to work meaning enjoins, is unacceptably arbitrary.[5]

Response: Erecting a rough cordon around essentially private—which is not to say, epistemically inaccessible—information is hardly arbitrary from a literary point of view. The making of literature is an individual, largely interior endeavor, but it is also a public, convention-governed one, bound by mutually understood rules for producing and receiving literary offerings. These rules might quite naturally specify that facts related to context of origin beyond what an ideally prepared and backgrounded reader could generally be expected to know are irrelevant to fixing or constituting the meaning of the work as an utterance in that context. The artist's *state of mind* is not our ultimate goal as interpreters of literary works, but rather what meaning can be ascribed to those works, albeit as the indissociable *products* of those very particular communicative agents; thus not all obtainable evidence as to the artist's state of mind is automatically germane to the project of delineating what the work issuing from that mind and presented in a literary setting arguably means.

Objection 2: Hypothetical intentionalism is committed to a communication model of the literary domain, but such a model does not sit well with the appeal to idealized, as opposed to actual, audiences that is a feature of sophisticated versions of hypothetical intentionalism.[6]

Response: The communicative model arguably presupposed by literary activity does not commit us to authors' projecting their works for specific and specifically envisaged audiences, ones contemporaneous with the author, rather than, less restrictively, whatever audiences, present and future, are well suited to receive and understand the work in its historical, cultural, and authorial context. Call the former the *narrowly* communicative model

5. See Anthony Savile, "Instrumentalism and the Interpretation of Narrative," *Mind* 105 (1996): 553–76; Paisley Livingston, "Arguing over Intentions," *Revue Internationale de Philosophie* 198 (1996): 615–33; and Robert Stecker, *Artworks: Definition, Meaning, Value* (University Park: Pennsylvania State University Press, 1997), chap. 10.

6. See Savile, "Instrumentalism and the Interpretation of Narrative."

of literary activity, if you like, and the latter the *broadly* communicative model. The point is that communication with appropriate readers— whoever, whenever, wherever they might be—is still communication, even when such readers are not narrowly identified or targeted in advance.

Objection 3: Allowing optimally hypothesizable intentions to trump actual ones, where the basic nature or status of a work is concerned, opens the door to an unacceptable level of indeterminacy regarding work content.[7]

Response: Hypothetical intentionalism regarding work content or meaning is rightly coupled with *actual* intentionalism as it pertains both to the *status* of works as literature and to their *categorial* or *genre* location within literature.[8] Note that category or genre specifications can be taken as tantamount to or generative of very general semantic, or perhaps metasemantic, intentions, indicating what *sorts* of meaning, at the least, are to be sought in a given work, which helps to dissipate the worry sounded by opponents of hypothetical intentionalism that hypotheticism regarding authorial semantic intentions will too readily issue in indeterminacy of meaning.

Furthermore, coupling actual and hypothetical intentionalism in this manner strengthens the claim of literature so understood to be communicative, in almost the narrower sense distinguished a moment ago, and for two reasons. First, readers who attempt to arrive at meaning by hypotheticist lights are entitled from the outset to know, and so ideally do know, at least what category of offering they are dealing with. Second, the actual author, in being obliged to show his opening hand, that is, vouchsafe to readers directly the approximate nature, if not the precise import, of his work, thus does not remain entirely behind a veil as far as the constitution of meaning is concerned.

Objection 4: The best hypothesis about authorial intention must, logically speaking, be that which is *correct;* thus there can in fact be *no* divergence between actual authorial intention and our best hypothesis as to what that intention is or was.

Response: This is a simple misunderstanding. Obviously, the "best" hypothesis in the formulation of hypothetical intentionalism cannot be taken to mean that which in fact happens to be correct, and so best in the sense of "true." Rather, the "best" hypothesis by hypothetical intentionalist lights is that which we would have most reason to accept or adopt *given* the total-

---

7. See ibid.

8. On the notion of categorial versus semantic intentions in relation to a work of literature, see my "Intention and Interpretation in Literature," and in a more critical vein, Paisley Livingston, "Intentionalism in Aesthetics," *New Literary History* 29 (1998): 831–46.

ity of evidence that is both available and admissible, that is, given the totality of what is derivable from the text and its legitimately invoked surrounding context.

Objection 5: Even if there is a distinction, regarding authorial intention, between a best hypothesis, in the sense invoked by hypothetical intentionalism, and a true hypothesis, why should we ever favor the former over the latter, once we have arrived at the latter, by whatever means we have at our disposal? Surely in science we would not prefer our methodologically soundest hypothesis regarding some state of affairs over what is in fact the case, were we to learn what that is.[9]

Response: This objection misunderstands the goal of literary interpretation as conceived by hypothetical intentionalism, which is not to discover, for its own sake, the author's intention in writing the text, as if criticism were at base a matter of detective investigation, but to get at the *utterance meaning* of the text, that is, what *it*—not *the author*—is saying, in its author-specific context. Utterance meaning just *is* constitutively tied to a most reasonable projection of utterer's intent in the given context and does *not* collapse into utterer's meaning. Thus, even when the latter is available, it does not displace the former as the object of literary interpretation—as opposed to biographical sleuthing.[10]

Objection 6: Hypothetical intentionalism that acknowledges the necessity for interpretation to ascertain actual intentions of a categorial or constitutive sort has already sold out the vaunted autonomy of the literary work—its independence in a fundamental respect from its creator—that it claims to safeguard.[11]

9. See Noël Carroll, "Interpretation and Intention: The Debate Between Hypothetical and Actual Intentionalism," *Metaphilosophy* 31 (2000): 75–95. Carroll charges that to proceed so would "appear to be fetishizing our method over what the method is designed to secure" (83).

10. Thus the charge that hypothetical intentionalism simply substitutes warranted assertibility for truth where literary interpretations are concerned (see Carroll, "Interpretation and Intention," 84) is similarly unjustified. Hypothetical intentionalism, at least when advanced with a background commitment to metaphysical realism, retains that distinction, but relocates it with respect to the items involved. For hypothetical intentionalism, a *true* literary interpretation of a *work* W by an author A writing in context C is one given by what is, so to speak, optimally warrantedly assertible about the *intention* with which A, writing in C, composed W's text. But if a literary interpretation is thus true, then *it* is more than just warrantedly assertible. (For further discussion of these issues, see Gregory Currie, "Interpretation and Objectivity," *Mind* 102 [1993]: 415–28.)

11. See Gary Iseminger, "Actual Intentionalism vs. Hypothetical Intentionalism," *Journal of Aesthetics and Art Criticism* 54 (1996): 319–26.

Response: This is not so. A restricted autonomy, to wit, regarding resultant meaning, is still autonomy; furthermore, it is arguably the only sort of autonomy—as opposed, say, to that requiring detachability from generative context—that it seems important to insist on where literature is concerned.

Objection 7: Hypothetical intentionalism, which identifies core work meaning with a best projection of authorial intention—where such projection may not in fact coincide with any meaning actually intended—thus appears in the last analysis to be not really concerned with either the author or his achievement. Hypothetical intentionalism unjustifiably severs the work from the agent who has created it.[12]

Response: Again, this is not so. Hypothetical intentionalism accords the semantic intentions of the actual author a crucial role; only it is a *heuristic,* rather than a *final,* one. Authorial intention is what truth-seeking interpretive activity necessarily *aims at,* the idea being that what one would most reasonably take to be that intention, on the basis of the text and a full grasp of its author-specific public context, yields a true interpretation of the literary work, understood as an artistic utterance, which is embodied in the text.

As to severing a work from its author, hypothetical intentionalism pleads not guilty; it simply insists that the meaning of a literary work, however informed its interpretation must be by the author's public identity, and even by certain of the author's actual intentions, is not constrained to being just what the author intended it to mean, even where that intention is fully compatible or consonant with the contextually situated text. And even though a literary work is inextricably the work of just that author, in that precise context, the author is not the ultimate arbiter of what his or her work means, that is, what it appears to convey or communicate to an appropriately backgrounded reader.[13] Finally, hypothetical intentionalism doesn't deny authors their achievements; it just locates those achievements in the utterance meanings their uttered texts attain, due for the most part to the ingenuity with which those texts have been contrived, and not in the utterer's meanings those texts also, in favorable cases, subserve.

Objection 8: The defense of hypothetical intentionalism ultimately rests on the claim that it accords better with current interpretive practices than does actual intentionalism, alleging that critics in framing interpretive

12. See ibid. and Livingston, "Arguing over Intentions."
13. Nor is the author in the best position to discern that, in any event. Authors, because of their unique perspectives on their own works, are generally very far from being ideal readers of them.

hypotheses do observe the proposed ban on inherently private information, such as direct but hidden authorial proclamations of intended work meaning. But in fact this is not the case.[14]

Response: Hypothetical intentionalism does not ultimately rest on an empirical claim about actual interpretive *practices,* taken in their full and motley variety, but rather on what are arguably *norms* underlying the most defensible of such practices, understood as ones that truly answer to our interests in literature as literature. It is on that elusive and highly contestable terrain that the dispute about the merits of hypothetical intentionalism must be conducted, rather than that of statistical conformity or nonconformity with current practice. Admittedly, a full case for hypothetical intentionalism on those grounds remains to be made.[15]

5. A literary work is an utterance, of course, but it is a sort of "grand utterance," one governed by different ground rules of interpretation than are ordinary utterances. Our interests in literature are *communicative* ones, where that is understood broadly, but they are not, *pace* certain recent writers, more narrowly *conversational* ones.[16] This means, in part, that in literary contexts, unlike conversational ones, we have a prior and independent

---

14. See Carroll, "Interpretation and Intention."

15. I note a further objection that is regularly raised against hypothetical intentionalism, one I find more troubling than those reviewed above. The objection is that the distinction presupposed by hypothetical intentionalism between *essentially public* and *essentially private* information regarding an author, where the former enters into the appreciatively relevant context for the work while the latter does not, is fundamentally untenable or fatally blurry (see, for example, Stecker, *Artworks;* Livingston, "Intentionalism in Aesthetics"; Carroll, "Interpretation and Intention"). Clearly, however this distinction is made out, it cannot be equated with that between *published* and *unpublished* information, if only because that would have the consequence that a work's meaning, that is, what is given by a correct interpretation of it, would implausibly change upon the publication of certain appreciatively relevant facts about how a work came to be that, it just happened, were not known outside of the author's immediate circle.

This is not the place to attempt a full reconstruction of the needed distinction, but one might begin to refine the concept of a work's appreciatively relevant public context by focusing on the idea of what the author *wanted* readers to know about the circumstances of a work's creation, beyond what is implicit in the author's previous work and the author's public identity. At any rate, such a thing obviously will not fluctuate with the contingencies of actual publication of the information in question. Finally, that the distinction, however reconstructed, might remain blurry is not fatal to its utility. We expect borderline cases for any difficult distinction, but the existence of such cases does not preclude a preponderance of clear-cut cases on either side.

16. See Noël Carroll, "Art, Intention, and Conversation," in *Intention and Interpretation,* ed. Iseminger.

interest in utterance meaning *entirely apart from* whatever utterer meaning may stand behind or parallel that utterance meaning as constituted. In conversation, if we don't understand what someone has said, we may quite properly get him to explain further what he meant or to qualify or retract his words. In literature, if we don't understand what a contextually situated text is saying, we cannot legitimately demand explication from the author or instruct him to modify his offering; at most we can ask him to confirm that the text he has given us is indeed the text he wants us to have, as we set about to interpret it as literature.[17]

17. For further defense of hypothetical intentionalism and criticism of actual intentionalism, see Saam Trivedi, "An Epistemic Dilemma for Actual Intentionalism," *British Journal of Aesthetics* 41 (2001), and Gregory Currie, "Interpretation in Art," in *Oxford Handbook of Aesthetics,* ed. Jerrold Levinson (Oxford: Oxford University Press, forthcoming).

Andy Kaufman and the Philosophy of Interpretation

Noël Carroll

I. Introduction

With respect to art, a current issue in the philosophy of interpretation—the issue to be addressed in this paper—is the debate between actual intentionalists and hypothetical intentionalists.[1] Insofar as both sorts of intentionalists *are* intentionalists, these two positions are ranged against anti-intentionalism—the view, influential since the 1940s—that maintains that considera-

1. Examples of actual intentionalists' arguments include E. D. Hirsch, *Validity in Interpretation* (New Haven: Yale University Press, 1967); idem, *The Aims of Interpretation* (Chicago: University of Chicago Press, 1976); Gary Iseminger, "An Intentional Demonstration," in *Intention and Interpretation,* ed. Gary Iseminger (Philadelphia: Temple University Press, 1992); idem, "Actual Intentionalism vs. Hypothetical Intentionalism," *Journal of Aesthetics and Art Criticism* 54 (1996); idem, "Interpretive Relevance, Contradiction and Compatibility with the Text," *Journal of Aesthetics and Art Criticism* 56 (1998); Noël Carroll, "Art, Intention, and Conversation," in *Intention and Interpretation,* ed. Iseminger; idem, "Anglo-American Aesthetics and Contemporary Criticism," *Journal of Aesthetics and Art Criticism* 51 (1993); idem, "The Intentional Fallacy: Defending Myself," *Journal of Aesthetics and Art Criticism* 55 (1997); idem, "Interpretation and Intention: The Debate Between Hypothetical and Actual Intentionalism," *Metaphilosophy* 31 (2000); Paisley Livingston, "Intentionalism in Aesthetics," *New Literary History* 29 (1998); William Irwin, *Intentionalist Interpretation: A Philosophical Explanation and Defense* (Westport, Conn.: Greenwood, 2000). The hypothetical intentionalist who will concern us in this essay is Jerrold Levinson; his position is set forth in "Intention and Interpretation in Literature," in *The Pleasures of Aesthetics* (Ithaca, N.Y.: Cornell University Press, 1996).

tions of authorial intentions for the purposes of interpretation are strictly irrelevant or inadmissible.[2] Actual intentionalism and hypothetical intentionalism, in contrast, allow a role for authorial intentions (or something like authorial intentions—namely, hypotheses about authorial intentions) in the interpretation of artworks.[3]

For anti-intentionalists, focusing primarily on the meaning of literary texts, the meaning of a work is determinable solely by reference to public resources, such as the conventions of language, including grammar and dictionary meanings, and, as well, the history and conventions of literature. From their perspective, reference to the meanings of the text intended by the author is not only extraneous—since it draws attention away from the text itself—but also logically inappropriate—since the text means what it says and cannot be made to say something else simply in virtue of an author's intention to mean otherwise.

Though formidable, these objections are not decisive. Against the anti-intentionalist's anxiety that concerns for authorial intention divert attention away from its proper object—the text itself—intentionalists can respond that holding the author's intentions to be relevant can enrich our interpretations of texts. That is, consideration of authorial intentions can redirect our reading of a text, enabling us to understand better the structural and semantic choices in the text and, thereby, enlivening our appreciation thereof.

Nor do the intentionalists agree that texts can be interpreted solely by means of attention to the conventions and history of language and literature—without reference to authorial intentions. The case of irony, for example, shows that in order to interpret a text as a complex utterance, one needs to identify the author's intention in presenting the text in a concrete context. For irony can obtain in texts bereft of conventional linguistic or literary markers. Moreover, the case of irony exemplifies a feature of utterances in general, namely: that utterances are connected to the utterer's intentions. Thus, it is not logically inappropriate to refer to authorial intentions in the

2. Statements of anti-intentionalism can be found in W. K. Wimsatt and Monroe C. Beardsley, "The Intentional Fallacy," in *The Verbal Icon* (Lexington: University of Kentucky Press, 1954); Monroe C. Beardsley, *Aesthetics* (Indianapolis: Hackett, 1981); idem, *The Possibility of Criticism* (Detroit: Wayne State University Press, 1970); idem, "Intentions and Interpretations: A Fallacy Revived," in *The Aesthetic Point of View*, ed. Michael Wreen and Donald Callen (Ithaca, N.Y.: Cornell University Press, 1982); George Dicke and W. Kent Wilson, "The Intentional Fallacy: Defending Beardsley," *Journal of Aesthetics and Art Criticism* 53 (1995).

3. An overview of the debates about artistic meaning and intention can be found in Robert Stecker's *Artworks: Definition, Meaning, Value* (University Park: Pennsylvania State University Press, 1997).

process of interpreting the texts when they are construed, as they should be, as the utterances of historically situated individuals.

Of course, the anti-intentionalists are correct in arguing that an author cannot make a word sequence mean just anything by simply willing it. One cannot make the word "purple" mean "orange" merely by intending it to be so. Consequently, we cannot interpret "purple" in the text in question by noting that the author says he intended it to mean "orange."

However, sophisticated intentionalists need not be committed to the notion that a text means simply whatever its author intends. Rather, the sophisticated intentionalist only maintains that authorial intentions are relevant to the interpretation of the meaning of texts where the intended meaning of the text is compatible with and/or supportable by what the author has written in terms of the conventions and histories of language and literature.[4] Thus, where the conventional meanings available in the text are open to more than one interpretation, the intentionalist sides with the interpretation that accords with the author's intention (or our best hypotheses of authorial intent). And when and if there is only one interpretation of the text, the intentionalist presumes, as we do in ordinary conversation, that that mirrors the author's intention. (Of course, where it is discovered that the author had some meaning in mind that is utterly incompatible with and/or unsupportable by what is written, the intentionalist agrees that the author has failed to realize his or her intention in the text).

Though sophisticated intentionalists have the means to address the leading objections of anti-intentionalists, they are nevertheless not in complete agreement among themselves. They are divided into at least two camps: actual intentionalists and hypothetical intentionalists. Roughly, the actual intentionalists contend that the authorial intentions that are relevant to the interpretations of artworks are the actual intentions of the pertinent artists.[5]

4. This version of actual intentionalism is suggested by E. D. Hirsch, who says: "Verbal meaning is whatever someone has willed to convey by a particular sequence of linguistic signs *and* which can be conveyed (shared) by means of those signs" (*Validity in Interpretation*, 31, emphasis added). See also Irwin, *Intentionalist Interpretation*, 4. Above, I say "compatible with and/or *supportable by*" in order to accommodate the case of irony.

5. In my own writings, I have tried to characterize this notion of relevance by saying that our best hypotheses about the author's actual intentions should constrain our interpretive activities. In his "Can Novel Critical Interpretations Create Art Objects Distinct from Themselves?" (an essay in this volume), Philip Percival, however, alleges that my contention that, given our conversational interests, hypotheses about actual authorial intention should constrain our interpretations is muddled. His argument is that it does not follow from my demonstration that aesthetic interests do not trump our conversational interests that conversational interests trump other values we might seek in interpretations. Percival's observation is true, but I never claimed the entailment he suggests. I only claimed that conversational interests

In contrast, hypothetical intentionalists claim that what is relevant for interpretation is merely our best-warranted hypotheses concerning the intentions of actual authors.

In this paper, I examine the debate between actual intentionalists and hypothetical intentionalists by taking a look at an extended case study: the comedy of Andy Kaufman. I argue that the best interpretation (the one that today most would agree is the correct interpretation) of one of the most important phases of Kaufman's career (his wrestling performances) can only be reached through actual intentionalism—and by ignoring what the hypothetical intentionalist argues are the special considerations of our interpretative practices with regard to literature, artworks, and the like. However, before explaining how Andy Kaufman represents an exemplary problem for hypothetical intentionalism, more needs to be said about what is involved in actual intentionalism, hypothetical intentionalism, and the dispute between them.

II. Actual Intentionalism

The variant of actual intentionalism that concerns me may be called "modest actual intentionalism." It should be understood to contrast with might be called "extreme actual intentionalism."[6] Extreme actual intentionalism is the view that actual authorial intentions fully determine the meaning and, therefore, the interpretation of artworks, such as literary texts. Extreme

---

constrain other interests. Nor does Percival bother to consider the sorts of reasons that I advance in favor of the constraint—some of which are ethical reasons, including mutual respect and self-integrity.

Another muddle that Percival attributes to me is this: if we have conversational interests in artworks, why should that stop the critic from introducing his own original line of thought? Percival notes: "He [the critic] might be so bold as to suppose he has something to say through the canvas of *The Potato Eaters* more interesting than what Van Gogh had to say."

This example is woefully underdescribed. Is it that the critic utterly disregards Van Gogh's intentions here, or does he work with them? If he works with them, then doesn't that satisfy my notion of constraint? But if what the critic says is completely irrelevant to Van Gogh's intentions, would we still consider the concept of a conversation to be applicable?

Moreover, if a critic uses an artwork to make his own point, in the way that a preacher in a sermon uses some news item as a parable of faith, why call that an interpretation rather than, as some say, an application?

6. Extreme actual intentionalism is represented in Steven Knapp and Walter Benn Michaels, "Against Theory," *Critical Inquiry* 8 (1982); idem, "Against Theory 2: Hermeneutics and Deconstruction," *Critical Inquiry* 14 (1987).

actual intentionalism is committed to the view that the text means what its author intends it to mean. Therefore, extreme actual intentionalism entails that if, by writing "purple" in the text, the author intends "orange," then "orange" is always what his inscription means.

The modest actual intentionalist avoids this counterintuitive commitment by denying that authorial intention fully determines meaning. Instead, authorial intentions are relevant to interpretation where the authorial intentions at issue are compatible with and/or supportable by what has been written—if we are speaking of literary texts—in accordance with the conventions and histories of language and literature. Where the author intends "orange" by writing "purple" and there is no ground for suspecting irony, the author fails in his intention instead of changing the meaning of his utterance of "purple." At the same time, where a text is open to several interpretations, the modest actual intentionalist argues that the correct interpretation is the one that takes the author's actual intention into consideration. Thus, while what is written constrains our interpretations, so authorial intention operates as a constraint on the interpretation of what has been written.

Modest actual intentionalism begins with the premise that, unless shown otherwise, we have no reason to suppose that our interpretation of artworks and literary texts differs in kind from our interpretation of everyday speaking and action. In everyday conversation, our interpretive goal is standardly to understand what our interlocutors intend to say. When, in a pacific tone of voice, we query, "What do you mean by that?" we are asking our interlocutor to clarify what he or she intends to say. The natural slide from "means" to "intends" here signals that our normal interpretive goal is to discover the meaning-intentions of other speakers. The modest actual intentionalist maintains that we have no grounds to presume that matters stand differently with respect to artworks and literary texts (though, as we shall see, this is perhaps the major bone of contention between modest actual intentionalists and hypothetical intentionalists).

According to the modest actual intentionalist, when we interpret an artwork or a literary text, we are attempting to discern the point the author intends, just as in a conversation we aim at determining what our informant intends/means to say. This, of course, does not entail that we ignore the relevant conventions, linguistic and otherwise, that obtain in the situation, but rather that we use them in order to interpret cospeakers.

The anti-intentionalist maintains that it is sufficient for the interpretation of artworks and literary texts that we attend to the pertinent linguistic and literary conventions, and that talk of authorial intentions is out of place.

This intuition is strongly (though not decisively) encouraged if we take as our prototype of artistic interpretation (the interpretation of artworks) the words and sentences of literary texts. However, two things should be said here.

First, not all, and perhaps even not most, instances of artistic interpretation concern the meanings of words or sentences. Even if words and sentences in literature could be adequately interpreted solely in light of linguistic and literary conventions, much art is not linguistic and, therefore, lacks the kind of determinate meaning conventions that words and sentences might be thought to possess.

Dutch still lifes, for example, juxtapose commonplace objects, like articles of food and watches, in a single scene; the viewer must fill in the meaning of these juxtapositions interpretively. There is no conventional algorithm that will give us the meaning of these juxtapositions—that tells us in a rulelike fashion that the food stands for our appetitive nature and the watch symbolizes a call for moderation. Rather, the viewer needs to try to make sense out of these juxtapositions by speculating about what the painter intended to communicate by means of them.[7]

Knowledge of the history of iconography, of course, is relevant here. But interpretation in such a case, and in so many others, is not a matter of subsuming the items in a literally grammarless painting under meaning conventions, but rather of inferring the point of what the painter, in his historical context, intended to get across. Since so much of artistic interpretation is concerned with interpretation in circumstances where there are no determinate meaning conventions and disambiguating grammars, much artistic interpretation cannot be construed as merely tracking and applying conventions, but must be construed as something else—striving to recognize the intentions of artists in the way we try to locate the intentions of interlocutors in everyday speech. Thus, at the very least, the modest actual intentionalist seems to propose a more comprehensive model of our interpretive activities than does the anti-intentional conventionalist.[8]

---

7. This example comes from Carolyn Korsmeyer, *Making Sense of Taste: Food and Philosophy* (Ithaca, N.Y.: Cornell University Press, 1999), 162.

8. One anti-intentionalist, Kent Wilson, has suggested that where there are no determinate meaning conventions of the sort found in language, we should not speak of interpreting the meaning of artworks at all. But this seems to be a very *ad hoc* way of settling the debate over intentionalism, since that debate has always been thought to be relevant to the interpretation of artworks in general. Standardly, nonlinguistic artworks are thought to possess meaning (e.g., montage in film and television). From the perspective of the philosophy of art, stipulatively to restrict the notion of meaning to linguistic matters not only seems arbitrary but, as well, fails to take seriously our interpretive practices. One does not explain the phenomenon

Of course, anti-intentionalists not only fail to model comprehensively the interpretation of the nonliterary arts. They also lack a comprehensive model for literary interpretation. For a great deal of literary interpretation (maybe most?) concerns the meanings not merely of words and sentences but of larger literary structures, like recurring or echoing motifs, whose communicative structure is not governed by determinate, grammar-like or dictionary-like conventions or rules.

Consider the recurring, overlapping, and expanding motifs of cannibalism, of eating, and of being eaten in Melville's *Moby Dick*.[9] There are no conventions or rules to tell us what these mean. Rather, we proceed by trying to figure out what Melville intended to say by means of these imagistic patterns. Thus, once again, the model of artistic interpretation that the anti-intentionalist advances is not even comprehensive for literature, even if it were always applicable to the interpretation of words and sentences. In this regard, modest actual intentionalism appears to be a superior account of artistic interpretation than anti-intentionalism, on the grounds that it is more comprehensive.

Second, there is also the question whether anti-intentionalism is even a comprehensive account of the way in which we interpret the words and sentences of literary texts. The problem of irony has already been mentioned. And similar issues arise over how to identify and interpret cases of allusion, since the attribution of an allusion will require, logically, that we have access to the author's knowledge stock (did the author really know the referent to which she is said to be alluding?) as well as to her ongoing artistic practice (is she the sort of artist for whom allusion is a likely option?).

In such cases, adverting to dictionary meanings and grammatical rules is not enough; one must go beyond the resources of the text and the pertinent linguistic and literary conventions and ask questions about the actual author—about what she knew or believed (or is likely to have known and believed) as well as what her inclinations, desires, and intentions were (or probably were). In order to interpret confidently many cases of irony and

---

by denying its existence. This is to give up the philosophical project of discovering the presiding conditions of possibility of our interpretive practices. Thus, Wilson's suggestion not only involves exiting the debate but also implies that Wilson himself, by effectively attempting to regiment our actual interpretive practices unrealistically, shirks the philosophical responsibility of reconstructing them. To declare, by fiat, that all nonlinguistic artworks lack meaning because they are not linguistic appears at root to beg the question. See W. Kent Wilson, "Confession of a Weak Anti-Intentionalist: Exposing Myself," *Journal of Aesthetics and Art Criticism* 55 (1997).

9. The example comes again from Korsmeyer, *Making Sense of Taste*, 194–200.

allusion, we need knowledge about who the author actually is, including knowledge about her mental states, including her intentions.

Moreover, the lessons illustrated by the cases of irony and allusion are applicable to the interpretation of literary words and sentences generally, since irony and allusion make evident that literary words and sentences are not just word sequences but utterances, and understanding utterances requires reference to authors and inferences about authorial or speaker's intention. At this point, the anti-intentionalist may suggest that there is some special problem epistemologically about securing access to authorial intentions, since authorial intentions are nonobservable mental states. However, these reservations seem scarcely compelling, since in everyday life we are usually extremely successful in excavating the intentions behind the words and deeds of others.

With regard to linguistic and expressive behavior, we have little difficulty in inferring (typically accurately) the intentions of conspecifics. So why does the anti-intentionalist imagine that there should be some special difficulty with respect to artistic and literary behavior? If there is no problem with interpreting ordinary utterances by reference to speakers' intentions in everyday life, why fear that some unique difficulty erupts when it comes to the utterance meanings of literary works?

Interpreting literary texts or the historically situated point of nonlinguistic artworks—construed as utterances—involves us largely in inferring authorial intentions. Contra anti-intentionalism, this mobilizes information about the actual creator of the artwork in question—information about who he was, his culture, the genre he worked in, his oeuvre, and his ideological, religious, intellectual (etc.) convictions. The practice of artistic interpretation is, in great measure, a process of inference about the actual intentions of artists.

This, of course, is not to deny that the primary evidence for these inferences is generally the artwork itself. But as in ordinary conversation, when we closely scrutinize the artwork, we are doing so in order to uncover the best clues we have for authorial intent. We are reading, looking, and/or listening, guided by the aim of identifying the intentions of the creator of the artwork. Tracking authorial intent need not send us "outside" the artwork; typically, attending closely to the artwork is our best avenue for approaching authorial intent.

Nevertheless, since an artwork, such as a piece of literature, is not simply an abstract sequence of words but a particular, historically located utterance, our search for authorial intentions requires that we often supplement the reading of the text with information concerning the context of its production, including knowledge of who the author was, his historical circumstances, his entire oeuvre, and the genre in which he was working. Access to this information does not supplant our reading of the text, but gives us the background necessary to understand its semantic and structural choices—the choices that make it the particular utterance it is—contextually.

This is a point upon which both modest actual intentionalists and hypothetical intentionalists agree. Where they disagree is about the range of information about the artist that is interpretively permissible as well as about whether our legitimate access to actual authorial intention is *always* restricted to all and only well-warranted inferences.

III. Hypothetical Intentionalism

For modest actual intentionalists and hypothetical intentionalists, the artwork is not an abstract concatenation of signs, symbols, and articulations whose meaning is decipherable solely in virtue of conventions. Each artwork is a situated, contextually concrete, and particular expression, the production of an individual artist with some point, and, therefore, best understood on the model of an utterance. But in order to understand an utterance, one requires a conception of the relevant historically located utterer.

A literary work, for example, is not simply a string of sentences; it is an organized whole, unified by a purpose, the source of which is the artist.[10] Thus, when we read, we read the text as a contextually situated utterance whose meaning must be connected to some definite speaker. We need to read this way in order to discover the specific point of the utterance in context. That is, literary works are concrete speech acts, not abstract word sequences, and, therefore, their meaning is, in part, relative to the speaker in question and his or her historical circumstances.

Modest actual intentionalists and hypothetical intentionalists share this starting point. They concur that, in treating artworks and literature as utterances, we are committed to essaying inferences about the actual author, including, notably, inferences about what she intended by her artwork. The

---

10. Even the apparent strings of sentences explored by surrealists are not merely strings of sentences; their seeming randomness is purposively driven by the desire to make a philosophical point.

inductive grounds for these inferences may include not only (though most importantly) the artwork itself but also public knowledge about the biography of the artist (her beliefs and experiences), historical knowledge about the conditions (both art-historical and social) in which the artwork was produced, knowledge about the genre to which the artwork belongs, and knowledge about other works by the same artist, up to and including knowledge of her entire oeuvre. From this, we form hypotheses about the actual intentions of the artist that both partially constitute and also further enable our interpretation of her concrete utterance contextually.

Because modest actual intentionalists and hypothetical intentionalists agree so extensively on the nature of interpretation, the two positions generally converge in their interpretations of artworks. However, the two positions are not equivalent, because, despite their broad consensus, they disagree over the range of "extratextual" information that is legitimately available to the interpreter, and, therefore, the two positions may, at times, render different interpretations.

The modest actual intentionalist allows the interpreter access to the private avowals of artists as found, say, in private notebooks, sketches, diaries, and interviews (both with the artist and his confidantes). According to the modest actual intentionalist, these may, when used cautiously, play a justifiable role in interpretation.

Contrariwise, the hypothetical intentionalist precludes invocations of authorial intention culled from such private sources, restricting the inductive grounds of interpretive inferences to authorial intention to the work itself, the author's publicly accessible biography, historical knowledge of the context in which the work was produced, the author's oeuvre, and the prevailing conventions of the genre of which the work is a member. For the hypothetical intentionalist, the best-warranted hypothesis indicated by these sources is the correct interpretation of the work, even if it diverges from the sincere assertions of authorial intention found in, for example, the artist's private papers, including his notes and letters about a specific work.

However, since the modest actual intentionalist allows access, albeit mindful, to private avowals of authorial intention, the modest actual intentionalist realizes that the best warranted hypothesis (concerning actual authorial intention as obtained by respecting the protocols of hypothetical intentionalism) may part company with the author's actual intention. And where this happens, if the author's actual intention is supportable by the artwork, the modest actual intentionalist will defend the interpretation consistent with the author's intention over the best-warranted inference derivable by the hypothetical intentionalist. For this is how we proceed in everyday interpretation, not only in our understanding of ordinary conversations but with respect to more formal discourse, like wills.

Though this difference between modest actual intentionalists and hypothetical intentionalists may not, in general, result in different interpretations, in certain circumstances it can. For example, as Paisley Livingston points out, we have evidence that Henry James intended *The Turn of the Screw* to be a ghost story.[11] That is what James said.[12] But, as is well known, there is also a popular interpretation of the novella that says that the story is purposefully ambiguous between being an example of a supernatural tale and being a psychological study of a disturbed governess who fantasizes the presence of ghosts.

Suppose that the latter interpretation is the best-warranted hypothesis available without consulting James's avowals about the story; then the hypothetical intentionalist will favor the ambiguity interpretation, whereas the modest actual intentionalist will favor the ghost interpretation.[13] Thus, though similar in many ways, modest actual intentionalism and hypothetical intentionalism are not the same, because in certain instances, they deliver different verdicts about the correct interpretation of given artworks.

Since modest actual intentionalists and hypothetical intentionalists agree that interpretive activity in large measure involves hypothesizing the actual intentions of authors, what accounts for their different attitudes toward the

11. Livingston, "Intentionalism in Aesthetics," 841–44.

12. It is true that James indicated this intention in the preface to *The Turn of the Screw* and that the hypothetical intentionalist might claim that publication of this authorial avowal renders it public rather than private and grants the hypothetical intentionalist legitimate access to it. On the one hand, it seems to me rather arbitrary to attempt to draw the line between admissible authorial avowals and inadmissible ones this way; suppose that James's preface was accidentally lost by the printer and never published in the text, surfacing only much later in James's private papers. Would that change the meaning of the text?

On the other hand, for purposes of explicating the difference between modest actual intentionalism and hypothetical intentionalism, let us just imagine that James never published the preface. It would still be the case that the modest actual intentionalist would be willing to weigh James's explicit intentions, once discovered, in this case, whereas the hypothetical intentionalist would not.

13. It is not strained to conjecture that the hypothetical intentionalist might think that the ambiguity interpretation is the best-warranted hypothesis on his grounds, since, where an inference is well supported epistemically, the hypothetical intentionalist allows to come into play aesthetic considerations concerning which rival interpretation makes the relevant work better aesthetically. Thus, if the hypothetical intentionalist takes the ambiguity interpretation to be well warranted and also believes it makes *The Turn of the Screw* aesthetically better (more interesting) than the ghost interpretation, he will favor the ambiguity interpretation. See Levinson, "Intention and Interpretation in Literature," 179.

admissibility of private avowals of authorial intention? From the perspective of modest actual intentionalism, the hypothetical intentionalist seems satisfied with the warranted assertibility of the relevant authorial intentions, even where the truth about said intentions is accessible and diverges from the hypothetical intentionalist's best inference. But why settle for the warranted assertibility of an interpretation where the truth of the matter diverges from our best hypothesis and, in addition, is available to us? We do not usually prefer warranted assertibility over truth where the difference is evident to us.[14] So, why should this be so when it comes to the interpretation of artworks?

The hypothetical intentionalist's answer to this query is straightforward: the interpretation of artworks and literature is a different form of inquiry from other sorts, so talk about what we "usually prefer" in other domains of acquiring knowledge is not germane to this debate. Jerrold Levinson, perhaps the leading hypothetical intentionalist of the moment, writes, for example:

> [I]t is arguably one of the ground rules of the game of literary decipherment that literary works are not supposed to require authors to explain what they mean, and thus that direct authorial pronouncements of meaning can be set aside by the reader devoted to the central job of interpretation. The task of intuiting our way to an optimal construal of authorial intention for a text emerging from a rich author-specific public context is simply different from that of arriving at the truth about the author's intention with respect to a given text, from all the available evidence no matter what sort—diaristic, journalistic, electroencephalographic. Though as appreciators of literature we are entitled and expected to construe an author's offering against the background of the author's earlier work and the author's public identity as a writer, and in light of the author's explicit intentions for how a work is to be approached on the categorical plane (e.g., as a historical novel), we are, I think, implicitly enjoined from allowing an author's proclamations of meaning achieved to have an *evidential* role in the construction of a picture of what the author is most reasonably thought to have been trying to convey through that text offered in context.[15]

14. This observation is pursued at greater length in Carroll, "Interpretation and Intention," 82–84.

15. Levinson, "Intention and Interpretation in Literature," 208. Moreover, Levinson's invocation of a literary language game in this quotation is not a wayward aside. He also adverts

That is, according to Levinson, the language game of literary interpretation excludes interpretive reliance on direct avowals of authorial intention. It is true that our interpretive activities revolve around formulating the best hypotheses of authorial intent, but this is not the goal of the game; it is, again according to Levinson, merely a "heuristic."[16] What we are really after—when all is said and done—is the best-warranted hypothesis concerning authorial intention within the inductive parameters described by hypothetical intentionalism. This is what the interpretation game asks of audiences.

The interpretation game does not require or even permit reference to actual authorial intentions that are derived from nonpublic authorial pronouncements and that diverge from our best-warranted inferences à la hypothetical intentionalism. This constraint is, allegedly, in the service of the special interests of our interpretive institutions and practices. In this regard, hypothetical intentionalism, rather than modest actual intentionalism, putatively best reflects the special rules and purposes of the institution of literary interpretation narrowly and the institution of artistic interpretation more broadly.[17] Adherence to the rules of interpretive practice, then, is the hypothetical intentionalist's bottom line.

But does hypothetical intentionalism really better reflect our prevailing interpretive practices than modest actual intentionalism? What is the evidence?[18] It cannot be that hypothetical intentionalism, but not modest ac-

---

to this language game on pp. 177, 178, 184, 194, 196, and 198, generally to iterate the point made above.

16. Ibid., 200.

17. Though the title of Levinson's article refers to literature and though he speaks of the special interests of literature, his hypothetical intentionalism can be taken to apply across the arts, since he discusses not only examples from literature but ones from music and film as well.

18. It should be noted that the interpretative-language-game argument is not the only objection that the hypothetical intentionalist may raise against actual intentionalism. Another may be that in countenancing authorial pronouncements of authorial intention, the actual intentionalist is unable to acknowledge and to account for failures of authorial intention—cases where the author fails to realize his or her intention in the text.

But this does not seem to be an apt objection to modest actual intentionalism, since, for interpretive correctness, modest actual intentionalism requires that the authorial intentions we take seriously for hermeneutical purposes square with the text. Thus, the modest actual intentionalist explains cases of failed authorial intention in terms of the distance between the author's avowed intention and what we find in the text or artwork. Unlike the extreme actual intentionalist, the modest actual intentionalist does not accept authorial pronouncements as always and exclusively decisive, but can admit and explain cases of failed intention. That is, failed intentions are not impossible within the purview of modest actual intentionalism.

Furthermore, because the preceding argument seems more appropriately aimed at extreme actual intentionalism rather than at modest actual intentionalism, in what follows I will tual intentionalism, describes interpretation primarily as concerned with framing well-warranted hypotheses about actual authorial intentions, since both approaches endorse this description of interpretation. Nor can hypothetical intentionalism claim as evidence in its behalf that, in general, audiences are satisfied with interpretations arrived at inferentially through the avenues enumerated by hypothetical intentionalism. For in most cases audiences are so satisfied because they presume that our best hypotheses of this sort coincide with actual authorial intention.

That is, they are reading, listening, or viewing for actual intention, and their natural default assumption is that, unless other pertinent evidence surfaces on the horizon, our best hypotheses—based on the work, its genre, and the author's public biography and oeuvre—probably zero in on the author's actual intention. However, that audiences usually embrace this rather natural default assumption hardly entails that they would not revise it should evidence—such as contrary authorial avowals of intention—appear that is at variance with the default assumption. For a provisional default assumption, no matter how natural, does not constitute an unbreachable rule of our interpretive practices.

And yet, the hypothetical intentionalist claims that it is a steadfast rule of our interpretive practices—such as the literary language game—that we forswear resort to authorial avowals of intention. To the modest actual intentionalist, of course, this sounds like an instance of begging the question

---

concentrate primarily upon challenging the interpretive-language-game objection rehearsed above.

However, before leaving this issue, another point must be broached. Perhaps the hypothetical intentionalist has in mind this objection: the actual intentionalist has no way of accounting for the meaning of a text where the actual authorial intention fails.

Suppose that the author's intended meaning does not correspond with what is written on the page. Does this entail that the modest actual intentionalist must say that what the author has written is meaningless, despite the fact that it is written in plain and intelligible English?

The modest actual intentionalist, however, is not driven to this counterintuitive conclusion. For the modest actual intentionalist here does acknowledge that there is such a thing as utterance meaning. In the case envisioned, the passage of writing in question has utterance meaning. Nevertheless, it does not follow from the likelihood that we will acknowledge that such a passage possesses utterance meaning that it is only utterance meaning that we ever do or should seek in literary texts. Where texts do possess authorial meaning, we do pursue it, and the literary institution, as I will argue, appears to license this as permissible. Moreover, as argued above, the search for authorial meaning is, by default, our operating assumption. Settling for utterance meaning is, I contend, a secondary and not altogether satisfying result.

Nor does it follow from the fact that sometimes we may just have to do with utterance meaning that utterance meaning is always what we are or should be after. The maxim that underwrites such a conclusion could not be generalized to other forms of life.

that elevates, through little more than confident assertion, hypothetical intentionalism as a deep rule that governs all our interpretive practices. Indeed, the modest actual intentionalist may ask why, if there is such a settled rule with respect to the institution of interpretation, there is nevertheless such a heated and protracted debate between modest actual intentionalism and hypothetical intentionalism.

After all, the participants in this debate are all competent interpreters. So, if there is a clear-cut rule here, then how can so many otherwise informed practitioners (i.e., the actual intentionalists) be so utterly unaware of its existence? What kind of *rule* escapes the notice of so many?

Needless to say, what might turn out to be the sheer ignorance of modest actual intentionalists about the rules of the interpretation game is not a conclusive argument against hypothetical intentionalism. However, inasmuch as the hypothetical intentionalist is invoking a supposed rule of our actual interpretive practices—a rule that allegedly says that reference to authorial intentions as evidence of interpretive correctness is *always* out-of-bounds—we are entitled to question whether such a rule does really seem to govern our interpretive practices.

And to adjudicate that question, it is fair to consider an illustrative counterexample that indicates that there is no ironclad rule here that, with regard to our actual interpretive practices, mandates that the best-warranted inference of authorial intent à la hypothetical intentionalism is, in fact, always to be preferred to the invocation of "private" authorial intentions. That is, if the hypothetical intentionalist is postulating a rule of our interpretive practices on the basis of a rational reconstruction of what we actually do, then it pays to consider empirical case studies.

IV. The Case of Andy Kaufman

The release of Milos Forman's film *Man on the Moon* (1999) has rekindled a great deal of interest in the work and career of the late comic Andy Kaufman (1949–84).[19] Kaufman, who called himself a "song-and-dance man"

19. At least two biographies have appeared recently: Bill Zehme, *Lost in the Funhouse: The Life and Mind of Andy Kaufman* (New York: Delacorte Press, 1999); Bob Zmuda (with Matthew Scott Hansen), *Andy Kaufman Revealed!* (Boston: Little, Brown & Co., 1999). Scholarly comment on Andy Kaufman's work includes Philip Auslander, *Presence and Resistance: Postmodernism and Cultural Politics in Contemporary American Performance* (Ann Arbor: University of Michigan Press, 1992), chaps. 7 and esp. 8.

rather than a "comic," was perhaps best known for his role as Latka Gravas on the television series *Taxi*. Kaufman also often appeared on *Saturday Night Live* and other variety formats, such as *Fridays;* was a frequent guest on Carson and Letterman; played the comedy-club circuit, the college circuit, and night clubs; and made two ill-fated feature motion pictures. He was particularly respected by other comics, including, notably, Robin Williams, Lily Tomlin, Steve Martin, and Michael Richards.

One of Kaufman's recurrent strategies was to make the audience think that they were witnessing a truly awful performance by an inept comic, only to reveal, on the turn of a dime, that they were in the hands of a master.

For example, he would begin a series of seemingly incompetent imitations of Nixon and Archie Bunker in a "foreign" accent so thick and so ill-timed that the audience would begin to become embarrassed for the performer: they had never seen anything so wretched. Then he would announce, still in character, that he was about to do an impersonation of Elvis Presley; the groans would be audible. But the imitation of Presley would be so gloriously on the money that the audience would not only be overwhelmed by its precision but also come to realize that they had been had by the earlier parts of the performance. The incompetence had been staged by a performer who could imitate anything—including an execrable stand-up routine. Laughter and applause would greet Kaufman's exit from the stage, not only for a perfectly observed rendition of the King but also in appreciation of the "practical joke" Kaufman had played on the audience.

Similarly, in his first performance on *Saturday Night Live,* Kaufman appeared nervous and fidgety. Silence loomed for what seemed an inordinate amount of time. It appeared that Kaufman either had forgotten his routine or was too frozen with fear to begin it. Then he fiddled with the record player beside him. It blared out the theme song from the old TV show *Mighty Mouse*. This garnered some titters, part nostalgia, part camp. But still the performer seemed lost—until we heard the refrain "Here I come to save the day," which Kaufman lip-synched with such perfection and bravura, transforming himself, in a single beat, from a vulnerable schlemiel to a matinee idol, that the audience exploded in laughter.

In both of these performances, and many others, Kaufman was exploring the boundary between theater and reality by first convincing (or nearly convincing) the audience that they really might be watching the most pathetic attempt at comedy ever, and then revealing that it was all an act. In this way, Kaufman's concerns correlated with those of contemporary performance artists—except that Kaufman was practicing his version of deconstruction on mainstream television far away from the lofts of Soho. Kaufman's use of pastiche and his preferred pop-culture iconography—especially the imagery of fifties' TV and music—also aligned Kaufman's sensibility with that of emerging postmodern performance art. But in some ways, Kaufman's investigation of the line between theater and reality was more effective than that of performance artists because, due to his adagio pacing, he often got people to believe or at least to take seriously the proposition that they were actually watching disasters of such embarrassing proportions that they would squirm in their seats. Kaufman would not begin these performances with a "wink"—or any other marker of comic framing that might cue the audience—and he unflinchingly stayed in his inept character for so long that viewers would start to worry that something was wrong, until he turned the tables.

Kaufman provoked a fight on the set of *Fridays* that left the newspapers speculating that it was real, while also developing a character, named Tony Clifton, who was the epitome of the crude, rude, conceited lounge singer. Clifton appeared in a number of shows, but Kaufman himself would deny that he was Tony Clifton, as would "Tony Clifton" when he (Clifton) was interviewed, though it became known eventually that Clifton and Kaufman were one (Clifton perhaps being the dark doppelgänger of Kaufman's Latka Gravas character, a naif of saccharine innocence). Through inventions like these, Kaufman was able to satirize the conventions of popular performance while also interrogating their conditions of credibility and the unwritten terms of the audience/performer contract.

Perhaps Kaufman's most ambitious experiment along these lines was his wrestling career. It began with his challenging women from the audiences at comedy clubs and colleges to come on stage and wrestle with him. And Kaufman and his wrestling partners really grappled—at least in the sense that they tried to pin each other. Kaufman brought this act to television, where he stoked the audiences' passions by making inflammatory, derogatory remarks about women and their abilities that would outrage both feminists and Daughters of the American Revolution. These wrestling matches were not popular, eventually getting Kaufman voted off *Saturday Night Live,* but he persisted.

Not able to find a home for his "Intergender Wrestling Championship" at Madison Square Garden, he traveled south to Memphis to challenge women. Here he ran into Jerry Lawler, a professional wrestler and beloved figure on the scene. Lawler taunted Kaufman into meeting him in the ring. Before their bout, Kaufman made a series of highly insulting videos of

Lawler, Memphis, and the South in general. Claiming that he was from Hollywood and had brains, Kaufman demeaned the intelligence and cleanliness of Southerners. At the time of the scheduled bout, the population of Memphis crowded into the amphitheater, screaming for Kaufman's head. Jerry Lawler complied, dealing Kaufman a series of pile drivers that resulted in Kaufman's removal from the ring on a stretcher.

Yet the debacle did not end there. Kaufman and Lawler appeared on the Letterman show, ostensibly to reconcile, but instead Lawler decked Kaufman, and Kaufman retaliated by throwing hot coffee at Lawler. Various rematches, grudge fights, and shouting exchanges ensued, often before cameras. Kaufman seemed out of control, gripped by an incomprehensible, obsessional fantasy that he really was a professional wrestler. His popularity suffered, but he persevered. The whole spectacle looked like a sorry mess, a descent into madness. After Kaufman's death, the 1989 "documentary" *I'm from Hollywood,* written and directed by Joe Orr and Lynne Margulies (Kaufman's former lover), reviewed the entire episode, leaving the strong impression that the affair was nothing short of pathological. Robin Williams and Tony D'Anza say as much on the videotape, and there is nothing else in the program to contradict them.

However, recently, several of Kaufman's close associates, including Bob Zmuda and Jerry Lawler, have come forward to bear testimony about Kaufman's actual intentions concerning what we might call his "wrestling project." As a result of this insider information, we can now say that, though the women Kaufman wrestled were genuinely committed to defeating him (and he them), thereby making that aspect of the project authentic, most of the rest of it (the matches with Lawler, the Letterman show, and possibly even *I'm from Hollywood*) was pure theater. The wrestling project was an opportunity for Kaufman to explore, reflexively and often parodically, the features of professional wrestling that fascinated him, such as the fact that, though "everyone knows" that professional wrestling is fake (theatrical), it is nevertheless able to move fans emotionally to the point of screaming seriously for blood. Through his wrestling conceit, Kaufman discovered a vantage position from which to survey, albeit comically, some of the rhetorical levers that make the engine of professional wrestling run.

It makes a big difference whether one watches tapes of Kaufman's wrestling career under the influence of the madness interpretation or the reflexivity interpretation. When I first saw Lawler smash Kaufman into the mat, it saddened and sickened me. Unaware of Kaufman's true intentions, Lawler struck me as a bully meting out excessive punishment to a weakling—admittedly an obnoxious weakling, but still a weakling, and probably a crazed one. It seemed wrong to crush such a demented wimp so mercilessly, though, of course, the wimp himself too bore some of the responsibility for the sordid event. How, one wondered, could anyone have allowed this situation to spiral as uncontrollably as this? Decency, it seemed to me, bade us to avert our eyes from the whole absurd, unhappy predicament in favor of remembering Kaufman's better days as a performer.

However, once apprized by insiders of Kaufman's actual intentions, I no longer avert my eyes. I pay close attention to Kaufman's stylistic choices and savor their comic resonances—his outlandish costume, for example, composed of thermal underwear and swimming trunks, and his "natural" fright wig, recalling some silent clown. Rather than turn away, I reflect on his brazen, subversive foregrounding of some of the deepest conventions of professional wrestling. Posing himself as the villain (what is called a Tar Heel), by extravagantly belittling women and the South, against the hero ("good guy") Jerry Lawler, Kaufman bared the données of professional wrestling by deploying them hyperbolically. Each one of Kaufman's choices, including his gestures and behavior ringside, once grasped with the comic-reflexive distance Kaufman intended (at least for his coterie), appears as an insight, telegraphed through exaggeration, into the practice of professional wrestling. Thus, like a work of what is often called high art, Kaufman's wrestling project and parts thereof sustain and reward repeated viewing and contemplation.

By now the relevance of Kaufman's wrestling project to the debate between modest actual intentionalism and hypothetical intentionalism should be evident. Without insider information with regard to private avowals of Kaufman's actual intentions, the madness interpretation is the best-warranted hypothesis concerning Kaufman's wrestling career. This is so because Kaufman planned it that way. He controlled the information about what he was doing and even planted disinformation about it so the interpretation that would most recommend itself to appropriately backgrounded viewers (those fully informed of all the contextually relevant information surrounding the wrestling project *except for* information about private avowals of authorial intent) would be the madness interpretation. That is, the madness interpretation is the one that the hypothetical intentionalist would proffer for acceptance.

On the other hand, if we are modest actual intentionalists, we may help ourselves to the insider information about Kaufman's authorial intentions, and this will incline us far more in the direction of the reflexivity interpretation.

But which interpretation is correct? The madness interpretation or the reflexivity interpretation? Without begging the question in this debate, I think we can say this much: the reflexivity interpretation is now at least the canonical interpretation of Kaufman's wrestling project.

Moreover, if the reflexivity interpretation is the canonical interpretation here, that may tell us something about the debate between hypothetical intentionalism and actual intentionalism. It may tell us this much: our interpretive practices have no rules that prohibit us from using insider information about private avowals of authorial intention in determining the outcome of our interpretive quandaries.

The hypothetical intentionalist primarily rests his case against weak forms of intentionalism on the claim that, given the nature of our interpretive practices, we *always* prefer well-warranted (à la hypothetical intentionalism) hypotheses about authorial intent over private avowals of authorial intent. This is a rule of the language game of interpretation. This premise of hypothetical intentionalism is, however, undermined if at least sometimes it is evident that in our actual interpretive practices we go with private avowals of authorial intent that are at odds with our otherwise best-warranted hypotheses about authorial intent. Furthermore, the example of Andy Kaufman's wrestling project, inasmuch as the reflexivity interpretation is presently canonical, shows that our actual interpretive practices are open to incorporating avowals of authorial intention in acceptable interpretations. There is no such rule as the one hypothetical intentionalists invoke against modest actual intentionalism. Andy Kaufman represents one counterexample to the hypothetical intentionalist's putative rule, though there are others.[20]

The hypothetical intentionalist may make the fair observation that usually artists will abide by the standard communicative conventions of their

20. Other cases are discussed in Carroll, "Interpretation and Intention," 87–94. In that article, I also point out that many feminist literary critics, taken pretheoretically as exemplars of our actual interpretive practices, very frequently employ biographical information, including avowals of authorial intention, derived from "nonpublic" sources. Is one to suppose that feminist critics are ignorant of the rules of the game in this regard? But one would have thought that the practice of these feminist critics is, in part, constitutive of our interpretive practices and their implicit rules. In his *Intentionalist Interpretation*, 27, William Irwin also cites tendencies in feminist criticism that favor actual intentionalism. He mentions, as an example, Paula Bennett's *My Life a Loaded Gun: Female Creativity and Feminist Poetics* (Boston: Beacon Press, 1986).

art forms just because this will enhance the probability that they will be understood, and that typically artists have an interest in being understood. Artists behave in this way because they presume that the audience expects them abide by said conventions. Thus, it is advisable—inasmuch as the artist desires uptake—for the artist to play within the conventions. But however *advisable,* there is no necessity here. An artist may eschew conventional approaches. The risk is his, and it is up to him whether he takes it or not.[21]

A poet may decide to proceed in a manner that is not usual, because his agenda diverges from the norm. And the results may fascinate readers so much that they will avail themselves of whatever resources they can locate, including private avowals of authorial intention, even if discovered in unpublished notebooks or through confidences bestowed by the artist on acquaintances.[22] This surely describes our actual interpretive practices better than the supposed rule recommended by the hypothetical intentionalist. And, with respect to comedic performance, something like this is the best description of what has happened with regard to Andy Kaufman's wrestling project.

Andy Kaufman's wrestling project, involving the comic-reflexive exploration of the nexus of theater, reality, and emotion, was an unusual one—one that for full effectiveness required that he draw spectators into his subterfuge (much in the way that an experimental psychologist misdirects his subjects). Because his aims were unusual, he broke, or at least waived, the so-called rules, denying his audience a knowing "wink." We may marvel that he was willing to risk so much in terms of popularity by continuing his wrestling project, though we probably would not think it quite so strange if he were categorized as an avant-gardist or conceptual artist addressing a small inner circle. And, in any case, we do not know how Kaufman would have continued the project had he lived. Perhaps somewhere down the line there might have been a "wink," and then everyone would have "gotten it." But what remains of the project is curious and intriguing enough that we want to understand it interpretively. And to do so, we take advantage of

21. The same point is made by William Irwin in *Intentionalist Interpretation,* 57, 59.

22. The above is offered merely as an argument against one of the central premises of hypothetical intentionalism's case against modest actual intentionalism. It is intended to show that, since sometimes interpreters will quite naturally heed private avowals of authorial intention, there cannot be an implicit rule governing our interpretive practices to the contrary. This argument does not show that authorial intentions always constrain our interpretations. In order to reach that conclusion, one must take into consideration the conversational and ethical issues discussed in Carroll, "Art, Intention, and Conversation," and Irwin, *Intentionalist Interpretation.*

the kinds of information about authorial intention that the hypothetical intentionalist rules "out of bounds." We do so because, in fact, there are no rules here. Only fascination with Kaufman and his art drives our interpretive enterprise.

V. Hypothetical Intentionalism Again: The Second Round

The hypothetical intentionalist maintains that his position respects an implicit rule of the language game of interpretation that modest actual intentionalism forgets. Supposedly that rule enjoins us to refrain from relying on private avowals of authorial intention when interpreting artworks, literature, and the like. The modest actual intentionalist responds that if there is such an implicit rule, then we would expect it to be reflected in our actual interpretive practices. But this does not appear to be the case. Elsewhere I have cited a number of reasons to question the existence of the hypothetical intentionalist's alleged rule.[23] Herein I have dwelt at length on the case of Andy Kaufman. However, insofar as the hypothetical intentionalist primarily advances the superiority of his view over that of modest actual intentionalism in virtue of the existence of this putative universal prohibition, one counterexample should suffice.

But, of course, it is hard to imagine that the hypothetical intentionalist will take this objection lying down. So let us spend some time proleptically speculating on how he might attempt to deal with the case of Andy Kaufman. Supposing that the hypothetical intentionalist agrees that the reflexivity interpretation is the canonical interpretation of Kaufman's wrestling project, he may argue that this is perfectly consistent with the terms of hypothetical intentionalism. So, can the hypothetical intentionalist take the reflexivity interpretation on board, and, if so, how?

First, for example, he might contend that the relevant insider information about Kaufman's intentions really is public. After all, it is now obtainable in published biographies. But, of course, it was not publicly accessible knowledge at the time of the wrestling matches. The madness interpretation was the best hypothesis back then. So what will the hypothetical intentionalist do here? Go relativist—claiming that the madness interpretation is the best-warranted interpretation relative to one time period and the reflexivity interpretation for another?

23. Carroll, "Interpretation and Intention."

Furthermore, if the hypothetical intentionalist regards private avowals of authorial intention (and confidential information thereof) to be public simply so long as it is published, one wonders whether there is an issue of principle here, since the boundary between private avowals and public ones will become so unstable. One would have thought that diaries stand as the epitome of the sort of private avowals that the hypothetical intentionalist aspires to bracket. But diaries can be published. Does that make them public? Does the publication of a diary suddenly make the authorial intentions legitimately available for interpretation, whereas just previously they had been "out of bounds"? That seems arbitrary. Publication seems too slender a criterion to support the kind of distinction between *private* and *public* the hypothetical intentionalist desires. It makes it just too easy to move private authorial pronouncements into the public realm.

Or consider the case of a critic who goes into the archive, uncovers an author's private-meaning intentions, and incorporates them into an interpretation that is then published. Are we to say that the critic's interpretation is illegitimate from the perspective of hypothetical intentionalism (since he adverts to unpublished authorial avowals), though references to the author's intentions by readers of the critic's article are acceptable, since said intentions have been published in the critic's very own essay? But that is certainly paradoxical.[24]

Another line of response that the hypothetical intentionalist may raise with respect to Andy Kaufman is to remind us of a distinction he draws between categorical and semantic intentions. Semantic intentions concern the meaning of an utterance and parts thereof, while categorical intentions pertain to the genre or class to which the utterance belongs. Hypothetical intentionalists allow reference to private avowals of authorial intentions when it is a matter of fixing the category of the work, but disallow it with respect to authorial semantic intentions. In this light, the hypothetical intentionalist might claim that the intentions of Kaufman that concern us are

24. In "Intention and Interpretation in Literature," Jerrold Levinson, a hypothetical intentionalist, offers an interpretation of Kafka's "Country Doctor." He notes that the substance of this interpretation derives from Walter Sokel's *Franz Kafka* (New York: Columbia University Press, 1966). Part of that "substance" includes references concerning Kafka's beliefs about writing. Interestingly, Sokel's information about Kafka's beliefs come from Kafka's personal documents, including his diaries and letters. How is it that the hypothetical intentionalist allows access to private avowals of belief, but not intentions? The question should be especially vexing, since a leading component of intention is belief. The distinction the hypothetical intentionalist is striving to sustain here seems remarkably thin, and perhaps porous. See Levinson, "Intention and Interpretation in Literature," 185; Sokel, *Franz Kafka,* 3–8.

categorical ones and, therefore, no threat to the hypothetical intentionalist position.

There are several problems with this tack. First, it is not clear what category Kaufman's wrestling career falls into. Whatever it is, it is pretty unprecedented. But the hypothetical intentionalist can say that it is irrelevant whether there is a preexisting category here, since what a categorical intention amounts to is the author's conception of how the work is to be approached. But the case of Kaufman complicates this tidy formula. It prompts us to ask, "Intended to be approached *by whom?*" The general audience or insiders? Clearly, if we are talking about the approach available to the general audience, as one supposes the hypothetical intentionalist would be, then the authorial intention was that the events be approached as typical wrestling matches and typical talk shows. But wouldn't that make the madness hypothesis more probable than the reflexivity interpretation?

Moreover, it is questionable whether the distinction between categorical intentions and semantic intentions, and the hypothetical intentionalist's divergent attitudes toward them, are genuinely defensible. What justifies the different attitudes? If it is merely the assertion that such difference in attitudes is one of the rules of the interpretation game, then that seems to beg the question.

Furthermore, categorical intentions and semantic intentions do not always seem to be distinct. Suppose the hypothetical intentionalist claims that the category to which Kaufman's wrestling project belongs is that of irony. Isn't irony typically treated as a semantic intention in debates about intentionalism? And, in any event, even if Kaufman had the categorical intention that the whole project be ironic, he also had the semantic intention that his various inflammatory remarks about women and the South be exaggerations of the competitive, confrontational braggadocio of professional wrestling. These semantic intentions must be taken to be relevant if the reflexivity interpretation is to be found comprehensive. Without them, the hypothetical intentionalist cannot fully embrace the reflexivity interpretation.

Finally, the hypothetical intentionalist may point out that, on his view, aesthetic considerations can enter into the determination of an interpretation. Where two epistemically well-warranted interpretations are in balance but one makes the work in question aesthetically better, the hypothetical intentionalist argues that the aesthetically more enhancing one is better. Why this should be so, the hypothetical intentionalist never says. But applied to the case of Andy Kaufman, the principle might work this way: given the madness interpretation and the reflexivity interpretation, the latter makes the work aesthetically better. Therefore the reflexivity interpretation is to be preferred.

Epistemically, it might be said that the reflexivity interpretation fits smoothly with other parts of Kaufman's oeuvre. Like his imitations, the wrestling project puts his audience in a quandary about the real status of what they are seeing. The only difference is that the wrestling project never broke frame—never let the viewers in on the gag—though the imitation routines did. Moreover, once one adopts the reflexivity hypothesis, it does a very comprehensive job of explaining the wrestling project. That is, the work supports the interpretation. So, inasmuch as the reflexivity interpretation can be motivated epistemically by the hypothetical intentionalist, he can invoke aesthetic considerations to argue in its behalf against the madness interpretation.

The modest actual intentionalist, of course, counts as significant the correspondence of the wrestling project with other parts of Kaufman's oeuvre, while also regarding it as imperative that the work support the reflexivity interpretation. And yet we question whether, using simply the resources of hypothetical intentionalism, this is enough to ground the reflexivity interpretation. For if we really believe that the madness hypothesis is compelling at all, then there is something morally and intellectually wrong with favoring the reflexivity interpretation solely on aesthetic grounds.

That is, if there are real grounds for regarding the wrestling project as pathological, then it seems morally callous and cruel toward the previously mentally disabled, now late Andy Kaufman, and dishonest to ourselves, to pretend that it is a brilliant feat of reflexivity. Nor do I think that most interpreters would feel comfortable doing so if they held reasonable suspicions that the work was really some kind of psychotic fugue or schizophrenic rampage. It would be like making believe the helpless spasms of a madman constituted jitterbugging.

We would, as I said earlier, prefer to turn away from the whole sorry mess. The only way to overcome this reluctance and to opt for the reflexivity interpretation is to satisfy ourselves about Kaufman's actual intentions, which, of course, are only available through the kind of insider information that hypothetical intentionalism precludes.[25]

---

25. Nor is it open to the hypothetical intentionalist to say that he can base his attribution of the reflexivity interpretation on the supposition that Kaufman's intentions were likely to have been the same as other comics working in this genre, since there were no other comics like Kaufman (though some other comics did appreciate what he was doing) and there is not (yet) a genre hereabouts.

For related reasons, the hypothetical intentionalist cannot absorb insider information about Kaufman's intentions by regarding that information as merely suggestive of an interpretation rather than as evidence for an interpretation, because, as I have argued, unless we are really satisfied (unless we take the insider information to be *evidentially sound*), we will not feel disposed to approach the wrestling project from an aesthetic or an artistic point of view. Perhaps we will agree that it is worthy of a medical or psychiatric interpretation/diagnosis. But that will not be stated in terms of reflexivity.

Thus, hypothetical intentionalism cannot—in comparison with modest actual intentionalism—lay equal claim to the reflexivity interpretation of Andy Kaufman's wrestling project. So, if the reflexivity interpretation is canonical in this case, hypothetical intentionalism does not afford an adequate model of the interpretive practices that gave rise to it.

VI. Conclusion

This paper has been narrowly concerned with the debate between modest actual intentionalism and hypothetical intentionalism. These two approaches share many points of tangency. Both, for example, conceive of interpretation as, in large measure, occupied with searching for the best-warranted hypotheses of authorial intent. However, they disagree about the range of data that may be consulted in the process of constructing these hypotheses. Specifically, the modest actual intentionalist permits information about the authorial intention to play a role in interpretation even if that information hails from insider or private sources. The hypothetical intentionalist rejects usage of such information about authorial intention, arguing that this would violate an implicit rule of our interpretive practices.

In order to assess the hypothetical intentionalist's argument against modest actual intentionalism, I have taken a long look at the comedy of Andy Kaufman. If the hypothetical intentionalist is correct about the implicit rules of our interpretive practices, then we would expect interpreters uniformly to abstain from relying upon insider information about Kaufman's intentions. Therefore, insofar as this appears unlikely, modest actual intentionalism is not endangered by the hypothetical intentionalist's invocation of his implicit rules of interpretation. If the hypothetical intentionalist wishes to argue that interpreters should not rely on Kaufman's avowals of intent, then he needs to do more than merely assert the existence of a prohibition.

Whose Play Is It? Does It Matter?

Annette Barnes

Samuel Beckett's death prompted speculation: would his death "lead to the liberation or the distortion of his works"? A Beckett scholar predicted that productions of his plays would proliferate—"the plays will now be more available for interpretation." An actress hoped there would not be a drive "to free Beckett's work to interpretation." "Great writers are free," she said. "All you have to find is how to get inside the work and the mind of the writer."

"To free Beckett's work to interpretation," in this context, means leaving people free to produce interpretations of Beckett's works that might be at odds with his own understanding of them. Beckett was well known for his disapproval of certain productions, having, for example, banned a director who staged *Endgame* in a subway from producing his other plays. But was Beckett's disapproval justified in terms of anything other than his likes or dislikes—did the productions fail in some way to be legitimate productions?

While I do not in this essay directly address the question of which performances of Beckett's plays are legitimate, the question I do try to answer—can a performance that is at odds with a playwright's own

I would like to thank Gerald Barnes for his constructive criticism of an earlier draft of this essay.

understanding of his or her play be a legitimate one?—partially answers the prior question.

I discuss a number of ways in which a performance can be at odds with a playwright's own understanding of his or her work. Specifically, I focus on the ways in which a performance can conflict with the realization of an author's intentions or with the realization of his or her desires.[1] The intentions and desires that I treat as ingredients of the author's understanding are those that have as their rational basis details of what would count, speaking more strictly, as the author's understanding (conception) of his or her play. I distinguish between performances that are faithful—roughly, those that are not at odds with a playwright's own understanding of his or her work—and performances that are genuine—very roughly, those that comply with the dialogue in a playwright's script. I argue that while faithful performances are always genuine performances (at least in cases where the author has not misunderstood the work), not all genuine performances are faithful performances. I then consider the different effects classifying a performance as nonfaithful can have in different circumstances.

I begin with the ways in which a performance can conflict with the realization of an author's intention. To keep the discussion's dimensions manageable, I concentrate on the author's intending to create characters with certain characteristics. Lewis Carroll, speaking as the originator of the characters in a stage production of *Alice,* says that "I may without boastfulness claim to have a special knowledge of what it was I meant them to be, and so a special understanding of how far that intention has been realized." He fancies further that some people might "be interested in sharing that knowledge and that understanding." Carroll knows, for example, that he meant the White Rabbit as a contrast to Alice—"For *her* 'youth,' 'audacity,' and 'swift directness of purpose,' read 'elderly,' 'timid,' 'feeble,' and 'nervously shilly shallying,' and you will get *something* of what I meant him to be"; that he meant the White Queen to be "gentle, stupid, fat and pale; helpless as an infant; and with a slow, maundering bewildering air about her, just *suggesting* imbecility, but never quite passing into it."[2]

I assume, as does Carroll, that it is possible for artists to know what they intend their characters to be—to know, for example, that they intend them

---

1. Anyone who balks at calling a conflict with desires a conflict with understanding can substitute other evaluative pro- attitudes for "desire," for example, "believe desirable."

2. Lewis Carroll, " 'Alice' on the Stage," reprinted in *Diversions and Digressions of Lewis Carroll,* ed. Stuart Dudgeon Collingwood (New York, 1961), 163–74. All the Carroll quotes, here and below, come from these pages.

to have certain characteristics—and to realize those intentions in their works. I also assume that a playwright's intention to create characters who have certain characteristics is successfully realized if it is possible for actors to play the characters as having these characteristics—that is, if it is possible for actors to behave in the ways characters with those characteristics would behave in the circumstances that are supposed to obtain.

Carroll's intentions regarding his characters, what he meant them to be, could be realized both in the *Alice* books and in the stage production based on those books. Their successful realization in the stage production would be good evidence that they had been successfully realized in the books. "I need not," he says, "try to describe what I meant the hatter to be, since, so far as I can now remember, it was exactly what Mr. Harcourt has made him; and I may say nearly the same of Tweedledum."

When a performance fails to realize the author's intentions, the failure may lie with the author. Brecht, when faced with comparisons of Mother Courage to Hecuba in his play's original performances, undertook to rewrite the play. He had not realized his intention to make Mother Courage unsympathetic; actresses were unable to play her as unsympathetic. Given this sort of possibility of failed intention, the answer to the question whether a performance at odds with a playwright's own understanding of his or her play can be a legitimate performance would have to be yes. If the playwright has misunderstood his or her own work, performances that are at odds with the author's understanding (which in this instance is a misunderstanding) can be legitimate. But a more difficult question remains. Suppose the failure with respect to the author's intention does not lie with the author but with the performance. Can a performance that is at odds with the author's own understanding of his or her work, assuming that he or she has not misunderstood the work, be a legitimate performance?

For example, consider a performance of Beckett's *Catastrophe* in which the Protagonist appears to appeal abjectly to the audience. While one may not be able to tell from the performance alone that the character's so doing is at odds with what Beckett intended him to do in any performance, and with what the character does in other productions, one could have learned of the disparity if one had read the play, seen those other performances, or read what Beckett had to say about his character. Is the performance of Beckett's play in which the Protagonist makes the abject appeal a legitimate one?

To simplify matters, let us imagine a case in which what the author—call him Jasper—intended regarding the characteristics of the characters he has created is easily discoverable. At the end of Jasper's play *The Doll's House,* a woman leaves her family. Statements in the play suggest that this woman will not prosper, that being a wife and mother are essential to any woman's well-being. The female character can be played in a way that emphasizes this suggestion, and Jasper confirms that this is how he intended the character to be played.

Jessica, a director, believes that the views about women suggested in Jasper's play, when the play is read in the way Jasper intended, are mistaken—a real-life analogue to the character would be able to prosper. In Jessica's production of Jasper's play, a production that uses all and only the dialogue that Jasper has written, the woman character, when she leaves her family, is able to prosper. It is not, I think, unrealistic, given the availability of irony and emphasis, to imagine that Jasper's woman character can be played in this way.

Since Jessica's reading of Jasper's play is at odds with Jasper's own understanding of his play, would Jasper have legitimate grounds for contending that there is something wrong with Jessica's production, namely, either that it does not generate genuine performances of his play or that it does not generate faithful performances? Is there something wrong with a feminist-inspired performance of a professed nonfeminist work even if there is nothing wrong with a feminist-inspired criticism of the work in terms of its mistaken beliefs about women or its failure to see that a real-life counterpart of the character could prosper? (Although I focus on feminist performances, my remarks apply *mutatis mutandis* to other familiar cases—Christian performances of professed non-Christian works, Marxist performances of professed non-Marxist works, and so on.)

Even if we assume, as I do, that it makes sense to talk about authors' realizing their intentions in works, whether there are grounds for either of Jasper's contentions (if they are in fact distinct contentions) depends upon a number of factors. Consider first the question whether there are legitimate grounds for contending that the feminist-inspired presentations of Jasper's play do not constitute genuine performances. It seems clear that in order to answer this question we need to answer the question what counts as a genuine performance?

That the actors' utterances comply with the written dialogue in a true copy of the playwright's script is a relevant condition for a genuine performance.[3] The radical noncompliance in a production of *Hamlet* that eliminated

---

3. Catherine Z. Elgin, *With Reference to Reference* (Indianapolis, 1983), 115–16. Cf. Nelson Goodman's *Languages of Art.* While they make such compliance a necessary condition, I

the first scene in order that the ghost of Hamlet's father could be played "as a projection of Hamlet's neurosis" prompted one commentator to contrast this *Hamlet* with "the real *Hamlet*." But this same commentator noted that the original typescript of Oscar Wilde's *Importance of Being Earnest* contains four acts, whereas the play as we know it has three acts.[4] Scripts from which true copies are to be generated may, therefore, be scripts edited in the production process, in the Wilde case by an actor-manager before initial rehearsals.

Moreover, even where the dialogue is not intentionally modified in the course of production by the playwright or director or actor, strict compliance with that dialogue is not assured. "Clarity of utterance" is a playwright's ideal, not always realized in practice: actors, we are told, for example, not infrequently neglect the conditional "if" at the beginning of sentences.[5] Another form of nonintentional failure of compliance occurs when actors forget their lines, leaving out those forgotten or improvising others.

Some argue that strict compliance with the dialogue is a necessary condition for a genuine performance,[6] although specifying what such compliance involves is not a simple matter. Merely saying all the words in the right order will not do; they must be said in such a way that they mean something. However, even if one were able to specify what compliance involves,

---

claim here a weaker relation. A relevant condition, for example, for pain is pain behavior, despite the fact that such behavior is neither a necessary nor a sufficient condition for pain.

4. Tom Stoppard, "Pragmatic Theater," *New York Review of Books* XLVI, no. 14 (1999): 8. Stoppard, considering whether a playwright's technique is controlling "the information that flows from a play to its audience, and in particular the ordering of the information," notes that interference with that order is a commonplace occurrence. He cites several examples. In a production of *Comedy of Errors*, a Syracuse T-shirt lets the audience know, before Shakespeare does, that one of the men in the duke's presence is the sort of enemy, if found in Epheseus, the duke condemns. Although Stoppard refers to this as "his [the director's] *Comedy of Errors*," Stoppard believes that it is also a successful production of Shakespeare's *Comedy of Errors*. However, in a production of *Hamlet* in which the ghost of Hamlet's father is but a figment of Hamlet's troubled mind and from which the first scene, in which the ghost appears and Hamlet does not, has been eliminated, Stoppard balks at its being Shakespeare's *Hamlet*. He says that "[i]n the real *Hamlet*, the real first scene" has an emotional impact lacking in what must be by contrast not the real, that is, Shakespeare's, *Hamlet*. Lest one think the cutting of a scene condemns a production to nonreal status, he cites Wilde's *Importance of Being Earnest*. Wilde wrote it as a four-act play, but the actor-manager of its first production cut the text down to the three-act play it has been ever since. Wilde wrote to the actor-manager: "The scene which you feel is superfluous caused me back-breaking labor, nerve-racking anxiety. And took fully five minutes to write."

5. Ibid.

6. Elgin, *With Reference to Reference*, 116.

performances that (on any reasonable specification of compliance) fail to comply strictly with the dialogue have in practice been, and will continue to be, regarded as genuine performances.

No one will in practice rule out as nongenuine a performance with a few words forgotten, that is, if they are not crucially important words. However, how much change is to be tolerated before one stops speaking of a performance as a performance of the real play is a question that practitioners in the field are constantly called upon to answer. Is, for example, a radio production of *Romeo and Juliet* in which "the director has changed some of the text" the real *Romeo and Juliet*?

Those who, despite practice, argue for the theoretical necessity of strict compliance with the dialogue in order for a performance to be genuine do not similarly argue for the necessity of strict adherence to the playwright's written stage directions or to all descriptions given of costumes, scenery, and props. Theory is in accord with practice in this regard, for wide variations in setting, costumes, scenery, props, and lighting is tolerated in performances taken to be genuine.

Let us turn from one of Jasper's possible contentions—the contention that Jessica's production does not generate genuine performances of his play (a contention that would be justified if, for example, Jessica's production failed in dramatic ways to comply with the dialogue in Jasper's script)—to the other: the contention that Jessica's production does not generate faithful productions of his play. When we ask whether there are grounds for ruling out feminist-inspired presentations of Jasper's plays as nonfaithful performances, we are faced with the question, what makes a performance a faithful performance? To answer this question, I propose a partial and, I think, nonarbitrary characterization of a performance's faithfulness. A performance is faithful when it is not at odds with an author's own understanding of his or her work. But what is it to be at odds with an author's own understanding of his or her work? I talked earlier about authors' realizing their intentions in their work. Would a performance be nonfaithful if it conflicted with the realization of an authorial intention?

It is reasonable to suppose that a playwright successfully realizes his or her intention to create characters having certain characteristics if actors can play the characters as having these characteristics. For example, Jasper's intention to create a female character who lacks the capacity to prosper on her own is realized when an actress can play the female character as lacking the capacity to prosper on her own. When Jessica produces performances in which the female character has the capacity to prosper on her own, these performances are not in conflict with the realization of Jasper's intention to create a female character who lacks the capacity to prosper on her own. That intention is realized if it is possible to play the woman character as lacking the relevant capacity in *some* performance and we stipulated that the woman character could be so played.

Although there may appear to be a paradox here, since I allow that one and the same character could both lack the capacity to prosper and have the capacity to prosper (the law of contradiction seems not to hold for character descriptions), the appearance of paradox disappears if one understands the character's having (or lacking) the capacity to prosper in terms of the character's being able to be played as having (or lacking) the capacity to prosper.

If Jessica's performances do not conflict with Jasper's realization of his intention to create a female character who lacks the capacity to prosper on her own, is there any authorial intention with which her performances do conflict? Playwrights may not only intend to create plays whose characters have certain characteristics, an intention that can be realized in the scripts they write, they may intend that their plays be treated in certain ways. They may intend, for example, that there exist at least *some* performances of their plays in which their characters are played as having the characteristics they intended those characters to have, or that their plays have *only* performances in which their characters are played as having the characteristics they intended those characters to have.

Let us suppose that Jasper intended that his play have some performances in which the woman character is played as lacking the capacity to prosper on her own. If Jessica's performances are the only performances of Jasper's play that will ever be staged, then she can prevent the realization of Jasper's intention that there be some performances that are not at odds with his understanding. In this sense her performances may conflict with the realization of Jasper's intention. However, if other performances are possible in which the woman character is played as lacking the capacity to prosper on her own, then Jasper's intention can be realized despite what Jessica does in her production.

If Jasper's intention was to write a play such that in *no* performance of it is the woman character played as having the capacity to prosper, then Jessica's production conflicts with the realization of that intention. Indeed it prevents it from being realized. However, if a playwright had such an intention, it is very unlikely that such an intention would be realizable.[7] For

---

7. I am limiting the kind of intention involved here. If Jasper had intended that his female character not be a centipede, that intention would of course be realizable in any production.

however many things a playwright does to ensure that all performances of his play conform to his intentions—he may direct his own play, impose restrictions upon other directors who stage his plays—performances are notoriously difficult to control even in an author's lifetime. As Tom Stoppard notes,

> [W]e are talking about what happens to the text from the moment it is shared out among the people who have to deal with it, and it should be said that in the case of a very few insistent playwrights, nothing happens to it, for better or worse. But the central paradox of theater is that something which starts off complete, as true to itself, as self-contained and as subjective as a sonnet, is then thrown into a kind of spin dryer which is the process of staging the play; and that process is hilariously empirical.[8]

While the intention to create a work whose characters have certain characteristics is successfully realized if the playwright has written a script that can be performed in a certain way, an intention over whose realization Jessica has no influence, Jessica has some influence over whether Jasper's intentions regarding how his work is to be treated are realized. That Jessica's production conflicts with the realization of authorial intention in the way described—that is, prevents the realization of the intention that no performance be at odds with the author's understanding—means that Jessica's production is at odds with Jasper's understanding of his own play. Performances that so conflict are not faithful performances.

Another way in which Jessica's production is at odds, or is in conflict, with Jasper's understanding of his own work concerns a conflict with his desires. Jasper not only has intentions with regard to his work, he also has desires about how his work should be treated, desires with which Jessica's production can conflict.

Playwrights who recognize the limits of their power to control productions of their plays may desire, even if they do not intend, that performances of their works not be at odds with their own understanding of their works. Let us restrict ourselves to those cases in which authors have not misunderstood their own works. Playwrights desire not only to have written a script that *can* be played in a certain way, they also desire it to *be* played that way. And their desire that performances of their plays have certain characteristics

8. Stoppard, "Pragmatic Theater," 8.

is a desire to which we grant legitimacy. For there is reason to value the playwrights' written words more highly than all other contributions to a production. There is reason to privilege the authorial desire that arises once the play is written, that is, once the intention to create characters with certain characteristics has been realized.

Since it seems clear that playwrights in writing their plays do something, and since we generally allow agents to have a say about what it is they are intentionally doing, it seems reasonable to give playwrights a say in determining what they are intentionally doing in writing their plays. If playwrights have this say—and it seems arbitrary to deny it to them if we allow it to agents generally—then if a playwright (e.g., Jasper) intentionally creates in his play a character who *lacks* a certain capacity (who can be played as lacking that capacity), it seems reasonable to say of a performance of that play in which the character is played as having that capacity that it is *for this reason* not a faithful performance. We are interested in what playwrights, like other agents, intentionally do, and classifying as faithful certain performances of their work that are not at odds with their own understanding reflects that interest.

To restrict faithful performances to those that are not at odds with the playwright's own understanding of his or her work is, in some sense, to confer an elevated status upon these performances. This elevation indicates that we recognize the legitimacy of playwrights' desires to have their plays treated in a certain way, but this elevation is limited. For not being a faithful performance does not entail that a performance is not genuine. Given this characterization of faithfulness, genuine performances need not be faithful performances; not being at odds with the playwright's own understanding of his work is not required for genuineness.

Are we justified in assuming that something that fails to be a faithful performance can nonetheless be a genuine performance? To see why we must assume that it can, let us assume the opposite; that is, let us assume that Jessica's nonfaithful production cannot generate genuine performances of Jasper's play. This assumption puts us in an untenable position, despite any difficulties we might have with specifying the relevant conditions for genuineness. Let us see why.

Playwrights, while intentionally doing certain things in writing their plays, may unintentionally do other things. A playwright may, for example, unintentionally create an ambiguous character, a character who not only may be played as lacking a certain capacity but also may be played as having that capacity. Given what I have said is required for a character to have a given trait (the character can be played as having that trait), Jasper could intentionally create a female character as lacking the capacity to prosper on her own and unintentionally thereby create a female character ambiguous with respect to the capacity to prosper. A staging of the play that is at odds with the playwright's intentions regarding performances of the play may not be at odds (indeed it may accord) with what he or she unintentionally did, but did nevertheless. I see no reason why such a staging, although not a faithful performance, could not be a genuine performance. If this is correct, it would be a mistake to link genuineness with not being at odds with a playwright's own understanding of his or her work in the way that I have linked faithfulness with this understanding.

If not being at odds with a playwright's own understanding of his or her work is not required for genuineness and if, as we have stipulated, in Jessica's production the actors' utterances comply with the dialogue that Jasper has written, then it is possible that Jessica's production generates genuine performances of Jasper's play. Let us assume, therefore, that it does generate genuine performances. As we have seen, however, her production does not generate faithful performances. The best explanation, or at least the most intuitively satisfying explanation of our inclination to call it nonfaithful, I suggested, is that Jasper had succeeded in his intention to write a play in which the woman character lacks the capacity to prosper on her own. He has succeeded in doing this when the character can be played as lacking that capacity. Jessica's performances in which the woman character has the capacity to prosper on her own can thus conflict with Jasper's intentions and desires about what sort of performances performances of his play will be.

If we can determine that Jasper successfully realized his intention to create a character who lacks the capacity to prosper, and if realizing this intention does not rule out the possibility that the character has the capacity to prosper in some conceivable genuine, although not faithful, performance, then Jessica's production, while not conflicting with this intention, can, as we have seen, conflict with other intentions or desires he may have. While her performances are not faithful performances of Jasper's play, they can nonetheless be genuine.

Suppose that Jessica's performances are not faithful, that Jasper has legitimate grounds for this contention. What force does this contention have?

Tom Stoppard, after describing Max Frisch's *Fire Raisers,* asks: "Is this a metaphor for Hitler taking over in the 1930's? The author, I'm told, was thinking of the Communist takeover in Eastern Europe in the 1950's. But, to me, his opinion carries no more weight than mine. Or yours, if yours happens to be, 'That's how so-and-so stole my business.' "[9]

Is Stoppard here suggesting that nonfaithful performances of *The Fire Raisers* are as good as faithful ones, that the charge of nonfaithfulness has no force? If we recall that performances are nonfaithful if they are at odds with the playwright's own understanding of his or her play, and if it is not required of a faithful performance that it *accord* with such understanding but only that it not be at odds with it, then the alternate performances suggested by Stoppard need not be nonfaithful performances. If they were not nonfaithful performances, Stoppard is not addressing the question, what force does a contention of nonfaithfulness have?

Like Stoppard, I believe that the question of meaning in this context has no answer that is the exclusively correct answer, although it is not clear that he would agree with me that there are many answers that can be correct. (He says that "[a]rt which stays news, in Ezra Pound's phrase, is art in which the question 'what does it mean?' has no correct answer.") I want to argue now that the force of the charge of nonfaithfulness is a variable force.

If, as our example assumes, Jessica's performances accord with true beliefs, in this case true beliefs about women, can this accord outweigh the nonfaithfulness of the performance? Consider for a moment the following dialogue between a long-married husband and wife.

MRS. EVERSOLONG: What a nice couple the Rochesters are. We should have them to tea.

MR. EVERSOLONG: You are absolutely right, my dear, they were despicable. I am glad that we shall never see them again.

MRS. EVERSOLONG: Oh, I am afraid that you have misunderstood me, Duncan. I meant what a nice couple they were.

MR. EVERSOLONG: I did not misunderstand you, my dear. On the contrary, I knew exactly what you meant, but you are quite wrong. By construing what you said in the way that I did, what you said was true, and I know, my dear, that you are interested above all in speaking truly.

At this point, Mrs. Eversolong might sigh inaudibly and resign herself to teas without the Rochesters. Let us imagine, moreover, that in the situation so described, Mrs. Eversolong is mistaken and Mr. Eversolong is not—the Rochesters *are* despicable. Let us also imagine that our playwright Jasper

9. Ibid., 10.

does not make a similar conciliatory response to director Jessica's correction. Imagine his response to be: "Damn it, I bloody well meant what I said, and I don't need you to correct me. Write your own play, don't tamper with mine." Might not even feminists see a virtue in a Jasperian, as opposed to a Mrs. Eversolongian, response?

But is a Jasperian response appropriate in either Mrs. Eversolong's case or in his own? Suppose, for example, that Mrs. Eversolong, amiable though she is, is a poor judge of character and Mr. Eversolong is, as usual, right. In this case, Mr. Eversolong's correction of his wife might be justified, for he might be rather skillfully, even if not very nicely, dealing with her shortcoming. An inaudible sigh might be just the appropriate response on his wife's part.

Moreover, might not a Mrs. Eversolongian response be more appropriate even for Jasper in his situation? If Jasper were a mediocre playwright and Jessica's production made what would have been a minor, muddled work on Jasper's reading into a minor, unmuddled and interesting work, a Mrs. Eversolongian response might be the more appropriate response even here. By being faithful to the letter, but not the spirit, of Jasper's words, Jessica might have improved Jasper's play, and, therefore, an inaudible sigh from Jasper might be a seemly response. Indeed, we could imagine Jasper in the course of time changing his mind about what he meant, a change of mind facilitated by the gradual realization that the play is a better play if construed as a feminist one. Good criticism, Norman Mailer said, kisses thought up another notch; Jessica's "correcting" performance might do the same. If we follow this line of thought, then being nonfaithful to the work seems not always to be a serious fault.

Suppose, however, that Mrs. Eversolong is not, as we have just imagined, a poor judge of character, but is a brilliant judge of character. However, in the case of the Rochesters, she is wrong. In the situation as now described, should we not take offense at Mr. Eversolong's summary dismissal of her judgment?

If Jasper had the stature of an Ibsen, we might want performances of his play not to conflict with what he meant (assuming we can determine what he meant) even if we decided that what he meant was false. Would not a Jasperian response be legitimate? If Shakespeare, for example, had, in *The Merchant of Venice,* intended to write a play in which anti-Semitism is sanctioned, and if it was possible both to determine that he had and to perform the play as sanctioning anti-Semitism, we might want such productions despite our rejection of anti-Semitism.

If we did, then cannot Jasper, assuming he is a major playwright, legitimately accuse Jessica of producing the kind of performance that we do not want? We want faithful performances, and hers are not that. But even here, although we want faithful performances of his play, it is not at all clear that we want *only* faithful performances.

If, for example, we adapt T. S. Eliot's view concerning a poem to a play—if, although there is a sense in which a playwright "knows better what his plays mean than can anyone else," nevertheless "what a play means is as much what it means to others as what it means to the author; and indeed, in the course of time a playwright may become merely an audience in respect to his own works forgetting his original meaning—or without forgetting, merely changing"[10]—then we may not want only performances that are faithful, even if the playwright is a major playwright. Stoppard, you will recall, echoes Eliot's sentiment that what a play means is as much a matter of what it means to others as what it means to the author in his claim that "to me, his opinion [the author's] carries no more weight than mine."

A major director's view, especially if she has true beliefs about women, might also be worth having. Though Jasper might not initially like Jessica's performances, his complaints against them need not have sufficient force to rule them out. If, on the other hand, the potential directors are mediocre, their beliefs muddled, then we may prefer performances that are not at odds with playwrights' own understanding of their works.

Even if Jasper has a legitimate complaint—a feminist-inspired performance of his play is not a faithful performance—how seriously his complaint should be taken varies, as we have seen, with circumstances. If one were interested in performances that portrayed the woman character in a way that showed what possibilities her real-life analogue would have, or if one wanted an interesting performance, then Jasper's complaint might not be taken very seriously. If, on the other hand, one were interested in what Jasper, an acknowledged master playwright, had intended to say, and had succeeded in saying, in his play, even if we ultimately decided that what he had to say was false, then Jasper's complaint might be taken more seriously. How seriously it should be taken depends on the details of the case.

I have thus far spoken of the propriety of performing as a feminist work a play intended not to be a feminist work. Suppose, however, that Jessica writes a feminist work and Jasper, a director, gives nonfeminist performances of it. It would, perhaps, be easier here for feminists to see that there

---

10. Eliot's views concerning a poem can be found in "The Modern Mind," *The Use of Poetry and the Use of Criticism* (Loudon, 1964), 130.

are legitimate grounds for authorial complaint, for this new case is in an important respect not strictly parallel to the earlier one. Whereas we supposed that the feminist performances of Jasper's play had the virtue of embodying true beliefs about women, we are not assuming that the nonfeminist performances of Jessica's have this virtue. However, we can imagine that even in this case there might in some circumstances be reasons for allowing performances of the sort Jasper proposes, assuming that although these performances are not faithful, they are nevertheless genuine.

The distinction between a faithful performance and a genuine performance is meant to reflect both that we are interested in what authors do intentionally—faithful performances are not at odds with an author's own understanding of his or her work—and that our interests in their works extend beyond what was done intentionally in them. Genuine performances need not accord with an author's own understanding of his or her work. I suggested, for example, that we are also interested in what works could show us about the possibilities real-life analogues to their characters might have.

We interested in plays for a variety of reasons, and factors other than the two I have discussed—the playwright and the director—influence what kinds of performances get produced. For example, audiences may exert influence, for they may be willing to entertain only certain kinds of performances at certain times. Thus it could happen that no matter what the author's successfully realized intention in the work was, performances faithful to that intention would not be tolerated by audiences at a given time, although they might be tolerated at another time.

While an insistent living playwright may be able to prevent major transformations of the script in the process of production, as Beckett during his lifetime was able to do, most playwrights living or dead cannot prevent this. Moreover, given that instances of dramatic works are performances, the different directors, actors, designers, and managers that are involved in the production process will inevitably produce different performances even where authorial control is tightest.

Consider, for example, two recent productions of O'Casey's *Juno and the Paycock*. Whereas one director emphasizes the O'Casey rhetoric and the family tragedy, another director focuses on the political tragedy, the "fierce tragicomedy of anger and exasperation" in Ireland. Whereas the Captain is in one production "a ruined chieftain, a sordid but magisterial whinger," in another he is "a fighter: one who fights dirty and whinges with the best, but still a fighter." While the relationship between Juno and the Captain can be made "almost like that between a harassed mother and an immature adolescent," who at moments "almost fight on level ground," in another the Captain may roar and fire-raise, while "the women provide stability, and hold both the psychological power and the purse strings."[11]

Although different performances need not conflict with the playwright's own understanding of a play, more than one interpretation of the play will surface in these productions. If what I have suggested in this discussion is correct, then, despite an author's misgiving, performances that embody interpretations of the play that conflict with the playwright's own understanding of the play can nevertheless count as genuine performances. Of course, determining which of those performances that are at odds with the playwright's own understanding are genuine and which are not genuine is, as I noted earlier, not an easy task.

My discussion has been a limited one, but it reaches a conclusion: it matters whose play it is, but, if the suggestions I offer are correct, how much it matters varies. The consequences of this discussion for the question of a single right interpretation in the dramatic arts should be clear. The search for a single right interpretation of a play's content would be misguided, whether the search were for the only genuine interpretation or, alternatively, for the only faithful interpretation.

11. John Peter, "Double Take," *Sunday Times Culture*, 26 September 1999, 20. All quotations about O'Casey's play appear on this page.

Tossed Salad: Ontology and Identity

Susan L. Feagin

Even relatively conservative accounts of interpretation and the ontological status of works of art may deny there is a single correct or legitimate interpretation of an artwork on the grounds that there is more than one appropriate perspective from which to interpret it. One might plausibly see a work as the product of a knowledgeable and skilled agent, while another might see it as part of a particular cultural matrix that abstracts over individual agents at a given point in or period of time. To the extent that the institutions, values, and practices within a culture are beyond the powers of any single agent to control, these two perspectives will yield significantly different interpretations. I am on record as holding a view such as this, that is, that one should identify such points of view as yielding different interpretations of the same object.[1]

I have come to believe, however, that there are cases where the identities of objects are more ambiguous than I previously thought. One type of case that displays this ambiguity fairly clearly takes shape when an object is created by individuals within and for a given cultural context and is at some

I thank Andrew Bergerson and members of the interdisciplinary faculty workshop for their questions and suggestions on an earlier version of this paper.

1. See "Incompatible Interpretations of Art," *Philosophy and Literature* 6, nos. 1 and 2 (1982): 133–46.

later point removed from that context and incorporated into another where it plays a quite different cultural role. One particularly clear example of such an "identity crisis" is described by Ajume H. Wingo, who spotted a mask that was made and used for sacred, religious purposes (in a culture very similar to his own in Africa) in a Berkeley art gallery.[2] His first reaction was to say that the mask did not belong there. In Africa, it was supposed to remain hidden from everyone except a small minority of people who had been "initiated as its custodians," and it was believed to have the power to harm the uninitiated who dared to touch it or even to look at it. In the Berkeley gallery, however, everyone was looking at it and felt free to touch it—ironically, constrained, if at all, by concerns that they might damage the mask. It finally occurred to Wingo that "the thing that didn't belong there was me."

I attempt in this paper to motivate the view that artifacts whose identities were once fixed as made or chosen by individuals in accord with a culturally recognized role or function acquire ontological tensions and ambiguities as part of their identity because of changes in cultural context. My discussion focuses on such objects in relation to particular aspects of American cultural life at the dawn of the twenty-first century, where this process of ontological change, I allege, is taking place right before our very eyes. Ultimately, I propose that the character of the cultural changes at work dictate that it is important to recognize the tensions and ambiguities in their identities rather than to try to resolve the tensions by choosing one side or the other, for example, in the case described above, either sacred mask or art.

For the purposes of this paper, interpretation includes any relatively deep, rich, and extended description, criticism, art-historical analysis, and so forth, of one or more works of art, written in the vernacular language(s) of the interpreter's culture. A case can be made for using "interpretation" as a technical term whose use is restricted to a relatively narrow and specific type of activity, as distinguished from description, criticism, analysis, review, and so on. This narrow use of the term preserves distinctions that are important for understanding the different audiences and objectives for writing about art. Yet, these distinctions between different types of writing about the arts tend to mask the significance of the property they share as *written*. I limit my discussion to interpretation as it exists in relation to (*a*)

2. Ajume H. Wingo, "African Art and the Aesthetics of Hiding and Revealing," *British Journal of Aesthetics* 38, no. 3 (1998): 251–64.

the *visual arts* alone, in those contexts (*b*) where there *is an assumption of general literacy* and (*c*), in principle, *widespread access* both to written interpretations and to the visual works of art that are interpreted. Each of these conditions has a rationale.

I limit my discussion to interpretations of the visual arts because they have had major personal and cultural roles and functions, historically speaking, for nonliterate viewers. Regardless of where one comes down in the debate over whether pictures possess their cognitive or representational contents by social construction or by virtue of some similarity to objects in the world (or to the way viewers see objects in the world), one needs to accommodate the fact that visual images, or pictures, have historically been employed in ways that do not require their viewers or the populace in general to be literate. They may require a certain cognitive stock and assume a certain range of prior visual experience, but not necessarily the abilities to read and to write. In Part Two, I describe why general literacy as it exists today in American life is a sufficiently important aspect of the cultural context that it can reasonably be seen as affecting the ontological status of visual works of art. I take general literacy to be a characteristic of those environments where the following three conditions are satisfied to an appropriately high degree and for an appropriately wide range of individuals. The three conditions are that a value is placed on literacy, that there is an assumption of literacy, and that literacy is a reality. General literacy in this sense has been rare in the course of human history, even though many today take their own literacy and numerous applications of it for granted.

It is also important that there is, at least in principle, widespread *access,* in some sense or other, to interpretations and the artworks that are interpreted. Not all works of visual art, on the one hand, are available to everyone in person, but much is available through reproduction. Acquaintance through reproduction is a complicating factor, since some works lend themselves to reproduction better than others. In addition, social, economic, and other factors affect what works we discuss and what we say about them. I in no way wish to deny that our acquaintance with the visual arts is partial (perhaps in both senses of the word) and affected by the judgments of whoever is writing the history and criticism of the arts. In fact, during the course of the twentieth century we have seen expansions in the concept of art to include, quite deliberately, types of objects that are available to a larger number of people, especially those who have not traditionally had a role in the art world or in academia. These include, but are not limited to, imagery from advertising, popular culture, and components of the material culture of ethnic groups that have otherwise been alien to those who encounter them—one might even say confronted by them—in galleries and art museums.

Each human being has an identity at multiple ontological levels. At one level, we are members of the biological category *Homo sapiens,* having evolved to be what we are over a vast period of time. Our brain structure reveals its evolutionary history in its accretions of new structures onto the old rather than by replacing an entire system or subsystem for another. As a consequence, some outcomes of our mental processes conflict with others, and hence fragment how we humans may experience ourselves and how we relate to the world. In Part One, I describe some examples of conflicts between perceptual experience and cognition that serve as a metaphor for the ontological tensions that exist in certain types of artifacts we typically consider to be art.

At another level, humans respond to other minds and are able to live in communities with others. We bond through cultural practices and receive the benefits of cooperation and diversity of abilities. An identity of a third ontological type is fed by opportunities to make one's own contributions to the well-being (or harm) of others and the community. That is, one is an agent who exercises choice and control, seemingly independent of outside cultural or inside biological influence, and as able to take responsibility for one's own actions.

The fragmentation of the individual is often described dramatically and with great existential angst while berating the Cartesian fantasy of a simple unified self. At the same time, other theorists describe personal identity as the construction of a coherent narrative out of the inconsistency and confusion experienced in the course of an ordinary life. But there is another way. Conflict among, and sometimes within, these ontological levels—biological, cultural, and individual personhood—is precisely what enables one to develop and grow as a person and as someone who should be seen as having value as an end in itself. Humans should not expect to integrate everything in one's experience into a coherent account of who they are, whether in the form of a Cartesian *res cogitans* or a temporally extended narrative. In Part Three, I propose that the ontological tensions that exist within human beings should be recognized as existing in some of the things human beings make, that is, artifacts that begin their lives as the product of human contrivance and become something very different when transported, along with similar types of objects, to a different culture.

Part One: Personal Identity and Visual Perception

> Tradition is the illusion of permanence.
> —Woody Allen as Harry in *Deconstructing Harry*

Plato noticed that conflicts occur within human minds and used this fact to argue for what can be usefully thought of as a proto-modularity thesis, that is, that each person's psyche has three parts. Consider a stick propped up in a transparent vessel half-filled with water. Visually, the stick appears to be notched and bent at a slight angle at the surface of the water. It will continue to appear this way no matter how deeply one concentrates on the fact that the stick is not notched and bent in the way it appears to be. Thus, this visual process is cognitively impenetrable, that is, impervious to higher-order cognition such as knowledge or understanding. In human beings, many modular units process perceptual stimuli in ways one is often unaware of and virtually entirely unable to control.

Not all visual experiences, much less other types of experiences, are cognitively impenetrable. Connoisseurship in the visual arts is possible in part because one can have different visual experiences without any alteration in the character of the proximal stimuli (the pattern of irradiation on the retina) or because, even when there are changes in the proximal stimuli, the changes in one's experience are not due to them. One becomes able to make finer discriminations, which improve one's ability to identify and individuate objects in the world and their properties. A great deal of learning in humans takes place at this basic perceptual level, often without even attending to it, which is an advance in major respects over perceptual systems that do not have that flexibility.

Visual experiences that are not cognitively impenetrable play an important role in relation to cognition precisely because there are some adjustments one's sensory system cannot and will not make, even when one knows the phenomenology of the experience does not accurately reflect the way the world is. Fortunately, we are not compelled to believe the world is as we visually experience it. A randomizing device might keep us from the fate of Buridan's fabled ass, immobilized, in our own case, because equidistant from conflicting but cognitively equally compelling states of mind: a visual experience, on the one side, and an otherwise justified belief, on the other. In the greater scheme of things, however, one would hope for something a bit more reliable, and Plato drove home the point that human abilities to reflect and reason are more useful than mere perception or chance. Thinking *requires* going beyond what is presented in sensation, beyond "the given" that refuses, phenomenologically, to budge. Just as people reach a stage where they can accept or reject part of the content of a given sense experience, they can accept or reject part of what is provided for them as part of their culture. In both cases the flexibility provided by reasoning is of greater advantage than a wholesale acceptance of (and certainly than a wholesale rejection of) the "given." The inconsistencies that arise within one's perceptual experiences themselves, as well as between beliefs and experience, serve as constant reminders that humans have the ability to take responsibility for their beliefs and actions, as epistemic, artistic, and moral agents. At a minimum, these are the types of situations that lead us to think of ourselves as such.

Immanuel Kant describes the feeling of the sublime as containing both pleasure and pain: pleasure in being able to have ideas that are not limited to those we can acquire through sense experience, and pain in realizing that the world extends beyond our powers to perceive it, that the world was not made "for us." A perception of "the starry heavens" above does not present us with a perceptual experience of infinity, but it "brings with it" the idea of infinity. An experience of irreconcilable internal conflict reveals something special about the minds of human beings as agents and hence as persons. Some philosophers have even grounded the concept of free will in the phenomenological fact *that we experience conflict* between duty and desire, between our knowledge of what we ought to do and the weakness of our will in getting us to do it.[3] The phenomenology of one's experience of conflict and freedom might of course be mistaken; it may seem to one that one is making a free choice when one isn't. Free will is no better off, yet certainly no worse off, in this respect than other properties we attribute to persons or to objects in the world on the basis of experience, since the phenomenology of *any* experience may not accurately reflect the way the world is.

I have moved from evolutionary facts about the brain to the modularity of mind in an effort to describe how tension and conflict within the workings of a human mind not only constitute an important aspect of human intelligence but also tell us something about the identity of human beings. We all try to make sense of things in the world, though some of us are better at this than others, as we try to figure out what evidence is reliable and what should be explained away. Successful illusionist paintings present us with this epistemic conflict in microcosm because the visual appearance of spatial depth persists even though we know it is an illusion.[4] Most people find such

3. See, for example, C. A. Campbell, "Is Freewill a Pseudo-Problem?" *Mind* LX, no. 239 (1951): 450–64. Kant's other favored example was, of course, "the moral law within."

4. Discussions of illusionist painting tend to focus on the issue of belief and hence become derailed when it comes to understanding both the nature of art and pictorial representation. I have argued that the nature and value of illusionist painting as used in works of art are predi-

illusions fascinating and somewhat amusing: we ponder the limits of our own perceptual capabilities as they are revealed in relatively everyday experience. The nature and value of illusion as it functions in works of art is predicated on a perceiver's being able at some point to realize that what is presented in the illusion is not real even though one cannot avoid seeing it that way. It is also common to overlook temporal and contextual factors at work in illusion. There is a type of Roman floor mosaic that is typically described as illusionistic, for example, those in fishmongers' shops, where they depict scattered fish parts on a white mosaic ground. It was unclear to me for a long time why anyone would think of such mosaics as illusionistic. Then one day in the kitchen, chopping vegetables, I accidentally brushed a piece onto the floor, knelt down to pick it up, and reached for what turned out to be not a piece of food but part of the grain in the wood flooring. The dawn broke. In the shop of the fishmonger the mosaics would occasionally and briefly be effective illusions. That is the point: not illusion anywhere, in any context, and for eternity; but momentarily, at that place, in that context. Many conflicts that confront us about who we are and how to understand an object in our environment are like these occasional illusions. They do not cause us to live an incoherent life or plunge us into existential angst, but provide an opportunity to reflect and to choose in relation to options we may have never otherwise considered. Ambiguities in the identity of cultural artifacts, discussed below, have the potential to be even more central to questions about personal and cultural identity.

General Literacy, Personal Identity, and the Visual Arts

Who's there?
—Bernardo in *Hamlet*

P. O. Kristeller's essay "The Modern System of the Arts" is justly held in high regard for its detailed and scholarly description of how "the modern system of the arts" gradually coalesced in Europe in the early eighteenth

---

cated on one's *not* believing that what is presented in the illusion is real. Rather, they are predicated on perceiving it as real even though one knows it isn't or even though one cannot tell. See Susan L. Feagin, "Presentation and Representation," *Journal of Aesthetics and Art Criticism* 56, no. 3 (1998): 234–40.

century.[5] One reason his essay is so persuasive is that it takes account of both synchronic and diachronic factors to show why this conceptualization of the fine arts is significant for understanding a culture, and the significant constituents of that culture, during a particular period of time. It also helps us understand the American cultural matrix of the latter half of the twentieth century (and beyond) insofar as it arises out of that "modern system of the arts," and how different it is from other cultural matrixes that do not involve a similar concept of the fine arts.

Differences between the cultural roles of the visual arts and literature are a central component of Kristeller's story. He shows that, historically, in more or less formally constructed educational systems within the Western world, the study of poetry and written language in general is typically linked with the study of mathematics. In contrast, painting is linked with carpentry and other skills that can be acquired through training and practice, for example, as an apprentice to a master, without the need to read and write. The prestige of the former assembly of areas of knowledge and study became embedded within the "fine" arts, and the lack of prestige that has accompanied the latter became linked with the "mechanical," or useful, arts. Whether or not one agrees that this distribution of prestige is appropriate, one feature that distinguishes the two groups goes a long way in explaining why the distinction in valuation persists. Linguistic symbol systems employed to record and convey information are virtually entirely conventional and must therefore be taught. A cultural investment has to be made in teachers and the paraphernalia of teaching, and a personal investment must be made to become a reader, for what turn out to be relatively abstract and long-term, rather than immediate, rewards. In contrast, images and paintings typically use many of the same features of a visual array that are used to identify and individuate objects in the world, such as color, overlap of forms, and decreasing size to show depth, and shading to show contour.[6] One can, without special training, identify the basic pictorial content of Chinese or Finnish landscape paintings but not the basic linguistic content of Chinese or Finnish writing at all. Indeed, some would argue that any

---

5. *Journal of the History of Ideas* xii, no. 4 (1951): 496–527, and xiii, no. 1 (1952): 17–46.

6. Some philosophers have held that, like writing, all pictorial representation is conventional and that what we call naturalism or realism is merely the mode of pictorial representation that is most familiar to us. I take the criterion offered in the text to provide a more plausible characterization of what makes a pictorial representation realistic. It has the additional advantage of cohering nicely with differences we observe between the cultural roles of pictures and of literature.

satisfactory account of the nature of pictorial representation must account for the relative ease of interpreting the subject matter of a painting in contrast with that of the written word.

Compare how paintings on the interior walls of European churches built between 1400 and 1650 C.E. originally functioned with how those paintings function now. As is well known, such images helped to focus the attention of those who were unable to read on the relevant religious ideas. I would venture that the majority of viewers today, such as American tourists, approach these images from the opposite direction, cognitively speaking: our easiest access to their meaning is through books or through someone who has read the relevant books. Words, we might say, are much more transparent to people today than those images. In addition, inscriptions of letters and words have and have had an almost magical significance in many cultures where general literacy is neither an assumption nor a reality. They often stand for the power of the unknown and meanings that are hidden. The same phenomenon occurs in cultures where few people can read the language in question. The "look" of inscriptions of words in an unknown language can be used for its emotive and expressive powers, quasi-mystical and religious, to allude to the exotic or to indicate a kind of global sophistication. Our "visual illiteracy" may not be as profound as the literal illiteracy in fifteenth- and sixteenth-century Europe, but it affects our relationship with visual images, as it does with "foreign" words, by making them more alien. When one comes from a culture that assumes literacy, and tries to understand paintings and images from a culture that does not, one pays a cognitive and emotional, not merely a perceptual, price. One is unable to appreciate the power of an image whose power depends on one's *not* having abilities that one takes for granted.

To the extent that one takes one's own literacy and a literate environment for granted, one is likely to underestimate their significance. For those reading this essay, imagine what your life would be like if you and those you have regular contact with, personally and professionally, could neither read nor write. Of course, in that case, you would not be reading this essay, and the thought experiment it asks you to conduct would not be possible. One may literally, without the hyperbole that usually accompanies the phrase, be unable to imagine such a thing, or able to imagine it only to a limited degree. For academics who work in areas traditionally included in "the arts and sciences" (sometimes "letters and sciences," sometimes "arts and letters"), the abilities to read and write are *sine qua non*; without them (or an agent to provide such services) one could not do the work. There are newspapers and popular magazines, advertising, street signs, driver's license exams, postcards and letters, tags on clothing identifying the fabric and instructions for care, legal contracts and agreements increasingly available to the general public in libraries and on the web, and on and on.

Today there is a huge cultural apparatus for the training of painters and for writing about them and their work. There are art schools and art departments in universities, as well as programs in the history and philosophy of art, in art education and in arts administration. There are galleries—for profit and not for profit—public and private art museums, and private collections and collectors who may open their doors by special arrangement. It is common for art museums to hire specialists to make sound judgments about how to expand their collections and to write catalogs about their holdings. There are appraisers who evaluate works for insurance and inheritance. There are volumes written on whether various works are authentic. There are books and journals for professionals, focusing on art history, philosophy, education, museum studies, studio practices, and art in relation to culture. There are books, textbooks, and magazines for the versed and unversed in the visual arts.

The social evolution of the visual arts into a specialized field of study over the last three hundred years of Western civilization has yielded benefits such as those that generally result from professionalizing a domain of study, made possible at least in part by the existence of written work that can be critiqued, rejected, or accepted, and built upon by others. Painting has come to employ ideas and methods that are not part of a visual common knowledge but instead a specialized area of understanding. The fact that so much is written about painting and the visual arts in general creates an intellectual environment within which artists can position themselves in relation to other artists and address a rich and intricate network of ideas about personal identity, culture, ethnicity, gender-linked perception, and the history and nature of art itself. It is perhaps needless to say that when a particular work stands in relation to other works and within some network of ideas such as these, its significance is not likely to become visible if one only looks (and looks only) at that individual painting. These days, the written word is the most efficient vehicle for any nonspecialist to learn what a work is about, what kinds of ideas might lie within it, and what personal or cultural phenomena it builds on or rejects.

Nevertheless, a significant portion of the public seems to believe that one should be able to appreciate a visual work of art without having to learn anything about it in particular or art in general. Clive Bell, writing in the early twentieth century, made an observation that continues to be relevant today. He noticed that people are often willing to admit their ignorance of music to explain why they don't respond to a particular piece, when they would deny any analogous ignorance to explain why a painting does not move them.[7] In spite of the fact that relevant and helpful information is available, many of those who do not have a professional interest in the visual arts appear to resent the idea that they may be expected to do some intellectual work to understand and appreciate a painting. Such resentment is not totally unjustified, not only because of, as mentioned, the nature of the medium as relatively transparent with respect to some of its representational content, but also because learning what one needs to know requires a level of commitment one might quite reasonably not be willing to make.

Our society spends significant resources, directly and indirectly, on teaching people how to read at both literal and deeper levels, and on individuals and institutions in which they exercise their skills. Labor specialization and the concomitant development of knowledge and skills specific to various specializations come to exist in subcultures having their own practices and argot. Within the subculture of academe that deals with the visual arts in particular, professorships, books, and journals are all parts of a cultural apparatus that de facto institutionalizes and underwrites the proliferation of interpretive theories and practices, each of which, as published, claims *per se* to have value. The same is true of the gallery and museum worlds. Astonishingly, however, there is no generally accepted view about the value of art, what value the multiplicity of interpreters and interpretations contribute to society, and, finally, whether art is worth it in the greater scheme of things.

It is reasonable to believe, however, consensus is lacking at least in part because the values and rewards of literacy and writing in general are more abstract, long-term, and indirect. For literacy to be of value it is not required that every essay or book be good or that each be totally comprehensible to every possible reader. The same is true of the value of writing about the visual arts: it is not required that every essay or book be good or helpful or that each essay or book—or painting—be totally comprehensible to every possible reader or viewer. Written language provides access to a greater variety of materials; from greater distances geographically, culturally, intellectually, and psychologically; in greater depth and detail; and with greater

---

7. Clive Bell, *Art* (London: Chatto & Windus, 1913; reprint, New York: G. P. Putnam's Sons, 1958), 31–32.

speed and efficiency than would be possible without it. It enables and encourages scrutiny of one's own thoughts—half-baked, confused, or insightful as they may be, and however difficult they may be to express. It also enables one to scrutinize others' writings both as part of the process of formulating one's own thoughts and understanding what one does not believe, and as a collection of volumes of information providing a depth and scope otherwise unavailable. In short, it changes the very nature of what is possible to do in and with the visual arts.

Abilities to read and write are for good reason connected with ideas of agency and personal identity. They afford validity to the ideas and perspectives of the individuals who read and judge the writing of others, and make it more difficult for those who lack them to be contributors to those aspects of the cultural life of a community. Thus, a commitment to general literacy reinforces a political ideal advanced by democracy, that individual persons have worth as ends in themselves. In fact, widespread literacy would seem to be necessary to any political system where each citizen and the well-being of each citizen are considered to be of value. The connection between valuing each person and providing an education for that person is so strong that it justifies requiring for all children a certain level of education, which equips them with the intellectual tools they need to be informed citizens and effective participants in the community. For any society larger than, say, the typical city-state of ancient Greece, widespread literacy would require a technology that allows relatively fast and inexpensive printing of a text, such as Johannes Gutenberg's invention of movable type in the mid–fifteenth century. His invention in fact also created a market for paper and hence an incentive to develop the technology to produce large quantities inexpensively, which, in turn, made it available to artists, who were then able to produce and keep their own sketchbooks and practice drawings, which show development of a personal style.[8] For our own time, it is especially significant that literacy is presumed and promoted for people who are different in gender, race, ethnicity, and social class from those who have traditionally held the reins of power (or at least of the illusion of power).[9] Information is made available through writing about the relevant aspects of ethnic experience or gender identity, facilitating the entrenchment of the

8. See Francis Ames-Lewis, *Drawing in Early Renaissance Italy* (New Haven: Yale University Press, 1981), chap. 1.
9. It hardly needs saying that requirements and prohibitions with respect to speaking and writing a vernacular language have long been used to manipulate people for political purposes.

work, as well as the ideas about ethnicity and gender, in the common understanding.

Though we think of democracy as having had its origins in ancient Greece—and in many ways, for good and for ill, it has—the Greek-derived "demos" does not quite capture the idea of a person described above. "Demos" means "the people" conceived as (*a*) the common people, a social class, or (*b*) a political unit, a voting block. Neither meaning has embedded within it the idea that value is in principle attached to each person rather than the idea that each person, as a mere component of a collective, is to be treated as a unit, for example, worthy of representation at the political level. Some sophisticated technologies do presume a value for each person simply as a person because they are developed to help individual people, as opposed to the demos. Many medical technologies, for example, vastly increase the likelihood that a patient will recover from an illness or other medical disorder. Our society has invested and continues to invest huge amounts of money in scientific research, technological development and manufacturing, training of individuals to use the technology and to provide care during a recovery period, not to mention the real estate and edifices where these services are provided. Such institutions can become subcultures in themselves, so that their practices contribute to the survival and welfare of the institutions rather to than the well-being of the persons who are treated as patients. Theoretically, however, we justify an institution and its practices at least in part in terms of the benefits accorded individual persons. Indeed, it is a commonplace that the value of the individual is incommensurable with the costs of the technology: no price tag can be put on a human life.

Suppose we accept the democratic ideal that each individual person is valuable as an end in itself. General literacy supports and entrenches this ideal. Literacy expands one's capacity for comprehension and production of many things and hence enables one to fulfill one's potentialities to a greater degree.[10] General literacy also expands the roles for visual art by exploiting its potential for interpretations whose content and context are made accessi-

---

10. I use the term "potentialities" instead of the more familiar "potential" or "capacities" because I agree with Joseph Margolis that the powers we are talking about are not mere capacities to learn, for example, a particular language or other, but exist at a more abstract level. See Joseph Margolis, *What, After All, Is a Work of Art?* (University Park: Pennsylvania State University Press, 1999), chap. 2. Several points in this paper arise from my preparation for the session on Margolis's book at the annual meeting of the American Society for Aesthetics in Washington, D.C., October 1999. I thank John Carvalho for inviting me to participate in that session and Margolis and Carvalho for their contributions to it.

ble only through writing. As words proliferate, the visual arts become a specialist area of study. Intellectual or professional specialization occurs at least in part when knowledge and understanding, crucial to the profession, are recorded in writing, accessed through reading, and perpetuated through more writing. The visual arts have become part of the subject matter of various professions, that is, for those who write about the arts (art historians, critics, etc.) and those who write about the writing about the arts (especially art theorists and philosophers). The visual arts are experienced and thought about in terms of ideas and issues that are best explored in writing, altering in a profound way their relation to any would-be appreciator because of an assumption of literacy.

Part Three: Individual Identity and Its Relation to Culture

> I come from the country of Show Business.
> —Christopher Walken, *Inside the Actors Studio*

Many interpreters of visual works of art write about them as products of an individual's efforts, skills, training, practice, beliefs, and intentions—in short, as that individual's work. On such a view, the nature and value of an artwork is established by how an artificer forms its structure and content. As is well known, Dürer proclaimed his own status as a creator in painting himself as Christ, and, during the Italian Renaissance, works of some artists, such as Piero and Michelangelo, were highly valued because they were produced by those particular much-lauded individuals. To the extent that written interpretations themselves and theories of art and its interpretation use and exploit this network of ideas, they are agent-centered, with the agent in the cases mentioned conceived as the artist. Artist-centered interpretation has room for restrictions imposed by and opportunities provided by cultural and historical circumstances, but only as percolated through the psyche of the artist.

Consider the case of Gene Davis. Many years ago, working as a reporter but ready for a change of career, he happened to see a couple of Barnett Newman's "zip" paintings in a Washington, D.C., museum. Newman's paintings are concerned with volumes pressing from the sides against a void, reduced in these paintings to a narrow slip of space in the middle. Davis, however, saw the paintings as containing central vertical stripes. He went on to have a successful career for over thirty years as a painter of "stripe" paintings of various widths and coloration. This phenomenon, which I shall call "aberrant influence," seems to be a perfect example of how an artist's "intentions" can be conflicting in ways unknown to the artist, and hence problematic in relation to how to interpret a work of art as an artist's work. In Davis's case, he presumably conceived of himself, while painting stripes, as extending something that Newman had done.

In looking for other examples of "aberrant influence" in contemporary art, one quickly notices that it is virtually ubiquitous, much closer to being the norm than to being an occasional aberration. More important, these types of misunderstandings do not seem to matter. We grant painters this degree of autonomy and freedom. Painters can and do pick up imagery, forms, and designs from a wide variety of sources and use them in ways that are alien to their original context, even if that imagery and so forth had specific well-known, public meanings within it. Some artists trade on established meanings, grounding a practice of artist-centered interpretation in relation to them, a practice that also charitably ignores an artist's minor misunderstandings or declares them irrelevant. Surely it is unreasonable to encumber an artwork with all of the original meanings and references that adhere to an image or mode of expression or visual affinity that the artist did not have in mind. Michael Baxandall affirms an artist-centered approach when he critiques the overused terminology of "influence" as employed by art historians, "primarily because of its wrong-headed grammatical prejudice about who is the agent and who the patient; it seems to reverse the active/passive relation which the historical actor experiences and the inferential beholder will wish to take into account."[11] If we think of the artist as agent, he continues, "the vocabulary is much richer and more attractively diversified." Some of his suggestions, along with a few others, are to ridicule, draw on, parody, appropriate, refer to, deliberately ignore, copy, dismember, revive, reject, play with, obsess over, and turn inside out.

Nevertheless, we can hardly grant artists dictatorial authority over what their paintings mean. At a more abstract level, features of the visual-art world of Gene Davis's day, which he may or may not have internalized, made it possible for him to succeed as an artist in making paintings of the sort he did. Paintings with simple forms were accepted and displayed as art. For all practical purposes, that acceptance was historically unique within

---

11. *Patterns of Intention* (New Haven: Yale University Press, 1985), 58–59. Baxandall also discusses here how the artist is not always thought of as the agent.

the course of Western civilization, a fact that Davis did not need to know in order to benefit from it.

Human beings are social beings who live out their lives with the advantages and disadvantages of the particular historical and cultural matrices that constitute the context for our own actions and thought. There are at least two relatively uncontroversial respects in which culture and history can appear in written interpretations of art, and as substantive with respect to the ontological status of the artwork itself, without being presented as having been percolated through the psyche of the artist. First, a work may have a cultural significance the artist cannot know or understand, such as when a work, after its artist has died, acquires historical significance for reasons the artist would not have been able to anticipate.[12] Second, a work may have a cultural significance one cannot control, because its meaning is established as part of (or not as part of) a system of practices identified at the cultural level where the actions and attitudes of any one person are insufficient to negate their reality. People's actions and the character of the objects they make may reinforce attitudes and practices within a culture, for good or ill, whether or not one intends it or is even aware of it. I have used the term "de facto significance" to refer to cases where meaning is established at a cultural or historical level so that an artist's individual intentions and denials, knowledge or ignorance, are irrelevant to imbuing a work with that meaning.[13] Neither artists nor anyone else has the power to remove just anything one does or makes from the cultural milieu by sheer force of will or personal intent.

It is one thing for people to live their lives in cultures and histories they cannot control. It is another to say that each person's identity is constituted, at least in part, by culture and hence that no person has full agency or personhood. Joseph Margolis writes, "We ourselves . . . are 'artifacts' of cultural history: 'second-natured' selves, first formed . . . by acquiring, in infancy (as the gifted members of *Homo sapiens* that we are), the language and practice of our enculturing society."[14] We are affected by innumerable technological advances that contemporary life affords us, increasing our comfort level and providing for the enrichment of our lives, all the product

12. See Arthur C. Danto, *Narration and Knowledge* (New York: Columbia University Press, 1985), chap. VIII, "Narrative Sentences," 143–81.
13. "Feminist Art History and De Facto Significance," in *Feminism and Tradition in Aesthetics,* ed. Peggy Zeglin Brand and Carolyn Korsmeyer (University Park: Pennsylvania State University Press, 1995), 305–25.
14. Margolis, *What, After All, Is a Work of Art?* 35.

of some of that labor specialization discussed above. We are affected by cultural mores as they are exhibited to us through our own parents and others we encounter. We are affected by language and engage in "language behavior" before we have a clue what it is and what we are doing. "Language behavior," a phrase I have often enjoyed ridiculing as an example of behaviorism gone amok, in fact captures something important about the early years of human development. Margolis sees the commonalties shared by each person with others in the culture, such as language, as essential to one's identity as an individual. As he puts it, "Human selves are individuals only insofar as they effectively share the collective practices of a common *Lebensform*."[15]

"Collective practices" and "common *Lebensform*" are a bit ambiguous, and I worry they require a bit too much homogeneity within a cultural environment. Members of a culture or society need not participate in all of its defining practices, and it is unlikely that there is any one practice everyone must participate in. Perhaps all that is necessary is for any individual to engage in some significant subset of practices, one or more of which are fairly central, though none essential, to the identity of any given culture. Something like this seems to be Ivan Karp's view when he writes that society can be seen "as a constantly changing mosaic of multiple communities and organizations. Individual identities and experiences never derive entirely from single segments of society—from merely one of the communities out of which the complex and changing social order is made."[16]

Individual persons negotiate their way within a culture as participants in it, engaging in sufficiently substantial subsets of practices that work within that culture and various subcultures also comprising networks of practices. Personhood may well require that one has this social or cultural dimension as something like a background condition for identifying any individual who has agency, even when it is "a complex and changing order," as Karp describes it. Agency, however, also requires accepting and rejecting various practices, which in turn require options and reflection on various possibilities, not just among what is culturally approved but as resistance or even in opposition to prevailing cultural practices. Not every agent will be rebellious; one may choose to conform and participate in this or that tradition, or

15. *Historied Thought, Constructed World: A Conceptual Primer for the Turn of the Millennium* (Berkeley and Los Angeles: University of California Press, 1995), 237.
16. Ivan Karp, introduction to *Museums and Communities: The Politics of Public Culture,* ed. Ivan Karp, Christine Mullen Kreamer, and Steven D. Lavine (Washington, D.C.: Smithsonian Institution Press, 1992), 3.

not. We're born with genetic predispositions and quickly become culturally embedded, learning a language, engaging in cultural practices that we may continue or later reject, even looking for cultural roots when they played no role in our upbringing, or making a highly visible rejection of cultural practices when they did. It hardly needs saying that people are not interchangeable; we differ biologically and with respect to our susceptibility to various types of cultural influence. One may adopt what is in fact only a peripheral and occasional accompaniment of a cultural practice, making it central in a way no one else does.

Though Margolis holds that we are artifacts, he denies that we are constructed *entirely* by forces outside ourselves. Instead, he says that persons are culturally apt agents, "second-natured" selves. We are formed only *at first* by our enculturing society. We bring the aptitude to be influenced by other minds, qua minds, and cultural significance, qua culture, with us into the world, and this aptitude, however it is instantiated in human beings, makes us more or less susceptible to influences at the abstract linguistic and cultural levels. It is an ontologically significant aspect of who we are. "[A] newborn child," Margolis writes, "can have learned any language as its own language if it can have learned the language it eventually acquires. And yet, at the point of mature competence, everyone is aware of the deep uncertainty of understanding the speech and behavior of others belonging to the same culture as well as to another culture."[17] If we understand what we do or create in terms of our cultural opportunities and constraints, abstracting over individuals (perhaps in the form of the demos), we lose the sense of agency that involves the knowledge and intentions of each person. For that, one must turn to the second-natured self.

Consider the case of an art historian who wishes to compare Ganesha figures made of painted, hardened but unfired clay, carried in religious processionals, with those made of stone or bronze that are located in Hindu temples in India and in art museums in the United States. Many groups of people speaking different dialects of Hindi participate in their own ceremonials, and there is no spelling (or pronunciation) for Ganesha common to them all. Sanskrit, the traditional language of scholars, is an ancient language no longer spoken and is perhaps for that reason appropriate when describing the bronze or stone figures as having a kind of timeless value. Yet, for that very same reason, Sanskrit is inappropriate for describing a disposable item used during a ceremony involving the general public.

17. Margolis, *What, After All, Is a Work of Art?* 41.

We should not assume that it is or is not appropriate to use the same term to refer to the two representations of Ganesha in the first place.[18] One could ignore the problem entirely by writing in English; indeed, unless one had been immersed in the culture to some extent, one would probably not even know there was a linguistic issue to be settled. Interestingly, to fill the need, contemporary researchers have concocted their own terms for the purpose, a kind of academic Esperanto of words not found in any natural language but similar to many. Those of us who come from the country of academe produce words for a living; that is one way we participate in the construction of our own culture. You know the joke: a scholar is a library's way of making another library.

Many of the decisions we make as responsible adults require reflection and choice and as such display similarities that arise from what human beings have in common despite extensive cultural differences. Thus, to the extent that our personal identity is defined by our second-natured selves, we may become more, rather than less, comprehensible as individuals. Consider one more example of how one can take advantage of an opportunity to exercise a linguistic choice that reflects a sense of one's own identity, only this time in an oral, rather than written, context. A sociologist colleague spent several years studying the changing social structures in the Southeast Asian community in Garden City, Kansas, in the western part of the state, where recent immigrants worked in the slaughterhouses and meatpacking plants. His assistant was a young Vietnamese woman who was the recipient of unwanted romantic attentions from a somewhat older and persistent Vietnamese male. When speaking to him in Vietnamese on the phone one day, she abruptly shifted into English. Why? In Vietnamese, there is no status-neutral term for "you," and, being both younger and female, there was no second-person-singular way to address him that did not embody an assumption that he had a social status superior to her own. She chose to use the resources of the English language available to her to define herself in a way not available in her first language.[19]

Some people identify themselves in ways that have been described, with some disparagement, as "hyphenated Americans": African-Americans, Mexican-Americans, Chinese-Americans, and so on.[20] Hyphenation recognizes and legitimates practices arising out of ethnic heritages that exclude

18. The example is from Vidya Murthy.
19. The example is from Kenneth Erickson.
20. In practice, one finds that some hyphenations, as in "Irish-Americans" or "Italian-Americans," are more acceptable than others.

those who have traditionally defined American culture. The continued use of the unqualified term "Americans," however, reinforces the idea of a homogeneous political and cultural identity. Similarly, the concept of the melting pot serves conservative social and political forces because the critical mass required to change its flavor must itself be relatively large. Human beings have rarely done a good job of harmonizing political, national, and ethnic identities in a way that doesn't simply remove differences. Perhaps a more appropriate culinary metaphor for contemporary American life, one that does not melt cultural differences into a homogeneous soup, is that of a tossed salad, which at least accommodates the complexity and variability of the identities of cultures, and especially of persons as agents who choose to identify themselves in a given way.[21]

From a first-person perspective, one assumes responsibility for something, including what one does and what one makes. "Assumes" is a particularly appropriate word to use here, because it allows one to skirt the thicket of debates about whether there really is free will, while recognizing that human beings, nevertheless, have to make decisions about how to act. From a third-person perspective, one holds persons responsible for their actions and does not allow them to avoid responsibility by claiming to be helpless victims of insuperable forces, whether from nature or culture, past experiences or unreasonable hopes for the future. Given the lack of any adequate analysis of what free will is, I suspect that the concept would not play the major role it does in the general scheme of things if we did not have first-person experiences of conflict in the face of a need to make decisions about how to act. This conflict exists at the moral level, in one's choice of actions, and at the epistemic level, in one's choice of what to believe, and at the aesthetic level, in one's choice of how to identify and interpret a work of art. I have been suggesting that, in the cases of transportation of artifacts across cultural boundaries of the sort describe above, it is best to retain the tension in the identity and interpretation of the artifact as art, or not, because that tension may constitute the most important aspect of its identity.

Susan Sontag remarks in her justly famous essay *Against Interpretation* that "interpretation is the revenge of the intellect upon art."[22] She wanted a brute experience to connect her with the world, though she also recognized

21. The term "tossed salad" was advocated by Richard McKinzie.
22. *Against Interpretation* (New York: Dell, 1961/1966), 7. In fairness, I should point out that Sontag relativized her claim to the value of interpretation *at that time,* which she characterized as suffering from "hypertrophy of the intellect at the expense of energy and sensual capabilities."

that once interpretation is pursued because of one's inability to see, it is not possible to return to the innocence of a pure, unmediated experience of an image, a painting, a work of art. That innocence was a fiction to begin with, of course; the relevant questions are about what mediations are appropriate and why. Physical objects acquire and lose meaning and significance as they enter and exit various cultures through time. A painting first formed and used as a visual representation of religious ideas may be bought, removed from its original site, and then displayed by people over five centuries later for having properties its new owners revere. To the extent that one's own literacy as part of general literacy is an aspect of our first-formed self we cannot remove, paintings from eras of general illiteracy have a significance that is virtually inaccessible. Interpretation produced through scrutiny and self-reflection, written and legible to the general public, does not destroy a visual work of art any more than a person's inventing a new word or using a word from a language of which one is not a native speaker destroys that person. General literacy provides a cultural environment where numerous interpretive practices flourish. These practices reveal the potentialities of paintings and sculptures that are as deep and complicated as people have come to show themselves to be, in part because we engage in such practices.

Wittgenstein and the Question of True Self-Interpretation

Garry L. Hagberg

Many find, I believe, that the intuitive plausibility of the doctrine that has been aptly termed interpretive multiplism,[1] that is, the belief that there can be more than one ideally admissible interpretation of a cultural entity, tends to expand when we are talking about others and to diminish when we are talking about ourselves. The reasons for this asymmetry in our pre-analytical intuitions are complex and extend into the philosophy of mind, the philosophy of language, and—most fundamentally—the vexing question concerning the nature of selfhood. Although it is impossible to cover all these areas at once, here I try to show some of the significance of Wittgenstein's writings on mind and language as they pertain to the self, and particularly to reconsider, in the light of Wittgenstein's remarks, not only the puzzle of true self-interpretation but also the metaphysical-linguistic presuppositions that are too often embedded within that puzzle's very formulation. The task at hand will thus entail a close reading of those remarks of Wittgenstein's most pertinent to this particular topic—and the remarks perhaps too little considered both within Wittgenstein scholarship and be-

---

1. Michael Krausz, *Rightness and Reasons: Interpretation in Cultural Practices* (Ithaca, N.Y.: Cornell University Press, 1993); see esp. chap. 2, "Cultural Practices and the Ideals of Interpretation: Singularism and Multiplism," 38–65.

yond—that concern not just the nature of linguistic meaning and especially the nature of, as speakers, our knowledge of that meaning, but more precisely the nature of *retrospective* meaning, that is, the very distinct nature of our knowledge, not just of what we mean, but of what we—from a position of hindsight (or, more accurately, a position of the future *vis-à-vis* that now-past language)—*meant*. And the task at hand will entail a look into some actual practices of self-interpretation (it was of course Wittgenstein who was most concerned among philosophers of language that we turn to our practices to counterbalance the impulse to theorize); here we return, if only briefly, to the author of the most influential and most philosophically sustained piece of self-interpretation. Indeed, passages of Augustine's *Confessions*[2] will prove as conceptually intricate, if in a rather different way, as Wittgenstein's: in some cases they will show the misleading power of the presuppositions regarding meaning in autobiographical understanding; in others they will show a mind beginning to break free from its own misleading metaphysical self-concept. But first things first: what can we say at present about the sources of the intuitive belief that interpretive singularism is the most plausible position with regard to self-knowledge?

First-person privileged access is of course a metaphysical picture of the self that has been, deservedly, subjected to a good deal of critical scrutiny. The philosophical picture of the mind, introspecting upon inwardly and directly observable contents to which it alone has direct access, is the problematic legacy of Cartesianism, and its immediate analogue in the philosophy of language is not difficult to identify: we, as speakers, have inwardly and directly observable access to the contents, indeed—as this pernicious picture of language unfolds—access to the meaning of our utterances. This dualistic picture of the mind and of language, as stated, is now defended by very few; the overt enfilades of Ryle,[3] and the undercover work of Wittgenstein in meetings with his inner interlocutor,[4] changed—one hopes forever—the reception of this picture. But, despite this, its influence, or its residue, continues to be detectable;[5] my point is of course that it is discern-

2. Saint Augustine, *Confessions,* trans. R. S. Pine-Coffin (Harmondsworth, Middlesex: Penguin, 1961). References to this work will be given parenthetically in the text.

3. Gilbert Ryle, *The Concept of Mind* (London: Hutchinson, 1949).

4. For an insightful study of Wittgenstein's employment of various voices within *Philosophical Investigations,* see Jane Heal, "Wittgenstein and Dialogue," in *Philosophical Dialogues: Plato, Hume, Wittgenstein,* ed. T. Smiley (Oxford: Oxford University Press; British Academy, 1995), 63–83.

5. This claim is made by many of those working inside the Wittgensteinian tradition but also by those outside of it. See, for example, Donald Davidson, "Knowing One's Own Mind," in *Self-Knowledge,* ed. Quassim Cassam (Oxford: Oxford University Press, 1994), 43–64:

ible in the intuitively plausible asymmetry between our self-interpretive singularism, our first-person belief in a single and ideally correct answer to any
question of self-knowledge (here particularly *linguistic* self-knowledge, that
is, knowledge of what we meant—and, equally important, of what we did
not mean—on a given past occasion), and the multiplism we may accept
with regard to the interpretations of others. It is the die-hard idea of privileged access at work (as it so often is in philosophical problems of selfhood)
behind the scenes, shaping our conception of introspection here, and that
die-hard idea exerts its influence in its presence and, perhaps less obviously
but no less significantly, in its absence, its denial. How so, precisely?

When facing the problem of true self-interpretation, three options readily
present themselves to any reasonably categorically tidy mind. First, we
might argue that there is, in any question concerning what we did and did
not mean, a determinate interior mental event and that the truth of the
matter just is a direct correspondence to this. And—crucially—it is here
thought that we can know the determinate mental event of having meant
one thing and not another (or a number of others, as multiplism as applied
to linguistic meaning would have it) via direct introspection: we have this
in mind when we utter the interpreted language, and we—with unique access—accurately recall having had it in mind when we later give the single
correct interpretation of our original meaning. This, as the first categorical
option, shows the influence of the dualistic-introspectionist picture of the
mind through its robust presence: the picture is intact, and one is affirming
direct and privileged access.

Second, we might argue that, while it is true that there is or was a determinate mental event that constituted the true meaning of our questioned
utterance, in fact we do not have direct introspective access to it (as Freudians of a linguistic persuasion might argue), so we must face (and overcome
through depth analysis for the Freudians) a distinctive variety of skepticism
here: we know that there is or was such a determinate interior event constituting the meaning, but we also know that we cannot (at least directly or
without a protracted and unguaranteed effort at self-interpretation) know
it. This shows the influence of the Cartesian-introspectionist picture of the
mind and language through a muted presence: the dualistic picture is intact,
but one is denying direct privileged access.

"There is a picture of the mind which has become so ingrained in our philosophical tradition
that it is almost impossible to escape its influence even when its worst faults are recognized
and repudiated" (61).

The third option is not, of course, the absurd claim that we can know a determinate inner mental event that is not there, but rather the claim that the inner determinate event is not there and thus that there is no possibility of our knowing it. Here, as an old-fashioned behaviorist might put the matter, there is no possibility of truth-as-correspondence-to-inner-facts precisely because there are no inner facts to which our interpretation might correspond. It is in this case that the dualistic-introspectionist picture shows its influence through its absence: the *underlying structure* of the picture is intact, and it is only reinforced in the denial of the inner determinate meaning-event. The robust introspectionist, the skeptical introspectionist, and the behaviorist all share the structure, the fundamental, presupposed, structure of the question of self-interpretation. But a fourth option, a thoroughgoing rejection of the very conceptual structure of this question, might now seem an interesting possibility—from that perspective we might indeed be able to contemplate our autobiographically interpretive practices without the prismatic distortion of theory. But this cannot be stated directly or succinctly: how would we formulate, with only the minimal tools before us, the question of true self-interpretation in a way free of the dualistic-introspectionist picture? And how could we describe the significance of looking both to the details of retrospective meaning and to autobiographical practices *before* the fact? Perhaps there is a kind of true self-interpretation not envisioned by, or envisionable within, these foregoing categories, and that may be one way of briefly characterizing what a close look into Wittgenstein's relevant remarks allows. If self-interpretive singularism has a lingering plausibility, this plausibility depends on our belief that, after all and regardless of what else is said, we (1) mean determinate things when we speak and (2) we must in some way know what it is that we mean. If those two elements are true, then—so we are strongly inclined (for reasons I've hinted at) to believe—there is a *right* answer to any question concerning what we did and did not mean. But how should that particular form of rightness be characterized? With that question, along with the foregoing introductory considerations, in mind, let us turn, in Sections I and II, to Wittgenstein on meaning, then, in Section III, to Augustine on self-interpretation, and finally, in conclusion, to a reconsideration of the embedded presumption within these introductory questions.

I. Meaning in Retrospect

Guessing at how a word functions, Wittgenstein has said and shown, will not yield valuable philosophical results. The necessary task, as he made clear, is to "*look* at its use and learn from that" (*Philosophical Investigations,*[6] § 340). It is evident that a vast repository of usage of philosophically troublesome, and indeed sometimes troubling, concepts such as the self, indeed what he called the mysterious "I," is to be found in literature (particularly of an autobiographical or semiautobiographical kind); the traditional categorization of some literature as *philosophical* literature[7] implicitly acknowledges this fact. But Wittgenstein's next remark, immediately following the foregoing assertion, concerns *prejudice,* specifically the prejudice that stands in the way of taking his philosophical advice, of looking—with the right background, interests, focus, and frame of mind. And this prejudice, or these conspiring prejudices, are, as he said, "not *stupid,*" and the philosophical difficulty lies in removing them. Wittgenstein made this remark in the context of his investigation into the question "What is thinking?" but he might have placed it with equal aptness in his discussion, at the very end of part I of *Philosophical Investigations* (but also pursued throughout his other writings),[8] of what it is—and what it is not—to *mean something.* For it is precisely the deeply seated belief, or again the pre-analytical intuition, that the mental phenomenon of meaning something not only underwrites self-interpretive singularism but also requires, or indeed proves, the prior existence of an inner point of consciousness, an inner (and again we might characterize it as a Cartesian) self that is the private place within which the act, state, or process of meaning something occurs.

Wittgenstein's investigation into this phenomenon in at least one very clear sense runs exactly parallel to his investigation of thinking itself: meaning something is, on examination, found not to be at all what we expected when coming to the subject with certain philosophical presuppositions, and the subject does not reduce to a single uniform mental act, process, or state. He finds, here too, various phenomena, not a phenomenon, and—de-psychologizing this subject as well[9]—he says they are not *mental* in the way we

6. *Philosophical Investigations,* 3d ed., trans. G. E. M. Anscombe (New York: Macmillan, 1953).

7. See, for example, the studies of *Middlemarch, Anna Karenina, The Brothers Karamazov,* and *Remembrance of Things Past,* in Peter Jones, *Philosophy and the Novel* (Oxford: Clarendon Press, 1975).

8. It is, instructively, impossible to list *all* of the passages devoted to the analysis of meaning throughout Wittgenstein's writings, precisely because the multidimensional nature of the topic—extending not only into explicitly linguistic investigations but also into privacy, intention, rule following, mental states, images, aspect perception, memory, and so forth through an indeterminate list—gives it a highly mobile boundary. Thus what is and is not relevant to the study, or the elucidation, of meaning within Wittgenstein's writings is determined (appropriately and as an illustration of its own larger message) by the context of the specific inquiry.

9. I have discussed broadly parallel "de-psychologizing" aspects of Wittgenstein's work in "The Self, Reflected: Wittgenstein, Cavell, and the Autobiographical Situation," in *Ordinary-*

might have expected. And this result, I want to suggest, pertains quite directly to our understanding of the nature of the self (although Wittgenstein did not draw this out explicitly either, and in this way too it runs parallel to the discussion of thinking) and removes one of the central prejudices against seeing the concept of the self perspicuously, which is, naturally, a precondition for correctly understanding the very question of self-interpretation. But there remains, of course, the possibility that the belief in the inner-self-as-necessary-location-of-meaning-something is *not* a prejudice, but instead is accurate; as we follow Wittgenstein's discussion, it will become clear that, along with his project of the de-psychologizing of our understanding of what it is to mean something, he retains a respect for first-person authority with regard to meaning something. In short, we find Wittgenstein taking a "middle way" between Cartesianism and its polemical partner, behaviorism; Wittgenstein's discussion escapes the misleading influences of the former without reducing the subject to the latter.

The first thought that might well strike us when reflecting on the experience of meaning something is, as indicated briefly above, that we can easily *remember* having meant something, and this memory gives us the content upon which to introspect. Again, it is by now no secret that this is already a heavily freighted—a *metaphysically* freighted—way of framing the issue; Wittgenstein thus starts at precisely this point. In *Philosophical Investigations*, § 661, he asks, in remembering having meant *him*, if we are thereby "remembering a process or state?" This is enough at least to unsettle the initial presumption that meaning something is a distinct mental process individuated within consciousness, and implicitly challenging this individuation, he follows it with the more pause-giving question "When did it begin, what was its course, etc.?" Is, indeed, meaning something the *kind* of thing that *has* a course? If a process, it seems that it should. But there must be, or so we are strongly inclined to think, a process or mental act that constitutes our meaning something; what else could constitute this? Against this intuitive sense (where this intuitive sense is itself caused by an unwitting subscription to an underlying philosophical picture) Wittgenstein asks us, in §

Language Criticism: Literary Thinking After Cavell After Wittgenstein, ed. K. Dauber and W. Jost (forthcoming); "The Self, Thinking: Wittgenstein, Augustine, and the Autobiographical Situation," in *Wittgenstein, Philosophy, and the Arts*, ed. P. Lewis (forthcoming); and "The Self, Speaking: Wittgenstein, Introspective Utterances, and the Arts of Self-Representation," in *Revue Internationale de Philosophie*, ed. Jean-Pierre Cometti (forthcoming). For a fine guide to the Fregean work that stands behind Wittgenstein's de-psychologizing projects, see Anthony Kenny, *Frege* (London: Penguin, 1995).

675, to imagine asking or being asked the question "what was going on in you when you uttered the words . . . ?" and adds, pointedly, that the "answer to this is not: 'I was meaning . . .'!" A statement about what one meant by a word, he tells us shortly (§ 676), is not equivalent to a statement about "an affection of the mind." It takes little reflection to see that Wittgenstein's points here are sound: we do not answer questions concerning what we meant in saying X, or what was going on in our heads when we said X, by "reporting" on inner processes—which in turn we find we are not anyway able to describe in terms of their beginnings, courses, and so forth.

But are these points compelling in any larger sense, beyond what appears to be their extremely limited scope? It seems not; that is, they are certainly not sufficient to dislodge the presumption, intuition, or belief that the Cartesian inner self is nevertheless behind, or required by, meaning something, precisely because we might well continue to hold that, despite how we would or would not answer such questions, we still mentally picture the person or thing we mean and that such a mental envisagement is precisely what "meaning something" amounts to, is constituted by. But Wittgenstein has a ready answer here: "If I say 'I meant *him*' very likely a picture comes to my mind . . . but the picture is only like an illustration to a story." And from the mental picture *alone,* or from being told of the existence of such a mental picture, it would, one can quite readily see, prove mostly "impossible to conclude anything at all," for only when one already knows the story that the picture illustrates, only when one is in a position to apprehend "the significance of the picture," would one be able to posit the picture as the content of that which was meant—which is of course the wrong way around. Such a mental picture should *constitute* the act of meaning something, not *follow* it, if the explanation is to have force. Still, this issue too seems preliminary; even if the mental act of producing mental pictures is much more problematic than we might initially have thought in giving content to the phrase "meaning something," does this really uproot the conception of the self behind it?

One might well insist that the matter of meaning something is in fact reducible to its essence and that this essence, most fundamentally, is a matter of *stipulation.* "Meaning something" is, one might argue, less mysterious than it is beginning to look; "by *this* I meant *that*" is as far as we need to go, and this ensures a correct—indeed *the* correct—answer to any question concerning what we really meant. But Wittgenstein worked extensively on the ordering and reordering of the entries that make up *Philosophical Investigations,* and it seems clear that this labor was often undertaken in order to capture, and to anticipate, the natural moves, the natural sequential un-foldings, of philosophical thought. It is thus not surprising that we find his well-known "abracadabra" section next (*Philosophical Investigations,* § 665):

> Imagine someone pointing to his cheek with an expression of pain and saying "abracadabra!"—We ask "What do you mean?" And he answers "I meant toothache."—You at once think to yourself: How can one "mean toothache" by that word? What did it *mean* to *mean* pain by that word? And yet, in a different context, you would have asserted that the mental activity of *meaning* such-and-such was just what was most important in using language.
>
> But—can't I say "By 'abracadabra' I mean toothache?" Of course I can; but this is a definition; not a description of what goes on in me when I utter the word.

This section tracks a number of important shifts or movements of thought on this matter. First, it gives voice to the strong impulse to posit *stipulation* as the essence of meaning; the speaker shows this by saying and then briefly explaining his having said "abracadabra." Second, the strong competing intuition *against* stipulation as the content of meaning something is recorded next; when we are shown in an actual example what we might endorse in the abstract, that is, pure stipulation, we react with a feeling of deep implausibility: *that* couldn't possibly go very far in explaining what it is *actually,* or indeed *ordinarily,* to mean something. Third, one wonders if the stipulation thesis, as shown to us here, even makes sense: what does it *mean* to mean that? Significantly, here we find yet another argumentative thread that is powerful but left unexpressed, or only implicit, by Witt-genstein: "Meaning something" is precisely what is in question, and we might try—successfully or otherwise, as we have just seen in the second stage of this section—to explain it by stipulation. But then *that* stipulation, as we see, goes unexplained ("what does it *mean* to *mean* pain by that word?"), and thus we have at least the hovering threat, if not the grounded reality, of an infinite-regress problem in regard to stipulation. Yet, fourth, we find a reconsideration from the vantage point of the concrete case of what we may have posited in the abstract; "in a different context" we would indeed have asserted the mental act of meaning something as the essence of the matter. In fact, at this fourth stage of movement, one seems to uncover again the seemingly inextinguishable plausibility of the stipulation thesis: can't we now just say we mean "toothache" by "abracadabra"?

And here, as the fifth and most important step, we see the *coup de grâce* to the stipulation thesis as an explanation, not of a momentary *encoding* of meaning, that is, determining momentarily to mean one word by another, but of the countless ordinary cases of meaning something: we *can* mean "toothache" by "abracadabra," but this is a definition and not, most significantly, a description of the inner mental act, state, or process that occurs when we utter a word and mean something by it. Advancing mystery is the one thing that *is* clear at this stage: in regard to a mental event that allegedly constitutes "meaning something," the matter is becoming increasingly mysterious. That which initially seemed obvious now looks implausible, and any thesis enjoying newly revived plausibility fails on closer inspection to provide the explanation we need. The truth of the claim we saw at the outset, that is, that a statement "I meant this by that word" is fundamentally different in *kind* from a statement "about an affection of the mind," is becoming ever more evident. Still, Wittgenstein has not yet given us enough to relinquish the presumption, which, despite what has been said, at least *in the abstract* seems unavoidable in giving an account of what it is to mean something, namely, that there is some kind of mental object to which we give our inward attention when meaning something in particular.

II. The Pain and the Piano

It must be with this sense of obviousness—a sense that is about to be unsettled along with the preceding cases—that Wittgenstein initiates the next part of the discussion by asking us to imagine that we are in pain while simultaneously hearing a piano nearby being tuned (*Philosophical Investigations*, § 666). In such a case, he reminds us of the obvious fact that it makes a great difference if, in saying "it'll soon stop," we mean the pain or the tuning. But he brings in this contrast in order more finely to focus the question "but what does this difference consist in?" He admits—and here the admission suggests that the philosophical presumption we naturally bring to such a case can be at least in part right—that in many cases a directing of the attention corresponds to meaning one thing or the other; interestingly, he likens this to a case of nonperniciously construed introspection, where a particular way of shutting one's eyes might be called "looking into one's self." But the argument, brought out in the following section, is that, while there may (just as there may not) be correspondence to a particular directing of the attention, such a correspondence does not in itself prove either necessary or sufficient for meaning something. First, one can perfectly well *mean* pain in saying "It'll get better soon" and yet be faking it; that the pain is simulated does not preclude the meaning of pain in saying that. One may say (reducing to the vanishing point the "object" of pain to which one is allegedly directing one's attention and which thus allegedly determines the content of "meaning something" in this case) "It's stopped now" and yet still perfectly well mean pain. One means pain, yet one is not—indeed one *could* not—be "concentrating his attention on any pain." And there is the parallel point in the honest case; if one genuinely has pain and then says "It has stopped now," one means something without the inner referent.[10] Moreover (and Wittgenstein adds this a bit later, in § 674), does one use the locus of attention and the strength of that attention as criteria for what we meant? Does one say, consistent with this thesis, "I didn't really mean my pain just now; my mind wasn't on it enough for that"? Or do we ask ourselves what we meant by the words "It'll stop soon" *because* our attention was divided between the pain and the piano? Wittgenstein admits that there can be a corresponding focusing of the attention, but that is never going to provide the essence of "meaning something."

Wittgenstein offers, not surprisingly, a partial diagnosis of the condition of believing that *some* kind of pointing, in this case through directed attention, is necessary for meaning something; the diagnosis is familiar. While believing, or clinging at some conscious or other level to the intuition, that ostensive definition is the essential element of meaning (Wittgenstein does not articulate this in the present discussion, but it seems indisputably implicit at this point), one might observe that it is possible to "refer to an object when speaking by pointing to it" (*Philosophical Investigations,* § 669). In such a case pointing is simply and unproblematically a part of the language-game.[11] But upon this base of incorporating verbal, behavioral, and intentional aspects, we then construct the analogy to the inner

10. This way of putting the matter, that is, positing an "inner referent," opens the way into the private-language argument (which is beyond the scope of my discussion here) and is, as stated, a conceptually dangerous formulation in that it could reinforce the very inner/outer dualistic picture that is being challenged by Wittgenstein's reflections.

11. In *Meaning and Interpretation: Wittgenstein, Henry James, and Literary Knowledge* (Ithaca, N.Y.: Cornell University Press, 1994), 9–44, I have discussed the concept of the language-game as it is developed in Wittgenstein's later thought.

case, that is, "And now it seems to us as if one spoke *of* a sensation by directing one's attention to it." But, to encapsulate what follows, the analogy from the outer to the inner case is hardly sound. Again, one *can* direct one's looking or listening to a particular thing, and this *can* constitute meaning when the particular move of focusing attention in this way as a form of meaning something is legitimated within the circumscribed language-game. But this is *in*essential; in telephoning someone to say "This table is too small" we may indeed point to the table as we speak. But the meaning is hardly *dependent* upon that; moreover, the hearer can obviously understand without witnessing either the physical pointing or any imagined inward directing of the speaker's attention as mental pointing. The analogy is not only unsound; it is here again misleading, in its power to establish conceptual expectations that need not in truth be fulfilled.

Wittgenstein considers the cases in which we ask if someone really meant what was said, for example, "When you were swearing just now, did you really mean it?" (§ 667), and this, he implicitly suggests, often does not concern "meaning something" centrally in the way that it appears to do. Thus it may be asking, rather, "Were you really angry?" Here again he invokes the innocent (i.e., non-Cartesian) conception of introspection, saying that the answer given to such cases is often a result of *this* kind of introspective reconsideration. And such answers fall along a wide spectrum: the examples offered include "I didn't mean it very seriously," "I meant it half-jokingly," and so forth. Similarly, and instructively (since the capacity to mean something is not literally halved in such cases; we still mean, if in a less unitary, or a less committed, way), we can say "I was half thinking of him when I said that."

That discussion leads directly to another vitally important section of *Philosophical Investigations,* in which again a layered or multistaged sequence of thought unfolds (§ 678): "What does this act of meaning (the pain, or the piano-tuning) consist in? No answer comes—for the answers which at first sight suggest themselves are of no use.—'And yet at the time I *meant* the one thing and not the other.' Yes,—now you have only repeated with emphasis something which no one has contradicted anyway." Here, first, the fundamental impulse to locate the essential mental act of meaning something is again given voice. This impulse is *very* hard to quiet, not only for the reasons thus far discussed but also because the impulse, or the insistence, seems to protect the conceptually linked notion of the inner self from being reduced out of existence by a thoroughgoing behavioristic account; it protects against the sense of loss that any such reductive or eliminative account brings in its wake. And because the phrase "meaning something" is after all widely used, and indeed a universal experience, *must* there not be something determinate in which this meaning something consists? Do we not, to reframe the matter in recursive terms, mean something when we use the phrase "mean something"? (Recall Wittgenstein's preceding question, "What does it *mean* to *mean* this?") But, second, now that we have followed Wittgenstein's argument to this point, he observes a new condition or reflective state, a new movement of thought: "No answer comes."

Well, of course answers do come—or rather they have. The various construals of meaning something we have seen thus far include (1) an easily remembered process or state, (2) a process that follows a course and upon which we can report, that is, an "affection of the mind," (3) a mental picture constituting the something we mean, (4) an act of stipulation, (5) a focused directing of inward attention on the inward referent upon which we concentrate, (6) an act of "pointing" analogous to pointing, and subsuming all the previous, (7) the essence of, the necessary and sufficient condition required by, the words "meaning something"—and they all fail; even though they all quite naturally suggest themselves in this problem area, they "are of no use." Yet there again comes a third, contrasting movement of thought, manifesting the irrepressible sense that there simply must be such an answer and that it is implicitly voiced within the explicit claim "And yet at the time I meant the one thing and not the other." This is indeed the case, but the matter is not dropped here by an author most concerned to examine human practices, to "look and see," precisely because, while he may want to "leave the world alone," he most assuredly does not want to leave our *thought,* our thinking about that world, alone.[12]

And the problem, as we see in the fourth stage of this section, is not with the simple truth that we meant one thing and not another, but with our *construal* of that truth. In saying "Yes,—now you have only repeated with emphasis" a claim that not a single element of what you have said thus far repudiates, we see that it is possible to retain the simple and undeniable truth of our meaning something while jettisoning all seven of these various misconstruals or attempts to reduce the phenomenon in question to a formula or mentalistic essence. What is thus striking about the fourth stage of *Philosophical Investigations,* § 678, is that we are left with a sense that meaning something, as a human practice that occurs inside of given lan-

---

12. For a searching discussion of this issue in Wittgenstein's philosophy, see Jonathan Lear, "On Leaving the World Alone," *Journal of Philosophy* 79 (July 1982): 382–403.

guage-games, is going to be clarified, or indeed *is* being clarified, through a layered process of confusion removal. This section, like so many before it, offers instructions in what *not* to think, but it also at this stage seems to promise a positive aspect—a clear view of the practice as it lies before us. And with this it reinforces the sense that there may be no answer, *of the kind for which we have been looking,* to the question "What does this act of meaning consist in?" And if there is no such answer *of this kind,* then the conceptual foundations undergirding our intuitive belief in self-interpretive singularism are seriously destabilized. Indeed, in this case of meaning something, just as in the case with the question "What is thinking?" there may be only a different *kind* of answer, an answer—or a distinctive conceptual satisfaction—that is, again, the result of having obtained a perspicuous overview of the matter. And that is precisely the kind of satisfaction available from philosophical-literary and -artistic interpretation. But to the point at hand, we want to ask how exactly Wittgenstein follows up this fourth stage: how does he further isolate and illuminate the phenomenon of meaning something, from which he has already carefully removed veils of misconstrual?

The next topic that we encounter is that of the *connection* between the "meaning" and the "something," that is, the mental connection that seemingly must link the mind of the speaker to the object, or thing, meant. Here too, as one can now predict, we see a seemingly inevitable philosophical presumption quickly unraveled. Noting that we do not ask of a speaker who has been cursing someone if the speaker is sure he cursed "*him,* that the connexion with him was established" (§ 681), Wittgenstein then gives voice to what he will shortly identify as the mistake of proceeding from this observation to the belief that the connection is thus "very easy to establish, if one can be so sure of it!" But that is, he suggests, to presume too much. To return briefly to the case of the piano and the pain, in saying that one was thinking of the piano, one is not thereby committed to saying that one thus had to *observe* that such a connection existed. And indeed—although here Wittgenstein's discussion is quite incomplete and can leave one with the mistaken impression that he is claiming that this might well *always* be the case—one can make the connection retroactively, a connection that did not at the time of speaking exist. Wittgenstein wants *not* to choose between (1) saying that such retrospective answers with regard to what one meant in a past utterance observe a preexisting connection or (2) that such retrospective answers create a connection that did not theretofore exist. He says, simply (§ 682), "Can't I say *both?* If what he said was true, didn't the connexion exist—and is he not for all that making one which did not exist?" This, it must be said even by someone largely sympathetic with Wittgenstein's philosophical undertakings, seems either strange, equivocating, self-contradictory, clearly erroneous, or all four.

The problem, as becomes increasingly clear through these final sections, is with the way in which the question is framed, particularly with its smuggled presumptions. *Given* that the idea is in place of a connection's being a mental linkage that somehow reaches out from mind to object, Wittgenstein wants to say "both"—although he might with greater help to his reader have said, more directly, "neither." What he does in the following passages is thus wholly to reconstrue the very concept of the connection. One strategy for making this reconstrual convincing (and he is up against the dead weight of deeply entrenched Cartesian or mentalistic presuppositions) is to show that we often take such retrospective answers with regard to past meaning *not* as reports on mental linkages but as hypotheticals concerning what *would* have been said had particular further questions been asked at the time of the initial utterance. "They say, for example, that I *should have* given a particular answer then, if I had been asked" (§ 684). But, even though this "does say something about the past," it is "only conditional"— thus weakening (or beginning to shift the great weight of) the sense that the mental connection must be there initially. This point is amplified in the following examples, particularly where it is observed that where we give someone an arithmetic rule for the expansion of a series, it will be correct to say in response to a question, for example, "Yes, I meant you to continue the series beyond 100," and yet the speaker, the giver of the rule, may have thought *no such thing*. Thus, highly significantly, the criterion for the truth of a claim concerning what speaker X meant will not invariably refer to the events in the mind of the speaker.[13] Some connection exists—he did after all mean something and not nothing or not just anything—yet it cannot be of the kind envisaged in the philosophical presumption behind the framing of

13. It is perhaps worth noting that the application of this point—that is, that the criterion for the truth of a retrospective-meaning assertion will not invariably be provided by events in the speaker's mind—to the arts of self-revelation, for example, autobiography, autobiographical fiction, and self-portraiture, instructively blurs the line between historical fidelity or accuracy and revisionism in self-description. This may suggest that there stretches a continuum of intermediate cases between the much-debated polar extremes of *ex post facto* objective accuracy and (relativistic) revisionism and that, if we are sufficiently attentive to the nuances of retrospective meaning, we will see that we are not forced to choose between these polarized or oppositional positions. On the value of considering such intermediate cases, see *Philosophical Investigations*, § 122.

the question. "Is it correct for someone to say: 'When I give you this rule I meant you to . . . in this case'? Even if he did not think of this case at all as he gave the rule?" (§ 692). Allowing no false doubt to seep into the investigation, Wittgenstein answers his own question quickly and unambiguously: "Of course it is correct." And then he adds, in a phrase, the heart of the matter (and this is the reason behind his apparently strange equivocation above)—"For 'to mean it' did not mean: to think of it." Thus, significantly, there may be no particular and determinate mental act of thinking that gives the singular correct answer to what we did and did not mean by a given utterance. The conceptual foundations for self-interpretative singularism have not just been destabilized, they have collapsed.

There is a sense in which such retrospective answers regarding initial meaning can be after-the-fact reinforcements of preexisting connections, and another sense in which they are, even though correct, created. Thus Wittgenstein's reply above, "Can't I say *both*?" is after all reasonable, if somewhat misleading at that particular stage of the discussion. But it is, naturally, the broader context, the particularization of the language-game within which the utterance has force, to which we must look for clarification of, and answers to, such questions. And indeed *meaning* will reveal itself not to be invariably at center stage throughout a consideration of numerous cases: "Instead of 'I meant him' one can, of course, sometimes say 'I thought of him'; sometimes even 'Yes, we were speaking of him.' " And suggesting that the intuitive sense of necessity of the (mysterious) mental link, the seemingly essential connection, uniting the "meaning" and the "something" will diminish through such an inquiry into cases, Wittgenstein adds, "Ask yourself what 'speaking of him' consists in" (§ 687), that is, look to the nuances of the circumscribed games in which we use these words without philosophical presuppositions—precisely the kinds of cases provided in literary, and specifically autobiographical, works.

But does all or any of this mean that such connections do not exist, that they are mythical? This, again, simply could not be the case: we do mean something and not nothing. The issue is indeed, as we can perhaps now see more clearly, one of removing layered misconstruals: "Certainly such a connexion exists, only not as you imagine it: namely by means of a mental *mechanism*." And then parenthetically reminding us again of the danger and power of misleading analogies, Wittgenstein adds, "(One compares 'meaning him' with 'aiming at him')" (§ 689). This position does not reduce to what is now widely discussed under the heading of externalism,[14] pre-

14. Broadly stated, I refer to a position that manifests itself in the philosophy of language

cisely because the first-person knowledge of the speaker is preserved. Yet it is certainly not any kind of post-Cartesian internalism either; "meaning something" is, on this view, de-psychologized. One way to attempt to state the point generally, if only as a corrective—although this too possesses a strong power to mislead in that it allows the removal of first-person authority and to too great a degree approximates externalism—would be to say that the connections are in the language, or in the language-game, not in the mind of the speaker. But that is to put forward a far more succinct definitional thesis than Wittgenstein allows in these final sections of *Philosophical Investigations*. What he does say, significantly—and in keeping with the claims made here that literary and artistic investigations are indispensable sources for the kind of understanding Wittgenstein strongly suggests we need—is that "[a]ll this points to a wider context" (§ 686). And the discerning examination of such contexts will prevent (or dispel after the fact) the philosophical confusions, impulses, and smuggled presumptions he has been exposing and diagnosing. Thus there may be a fourth option as outlined in the introduction above, one that rises from the ashes of the thoroughgoing rejection of the very conceptual structure that the robust introspectionist, the skeptical introspectionist, and the behaviorist all explicitly share. Thus, while the fourth option, as we shall see, in a sense rises from the ashes, it does *not* assume a form that is similar to that which it replaces. If, indeed (as we shall see below) the fourth option were a *theory*, succinctly expressed, it would most assuredly be anti-Wittgensteinian in character, and it would, as a theory of retrospective self-knowledge, surely elide the context-specific detail that is indispensably prerequisite to the attainment of an overview of relevant particularities. Without these assembled particularities, the fourth option would have no content other than a general (and thus in this way self-contradictory) gesturing to pragmatics. With them, the never-completed awareness of contextualized particularities constitutes precisely the "assemblage of reminders" of which Wittgenstein wrote, and the therapeutic value

---

in the view that the meaning of what is said is dependent upon features, facts, or circumstances external to the mind of the speaker, and in the philosophy of mind in the view that the phenomenological content of an experience similarly depends on features, facts, or circumstances external to the mind of the experiencing subject. (A related position arises in epistemology, where a person may be said to know a given thing without that thing being presently in, or in some cases available to, the mind of the knower; this would lead into the related examination of Wittgenstein's response to Freudian theory. In this connection, see Frank Cioffi, "Wittgenstein's Freud," in *Studies in the Philosophy of Wittgenstein*, ed. Peter Winch [London: Routledge & Kegan Paul, 1969], 184–210, and Jacques Bouveresse, *Wittgenstein Reads Freud* [Princeton: Princeton University Press, 1995].)

of them, of which he also wrote, is evident.[15] With this in mind let us look to—of all things—the telling particularity of the price of butter.

Butter can obviously rise in price, but it would be an extreme misconstrual to say that this is an *activity* of butter (or an inward process or inner state). "Meaning something" is a phrase whose grammar can be much more easily, and far less obviously, misconstrued. The "album" of the *Philosophical Investigations* was, again, carefully assembled. All of the foregoing—the entire discussion that collectively points not to a hidden linkage, connection, process, state, or act in the mind of the speaker but to a wider context—is neatly compressed into the final section (§ 693):

> "When I teach someone the formation of the series . . . I surely mean him to write . . . at the hundredth place."—Quite right; you mean it. And evidently without necessarily even thinking of it. This shews you how different the grammar of the verb "to mean" is from that of "to think." And nothing is more wrong-headed than calling meaning a mental activity! Unless, that is, one is setting out to produce confusion. (It would also be possible to speak of an activity of butter when it rises in price, and if no problems are produced by this it is harmless.)

15. A number of writers have paid special attention to the remarks Wittgenstein wrote that suggest a deep affinity between the difficulties and conceptual dangers inherent in philosophical investigation on the one hand and in the achievement of self-knowledge on the other. Thus the therapeutic value to which I refer would have both philosophical and personal senses. See, e.g., James Conant, "Putting Two and Two Together: Kierkegaard, Wittgenstein, and the Point of View for Their Work as Authors," in *Philosophy and the Grammar of Religious Belief*, ed. Timothy Tessin and Mario von der Ruhr (London: Macmillan; New York: St. Martin's, 1995), where it is argued that, within Wittgenstein's later work, "the etiology of philosophical confusions is as complicated—and as difficult to survey—as our lives and our language. So the procedure of uncovering our individual confusions must remain a piecemeal one" (303). For a contrasting view (which houses a number of Wittgenstein's remarks of immediate relevance to present concerns, regardless of this debate concerning the similarity or difference between philosophical work and life-interpretive work), see D. Z. Phillips, *Philosophy's Cool Place* (Ithaca, N.Y.: Cornell University Press, 1999), 46: "But in saying 'You cannot write anything about yourself that is more truthful than you yourself are,' 'Nothing is so difficult as not deceiving oneself,' 'If anyone is *unwilling* to descend into himself . . . he will remain superficial in his writing,' and 'Working on philosophy is really more like working on oneself,' Wittgenstein is referring to difficulties in *doing philosophy*, difficulties in giving the problems the kind of attention philosophy asks of us." It is in the problems—the *philosophical* problems—of the nature of the self, and particularly self-interpretation, that the two positions converge: gaining conceptual clarity about the (philosophical) concept of self-knowledge is part of the attainment of (personal) self-knowledge.

But we must return to the fundamental question raised earlier and, of course, central to any attempt to understand the self's past thought and meaning in the larger context of autobiographical or biographical self-interpretive inquiry: Does this investigation into the problem of "meaning something," like the parallel investigation into the question "what is thinking?" give us clear reason to abandon with finality the broadly Cartesian conception of the self with which we have now seen Wittgenstein interact in numerous ways? The answer is probably a hesitant no—hesitant because these reflections, in de-psychologizing "meaning something" and showing the construals to which Wittgenstein is opposed ultimately to be "wrong-headed," do in one sense argue against the broadly Cartesian conception of the self, and this seems to suggest a "yes"; and "no" because they do remarkably *preserve*, rather than obliterate, first-person authority with regard to retrospective meaning, if of a kind very much unlike what we might have initially envisaged when coming to the problem of self-interpretation with the dualistic-introspectionist conceptual structure, or philosophical picture, in mind. Again, Wittgenstein is charting a middle way—although we must bear in mind that his *via media* does not synthesize the polar opposites, it rejects their mischaracterizations and more accurately tunnels under, rather than strides between, them. And so a final important question also wants answering: Does anything intrinsic to the phenomenon—or phenomena—of meaning something necessitate the *preservation* of any Cartesian or post-Cartesian conception of the self? The answer to that, quite against one's natural first impressions and intuitions—the ones with which we began this inquiry into the substance of Wittgenstein's final sections of *Philosophical Investigations*—is, remarkably, no.

III. Augustine in Retrospect

In his recounting of the famous episode in which he steals pears from a pear tree with a gang of juvenile acquaintances, we find the older Augustine reflecting—as we so often do throughout the *Confessions*—on the misdeeds of his youth. In this recounting, we find Augustine not directly stating what he was thinking at the time of his earlier misdeeds but—as we also see him often doing throughout the *Confessions*—*speculating* on what he may or may not have had in mind. And, characteristically, he makes a distinctively significant theological-epistemological assertion: "No one can tell me the truth of it except my God" (52). Unable to subscribe, in this episode, to the view of robust introspectionism and perform the requisite act of retrospective introspection, he puzzles over his intentions: "It is true that if the pears which I stole had been to my taste, and if I had wanted to get them for myself, I might have committed the crime on my own if I had needed to do no more than that to win myself the pleasure. I should have had no need to kindle my glowing desire by rubbing shoulders with a gang of accomplices." And then he concludes, on the basis of this hypothetical concerning what he would have done if his desire for the fruit had been the central motivation, "But as it was not the fruit that gave me pleasure, I must have got it from the crime itself, from the thrill of having partners in sin" (52). This "must" is obviously significant for the problem of true self-interpretation. Augustine is indeed reflecting on his own past as from the vantage point of another, indeed speculating on the self—on what his earlier words and deeds meant—as would (in the terms introduced above) the multiplist. And a moment later, he asks himself how he might explain his own "mood" at the time of his thieving: "[H]ow can I account for it? *Who knows his own frailties?*" (52). This autobiographical skepticism is, then, clearly not indicative of robust introspectionism, but neither is it, clearly, any kind of interior-denying behaviorism—he is not looking at his own behavior solely, as from the vantage point of another person, but rather is pursuing a grasp of his (hidden or presently obscured) intentions. But his voiced skepticism, "Can anyone unravel this twisted tangle of knots?" (52), does, as we have seen, have for him an answer: "No one can tell me the truth of it except my God." Here his philosophical thinking is clear: he believes, like the muted or skeptical introspectionist, that there *is* a single determinate fact of the case concerning what he meant or intended in committing the deed, but that it is hidden. Indeed, a bit later he articulates this position in connection with the Platonic distinction between moral appearance and reality, observing that "the appearance of what we do is often different from the intention with which we do it," suggesting precisely that he is in the grips of the sceptical-introspectionist picture of the mind. And the manifestations of this picture are evident throughout: later he says, "My heart lies before you, Oh my God. Look deep within. See these memories of mine" (77). Although God is here cast in the role of analyst (critics of psychoanalysis may say just the reverse), the conceptual picture at work is identical to that outlined in the introduction above.

Yet, intriguingly, he adds—and here we may see a mind beginning to free itself of its own misleading self-image—"and the circumstances at the time may not be clear" (67), suggesting, in a brief brilliant flash of this text, that—in a fashion anticipatory to Wittgenstein's observations above—it may be circumstantial, contextual matters that determine meaning as much as, or more than, an (alleged) process of thought, and that, in searching for the determinate singular thought, we may be misdirecting our attention if we want to grasp what is significant for the determination of meaning as the core of self-interpretation. And as such, this passage points to the fourth option mentioned at the outset, the opening possibility of a thoroughgoing rejection of the conceptual structure, a rejection of the architecture (to which we will return in the conclusion below) that would lead us to satisfy only the impulse to theorize and, in encapsulating a new position succinctly that merely replaces the one before it, answer to the demands of an underlying domineering philosophical picture of the mind or the self. A deeper, far less superficial conceptual satisfaction, precisely the kind of which Wittgenstein wrote in his various passages on the nature of philosophy, would prove accessible only subsequent to the removal of distorting conceptual models, indeed only to a mind reflexively set free of its severely prismatic self-image.[16]

There are numerous further flashes of insight, in which, distinctively, Augustine sees, and says, that it is a particular model or conception of the mind that has been misleading him in his self-examination, making certain theses seem unavoidable or obviously true that in fact are merely epistemic mirages. He, for example, now comprehends in retrospect that he "thought of evil not simply as some vague substance but as an actual bodily substance, and this was because I could not conceive of mind except as rarified body somehow diffused in space" (105). And later again, he speaks of his wits having been blunted by a misleading presumption—not unlike Wittgenstein's analysis of the "stupid prejudice" above—that precluded clear thinking: "My wits were so blunt and I was so completely unable even to see clearly into my own mind, that I thought that whatever had no dimensions in space must be absolutely nothing at all. . . . For my mind ranged in imagination over shapes and forms such as are familiar to the eye, and I did not realize that the power of thought, by which I formed these images, was itself something quite different from them" (134). Yet this is layered in its significance: on one level it is a mind, within the course of a sustained effort

16. The title of a fine study of Wittgenstein's development, David Pears's book *The False Prison* (Oxford: Clarendon Press, 1987), nicely encapsulates the kind of intellectual incarceration to which I here refer; in the matter of self-interpretive retrospective reflection the conceptual imprisonment can be unwittingly self-imposed.

of philosophical self-interpretation, again struggling to free itself from its own false self-image in a way consistent with (and again anticipatory of) Wittgenstein's analysis of retrospective meaning. On another level he does still—and this is what makes it a *struggle*—write of his inability to see clearly into his own mind, which revivifies the dualistic-introspectionist picture at issue.

There are, of course, contexts in which one may ask oneself if it is not true that one was doing a certain thing at a certain time for a reason that was unknown or (perhaps more interestingly and like Wittgenstein's example of "half thinking of him" above) half-known to oneself at the time; the very question of true self-interpretation often arises in just such cases. Augustine naturally provides a number of these; in one place he examines cases of a delay in closure, gratification, or consummation of an event, determining the depth of the delayed gratification, and suggests a simple possible correlation: the more protracted the one, the deeper the other. Involuntary cases of delay show the principle, such that the victorious general experiences the greater triumph after a lengthier and more dangerous battle; sailors experience more profound joy at their survival after a terrifying storm in which their fear of impending death was, in a causally linked way, just as profound. And, somewhat strangely, we are, he observed, happier at the partial health of a friend who, at first extremely ill, is now in partial recovery than we were at the full health of the friend prior to the illness (162). In such involuntary cases, no one speculates as to whether the delay, itself causally determinative of the depths of the subsequent joy, triumph, happiness, and so forth, was in some sense deliberate. But in cases in which persons prepare for their eating and drinking with (unnecessitated) hunger and thirst, or "drunkards eat salty things to make their throats dry and painful so that they may enjoy the pleasure of quenching their thirst" (162), or persons "who are engaged to be married . . . delay the wedding for fear that the betrothed have not 'suffered the trials of a long courtship' " (162), we might well have an open question concerning the motivation. And the questions of this kind, asked of one's self, indeed strongly suggest both that the robust-introspectionist model cannot accommodate such cases (and such cases are central to genuine self-interpretation) and that the behaviorist model would eliminate out of existence the very possibility of a half- or unknown meaning to our actions. Is then the muted or skeptical-introspectionist model supported here? No, precisely because the cases of the kind in question preserve the possibility not only of there having been a hidden intention (which "half-known" cases *would* suggest) but also of after-the-fact explanations arising not from the determinate thought of the speaker or actor but rather—again as Wittgenstein's analysis leads us to see—from the context, the very circumstances which, as Augustine says, may not initially be clear.

Many further case show this, not only in Augustine's autobiographical practice but also in the episodes of others that he relates. There is another famous episode, that in which Augustine's mother, Monica, is transformed by an angry word. Her servant-girl, in the context of the quarrel, calls Monica a "drunkard": as it happens, Monica took daily sips from the wine barrel, initially only a drop but gradually increasing to a semi-inebriating quantity. Monica herself had not, during the course of this advancing "disease," as Augustine describes it, been aware of the progression. With the one "harsh word of rebuke," and—significantly—intended as "a most bitter insult," the servant-girl, with words cutting like a "surgeon's knife," corrected Monica in a single stroke. Any full account of what transpired would include the epiphany-like suddenness of self-awareness that the rebuke occasioned; this would indeed be one aspect of the meaning of the linguistic action. Yet it was not intended, *in terms of a determinate mental event,* as a corrective, but rather, as Augustine precisely specifies, "to provoke her . . . , not to correct her" (194). We cannot know how the servant-girl would have replied to the question "But even so, was it not in the larger context clearly within the scope of your idea, your remark, that it should or could bring about a new self-awareness on the part of Monica, and that this would reform her?" But in very many similar cases in our ordinary experience we can know: the answer is yes. One might indeed say that in one way such a meaning was clearly not intended, but in another way, and at the same time, it was; it is likely that doubled answers of this kind indicate that the model or conceptual picture we are presupposing in the formulation of the question is either misleading or insufficiently subtle to capture the nuances of our self-descriptive practices. And in the larger context of Augustine's autobiographical practice, these models and conceptual pictures embedded within questions of self-interpretation fare no better, in the end, than they did within the context of Wittgenstein's investigations into retrospective meaning.

In conclusion, let us stand back and take a broader view. We began by observing a presumption that one very often, if not invariably, encounters in those questions in which the subject takes itself as its own object of investigation: that is, questions of self-interpretation. That presumption, variously manifested in contrasting positions, for example, that of the robust introspectionist and that of the skeptical introspectionist, was, simply stated, that in any such questions there will be a determinate and fixed mental event of meaning that originally determined the absolute and singularly correct answer to any question concerning what we meant in a given utterance or action (or, although this is a subject for another day, a pattern of action over time). And there was, I suggested, a conceptual template or picture of the self beneath this presumption that the mental-event-denying behaviorist also shares, that is, the fundamentally dualistic ontological separation of outward verbal or gestural behavior from the hidden inward mental actions or content that gives the meaning to those outward, physical actions.

But this presumption, however intuitively plausible it may seem at the outset of any inquiry into the nature of self-interpretation, did not survive the scrutiny given it within Wittgenstein's investigation into the initially seemingly curious nature of retrospective meaning. Indeed, we now, given those reflections and observations on the facts of our practices, have reason to believe that the presumption is misplaced and that, as Wittgenstein puts it, the logic, or the philosophical "grammar," of meaning *is* very different from the logic, or grammar, of thinking. And, similarly but more deeply, the dualistic-introspectionist conceptual picture upon which this presumption is founded and which undergirds the very formulation of the question of singularism in true self-interpretation is similarly unearthed (although its *full* analysis and removal could not be completed here).

Our turn to practices, to Augustine, showed two things: first, we saw cases in which a remarkably powerful philosophical mind was laboring under the self-misapprehension that the presumption enforces; second, we saw that powerful mind beginning, in places, to break free of that presumption. The false presumption, what we might in shorthand call "mental-event singularism," in truth survived neither Wittgenstein's philosophy nor Augustine's autobiography. But does this mean that we should enthusiastically embrace a parallel "mental-event multiplism," that is, the view (indeed hinted at in a few places within Augustine's text) that the question of the meaning of an utterance or action will have multiple true answers because the utterance or action is an outward manifestation of multiple inward mental events? The answer is a resounding no: that would be to remain a captive, to stay within the misleading conceptual template or picture from which reflections such as those reconsidered here might free us.

There is a real sense in which Wittgenstein's observations, since they are significant for self-interpretation, tell us what *not* to think. Should we not ask for another, better conceptual picture to replace the one that these considerations would remove? The answer here too is a resounding no, although this is perhaps less immediately clear. For the impulse to theorize is not easily diminished. The robust introspectionist has a bold and clear thesis to advance: simply look inward, transparently and immediately, at the meaning-content of the utterance, and report it accordingly. The skeptical introspectionist similarly has something, with equal boldness and only slightly less concision, to say: look inward, but with an awareness that the mental meaning-content, although wholly determinative of the significance of the overt utterance in question, may be initially obscured from our inner view, our introspective gaze. These twin positions (they share the same conceptual parentage in the foundations of Cartesian dualism) posit, indeed take as a given, that the determinative mental meaning-content is the *kind* of thing for which we should be looking in any question of retrospective verbal self-interpretation, and that, once found, the singular truth will be unproblematically in front of us. And the behaviorist, something of a younger sibling (with the same conceptual parentage but deriving its identity from its direct and forceful opposition to the older pair), also has a perhaps even more bold, and now antithetical, thesis to advance, with bracing concision. Asking for a new, concise, fourth conceptual model or picture to replace the ones that the foregoing considerations have removed—one that would display an equal measure of boldness and concision—is to ask to satisfy a philosophical desire we would do better to quell. It is to satisfy an impulse, of long and distinguished standing in philosophy, to preserve the edifice of an explanatory structure by replacing any removed element with a newly chiseled element that takes the same place. But there is an alternative, shown in the collection of strategies Wittgenstein developed within his middle and late philosophical writings (he referred to "a new method" that had been found), to the incremental restoration of conceptual architecture. Wittgenstein also wrote of razing to the ground such structures and removing from our conceptual landscape the impediments to a clear view of our practices, in our present case, of the self-descriptive practices that would, if assembled into a perspicuous overview or a conceptual mosaic of particularities, dissolve philosophical puzzlement.[17] This *kind* of

---

17. One might usefully reconsider the methods employed by John Wisdom in his once widely discussed *Other Minds* (Oxford: Blackwell, 1952), work that is still of considerable value in diagnosing the motivations to picture the mind in a way still very much in evidence in

philosophical solution—indeed dissolution—is *very* unlike a new, sharply cut theory to advance in place of those which have been supplanted. And one finds such a position—one of a very different kind that pragmatically turns to the particularities of our practices within actual contexts of self-investigation—satisfying only *after* the investigation, which in this case involves the close reading of Augustine but might also include any other of a vast number of philosophically relevant autobiographies, memoirs, and any other form of self-interpretive writing containing retrospective meaning-determination.[18] Fittingly, the proof of any such claim will be, indeed, in the pragmatics. Augustine realizes in retrospect that his own beliefs—in his case theological, but the point applies across the board to any self-interpretive question concerning love, affection, commitment, life choices, and so forth—were put to the test *in extremis,* at the death of his mother (200). His autobiographical report on what he did and did not believe was verified not in reference to an inner mental event but in reference to the pragmatic, circumstantially situated and personally engaged belief that manifested itself within and throughout the emergent patterns of his actions, words, hopes, fears, aspirations, regrets, and many other irreducibly human events and experiences. And in some cases, the truth—as in this case—is singular: his belief, as he expressed it most succinctly, was *real.* In other cases, the truth is multiple, in the sense that the meaning, the significance, of a given utterance or action will have multiple trajectories with regard to emergent patterns of actions or linkages to other utterances and actions. And in some

---

contemporary philosophy. In connection with these methods, see also R. W. Newell, *Objectivity, Empiricism, and Truth* (London: Routledge & Kegan Paul, 1986), esp. chap. 5, "Reason and Particular Cases: John Wisdom," 85–100. A more recent study, showing both an awareness of the great value of the Wisdomian variety of patience I am endorsing and the relation between particularity and clarity, is Paul Johnston, *Wittgenstein: Rethinking the Inner* (London: Routledge, 1993).

18. There are many recent volumes of and about autobiography and memoir, and no sign of a slowing of material relevant to the attainment of an overview of our multiform self-reflective practices. See, for a few examples, Jill Ker Conway, *When Memory Speaks: Reflections on Autobiography* (New York: Knopf, 1998); Leigh Gilmore, *The Limits of Autobiography: Trauma and Testimony* (Ithaca, N.Y.: Cornell University Press, 2001); and Paul John Eakin, *How Our Lives Become Stories: Making Selves* (Ithaca, N.Y.: Cornell University Press, 1999). For a collection of papers from various disciplines on the relation between self-narration and selfhood, see Ulric Neisser and Robyn Fivush, eds., *The Remembering Self: Construction and Accuracy in the Self-Narrative* (Cambridge: Cambridge University Press, 1994). For a recent study showing the need for, and providing, a significant expansion of the personal-identity problem, see Marya Schechtman, *The Constitution of Selves* (Ithaca, N.Y.: Cornell University Press, 1996).

cases, only seemingly paradoxically, the single truth is that one is genuinely divided or ambivalent,[19] or an utterance or action is genuinely ambiguous. But what all these answers have in common is that they are—as Wittgenstein says and Augustine shows—true *not* by virtue of a verified correspondence to a determinate meaning-giving mental event, but true on the level of pragmatic *use*. And we can only see the philosophical significance of those practices clearly if our minds are freed from distorting presumptions and misleading overgeneralized conceptual pictures.[20] In that sense, being shown what *not* to think is, remarkably, at the same time being shown what to think—without the imposition of another conceptual picture to replace the one we must labor to remove. Indeed, this too-little-discussed stretch of Wittgenstein's philosophy might successfully serve to remove a particularly pernicious conception of self-interpretation that in practice proves, somewhat ironically, only self-defeating. And as such, these considerations may in practice prove, fittingly, to be indispensable tools in the structuring of the mind's true image of itself.

19. At one point Augustine provides a perfectly lucid, and perfectly human, example of this genuinely divided ambivalence. He likens his thought at one stage of his life to "the efforts of a man who tries to wake but cannot and sinks back into the depths of slumber. No one wants to sleep forever, for everyone rightly agrees that it is better to be awake. Yet a man often staves off the effort to rouse himself when his body is leaden with inertia. He is glad to settle down once more, although it is against his better judgment and is already time he were up and about" (*Confessions*, 165). The truth, of course, is that in practice *both* seemingly antithetical claims—he does and does not want to rise—are correct descriptions of such a person and, of a person of Augustine's state at that time, are (seemingly paradoxically) singly multiply true. See also Augustine's similarly intriguing descriptions of a mind that will not obey itself (171, 173); it only appears to be "the strange phenomenon" Augustine says it is when in the grip of a misleading picture of the self.

20. One might usefully compare here Nietzsche's characteristically extreme and reorientingly insightful remarks on the mind's impulse to create false images of its own workings, what he calls "the antecedentia of action," in *Twilight of the Idols* (Harmondsworth, Middlesex: Penguin, 1968), esp. "The Four Great Errors," §§ 3–5, pp. 48–52. These passages offer, I would suggest, a rather blunt diagnosis of how we can eventuate in a "haunted" condition in which we puzzle over the hidden real meaning of an earlier utterance or action that would (allegedly) provide the singular self-interpretive truth.

Contributors

ANNETTE BARNES is professor emeritus of philosophy at the University of Maryland. She is the author of *On Interpretation: A Critical Analysis* (1988) and *Seeing Through Self-Deception* (1998).

NOËL CARROLL is Monroe C. Beardsley Professor of the Philosophy of Art and Hilldale Professor at the University of Wisconsin–Madison. His most recent books include *Philosophy of Mass Art* (1998), *Philosophy of Art: A Contemporary Introduction* (1999), and *Beyond Aesthetics* (2001). Professor Carroll is a former president of the American Society for Aesthetics.

STEPHEN DAVIES teaches philosophy at the University of Auckland. He is the author of *Definitions of Art* (1991) and *Musical Meaning and Expression* (1994), *Musical Works and Performances* (2002), and he is the editor of *Art and Its Messages* (1997).

SUSAN FEAGIN is professor of philosophy at the University of Missouri–Kansas City. She is the author of *Reading with Feeling: The Aesthetics of Appreciation* (1996) and co-editor, with Patrick Maynard, of *Aesthetics* (1997). She has served on the board of trustees of the American Society for Aesthetics and on the editorial board for the *Encyclopedia of Aesthetics* and of the *Journal of Aesthetics and Art Criticism*.

ALAN GOLDMAN is professor of philosophy at the University of Miami. He is the author of *Empirical Knowledge* (1988), *Moral Knowledge* (1988), *Aesthetic Value* (1995), and *Practical Rules: When We Need Them and When We Don't* (2002).

CHARLES GUIGNON is professor of philosophy at the University of South Florida. He has taught at Princeton, Berkeley, the University of Texas, and the University of Auckland. Guignon is the editor of *The Cambridge Companion to Heidegger* (1993) and author of *Heidegger and the Problem of Knowledge* (1983), *Dostoevsky's "The Grand Inquisitor,"* (1993), and *Re-envisioning Psychology: Moral Dimensions of Theory and Practice* (with F. Richardson and B. Fowers) (1999). His primary interests are existentialism and hermeneutics.

CHHANDA GUPTA is professor in the Department of Philosophy at Jadavpur University, Calcutta. Her publications include *Essays in Social and Political Phi-*

losophy (1989), *Philosophy of Science* (1992), *Realism versus Realism* (1995), and *Cultural Otherness and Beyond* (1998).

GARRY HAGBERG is professor of philosophy at Bard College, where he also directs the Program in Philosophy and the Arts and chairs the Division of Social Studies. His books include *Art as Language: Wittgenstein, Meaning, and Aesthetic Theory* (1998) and *Meaning and Interpretation: Wittgenstein, Henry James, and Literary Knowledge* (1994), and he has contributed to numerous journals, collections, and reference works in philosophy and aesthetics. He recently edited a special issue of the *Journal of Aesthetics and Art Criticism* on "improvisation in the arts."

MICHAEL KRAUSZ is Milton C. Nahm Professor and chair of the Department of Philosophy at Bryn Mawr College. He is the author of *Rightness and Reasons: Interpretation in Cultural Practices* (1993), *Varieties of Relativism* (with Rom Harré) (1995), and *Limits of Rightness* (2000). As well, Krausz is contributing editor of eight previous volumes on such topics as relativism, rationality, interpretation, cultural identity, metaphysics of culture, creativity, interpretation of music, and the philosophy of R. G. Collingwood. He has served on the board of trustees of the American Society for Aesthetics. Krausz is cofounder of the Greater Philadelphia Philosophy Consortium.

PETER LAMARQUE is professor of philosophy at the University of York in England. From 1995 to 2000 he was Ferens Professor of Philosophy at the University of Hull and before then senior lecturer in philosophy at the University of Stirling. He is editor of the *British Journal of Aesthetics,* author of *Fictional Points of View* (1996), and co-author, with Stein Haugom Olsen, of *Truth, Fiction, and Literature: A Philosophical Perspective* (1994). He also edited the *Concise Encyclopedia of Philosophy of Language* (1997) and *Aesthetics in Britain* (2000), a special issue of the *British Journal of Aesthetics.* He was philosophy subject editor of the ten-volume *Encyclopedia of Language and Linguistics* (1994).

JERROLD LEVINSON is professor of philosophy at the University of Maryland, College Park. He is the author of *Music, Art, and Metaphysics* (1990), *The Pleasures of Aesthetics* (1996), and *Music in the Moment* (1998), as well as editor of *Aesthetics and Ethics* (1998), co-editor of *Aesthetics Concepts* (2001), and editor of the forthcoming *Oxford Handbook of Aesthetics* (2002). A volume of Levinson's essays has appeared in French translation (*L'art, la musique, et l'histoire,* 1998), and he has contributed articles to numerous reference works in philosophy and aesthetics. Levinson is currently president of the American Society for Aesthetics.

JOSEPH MARGOLIS is Laura H. Carnell Professor of Philosophy at Temple University. He is past president of the American Society for Aesthetics, honorary president (past) and honorary life member of the International Association for Aesthetics. He has authored and edited thirty books, including most recently *What, After All Is a Work of Art?* (1998), *The Philosophy of Interpretation* (co-edited with Tom Rockmore) (1999), *Historied Thought, Constructed World* (1995), and *Selves and Other Texts* (2001).

REX MARTIN is professor of philosophy at the University of Kansas and was professor of political theory and government at the University of Wales, Swansea. His teaching appointments have included the University of Auckland, University of Sydney, and others. Martin is the author of *Historical Explanation: Re-enactment and Practical Inference* (1977), *Rawls and Rights* (1985), and *A System of Rights* (1993). He has edited the revised edition of R. G. Collingwood's *Essay on Metaphysics* (1998); and with Mark Singer he edited G. C. MacCallum's *Legislative Intent and Other Essays on Law, Politics, and Mortality* (1993). Martin has served as chair of the American Philosophical Association's Committee on Philosophy and Law.

JITENDRANATH MOHANTY is professor of philosophy at Temple University and Woodruff Professor of Philosophy and Asian Studies at Emory University. He has written on phenomenology as well as on Indian philosophy. His latest book is *Classical Indian Philosophy: An Introductory Text*. His two volumes of *Explorations in Philosophy* are forthcoming.

DAVID NOVITZ was reader in philosophy at the University of Canterbury, New Zealand. He is the author of *Pictures and Their Use in Communication* (1977), *Knowledge, Fiction, and Imagination* (1987), and *The Boundaries of Art* (1992), as well as many articles in the philosophy of art.

PHILIP PERCIVAL held lectureships at the University of Cape Town and various colleges of the University of Oxford before taking up a lectureship in the Department of Philosophy at the University of Glasgow in 1996. He has published articles in the philosophy of art, philosophical logic, and metaphysics, most recently in the journals *Mind* and *Analysis*.

TORSTEN PETTERSSON has held posts at several Scandinavian universities and is now professor of literature at the University of Uppsala, Sweden. He has published *Consciousness and Time: A Study in the Philosophy and Narrative Technique of Joseph Conrad* (1982), *Literary Interpretation: Current Models and a New Departure* (1988), as well as books in Swedish on the Swedish Nobel Prize winner Eyvind Johnson (1986) and on the oeuvres of nine pioneers of Scandinavian literary modernism (2001). For his work in literary history, he was awarded the Schück Prize for the year 2000 by the Swedish Academy. He has also published a collection of short stories and five collections of poetry.

ROBERT STECKER is professor of philosophy at Central Michigan University. He is the author of *Artworks: Definition, Meaning, Value* (1996) and co-editor of *John Locke's Essay Concerning Human Understanding in Focus* (1998). He has also published numerous papers on aesthetics, the philosophy of mind, and the history of modern philosophy.

LAURENT STERN is professor of philosophy at Rutgers University. He has published articles on interpreting and translating and is working on a book on these topics.

PAUL THOM is professor of philosophy and executive dean of arts at Southern Cross University, New South Wales, Australia. His publications in the field of philosophy of the arts include *For an Audience: A Philosophy of the Performing Arts* (1993) and *Making Sense: A Theory of Interpretation* (2000), along with many journal articles. He has also published widely in the history of logic and Greek philosophy. He is a musician and occasional opera director.

Index

aberrant influence, individual identity and culture and, 374–80

Abhinavagupta, 73–74

acceptable interpretations, contextual variables and, 168–69

access, identity and ontology in visual arts and, 362–63

actional-emotional meaning, intentionality and, 66–68

actual intentionalism: versus hypothetical intentionalism, 287–91; Kaufman case study of, 334–44; philosophy of interpretation and, 322–27

adequation argument: defense of interpretation and, 27; versus natural symbols, interpretation of, 29–30

adhibhautika (naturalist-social interpretation), 73

adhidaivika (pertaining to the gods), 73

adhyatmika (pertaining to inner spiritual life), 73

adjudication, Dworkin's theory of, 252–62

aesthetic theory: computer recognition of, 303 n. 41; contestable interpretations and, 15–16, 19–23; Gadamer's theory of hermeneutics and, 275–79

Against Interpretation, 379–80

agency: Heidegger's concept of, 268–73; individual identity and culture and, 376–80; literacy and personal identity and, 371–73

aims of interpretation, art interpretation theory and, 160–65

Alice in Wonderland, 346–47

allusion, actual intentionalism and, 325–27

alternative interpretations, definitive interpretations versus, 96–98

ambiguity: editorial interpretation of music and, 235–37; hypothetical intentionalism and, 329–33; jurisprudence and, 253–62; performative interpretation of music and, 239–41

ambivalence, self-interpretation and, 406

"antecedia of action," 406 n. 20

anti-intentionalists: actual intentionalism and, 323–27; philosophy of interpretation concerning, 320–44

apauruseyatva, intentionality and, 71–74

appreciation: literary interpretation and, 286–91, 301–6; utterance model of interpretation and, 173 n. 17

Arena fresco (Giotto), 34–35

Aristotle, 28–29

artifacts: identity and ontology in, 361–80; individual identity and culture and, 377–80

artist/critic parity: novel interpretations and, 198–205; radical constructivism and, 190–93

art-value, characteristics of, 202, 204–5

artworks: actual intentionalism and, 322–27; art-value of, 204–5; constructive realism concerning, 148–51; constructivist interpretation of, 169–73; Gadamer's theory of hermeneutics and, 275–79; Heidegger's hermeneutics and, 271–73; hypothetical intentionalism and, 327–33, 338–44; identity and ontology in interpretation of, 360–80; intentionality in interpretation of, 68–74; interpretative strategies and, 20–23, 29–30; Levinson's theory of meaning concerning, 176–80; limits of critical pluralism concerning, 101–21; modification

artworks *(cont'd)*
    of, through critical interpretation, 193
    n. 12; novel critical interpretations of, 181–
    207; ontology of, interpretation and, 56–
    61, 159–80; philosophy of interpretation
    concerning, 320–44; radical constructiv-
    ism and interpretation of, 182–86; realism
    about critical meanings, 186–89; structure
    of interpretation and, 52–56; symboliza-
    tion in, 206–7; text/work distinctness,
    193–98; theory of interpretation concern-
    ing, 160–65; utterance model of meaning
    and, 175–76; work versus "text," 165–69.
    See also performing arts; visual arts; *spe-
    cific media, e.g., painting*
atomism, literal meaning and, 69
Augustine (Saint), 382, 398–406
Aurobindo, Sri, 72
Austen, Jane, 106, 120, 194
authorial intent: hypothetical intentionalism
    and, 310–18, 328–33; intentionalist theory
    and, 320–22; interpretative strategies ver-
    sus, 22–25, 33; Kaufman case study of,
    334–44; literal meaning and, 70–74;
    literary interpretation and, 214–17; play-
    wright's intent, 345–59; poetic interpreta-
    tion and, 161–65; public versus private
    intent, 340–44; relevance and, 321 n. 5;
    unique interpretation thesis and, 36–38
autobiography, self-interpretation and,
    405–6

Barnes, Annette, 2, 345–59
Barthes, Roland, 107–8, 293
Bateson, F. W., 30–31
Baxandall, Michael, 374
Beardsley, Monroe, 27, 36–37, 39, 212–13,
    216–17, 290–91, 293–97
Beckett, Samuel, 311, 345–59
Beethoven, Ludwig, 128–29, 195, 232 n. 2;
    descriptive interpretations of, 249; *Grosse
    Fugue* of, 242–50; performative interpreta-
    tion of works of, 240–41; quartets of,
    235–36
behavior: art interpretation in context of,
    160–66; intentionality of interpretation
    and, 65–68
Being and Time, 266–73
"being-in-the-world," 268–73
belief box, definitive interpretations and,
    95–96

beliefs: alternative interpretations and,
    97–98; historical interpretation and,
    113–14; understanding and interpretation
    and, 94–96
Bell, Clive, 369–70
Berger, Melvin, 244–45, 247
BH Guessing Game, 49–51
bivalent logic: acceptance of, 92; incompati-
    bility of interpretations and, 115–18,
    124–25; incongruence of interpretation
    and, 125–26; jurisprudence and, 253–62
Blackburn, Simon, 57–58
Blake, William, 162–65, 167, 169–70
Brahmasûtras, 74
Brahms, Johannes, 45–51, 54–57, 59–60,
    238–39
Brecht, Bertolt, 347
Brentano, 64
Brooks, Cleanth, 30–31
Buddhism: hermeneutical strategies of,
    73–74; incongruence of interpretation con-
    cerning, 126–27

canonical interpretations, jurisprudence and,
    251–62
Carroll, Lewis, 346–47
Carroll, Noël, 4, 202–3, 204 n. 20, 287–91,
    315 n. 9, 319–44
Cartesianism, 382–84, 397–98, 404
Carvalho, John, 372 n. 10
Castle, The, 311
Catastrophe, 347
categorical intentions, hypothetical intention-
    alism and, 340–44
character development, lack of, in *Sun Also
    Rises,* 11–15
Christianity, *King Lear* and theme of, 226–28
classism, literacy and personal identity and,
    371–73
Clinton, Bill, 188–89, 197 n. 15
Clockwork Orange, A, 19
cognitive meaning: incongruence of interpre-
    tation and, 125–26; intentionality and,
    66–68; interpretive theory and, 63–64;
    personal identity and visual perception,
    364–66; retrospective meaning as, 385–89;
    self-knowledge and, 382–84
"collective practices," individual identity and
    culture and, 376–80
comedy, authorial intent in, Kaufman case
    study, 334–44
Comedy of Errors, 349 n. 4

commendations, interpretations as, 125–26
commonness, multiplism versus singularism
    and, 132–34
communicative interpretation, hypothetical
    intentionalism and, 313–18
composer's intent, musical interpretations
    and, 231–34
comprehensive interpretations: of artworks,
    assumptions concerning, 166–69; limits of,
    164–65
Conant, James, 397 n. 15
conceptual relativism, 156
Confessions, 382, 398–406
conflict, deep-level interpretation and, 89–91
constraints on interpretation: incompatibility
    of interpretations and, 115–18; role of
    facts in, 78–79
constructive realism, 55–56; imputation and,
    145–58; internal versus external forms,
    136–44; objects of interpretation and,
    122–23; realism and constructivism and,
    134–44; table of categories of, 154
constructivism: artworks' interpretation and,
    169–73; cultural context of, 43–44; Levin-
    son's interpretation of, 176–80; literary
    works and, 217–19; multiplism and, 3–4,
    122–23; object of interpretation and,
    148–51; radical constructivism, 182–86;
    realism and, 134–44, 146–48
contextual variables: Heidegger's Dasein and,
    267–73; monistic interpretation and,
    213–17; in work's identity, 166–69
contract, principles of, jurisprudence and,
    255–62
conventionalism: art interpretation in context
    of, 161 n. 3; realism about critical mean-
    ings and, 188–89
conversation: hypothetical intentionalism
    and, 317–18; literary interpretation and,
    287–91
"conversational hypothesis," artist/critic par-
    ity and, 203–5
core meanings, artistic interpretation and,
    178–80
Corngold, Stanley, 213 n. 2
Crime and Punishment, 61
critical interpretation: appreciation and liter-
    ary interpretation, 285–6; artist/critic par-
    ity, 198–205; defined, 181–82; descriptive
    interpretation as, 241–42; modification of

art and, 193 n. 12; philosophical jurispru-
    dence and, 251–62; realism concerning,
    186–89; variety of, 206–7; verbal meaning
    in, 291–94
critical monism. *See* singularism
critical pluralism. *See* multiplism
cultural symbols and context: constructive re-
    alism and, 151–53; critical pluralism and,
    101–21; historical interpretation and,
    113–14; identity and ontology and, 363;
    incompatibility of interpretations and,
    115–18; individual identity and, 373–80;
    intentionalist theory and, 41–44, 66–68;
    interpretative strategies and, 2–5; literacy,
    identity, and visual arts and, 367–73; ver-
    sus natural symbols, interpretation of,
    28–35; properties of, 118–20; "writerly"
    response to, 107–8
Currie, Gregory, 194, 295

Danto, Arthur, 30 n. 8, 37–39
D'Anza, Tony, 336
Dasein: Heidegger's concept of, 266–73; on-
    tology of interpretation and, 64
David Letterman Show, 334, 336
Davidson, Donald, 114
Davies, David, 166 n. 11
Davies, Stephen, 3, 229 n. 29, 231–50
Davis, Gene, 373–75
deconstructivism, performance art and, Kauf-
    man case study, 334–44
deep-level interpretation: conflict and,
    89–91; versus natural interpretation,
    86–89; painting analysis and, 85–86;
    translations and, 93–94
"de facto significance," individual identity
    and culture and, 375–80
definitive interpretation: alternatives to,
    96–98; conflicts and, 89–91; constraints
    on, 77–79; envoy of, 98; hedging concern-
    ing, 91–92; painting criticism as example
    of, 84–86; persuaders and, 79–84; theories
    of, 76–98; understanding and, 94–96
Defoe, Daniel, 173 n. 17, 300–306
DeKooning, 250, 311
democratic principles: jurisprudence and,
    256–62; literacy and personal identity and,
    371–73
denotata: determinability of interpretation,
    40–41; interpretive strategies and, 29–30;
    natural versus cultural aspects, 43–44

descriptive interpretation, musical works, 241–50

determinability of interpretation, 3; artist/ critic parity and, 190–93; elucidation and, 295–97; monism in literary works and, 212–17; natural *denotata*, 40–41; realism about critical meanings and, 187 n. 7

Dewey, John M., 151

dialogue, compliance with, intentionalism and, 349–50

Dickens, Charles, 173 n. 17, 289

Dilthey, Wilhelm, 264

disambiguity, intentionalist interpretation and, 214 n. 6

disclosedness, truth as, 266–73

diversity of interpretation: descriptive interpretation of music and, 242–50; of literary works, 211; monism and, 212–17

dogmatism: beliefs and, 96; persuaders of interpretation and, 81–84

Dollimore, Jonathan, 304 n. 46

Doll's House, The, 348

Donovan, Robert Alan, 301

due process, jurisprudence and, 256–62

Dürer, Albrecht, 373

Dworkin, Ronald, 3, 251–62

editorial interpretation, musical works, 234–37

education, literacy, identity, and visual arts and, 369–73

elaborative interpretations: critical pluralism concerning, 105–8; versus elucidative interpretations, 47–51; history and, 113–14; musical interpretation as, 130–34

Elegy in a Country Churchyard, 31–32, 215

Elgin, C., 194

El Greco, 41

Eliot, T. S., 357

elucidative interpretations: critical pluralism and, 120–21; versus elaborative interpretations, 47–51; incompatibility and, 117–18; literary interpretations as, 291, 294–97; musical interpretation as, 130–34; potential plurality thesis and, 52

Emma, 106–7

empirical knowledge, epistemic access and interpretation, 110–12

Empson, William, 293

Endgame, 345–59

envoys, definitive interpretations and, 98

epistemology: critical pluralism and, 108–12; hermeneutics and, 265; hypothetical intentionalism and, 342–44

Erased de Kooning Drawing, 176

Eroica symphony, 128–29

esoteric knowledge, literary interpretation and, 304 n. 45

exemplification, in artworks, 61

existence, objecthood and, 138–40

explication: literary interpretations as, 291, 296–97; verbal meaning recovered through, 291–94

expressivist ontology, multiplist realism and hermeneutics, 280–84

external constructive realism, 136–44, 154–57

external interpretation: versus internal interpretation, 45; structure of interpretations and, 52–56

facts: alternative interpretations and, 97–98; interpretation and role of, 78–79; persuaders of interpretation and role of, 80–84; understanding and interpretation and, 94–96

Faulkner, William, 218–19

faute de mieux interpretive strategy, 27

Feagin, Susan, 3, 360–80

feminist theory: actual intentionalism and, 338 n. 20; intentionalism in performance art and, 348–59; literary interpretation in context of, 162–65

fiction. *See* novels

film, hypothetical intentionalism and interpretation of, 331 n. 17

Finkelstein, Sidney, 245, 247

Fire Raisers, The, 354–55

Fish, Stanley, 217–19

Fiske, Roger, 242, 247

"fore-structure": Gadamer's hermeneutics and, 277–79; Heidegger's Dasein and, 268–73; multiple realism and hermeneutics concerning, 282–84

Forman, Milos, 333

Forster, E. M., 300

free will, personal identity and visual perception, 365–66

Freud, Sigmund, 33, 88, 170

Fridays, 334–35

Frisch, Max, 354–55

Furtwängler, Wilhelm, 128–29

fusing of horizons, Gadamer's theory of, 277–79
fuzzy-set theory, ontology of interpretation and, 57–58

Gadamer, Hans-Georg, 3, 114, 131, 264–66, 273–84
Ganesha figures, individual identity and culture and, 377–80
Giotto, Arena fresco of, 34–35, 40
global interpretive strategy, 138; hypothetical intentionalism and, 311–18
Goldman, Alan, 2, 9–25
Goldstein, Leon, 109
Goliath statue, 195–98
Goodman, Nelson, 59–60, 136–37, 140–41, 194
Gray, Thomas, 31–32, 215
Great Tradition, The, 300
Grosse Fugue (Beethoven), descriptive interpretations of, 242–50
Guignon, Charles, 3, 131, 264–84
Gupta, Chhanda, 4, 132 n. 19, 140, 145–58
Gutenberg, Johannes, 371

Hagberg, Garry, 3, 381–406
Haigwood, Laura, 162
Hamlet, 43, 112, 170, 217–18, 220–28, 295–96, 348–59
"Hard Cases," 252–53, 255
Harnoncourt, Nikolaus, 59
Harrison, Bernard, 140 n. 34
Hart, H. L. A., 252
Haydn's Symphony no. 100, 231–34
Haydn variations, 54–56, 59–60
hedging, definitive interpretation and, 91–92
Hegel, G. F. W., 74–75
Heidegger, Martin, 3, 131; Gadamer compared with, 276–79; hermeneutics and, 264–73; multiplist realism and hermeneutics of, 280–84; phenomenology of interpretation and, 64
Hemingway, Ernest, 9–25
Herculean jurisprudence, 259–62
hermeneutics: Gadamer's theory of, 273–79; Heidegger's Dasein and, 266–73; interpretive strategies, 2; multiplism and, 131–32; multiplist realism and, 279–84; truth in interpretation and, 264–84. See also romantic hermeneutics

heuristic intent, hypothetical intentionalism and, 316, 331–33
Hillis Miller, J., 173 n. 17, 289, 302–3
Hinduism, incongruence of interpretation concerning, 126–27
Hirsch, E. D., 26, 38–41, 214–17, 321 n. 4
historical context (historicity): art as object of interpretation and, 165–69, 179–80; constructivist interpretation and, 171–72; Gadamer's theory of hermeneutics and, 274–79; Heidegger's historicity of interpretation, 283–84; individual identity and culture and, 375–80; literary interpretation and, 163–65; monistic interpretation and, 213–17
history, interpretation and, 112–14
holistic interpretation, realism about critical meanings and, 187–89
Holland, Norman, 217–19
homosexuality, in Sun Also Rises, 10, 15–18
Hopkins, Gerard Manley, 214 n. 6, 292
Housman, A. E., 175 n. 19
human existence, Heidegger's concept of, 266–73
Hume, David, 93, 298
hyphenation, individual identity and, 378–80
hypothetical intentionalism: versus actual intentionalism, 287–91; artistic media compared with, 23–25; Kaufman case study of, 334–44; Levinson's theory of, 309–18; meaning and, 176–80, 214 n. 6; ontology of art interpretation and, 1661 n. 4; philosophy of interpretation and, 319, 327–33; public versus private intent and, 340–44

Ibsen, Henrik, 356
ideal audience, hypothetical intentionalism and, 177–78
"ideally admissible interpretations," critical pluralism and, 102–3
identity: contextual variables and, 166–69; culture and individual identity, 373–80; historical origns and, 171–72; literacy and visual arts and, 366–73; ontology of interpretation and, 360–80; visual perception and personal identity, 364–66
illusionist painting, interpretation of, 365 n. 4
I'm from Hollywood, 336
Importance of Being Earnest, 349
imputational interpretation: constructive realism and, 145–58; critical pluralism con-

imputational interpretation *(cont'd)*
cerning, 105–8; cultural properties and,
118–20; history and, 113–14; multiplism
and, 131–32

Incarnationist theology, interpretive strategy
based on, 32–33

incompatibility of interpretations: conflict
and, 90–91; constructivist theory and,
217–19; critical pluralism and, 114–18;
history and, 112–14; literary criticism and,
305–6; multiple realism and hermeneutics
concerning, 281–84; realistic literary interpretation and, 228–30; singularism versus
multiplism and, 123–34; unique interpretation thesis and, 35–38

incongruence. *See* incompatibility of interpretations

indefiniteness, editorial interpretation of
music and, 235–37

indeterminacy. *See* determinability of interpretation

Indian philosophy, intentionality of interpretation and, 68–74

"indicated" structures, text/work distinctions
and, 196–98

individual identity, culture and, 373–80

inner referents, meaning and, 390–98

"inputs," objecthood and existence and,
139–40

instability of interpretation, translations and,
93–94

instrumental aims, literary interpretation
and, 162–65

integrity, of law, 255–62

intelligibility, constructive realism and,
156–57

intentionalist theory: art interpretation in
context of, 161 n. 3; artist/critic parity and,
191–93; art-value and, 204–5; fictional
truth in context of, 20–25; hypothetical intentionalism versus, 314–18; interpretation
of natural versus cultural phenomena and,
28–35; Levinson's theory of meaning and,
176–80; linear versus punctal nature,
41–44; linguistic meanings and, 191 n. 11;
literary works and, 287–91; monistic interpretation and, 213–17; non-Intentional
properties and, 39–41; ontology of interpretation and, 58–61; philosophy of interpretation and, 319–41; realism about
critical meanings and, 186–89; unique in-

terpretation thesis and, 36–38. *See also* authorial intent; authorial intent, performer's
intent; hypothetical intentionalism

intentionality, ontology of interpretation and,
64–75

"Intergender Wrestling Championship,"
335–36

internal constructive realism, 136–45,
154–57

internal objects: versus external objects, 45;
ontology of interpretation and, 57–61;
structure of interpretations and, 52–56

interpretation: compatibility and convergence of, theories concerning, 27–44; creation of works through, 15–25; critical
pluralism and, 104–21; distinctiveness of,
in literary works, 287–91; epistemic access
and, 108–12; Heidegger's hermeneutics
and, 269–73; history and, 112–14; identity
and ontology in, 361–80; independence
from, 148–58; internal/external distinction, 45; multiple realism and hermeneutics
concerning, 280–84; paradigms of, in *Sun
Also Rises*, 14–15; philosophical issues
concerning, 1–5, 319–44

interpretive acts: characteristics of, 3; open-
ended interpretations, 63–75

interpretive anarchism, 266

interpretive authority, natural versus deep-
level interpretation, 86–89

intolerance, many-valued logic and, 92

irony: actual intentionalism and, 325–27; intentionalist theory and, 320–22; utterance
model of meaning and, 175 n. 19

Irwin, William, 338 n. 20

Iseminger, Gary, 214 n. 6, 291

James, Henry, 161, 216, 311, 329

Jefferson, Thomas, 90

Johnston, Paul, 405 n. 17

Joyce, James, 189, 300

Juhl, P. D., 26, 30–31, 38–41, 214

Julius Caesar, 204 n. 22

Jungle, The, 216 n. 10

Juno and the Paycock, 358–59

jurisprudence, interpretive strategies and, 3,
251–62

justice, jurisprudence and, 256–62

Kafka, Franz, 179, 311

Kant, Immanuel, 93, 142, 150, 153, 155–57,
365

Karp, Ivan, 376
Kaufman, Andy, 319, 333–44
Kelly, Paul, 252
Kettle, Arnold, 301
Kinderman, William, 243, 247
King Lear, 212, 220–28
Knapp, Steven, 214
Knight, Wilson, 298
knowledge: constructivist view of, 146–47;
    epistemic access and interpretation and,
    109–12
Koch, Carl, 33
Korsmeyer, Carolyn, 324 n. 7, 325 n. 9
Krausz, Michael, 39 n. 27, 45, 51–56, 102–
    53, 156–58, 184, 228–30, 286 n. 1, 306
Kristeller, P. O., 366–73
Kuhn, Thomas S., 40 n. 28, 149

Lamarque, Peter, 2, 4, 60, 129, 173 n. 17,
    204 n. 20, 206, 285–306
language and linguistics: actual intentional-
    ism and, 325–27; constructivist view of,
    172–73; cultural properties of, 118–20; hy-
    pothetical intentionalism and, 329–33; in-
    dividual identity and culture and, 375–80;
    intentionality of interpretation and, 65–68;
    literacy, identity, and visual arts and,
    367–73; literal meaning and, 69–74; radi-
    cal constructivism and, 183–86; realism
    about critical meanings and, 187–89; ret-
    rospective meaning and, 384–89; self-
    knowledge and, 382–84; translations and,
    93–94; Wittgenstein's philosophy of lan-
    guage and, 394–98, 403–6
language-game, Wittgenstein's use of,
    390–98
Lawler, Jerry, 335–37
Law's Empire, 259–62
Leakey, Louis, 28
Leavis, F. R., 300
Lebensform, individual identity and culture
    and, 376–80
Leibnizian view, multiplism versus singular-
    ism and, 132–34
Leonardo da Vinci, 33
Levinson, Jerrold, 4, 24 n. 8, 164 n. 9, 172
    n. 15, 191, 329 n. 13; actual intentionalism
    and, 287–91; hypothetical intentionalism
    of, 176–80, 309–18, 330–33, 341 n. 24
Lewis, David, 295
liberalism, interpretive theory and, 251

Limits of Rightness, 145–46
literacy: identity and ontology and, 362–63;
    personal identity and visual arts and,
    366–73
literal interpretative strategies: fictional truth
    and, 17–19; Indian theories of, 68–74
literary works (literature): actual intentional-
    ism and, 322–27; appreciation and inter-
    pretation of, 285–306; characterization of
    qualities in interpretation of, 297–306;
    constructivist interpretations of, 217–19;
    distinctiveness of, 286–91; hypothetical in-
    tentionalism and, 327–33; intentionalist
    theory and, 320–22; pliability of, 211–30;
    poetic interpretation and, 161–65; realistic
    interpretations of, 219–28; retrospective
    meaning in, 385–89; textual interpretation,
    166–69; text/work distinctness and,
    194–98; themes/theses distinction in, 297–
    306; utterance model of meaning and, 173
    n. 17, 199–205; verbal meaning and expli-
    cation in, 291–94
Livingston, Paisley, 214 n. 4, 329
Locke, John, 93
lucidic interpretation, critical pluralism and,
    106–8

Macbeth, 293 n. 17, 298
Mahler, Gustav, 178–79
Man on the Moon, 333
Manu's Law Book, 71–74
many-valued logic, hedging and, 92
Margolis, Joseph, 2–3, 58, 61, 87 n. 1, 107
    n. 6, 372 n. 10, 375–77; interpretive theory
    of, 26–44, 229–30; Krausz debate with,
    135 n. 24; multiplism and, 118–20, 125,
    131
Margulies, Lynn, 336
Martin, Rex, 3, 251–62
Martin, Terence, 301
Marxism: deep-interpretation theory and, 88;
    monistic interpretation of, 213; Vedic in-
    terpretations and, 73
Mary, cult of, 32–33
Matter of Principle, 253–55
McCormick, Peter, 136 n. 28, 138
McLoughlin v. O'Brian, 256 n. 5
meaning: actual intentionalism and, 323–27;
    Augustine's discussion of, 398–402; eluci-
    dation and theories of, 295–97; Gadamer's
    theory of hermeneutics and, 275–79; inten-

meaning *(cont'd)*
  tionality and, 68–74; pain and analysis of,
  389–98; physical versus psychological,
  72–74; realism about critical meanings
  and, 186–89; retrospective meaning, Wittgenstein's view of, 382–89; themes/theses
  distinction in literature and, 298–306; variety of, 206–7; verbal meaning, explication
  and recovery of, 291–94
Meiss, Millard, 33
Melville, Herman, 179, 325
memoir, self-interpretation and, 405–6
Merchant of Venice, 356
Merleau-Ponty, Maurice, 268–73
meta-interpretation, epistemic access and,
  108–12
metaphysical interpretation, artist/critic parity and, 200–5
"methodologism," hermeneutics and, 265
Michaels, Walter Benn, 214
Michelangelo, 34–35, 42, 373
Mighty Mouse, 334
"Milton," 164, 167
mind, philosophical view of, 382–84
mirror symbolism, literary interpretation
  concerning, 302–4
Moby Dick, 325
"Modern System of the Arts, The," 366–73
modest actual intentionalism, 4, 322–27; hypothetical intentionalism and, 327–33, 339
  n. 22, 341–44
Mohanty, Jitendranath, 2–4, 63–75
Moll Flanders, 173 n. 17, 300–306
Mondrian, Piet, 178–79
monism: literary interpretation and, 212–17;
  pliability of literary works and, 219–28
Moore's paradox, 54
moral development, in *Sun Also Rises,* 9–15
Moses, 42
Mother Courage, 347
Mozart, Wolfgang Amadeus, 194
multiple interpretability: authorial intent
  and, 216–17; constructivist theory and,
  217–19; hypothetical intentionalism and,
  310–18
multiplism: appreciation and literary interpretation and, 286; consensus concerning,
  103–4; constructive realism and, 142–44;
  critical pluralism and, 102–4; cultural
  properties, 118–20; defense of, 102–3; epistemic access and interpretation, 108–12;

history and interpretation and, 112–14; incompatible interpretations and, 114–18;
  incongruence of interpretation and,
  122–34; interpretative strategies and, 1–5,
  39 n. 27; limits of, 101–21; philosophical
  principles of, 381–84; realism and constructivism and, 134–44; self-interpretation and, 403–6; versus singularism,
  123–34
multiplist realism, hermeneutics and, 279–84
Musical Joke, 194
musical works: critical pluralist theory concerning, 104–21; descriptive interpretation, 241–50; editorial interpretation,
  234–37; hypothetical intentionalism and,
  178–79, 331 n. 17; intentionalism in,
  204–5; literacy concerning, 370; multiple
  interpretability of, 231–50; notational interpretation, 231–34; performative interpretation, 237–41; singularist versus
  multiplist theory concerning, 128–34;
  "sound structure" and, 166–69; text/work
  distinctions in, 194–98
Mutual Belief principle, elucidative interpretation and, 295 n. 22

narrative interpretation, 295 n. 21; hypothetical intentionalism and, 313–18
natural interpretation: conflict and, 90–91;
  versus cultural symbols, 28–35; versus
  deep-level interpretation, 86–89
nature symbolism, in *Sun Also Rises,* 10
Newell, R. W., 405 n. 17
Newman, Barnett, 373–74
Nietzsche, Friedrich, 88, 272–73, 406 n. 20
nihilism: in *King Lear,* 226–28; literary interpretation and, 303–4
noema, intentionality of interpretation and,
  64–68
nominalism, constraints on interpretation
  and, 78–79
nonepistemicity, constructive realism and,
  157–58
non-intentional properties: physical versus
  cultural contexts, 41–44; validity of,
  39–41
"No Right Answer," 254–55
normative constraints: artist/critic parity and,
  201–5; hypothetical intentionalism and,
  317–18; interpretation and role of, 79; jurisprudence and, 254–62; performative in-

terpretation of music and, 237–41; persuaders of interpretation and role of, 80–84

"Northanger Abbey," 194

notational interpretation, musical works, 231–34

noumenal realism, Kant's theory of, 142, 150, 153, 155–57

novels: incompatible interpretations of, 9–25; multiple interpretations of, 250; utterance model of meaning in, 300–301; verbal meaning in, 289, 292–94

Novitz, David, 2–3, 47–52, 101–21, 124–25, 129–34

object of interpretation: versus act of interpretation, 63–64; artist/critic parity and, 198–205; artworks as, 165–69; constructive realism and, 148–51; constructivism and, 172; intentionality and, 64–68; multiplist/singularist theories concerning, 122–44; novel critical interpretations and, 181–82; ontology of art and, 159–80

O'Casey, Sean, 358–59

Oedipus complex, *Hamlet* in context of, 170

Olsen, Stein Haugom, 290 n. 11, 298, 303 n. 41, 304 n. 45, 305

O'Malley, J. W., 32–33

one right answer thesis. *See* "single right interpretation" thesis

On the Veda, 72

ontological hermeneutics, 265–66; Gadamer's theory of, 273–79; multiplist realism and, 279–84

ontology of interpretation: art and, 56–61, 159–80; Heidegger's theory concerning, 64; identity and, 360–80; multiplism versus singularism and, 133–34; objects of interpretation and, 135 n. 25

opposition without exclusivity, incongruent interpretations, 123–34

"Origin of the Work of Art, The," 271–73

Orr, Joe, 336

Othello, 217–18, 220–28

Other Minds, 404 n. 17

Our Mutual Friend, 173 n. 17, 289, 292, 301–4

overdefiniteness, editorial interpretation of music and, 235–37

pain, Wittgenstein on self-interpretation and, 389–98

painting: actual intentionalism and interpretation of, 323–27; definitive interpretation and, 84–86; hypothetical intentionalism and, 178–79; individual identity and culture and, 373–80; interpretive strategies concerning, 20–23, 29–30, 32; literacy, identity, and visual arts and, 367–73; multiple interpretations of, 250; personal identity and visual perception, 365 n. 4; utterance model of meaning and, 175–76

Paratrisika, 73–74

Pears, David, 400 n. 16

perception, intentionality and, 64–68

Percival, Philip, 2–3, 173–76, 181–207, 321 n. 5

performance art: boundaries of, Kaufman case study, 334–44; critical pluralism concerning, 104–21; descriptive interpretation, 249–50; interpretations of, 59–61; limits of comparison using, 246–47; multiple interpretability of, 231–50; of musical works, 237–41; performative interpretation strategies and, 237–41; playwright's intent and, 345–59; radical constructivism and, 182 n. 2

performer's intent: descriptive interpretation and, 241–50; editorial interpretation of music and, 236–37; musical interpretation and, 232–34; performative interpretation and, 239–41; versus playwright's intent, 348–59

personal identity: literacy and visual arts and, 366–73; visual perception and, 364–66

perspective, ontology of interpretation and, 67–68

persuaders, interpretation and role of, 79–84

Peter and the Wolf, 248

Petrushka, 235

Pettersson, Torsten, 2–4, 31–32, 211–30

phenomenology: Gadamer's theory of hermeneutics and, 276–79; hermeneutics and, 265; interpretive theory and, 63–68

Phenomenology of the Mind, 74–75

Phillips, D. Z., 397 n. 15

Philosophical Investigations, 42, 385–98

philosophy of interpretation, 1–5, 319–44; in Augustine's *Confessions,* 398–402; retrospective meaning and, 384–89; self-knowl-

philosophy of interpretation *(cont'd)*
edge and, 397 n. 15; Wittgenstein's
discussion of, 390–98
physical properties, realism about critical
meanings and, 188 n. 9
piecemeal interpretive strategy, 138, 154
Piero, 373
Pietà, 29–30
plagiarism, interpretive strategy as, 22–23
plastic arts, text/work distinctions and,
194–98
Platonism, 41–42
plays and playwrights, intentionalist theory
and, 345–59
pliability, of literary works, 219–28
pluralistic realism, 228–30; hermeneutics
and, 279–84
pluralist interpretations: artist/critic parity
and, 201–5; of literary works, 211–30; poetic interpretation and, 161–65
poetry: authorial intent in, 339; intentionality
and interpretation of, 69–74; ontology of
interpretation, 161–65; plays versus, 357;
utterance model of meaning and, 176; verbal meaning in, 292–93
Political Liberalism, 252
Portrait of Picasso, 195
Potato Eaters, The, 52, 60, 171, 203–5, 322
n. 5
potentialities, literacy and personal identity
and, 372–73
Potential Plurality thesis, structure of interpretation and, 46, 51–56
Pound, Ezra, 355
practice-independent objects, critical pluralism and, 103
pragmatism, jurisprudence and, 260 n. 7
prejudice: Gadamer's hermeneutics and,
277–79; multiple realism and hermeneutics
concerning, 282–84; retrospective meaning
and, 385–89
preunderstanding, Heidegger's hermeneutics
and, 269–73
Pride and Prejudice, 47–48
"privileged fact," understanding and interpretation and, 94–96
projection: constructive realism and, 157–58;
Heidegger's Dasein and, 268–73
Prokofiev, Sergei, 248
Putnam, Hilary, 4, 132 n. 19, 136, 138–41,
145, 153, 155–57

Radcliffe, Ann, 194
radical constructivism: artist/critic parity
and, 190–93; realism about critical meanings and, 186–89; structure of, 182–86;
text/work distinctness, 193–98
Ramanuja, 74
rational inquiry, incompatibility of interpretations and, 115–18
Rauschenberg, Robert, 176
Rawls, John, 251–52, 255
reader-based interpretation, monism in literary works and, 212–17
realism: constructivism and, 134–44,
146–48; critical meanings and, 186–89; jurisprudence and, 256–57; literacy, identity,
and visual arts and, 367 n. 6; literary interpretation and, 211–30; in performance,
334–44; singularism and, 3–4, 122–23,
133–34
Reality principle, elucidative interpretation
and, 295 n. 22
redemptivism, in *King Lear,* 226–28
reference, artwork interpretation and, 107–8
reflexivity, hypothetical intentionalism and,
342–44
relativism: constructive realism and, 145–46,
152–53, 155–58; hypothetical intentionalism and, 340–44; incongruence and,
125–26; unique interpretation thesis and,
37–38
relevance, actual intentionalism and, 321 n. 5
religious practices, incongruence of interpretation concerning, 126–27
Rembrandt, 175
Renaissance studies, cultural materialism
and, 304 n. 46
representation: constructivism and, 137; independence from, 148–58; internal versus
external approaches, 52–56; literacy, identity, and visual arts and, 367 n. 6; object of
knowledge and, 147
reproduction, identity and ontology in visual
arts and, 362–63
Restrictive principle: beliefs and, 95–96; hedging on interpretation and, 92; natural versus deep-level interpretation, 86–89;
painting interpretation and, 85–86; persuaders of interpretation and, 80–84
retrospective meaning: defined, 382–84; truth
and, 394–98; Wittgenstein's philosophy of,
384–89

"right-answer" thesis, 3, 252–62
right understanding: jurisprudence and, 253–62; natural versus deep-level interpretation, 87–89
Rilke, Ranier Maria, 88
Risen Christ, 34–35
Rise of the Novel, The, 300
"robust relativism," pluralist realism and, 229–30
Romantic hermeneutic doctrine, interpretive strategy and, 26–44
Romeo and Juliet, 350
"Rose for Emily, A," 218
Rosen, Charles, 243–44, 247
Rubens, 41
Ryle, Gilbert, 382

Saint Anne, cult of, 32–33
Saint Antony Chorale, 45–51, 54–56, 59
Samkara, 74
Sanskrit, 72–74, 377–80
Saturday Night Live, 334–35
Schapiro, Meyer, 33–35, 40
Schleiermacher, Friedrich, 264
Schuller, Gunther, 128–29
Schumann, Robert, 48
scientific knowledge: Gadamer's theory of hermeneutics and, 274–79; sociological view of, 146
Scruton, Roger, 304–5
Searle, John, 136
secondary meaning, intentionality and, 69–74
self-deception: natural versus deep-level interpretation, 87–89; persuaders of interpretation and, 82–86
self-interpretation: in Augustine's *Confessions,* 398–402; pain as device for, 389–98; philosophy and, 397 n. 15; retrospective meaning and, 384–89; Wittgenstein's philosophy of, 381–406
"semantical thickness," 293–94
semantic intentions, hypothetical intentionalism and, 340–44
Sense and Sensibility, 120
sentential meaning, utterance meaning and, 299–306
Sessions, Roger, 130–31
sexuality, of Christ, 32–34. *See also* homosexuality

Shakespeare, William, 170, 204 n. 22, 217, 219–28, 304 n. 46, 349 n. 4, 356
Shelley, Percy Bysshe, 291
Shostakovich, Dmitri, 205
Showalter, Elaine, 296
Sibley, Frank, 303
Simpson, David, 162
Sinclair, Upton, 216 n. 10
"single right interpretation" thesis: elucidation and, 295–97; jurisprudence and, 254–62; literary interpretation and, 290–91, 302–6; verbal meaning and, 294
singularism: appreciation and literary interpretation and, 286; constructive realism and, 142–44; critical pluralism versus, 102–21; incompatibility of interpretations and, 115–18; incongruence of interpretation, 122–34; interpretative strategies and, 1–5, 39 n. 27; versus multiplism, 123–34; realism and constructivism and, 134–44; self-knowledge and, 382–84
situatedness, Heidegger's concept of, 267–73
skepticism, realism and, 146
"Slumber did my spirit seal, A," 30–31, 161
social evolution: individual identity and, 378–80; literacy, identity, and visual arts and, 369–73
Sontag, Susan, 379–80
speciment theory of interpretation, 30–35
"staccato" style, of Hemingway's work, 12
Starmaking, 136 n. 28, 138
statutory interpretation, jurisprudence and, 256–62
Stecker, Robert, 3–4, 39 n. 27, 114 n. 14, 150–51, 190, 200–202; art of interpretation and, 159–80, 311 n. 4; on critical monism/pluralism, 305–6; on Olsen's theory of appreciation, 303 n. 41; radical constructivism and, 182–87; utterance model of meaning and, 291, 295 n. 20, 298–99, 301
Steinberg, Leo, 32–34
Stern, Laurent, 4, 76–98
stipulation thesis, meaning and, 388–89
Stoppard, Tom, 349 n. 4, 352, 354–55
Stowe, Harriet Beecher, 216 n. 10
Stravinsky, Igor, 235
structure of interpretation, 45–46, 51–56
sublime, personal identity and visual perception of, 365–66

subsumptive interpretation, hypothetical intentionalism and, 312–18
Sullivan, J. W. N., 245–47
Sun Also Rises, The, 9–25
surface-level interpretation: versus deep-level
interpretation, 86–89; painting analysis
and, 85–86
sûtra texts, 71–74
symbolization: in artworks, 206–7; in musical works, 232–34

tautologies, epistemic access and, 109–12
Taxi, 334
Tchaikovsky, Peter I., 194, 241
technical analyses, descriptive interpretation
and, 248–49
technology, literacy and personal identity
and, 372–73
tempo: editorial interpretation and, 235–37;
notational interpretation and, 233–34; performative interpretation and, 237–41
Terry, Ellen, 296
textual interpretation: actual intentionalism
and, 322–27; art as work versus, 165–69;
artworks compared with, 20–23, 33; Gadamer's theory of hermeneutics and,
276–79; Heidegger's hermeneutics and,
270–73; hypothetical intentionalism and,
309–18; intentionalist theory and, 68–74,
287–91, 320–22; literal meaning and,
69–70; of literary works, 211–17; ontology of art and, 159–80; pliability of literary works and, 222–28; primacy and
autonomy of texts, 71–74; radical constructivism and, 182–86; strategies for,
14–19; theoretical assumptions concerning, 166–69; "violence" to the text, 283
n. 15
text/work distinctness: artist/critic parity and,
190–93; radical constructivism and,
193–98
themes/theses distinction, 297–306
Theory of Justice, A, 251
Thom, Paul, 2, 4, 148–52
thrownness, Heidegger's concept of, 267–73
time, Heidegger's concept of being and,
267–73
Toscanini, Arturo, 128–29
tragic dimension, Gadamer's theory of hermeneutics and, 275–79

transformation of interpretation, translations
and, 93–94
translation: definitive interpretation and,
93–94; interpretation and, 77–79
truth: as disclosedness, 266–73; elucidation
in literary interpretation and, 295–97; Gadamer's theory of hermeneutics and,
273–79; hedging on interpretation and, 92;
hermeneutics of interpretation and,
264–84; hypothetical intentionalism and,
315 n. 10; literary interpretation and, 163–
65, 304–6; multiplist realism and hermeneutics concerning, 279–84; self-
interpretation and, 405–6; Wittgenstein on
meaning and, 392–98
Truth and Method, 273–79
Turn of the Screw, 9, 161, 212, 216, 305–6,
311, 329
Twilight of the Idols, 406 n. 20

Ulysses, 189, 195
Unbestimmtheitsstellen, literary criticism
and, 222–28
Uncle Tom's Cabin, 216 n. 10
understanding: definitive interpretation and,
94–96; Gadamer's theory of hermeneutics
and, 273–79; Heidegger's hermeneutics
and, 266–73; interpretation and, 77–79;
literary interpretation and, 289–91, 300–
306; multiplism and, 124–25
unique interpretation thesis, interpretive
strategies and, 35–38
Universalizability principle: beliefs and,
95–96; conflict and, 90–91; hedging and,
91–92; painting interpretation and, 84–86;
persuaders of interpretation and, 80–84;
translations and, 93–94
Universalizability principle: natural versus
deep-level interpretation, 86–89
Upaniṣads, interpretation of, 69–71, 73–74
utterance model of meaning, 172–73, 173
n. 17; actual intentionalism and, 325–27;
elucidation in interpretation and, 295
n. 20; hypothetical intentionalism and,
309–18; Levinson's interpretation of, 176–
80, 291; literary interpretation and,
287–91; Percival's examples of, 173–76;
performance of dialogue and, 349–50;
philosophical view of, 382–84; textual interpretation and, 320–22; themes/theses
distinction and, 298–306

value-neutral explication, 294, 300–306
Van Gogh, Vincent, 52, 60, 171, 203–4, 322 n. 5
Vedas, interpretation of, 71–74
verbal meaning: actual intentionalism and, 321 n. 4; explication and recovery of, 291–94
"Visions of the Daughters of Albion," 162
visual arts: culture and individual identity, 373–80; identity and ontology in interpretation of, 362–80; literacy and personal identity and, 366–73; personal identity and perception of, 364–66

Waiting for Godot, 311
Walter, Bruno, 131
Walton, Kendall, 295
Warnke, Georgia, 280
Watt, Ian, 300–301
Webster, Brenda, 162–65
Whitehead, Frank, 226

Wilde, Oscar, 349
Williams, Robin, 336
Wilson, Kent, 324 n. 8
"Windhover, The," 292, 305
Wingo, Ajume H., 361
Wisdom, John, 404 n. 17
Wittgenstein, Ludwig, 42, 45–51, 133, 381–406; pain as metaphor for interpretation, 389–98; on retrospective meaning, 384–89, 400–402
Woman paintings, 311
Woolf, Virginia, 300
Wordsworth, William, 30–31, 161, 212–13
Wright, John, 228–29
"writerly" interpretations, 107–8, 120–21; history and, 113–14
"1887 written on the occasion of Queen Victoria's Golden Jubilee," 175 n. 19
Wygralak, Maciej, 57

Zmuda, Bob, 336